RUNNING ON EMPTY

Transport, social exclusion and environmental justice

Edited by Karen Lucas

To my daughter Niaomh

"Just the two of us...."

First published in Great Britain in 2004 by

The Policy Press
University of Bristol
Fourth Floor
Beacon House
Queen's Road
Bristol BS8 1QU
UK
Tel +44 (0)117 331 4054
Fax +44 (0)117 331 4093
e-mail tpp-info@bristol.ac.uk
www.policypress.co.uk

North American office:

The Policy Press
c/o The University of Chicago Press
1427 East 60th Street
Chicago, IL 60637, USA
t: +1 773 702 7700
f: +1 773-702-9756
e:sales@press.uchicago.edu
www.press.uchicago.edu

© Karen Lucas 2004

Transferred to Digital Print 2012

British Library Cataloguing in Publication Data
A catalogue record for this book is available from the British Library.

Library of Congress Cataloging-in-Publication Data
A catalog record for this book has been requested.

ISBN 978 1 86134 569 1 paperback
ISBN 978 1 86134 570 7 hardcover

The right of Karen Lucas to be identified as editor of this work has been asserted by her in accordance with the 1988 Copyright, Designs and Patents Act.

All rights reserved: no part of this publication may be reproduced, stored in a retrieval system, or transmitted in any form or by any means, electronic, mechanical, photocopying, recording, or otherwise without the prior permission of The Policy Press.

The statements and opinions contained within this publication are solely those of the editor and contributors and not of The University of Bristol or The Policy Press. The University of Bristol and The Policy Press disclaim responsibility for any injury to persons or property resulting from any material published in this publication.

The Policy Press works to counter discrimination on grounds of gender, race, disability, age and sexuality.

Cover design by Qube Design Associates, Bristol
Front cover: image kindly supplied by www.third-avenue.co.uk

Contents

List of figures and tables	iv
Acknowledgements	vi
Notes on definitions and spellings	viii
Notes on contributors	x
List of abbreviations	xiii

Introduction   1
Karen Lucas

Part One: Setting the context

one   Locating transport as a social policy problem   7
    Karen Lucas

two   Examining the empirical evidence of transport inequality in the US and UK   15
    Kelly Clifton and Karen Lucas

Part Two: The UK perspective

three   Transport and social exclusion   39
    Karen Lucas

four   Ensuring access and participation in the Liverpool city region   55
    Murray Grant

five   Halton Neighbourhood Travel Team   69
    Julian Westwood

six   BraunstoneBus: a link with the future   95
    Mike Preston

seven   A road less travelled: case studies from community transport   119
    Martin Jones

eight   Conclusions from the UK experience   145
    Karen Lucas

Part Three: The US perspective

nine   Transportation and environmental justice   155
    Lori G. Kennedy

ten   Job isolation in the US: narrowing the gap through job access and reverse-commute programs   181
    Robert Cervero

eleven   Community impact assessment for US17   197
    Anne Morris

twelve   Crossroad blues: the MTA Consent Decree and just transportation   221
    Robert García and Thomas A. Rubin

thirteen   Women's issues in transportation   257
    Stephanie Ortoleva and Marc Brenman

fourteen   Conclusions from the US experience   281
    Karen Lucas

Part Four: Transferring the lessons

fifteen   Towards a 'social welfare' approach to transport   291
    Karen Lucas

Index   299

List of figures and tables

Figures

2.1	The dynamics of diminishing accessibility	16
2.2	Increased distance of local facilities in urban and rural areas in the UK (1989-99)	17
2.3	Average distance travelled per person per annum in the UK by mode of transport and level of household income	19
2.4	Journey distances and travel time in the UK by income quintile	20
2.5	Journey distances and travel time in the US by income quintile	20
2.6	Car ownership in the UK by income quintile (2000)	22
2.7	Car ownership in the US by income quintile (2000)	22
2.8	People with driving licences in the UK by age and gender (1975-2001)	23
2.9	People with driving licences in the US by age and gender	23
2.10	US households without a car by race/ethnicity	24
2.11	Journey to work in the UK by mode and ethnic origin	24
2.12	Journey to work in the US by mode and ethnic origin	25
2.13	Average miles driven per year by income quintile	26
2.14	Bus fares and motoring costs (1974-2000)	26
3.1	Factors affecting accessibility	43
4.1	Drawing together the transport and social exclusion agendas	58
4.2	Differences in trip rates across income bands	59
4.3	Trends in public transport fares, motoring costs and the Retail Price Index	59
4.4	Pathways areas and Strategic Investment Areas (SIAs)	62
4.5	Job Link network December 2003-June 2004	65
5.1	Halton Borough Council geographical area	71
5.2	Alterations to 200 bus service following analysis of Personalised Journey Plan (PJP) requests	87
5.3	Patronage on route 200 (2003)	88
6.1	Defining the routes	106
6.2	A cartoon highlighting the arrival of the two new bus services	108
6.3	A bus used on the 317 route	109
6.4	Customer feedback from on-board surveys	110
6.5	Braunstone bus map route 302	114
6.6	StarTrak early warning information system	115
10.1	Percentage of reverse commuters who patronize public transport: low versus non-low-income households across four Californian metropolitan areas	186
10.2	Relative frequency of job access and reverse commute in California (2002)	188
10.3	Clean natural gas bus picking up employees at front door of Cache Creek Casino in Yolo County, California	189
11.1	Project area	199
12.1	Los Angeles population by ethnicity (1970-2040)	226

| 12.2 | Proposition A rail plan | 228 |
| 12.3 | Los Angeles County MTA passenger trips: fiscal year 1985-2002, with and without Consent Decree | 249 |

Tables

2.1	Trips and miles travelled per day by income in the US	21
3.1	Key concerns about transport by social group	45
4.1	LTP objectives for Merseyside	61
5.1	Snapshot of achievements for the first year of the NTT	89
6.1	Data on usage and customer satisfaction (by number)	111
9.1	Percentage and number of households by income	159
9.2	People with disabilities	160

Acknowledgements

The authors would like to thank a number of individuals and organisations who have been as passionate as we have about writing and publishing this book and for supporting the research, policy development, advocacy, campaigning and practical project delivery work we have all been involved in. First, thanks go to our publishing team at The Policy Press, who had the foresight to recognise the value and relevance of such a text when many others did not and have been extremely supportive and encouraging throughout its evolution. Second, thanks to Andrew and Catherine Ross at Final Draft Consultancy Ltd, who have taken a lot of the hard work out of the post-writing process with their excellent proofreading skills, textual advice and script preparation services.

In addition:

Kelly Clifton would like to express her gratitude and highest appreciation to Sandi Rosenbloom for inspiring her to think about the social implications of transportation policy and to thank her parents for their encouragement.

Julian Westwood offers his many thanks to John Mooney, Section Leader Transport Coordination at Halton Borough Council, for providing the support and allowing us the space for the Neighbourhood Travel Team (NTT) to succeed. He also wishes to acknowledge the other members of the Halton NTT who have helped in achieving the success of its first year, namely: Kath Tierney, Karen Dennis, Lyndsey Ryder, Paula Coppell, Paul Antrobus, Joanne Jackson and Bill Relph.

Mike Preston would like personally to thank Mark Carrara, Project Coordinator at BraunstoneBus, for his support and attention to detail in telling the BraunstoneBus story. The Braunstone Community Association (BCA) would also like to thank Dr Karen Lucas at the University of Westminster for her early case study research supporting the BraunstoneBus Urban Bus Challenge bid and Julian Heubeck, the public transport coordinator at Leicester City Council, for his personal commitment and professional support of the transport projects being developed by the BCA.

Martin Jones wishes to thank the Community Transport Association for their cooperation and support in writing this chapter and the individual projects cited in these pages for their time and interest.

Robert Cervero thanks Yu-Hsin Tsai, Joulia Dibb, Andrew Kluter, Cornelius Nuworsoo and Irina Petrova of the University of California at Berkeley for providing him with research assistance on the California case materials.

Acknowledgements

Anne Morris offers her thanks to Ms Gail Grimes of North Carolina Department of Transportation who trusted us to bring home the product, and to Ms JoAnne Stone, Principal of Pollocksville Elementary School, who allowed us to come into her classrooms and be creative.

Robert García and Thomas A. Rubin thank Sophia Chang, Amber Richer and Julie Ehrlich at the Center for Law in the Public Interest for their invaluable research assistance.

Stephanie Ortoleva and Marc Brenman thank the members of the Women's Issues Committee of the US Transportation Research Board for their longstanding commitment to women's transportation equity. They also thank Joanne Tosti-Vasey for her editorial assistance in their chapter.

Finally, on a personal note as editor and instigator of this volume, I would like to sincerely thank my fellow authors on both sides of the Atlantic, who have given of their extremely valuable and scarce time, freely, willingly and without complaint. Without you, my 'idea for a book' would never have been more than a pipe dream. The continuous support and guidance of Professor Peter Jones, Director of the Transport Studies Group at the University of Westminster and my long-suffering boss and mentor is, as ever, greatly appreciated. My thanks also go to my research assistants, Sara Fuller and Joanna Machin, and Dora Wheeler, the Transport Studies Group administrator, for their help and patience. Many thanks also go to my daughter Niaomh who knows far more about transport, social exclusion and environmental justice than a girl of her age really has any reason to!

Notes on definitions and spellings

In editing a comparative US and UK collaborative text, the issue of definitions and spellings arises, despite the common language. Even the use of 'transport' in the title has raised concerns with our publishers, because the term 'transportation' is seen to have more relevance in the US context. Most people reading this book will be familiar with the slightly differing English and American spelling, such as color/colour, recognized/recognised, center/centre, and so on. In other instances, however, entirely different words are used to describe the same thing; for example, the term 'mass transit' is used in the US to describe what is referred to as 'public transport' in the UK (although both are actually a combination of commercially-run and state-subsidised services).

In the interests of serving both audiences, the book uses English spellings in the three introductory, two concluding overview chapters and the UK case study chapters. American spellings are then used in Chapters Nine to Twelve, which refer directly to the US circumstance. 'Transport' and 'transportation' are used interchangeably throughout the text, and when using these terms, the authors generally refer to the privately owned and commercial and state-funded public transport that is available to individuals for normal daily travel purposes, rather than the movement of goods and services or longer distances and occasional travel, although it is recognised that this can also have implications for social equity.

Some other terms require some early definitions, although these are discussed in greater detail in the main text of the book. These include:

Accessibility planning (UK)	Analysis of whether people experiencing social exclusion (see below) can access key goods and services.
Community impact assessment (CIA) (US)	Analysis of whether low-income and minority populations are unfairly impacted upon by proposed (transportation) developments.
Community transport (UK)	A wide spectrum of bespoke community and voluntary-run and owned, transport services, including motorbikes and scooters, voluntary car schemes, vans and minibuses to meet the needs of communities and individuals excluded from conventional transport services.
Environmental justice (US)	Policies and programmes to address the unequal impact of development on minority and low-income communities.
Jitney services (US)	Private semi-fixed route minibus operations, similar to many informal transport services found in the developing world.

Notes on definitions and spellings

Paratransit (US)	Flexibly routed transport services designed to get people without their own transportation to essential activities, such as employment and health care.
People of color (US)	The term used in the US to refer to people from black and minority ethnic origins. Other similar terms include 'communities of color' and 'women of color'.
Reverse commute (US)	Journeys to work originating from the central city are to destinations in the suburbs and urban fringe.
Social exclusion (UK)	The inability to fully participate in the economic and social activities that are necessary to maintaining a reasonable quality of life.
Social inclusion (UK)	Policies and programmes to address social exclusion (as above).

Notes on contributors

Note: The notes on contributors are given in chapter order.

Dr Karen Lucas is a Senior Research Fellow with the Transport Studies Group at the University of Westminster (UK). Her specialist research interest is in exploring the interface between economic, social and environmental policies and programmes. She recently acted as a policy advisor to the government's Social Exclusion Unit (SEU) to address the issue of transport and social exclusion in the UK and was involved in the pilot studies to facilitate the national roll-out of this new policy framework for local transport planning and service sector delivery that resulted from this work. She is an international member of the US Transportation Research Board's (TRB) Environmental Justice Task Force.

Dr Kelly Clifton is an Assistant Professor at the University of Maryland (US) with a joint appointment in the Department of Civil and Environmental Engineering and the Urban Studies and Planning Department. She is an affiliate of the Maryland Transportation Initiative and National Center for Smart Growth. She is a member of the Transportation Research Board Committee on Traveller Behaviour and Values and chair of the Qualitative Methods Subcommittee. Her research has focused on the intersection of poverty, land use and transportation policies.

Murray Grant is Chief Policy Officer at Merseytravel (Liverpool, UK). He leads the multidisciplinary Policy and Planning Team, and has responsibility for forward planning, policy development and the Community Links Team. He has always been committed to linking transport with wider social policies, and this has led to his particular involvement with the developing agenda, linking transport provision to measures to address social exclusion. He was a senior policy advisor to the government's SEU examination of these issues and is currently a member of the Department for Transport's working group examining how the SEU recommendations can be implemented.

Dr Julian Westwood was previously the project manager for the innovative Neighbourhood Travel Team (NTT) in Halton (UK). He has managed numerous social inclusion projects working with the voluntary, youth and community sectors. His current work as TravelSafe Policy Officer for Merseytravel Public Transport Executive (PTE) involves addressing issues of crime and disorder on public transport and its immediate environment. He has a particular interest in the impact of these issues on socially excluded communities.

Mike Preston is Programme Manager at Braunstone Community Association (Leicester, UK). Starting work in social housing in 1985, he has focused increasingly on neighbourhood renewal since the mid-1990s, commencing work for Braunstone Community Association in 2000.

Martin Jones was previously director of communications and deputy director of the Community Transport Association (CTA). He played a key role in the CTA's involvement with the government's study on transport and social exclusion and edited *Community Transport* magazine from November 1998 until January 2004. He is now Senior Campaigns Manager at Arthritis Care.

Lori G. Kennedy is the owner and President of Kennedy Engineering and Associates Group LLC, a transportation engineering consulting firm based in Atlanta, Georgia (US). Lori was the former chair for nine years of the Transport Research Board (TRB) Task Force on Environmental Justice in Transportation. Lori is presently the Chair of TRB's Section on Social, Economic and Cultural Issues under the TRB Planning and Environment Group.

Professor Robert Cervero is Professor of City and Regional Planning at the University of California Berkeley (US). He has authored five books and numerous articles and monographs on transportation and land-use policy and planning. He presently chairs the National Advisory Committee of the Active Living Research program under the Robert Woods Johnson Foundation, and is a Fellow with the Urban Land Institute and World Bank Institute. He recently won the 2003 Article of the Year Award from the Journal of the American Planning Association.

Anne Morris is a Senior Consultant with PBS and J Consultants, Columbia SC (US). She has recently been selected as part of a three-woman team to design the US Federal Highway Administration's national training course on Community Impact Assessment (CIA). In addition, she is completing a national scan for the US Federal Highway Administration on best practices on how to identify and engage the low literacy and limited English proficiency population in the transportation decision-making process. She is a member of the US TRB's Environmental Justice Task Force and a founding member of its CIA Joint Subcommittee.

Robert García and **Thomas A. Rubin** worked together on the Los Angeles Metropolitan Transport Authority (MTA) litigation case referred to in Chapter Twelve. García is Executive Director of the Center for Law in the Public Interest in Los Angeles (CA). He was one of the lead attorneys in the MTA case. Rubin is a public finance consultant in Oakland, California. He was the lead financial expert for the plaintiff class in the MTA litigation and continues to serve as an expert in monitoring compliance with the Consent Decree.

Stephanie Ortoleva and **Marc Brenman** developed an innovative project to study women's issues in transportation together while working for the US Department of Transportation. The issue had been studied relatively little, and Ortoleva and Brenman brought their combined skills and experience in civil rights and feminist issues to this research. At present, Ortoleva is employed by the US Federal Agency as a civil rights attorney and Brenman is the Executive Director of the State of Washington Human Rights Commission.

List of abbreviations

ADA	Americans with Disabilities Act
AFDC	Aid for Families with Dependent Children
BART	Bay Area Rapid Transit
BRU	Bus Riders Union
CalWORKs	Californian Work Opportunity and Responsibilities to Kids
CBA	cost benefit analysis
CCT	Coalfield Community Transport
CEQ	Council on Environmental Quality
CIA	community impact assessment
DfES	Department for Education and Skills
DfT	Department for Transport
DOT	Department of Transportation
DWP	Department for Work and Pensions
EC	European Community
ECT	Ealing Community Transport
ERA	Equal Rights Advocates
FHWA	Federal Highway Administration
FTA	Federal Transit Administration
GIS	geographical information systems
HAZ	Health Action Zone
HCT	Hackney Community Transport
IGA	Independent Grocers Association
ISTEA	1991 Intermodal Surface Transportation Efficiency Act
ITCC	Interagency Transportation Coordinating Council
JARC	Job Access and Reverse Commute
JET	Job, Enterprise and Training Centre
LACTC	Los Angeles County Transportation Commission
LCSC	Labor/Community Strategy Center
LDF	Legal Defense and Educational Fund
LIFT	Local Initiative for Transport
LSP	local strategic partnership
LTA	local transport authority
LTP	Local Transport Plan
MPO	Metropolitan Planning Organization
MSBA	Metropolitan Suburban Bus Authority
NCDOT	North Carolina Department of Transportation
NCNW	National Council of Negro Women Inc.
NDC	New Deal for Communities
NEPA	National Environmental Policy Act
NTC	neighbourhood travel coordinator
NTT	Neighbourhood Travel Team

NWACTA	North Walsham Area Community Transport Association
ONS	Office for National Statistics
PAT	policy action team
PJP	Personalised Journey Plan
PRWORA	Personal Responsibility and Work Opportunity Reconciliation Act
PTA	Public Transport Authority (UK)
PTA	passenger transport authority (US)
SCAG	Southern California Association of Governments
SEPTA	South Eastern Pennsylvania Transportation Authority
SEU	Social Exclusion Unit
SIA	Strategic Investment Area
SIP	Social Inclusion Partnerships
SMR	standard mortality ratio
SPD	Single Programming Document
SRB	Single Regeneration Budget
TANF	Temporary Assistance for Needy Families
TDM	Transportation Demand Management
TEA-21	Transportation Equity Act for the 21st Century
UBC	Urban Bus Challenge
UCLA	University of California, Los Angeles
UMTA	Urban Mass Transportation Administration
WtoW	Welfare-to-work program

Introduction

Karen Lucas

Structural unemployment, poor educational achievement, ill-health, high crime rates and poor social integration remain a major focus of the social welfare agenda in most advanced industrial societies. Transport is increasingly being recognised as having a significant role to play in both the creation and alleviation of such problems. Although mass car ownership has brought huge benefits to the majority of people, a significant minority of the population still do not own or are unable to drive cars. In both the US and UK, non-car ownership is overwhelmingly concentrated among low income and other disadvantaged sectors of the population. There is a growing body of evidence to suggest that these people are finding it increasingly difficult to carry out the basic daily activities that the rest of the population take for granted. Furthermore, car drivers from the lowest income quintile are spending a large proportion of their income on travel-related costs and may be making considerable financial sacrifices in order to purchase and operate their vehicles.

Poor people are also predominantly concentrated in neighbourhoods that are disproportionately affected by the negative impacts of road traffic, such as pedestrian accidents, noise and air pollution and severance. They travel less often and over shorter distances than the average population, but the social and economic consequences of this behaviour, such as reduced work and educational opportunities and poor access to healthcare and other essential services, all too often have been overlooked. In part, this is because the policy professionals have poorly understood 'transport poverty' and its impact on social welfare. Traditionally, transport has not appeared as a topic of analysis in the social sciences; equally its social effects have tended to be overlooked by the transport disciplines. A key aim of this book, therefore, is to begin to encourage greater cross-fertilisation between these two disciplines. Although the main focus of the text is policy and practice in England and the US, much of its content and analysis will also be applicable to the rest of Europe and most other advanced industrial nations.

The term 'social exclusion' has gained common parlance in UK policy from the late 1990s, being widely adopted by the New Labour government to describe the linked economic, social and environmental problems experienced by people living on low incomes in some of England's 'worst estates'. As later chapters of this volume demonstrate, the problem of poor transport and access has only recently been recognised as part of this problem in the UK context, and policies and programmes are still very much at their developmental stage. The case study chapters in Part Two offer some early examples of the types of initiatives that are being developed and delivered across England to address this issue. It is evident that this policy agenda is still in its infancy in the UK and there is much to be learned about what might work most effectively in terms of practical delivery.

At first glance, a UK and US comparison of these issues may not appear to be a very fruitful line of enquiry. Social exclusion is not a generally recognised term in the US and there are quite clearly fundamental differences between patterns of land use and the transportation systems in the UK and the US, as well as quite major differences in the political, legislative, financial and administrative frameworks of each country. This book demonstrates that these differences do have an effect on the demographic nature of the problem of poor transport and access, as well as its geographical distribution and its level and intensity among the population of the two countries. As a result of these and other factors, the policy focus in each country is markedly different at times.

However, since the early 1990s, US policies and programmes for 'environmental justice' have been increasingly concerned with addressing the problem of unequal access of minority ethnic populations and low-income households to transportation. Although both the US concept of environmental justice and the policy framework in which it is delivered differ significantly from the UK transport and social exclusion agenda, in the field of transport at least, there are some striking similarities between the two policy agendas, as Part Three demonstrates. This means that there is already a strong body of knowledge in the US about addressing the transport problems of low-income and minority ethnic populations as part of a welfare agenda, which does not really exist elsewhere, and which can usefully serve to inform policy development in this area. A second aim of the book, therefore, is to assist in this knowledge transfer.

Perhaps more interestingly, however, considerable insights can also be gained by considering key differences between the two policy approaches. The final and fourth part of this volume, entitled 'Transferring the lessons', argues that, at present, neither the UK nor the US has the problem entirely solved, highlighting the inherent strengths and weaknesses of each policy approach and identifying a number of more fundamental, shared policy constraints. This provides a platform to offer a broader evaluation of existing and planned policies and assess whether these are capable of reversing the inequalities that have been a definitive, if unintentional, feature of past policies on both sides of the Atlantic.

This volume is specifically designed to appeal to both newcomers to the subject and those who are already familiar with this area. Part One ('Setting the context') is primarily designed to provide a broad-based introduction to the subject: Chapter One offers a brief overview of the intended role of social and public policy within advanced industrial societies and the position of the state in relation to this. It outlines the importance of transport in the welfare of citizens, both as an enabler of access to goods and services and in terms of the negative social and health impacts it can have on people's lives. In this way, it presents the basic case for adopting transport as a social policy concern and suggests some reasons why this approach has not been taken up in the past.

On the basis that most social policy is concerned with addressing the unequal effects of the market distribution of goods and services in the interest of the welfare of citizens, Chapter Two presents the empirical evidence of transport inequality in the UK and US. It draws out the similarities and differences in transport access and travel behaviour between the average population and different social groups within each country. Where the data allow, it makes direct comparisons between the UK and the US circumstances. It moves on to consider the implications of these inequities in relation to wider quality of life issues such as access to work, education, healthcare and other basic amenities, identifies how widely these issues have been examined within the existing body of research and highlights gaps in this knowledge base.

Part Two ('The UK perspective') is dedicated to the UK policy approach, with a particular focus on policy development and practice in England (under the devolved UK parliamentary system, English policy in this area no longer applies to the rest of the UK). Chapter Three introduces the social exclusion policy agenda; initially, it offers a definition of social exclusion as it is presented by the policy literature, and moves on to present the key components of the UK government's emerging strategy for addressing the problem of poor transport in England through accessibility planning.

The chapter is supported by the four case study chapters that follow it. The first (Chapter Four) focuses on the work undertaken by Merseytravel, the Public Transport Executive (PTE) for Liverpool and Merseyside, in linking major areas of regeneration with areas of high unemployment. The second (Chapter Five) describes the personalised travel planning programme that is being delivered to job seekers in Halton, a small local authority located to the south of Liverpool in the north west of England, as part of its return-to-work programme. The third (Chapter Six) presents the BraunstoneBus initiative, where Braunstone Community Association in collaboration with Leicester City Council has been successful in securing government funding for new bus services to provide access to major employment as well as the hospital and leisure destinations in the urban periphery. The fourth (Chapter Seven) describes a number of examples of community- and voluntary-based transport services that have been specifically introduced to fill a gap in mainstream transport services in deprived communities. Chapter Eight summarises the main points raised in the UK chapters and identifies the overall strengths and weaknesses of the social exclusion and accessibility planning approach.

Part Three is a reflection of Part Two in the US context. Chapter Nine discusses the way in which transport inequalities have moved to the forefront of the US transport policy agenda in recent years under the banner of the environmental justice movement. It describes the origins of environmental justice through the American Civil Rights movement and identifies the mechanisms by which concerns about transport inequity have increasingly influenced this agenda and been taken up by US Federal Law.

Chapters Ten to Thirteen offer four US-based case studies, each demonstrating some of the practical initiatives that have emerged to address transport inequities in the US. Chapter Ten describes and evaluates initiatives that have been introduced in the State of California in response to the Job Access and Reverse Commute (JARC) programme as part of the US 'welfare-to-work' agenda, which aims to assist low-pay workers to access entry-level employment. Chapter Eleven presents a community impact assessment (CIA) that was initiated in response to road-widening proposals for route US17, one of the oldest highways in the US. The assessment method was modelled on Federal Highways Administration guidance and involved nine minority ethnic and low-income communities that would be impacted upon by the proposals. Chapter Twelve describes how a team of US civil rights attorneys worked with grassroots organisations to file and win a landmark environmental justice class action against the Los Angeles Metropolitan Transport Authority. Chapter Thirteen looks at transportation issues from a women's rights perspective. Women are not included as a separate category in the civil rights legislation surrounding transport provision and spending. This chapter asserts that they should be, on the grounds that women are persistently disadvantaged by the transport system. Chapter Fourteen summarises the main points raised in the US chapters and draws out some key issues and concerns in relation to the approach that is being applied to the transport equity agenda in the US.

The final section draws comparative lessons between the UK and the US, in order to identify how the social and transport policy agenda on both sides of the Atlantic can better embrace the issue of social equity in the future.

Part One:
Setting the context

ONE

Locating transport as a social policy problem

Karen Lucas

In order to understand the relevance of looking at transport from a social policy perspective, it is important to first have some basic understanding of the intended role of social policy in advanced industrial societies. This chapter offers a brief overview of the main foci and interests of social and public policy as an academic discipline, especially for those who may be unfamiliar with this. It then takes the reverse perspective to look at the role of transport in modern societies and examine the transport policy-making tradition. The chapter identifies some additional reading in both these areas for those who may wish to further pursue this line of enquiry.

What is the role of social policy?

There are numerous texts tracing the origin of social and public policy making and analysis. It is clear that the subject is far from straightforward and open to a number of different interpretations. Professor Michael Hill, has written several useful books on this topic and provides a helpful background discussion in this respect in his 1996 volume, *Social policy: A comparative analysis*.

Hill broadly defines social policy as concerned with the role of the state in relation to the welfare of its citizens. Clearly, this is affected not only by their own actions, but also the actions of other individuals (over whom they may have little or no influence), as well as the behaviour and decisions of businesses. Other organisations and key institutions are all equally (and often more) important in affecting a person's welfare.

Hill identifies, on the one hand, that there is a philosophical position that sees 'markets' as the key organising factor in social activities. This perspective is commonly referred to as 'classical market theory', because the welfare of citizens is seen as appropriately determined by the distribution of income through free-market activity. The individual secures an income through work or investment activities and purchases goods and services, including health, education and other 'welfare' services, as necessary according to their needs. From this perspective, the regulation of economic activity and social order arises naturally from pricing mechanisms and out of individual self-interest.

On the other hand, there are those who argue that economic relationships cannot be governed by free-market exchange because of the inequities that arise, and that it is more appropriate for the state to intervene in the distribution of goods and services.

In practice, most advanced industrial societies have a 'mixed economy of welfare' (Kamerman, 1983), and the main decisions of government lie with the balance of this mix. All governments in advanced industrial societies are, in fact, heavily involved in the development and delivery of social welfare policies. One of the most common ways that states intervene to ensure the welfare of citizens is through the provision and/or funding of services. There are two key ways that this intervention manifests itself:

- By enhancing the income of individuals who are unable to purchase the services they need on the free market in order to enable them to do so. (This could take the form of increased tax allowances, benefit payments or vouchers and other non-cash subsidies.)
- The state can use its regulatory powers to encourage or compel the provision of services by appropriate institutions, which it must then usually wholly fund or subsidise.

There are mixed opinions about whether policy should be solely concerned with correction of malfunctions in the economic operation of society as and when they occur, or have some pre-emptive role in ensuring this happens.

Increasingly, there is also debate about the extent to which concerns about the welfare of citizens are, or even should be, the responsibility of the state. Rogers (2000) finds that, in the 21st century, modern states are gradually withdrawing from the concept of a welfare state that provides for most of its citizens towards one in which families and communities are increasingly being made responsible for sustaining the well-being of their members. He suggests that this is largely in response to the need to save on public expenditure.

Most commonly, the study of social policy has concerned itself with income maintenance and the welfare benefits system. Increasingly, there has been a tendency to add the study of health and social care provision to this list and, less frequently, education as well. Hill (1996, p 14) presents the case for including housing, employment and environmental policy, arguing that, although welfare-oriented interventions in the market are the exception rather than the rule, jobs and housing are vital for individual welfare. Environment is included because of "a dissatisfaction with the narrow approach to the study of social policy", and because the author considers it

> ... a little odd for discussions of social policy to disregard issues about dangers to individuals' health and safety which get right to the heart of the traditional role of the state in protecting its citizens....

However, he recognises that,

> ... in including only environmental policy among a range of issues where the regulation of economic activities is important the author is laying himself open to the charge that he is trying to redraw the boundary between social and other aspects of policy at a particularly unsatisfactory place.

Hill identifies that two additional topics were omitted from his comparative analysis: energy and transport policy.

In her introduction to *Delivering sustainable transport*, Root (2003) finds that failure to apply social science perspectives to transport policy has meant that transport studies have consistently failed to address public concerns about mobility and to make the links between progressive democratic aspirations, such as reducing unemployment or addressing health inequalities, and the system of transport delivery in advanced industrial societies.

In their earlier scrutiny of transport from a social sciences perspective, Banister and Hall (1981) also raised this criticism of transport policy. They assert that transport clearly has an important role to play in all modern societies and both the absence of adequate transport provision and the impacts of the transport system on individuals have important consequences for employment, education, housing and land use policy and thus the way in which economic activity is distributed as well as the health, safety and, thereby, more general quality of life of individuals and communities.

Understanding the role of transport in society

The history of transport has always been closely allied with that of urban development. Transport infrastructure is often responsible for shaping the layout of towns and cities, and thus determining where people live, work, shop, go to school, and carry out their leisure activities. It is easy to see the way in which the geographical layout of many urban areas in both the US and UK reflect the transport technologies dominant at the different stages of their development. For example, the coming of the railways permitted increased decentralisation, and marked the start of the trend towards lower residential densities in inner cities. The era of the motorcar added a further dimension; the increase of motorised urban mobility combined with economic and demographic changes has seen increasing suburban housing, and the move of industrial and commercial activities from the centre of cities to the periphery in most western societies.

Bruton (1993, p 13) outlines this shaping role of transport in society thus:

> It influences the location and range of productive and leisure activities; it affects the location of residence; it influences the range and provision

of goods and services available for consumption. It inevitably influences the quality of life.

Described in this way, transport and mobility can be seen as a stimulant to economic and social life. Troy (1996, p 208) goes as far as to argue that:

> Enhanced mobility gives people greater access to a wider range of interests and activities and allows them a higher degree of engagement with other like-minded members of the various communities to which they belong, thus enriching their lives and contributing to social and economic vitality.

Arguably, however, transport is often only a means to enable individuals to participate in the normal economic and social activities that would traditionally be reached by walking. More often than not, people use transport because they want to get somewhere and not because they wish to travel for its own sake. Root (2003) notes the odd exceptions to this, such as joyriding and the Sunday afternoon drive in the countryside. Nevertheless, the social benefits of transport and mobility are perhaps better understood in terms of their 'enabling accessibility function'.

In most modern societies, some form of transport is usually necessary if an individual is to gain access to education, employment, shops, essential services, leisure and the other social activities that are necessary to securing a good quality of life. In this way, it can be identified as a 'merit good' (Goodwin, 1990) and thereby worthy of policy intervention where the 'natural' distributional effects of the system disproportionately disadvantages certain groups or communities.

The growing importance of transport in enabling access to essential goods and services is increasingly being recognised within the transport literature. For example, Elkins et al (1991) note the steady decline in the number of services such as health and education and shops that can be accessed within walking distances. This means that people in advanced industrial societies are increasingly reliant on the transport system to access even basic services and amenities. In this way, as later chapters of this book demonstrate, transport is becoming a basic human necessity. Thus, ensuring that everyone has adequate access to it is a valid area of concern for public policy.

Public policy also has a key role to play in controlling any negative impacts arising from the transport system. Recent years have seen a considerable rise in public concern about the negative impacts of a car-dominated transport system, in terms of accidents, noise and air pollution and community severance (see Gorz, 1988; Whitelegg, 1993).

The transport policy-making tradition

There has, in fact, been a long history of state intervention in both the provision of transport and control of its negative effects on society in the UK and US.

Since medieval times, a government Act has required parishioners in the UK to pay a levy to maintain the roads (Truelove, 1992). In the US, the Interstate Highway Network was instigated by President Eisenhower as an act of defence following the Second World War, and governments on both sides of the Atlantic have enacted literally thousands of policies to regulate their transport system in the interests of public and passenger safety.

Even in the predominantly free-market system for transport provision in the UK and the US, some public transport or mass transit routes are supported by the state on the basis that they are considered 'socially necessary'. State funds are also made available to support specialist transport or paratransit services for people who are unable to access the public system because of disability or for particular journeys, such as the school trip or hospital outpatient visits. Transport, therefore, is an expensive item of government expenditure. In 2002/03, it accounted for approximately £12 billion of UK government spending, with a commitment to increase this to around £16.5 billion by 2005/06 (HM Treasury, 2002), and an estimated $56 billion of the 2003 US Federal budget, rising to approximately $58 billion in 2005 (US Department of Transportation, 2003).

Decisions about how the state spends money on transport have traditionally been made on the basis of cost benefit analysis (CBA). Cost benefit analysis takes different forms in different countries, and it is not appropriate or necessary to discuss the method in any detail in the context of this book. (For those with an interest in exploring the subject further, a comprehensive explanation of the method can be found in numerous publications on transport economics; for example, see Button, 1993). It is important to note, however, that there is a tendency for CBA to favour transport projects that bring small journey-time savings to a large number of travellers. Traditionally, therefore, transport-spending decisions have tended to favour road-building projects over public transport services and cycling and walking amenities. As later chapters of this volume demonstrate, the overall effect of the application of these methods has tended towards offering the greatest benefits from state transport spending to those who are already well-off in terms of their transport provision (mainly motorists), and least benefits to those who are least well provided for in this respect (mainly people who do not or cannot drive).

In transport planning, too, the main focus of activity has been geared towards improving operating conditions for vehicles. Until quite recently, the accepted transport planning method in both the US and UK has been to assess the likely demand for travel and cater for that demand through extensions to the capacity of the road and rail networks. Despite wide and long-standing criticism of the method and the incremental introduction of legislation requiring the transport planning process to consider wider social and community needs (dating as far back as the Ministry of Transport and Ministry of Housing and Local Government circular of 1964 in the UK, and the US Highway Act of 1962) (cited in Bruton, 1993, pp 56), only lip service has tended to be paid to the needs and values of communities themselves. This has resulted in a general tendency for transport systems to cater for physical movement rather than improving access to goods and services for the population as a whole or for minority ethnic and low-income groups.

More recently, however, transport policy making on both sides of the Atlantic has been undergoing some fundamental changes in its approach at both the national and local levels of government. In both the UK and the US, new policies and programmes are emerging which are recognising and attempting to address the negative consequences of poor transport, particularly on low-income and other disadvantaged groups. An important question that is addressed in later chapters of this book is whether or not these will be sufficient to reverse the negative trends that have been set in motion by the previous policy oversights in this respect.

Conclusion

The social costs of poor transport and the benefits of reducing these as part of a welfare agenda are often poorly understood and even more poorly monitored. One of the problems has been that providers of key services, including employers, educators, health workers and housing suppliers, have failed to understand the important role that transport plays in the distribution of the 'merit good' of their services across the populations they serve. The result has been that increasingly essential services such as jobs, hospitals, schools and shops are situated in places that are virtually impossible to access without a car. This means that those people in the population that most need these services are often the least able to reach them, and yet transport and access considerations rarely play a part in decisions about the location of these services.

In the main, these considerations do not play a part in mainstream transport planning decisions either, and the recent shift away from a demand-led planning model has generally not facilitated wider consideration of the social costs of transport policy. Equally, transport policy has been seen as 'falling outside' of this realm of social policy inquiry, either because it has been overlooked as a basic commodity or because the market system of delivery, supported by the state subsidies that are already in place, are presumed to be adequate for meeting people's travel needs. Chapter Two that follows, examines empirical evidence of the distribution of transport provision in the UK and the US in an attempt to gain a better understanding of how the travel behaviour of different social groups affects their life chances.

References

Banister, D. and Hall, P. (eds) (1981) *Transport and public policy planning*, London: Mansell.

Bruton, M. (1993) *Introduction to transportation planning* (3rd edn), London: UCL Press Ltd.

Button, K.J. (1993) *Transport economics* (2nd edn), Aldershot: Edward Elgar Publishing Company Ltd.

Elkins, T., McLaren, D. and Hillman, M. (1991) *Reviving the city: Towards sustainable urban development*, London: Friends of the Earth.

Goodwin, P. (1990) 'Demographic impacts, social consequences and transport policy debate', *Oxford Review of Economic Policy*, vol 6, no 2, pp 76-90.

Gorz, A. (1988) *Critique of economic reason*, London: Verso.

Hill, M. (1996) *Social policy: A comparative analysis*, Essex: Prentice Hall.

HM Treasury (2002) *2002 Spending review*, Chapter Eight (www.hm-treasury.gov.uk/SpendingReview/spend_sr02/report/spend_sr02_repchap08.cfm).

Kamerman, S.B. (1983) 'A mixed society of welfare', *Social Work*, vol 28, pp 5-11.

Rogers, J.J. (2000) *From a welfare state to a welfare society: The changing context of social policy in a postmodern era*, Hampshire: Macmillan Press Ltd.

Root, A. (ed) (2003) *Delivering sustainable transport*, Oxford: Elsevier.

Troy, P. (1996) 'Environmental stress and urban policy', in M. Jenks, E. Burton and K. Williams (eds) *The compact city: A sustainable urban form?*, London: E. & F.N. Spoon.

Truelove, P. (1992) *Decision making in transport planning*, Essex: Longman Scientific and Technical.

US Department of Transportation (2003) *2005 Budget Brief* (www.dot.gov/bib2005/tables).

Whitelegg, J. (1993) *Transport for a sustainable future*, London: John Wiley and Sons.

TWO

Examining the empirical evidence of transport inequality in the US and UK

Kelly Clifton and Karen Lucas

In order to argue the case for taking a social policy approach to transport, it is important to first gain a better understanding of the inequalities that arise from the present system of transport delivery. This chapter presents the statistical and qualitative evidence for this in the UK and the US. It should be noted, however, that distributional inequities in and of themselves do not necessarily justify the need for social policy intervention. It is generally accepted that such intervention is only appropriate where the welfare of citizens is already (or may become) undermined. With this in mind, the later sections of the chapter examine the evidence for this with particular emphasis on the effects of transport inequalities on people's ability to access the key activities that are considered essential to the welfare of citizens, namely employment, education and training, healthcare and social, leisure and cultural activities.

The combination effect

It is important to recognise from the outset that many of the inequalities that this chapter identifies have arisen over time as the result of a complex set of interactions between transport and land-use patterns. Figure 2.1 demonstrates how this combination effect works to both perpetuate transport inequalities over time and encourage increased car ownership and use by low-income groups, with its associate economic, social and environmental effects.

The overall effect is to create an 'accessibility deficit' among many low-income and excluded groups, which serves to 'lock them out' of the activities that support a reasonable quality of life and thus both contributes to and reinforces their social exclusion.

Dispersed land-use patterns and declining local services

As a starting point, it is important to recognise the dramatic growth in both vehicle numbers and the distances driven in all advanced industrial societies over the last 30-50 years. Mass car ownership, combined with other economic and socio-demographic changes in our society, has encouraged more dispersed land-

Figure 2.1: The dynamics of diminishing accessibility

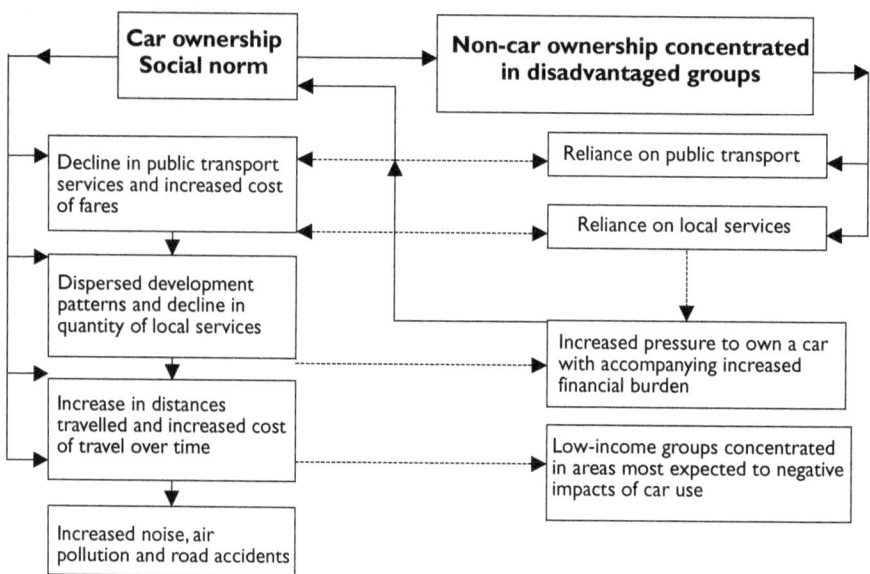

use patterns. This in turn has meant an increasing shift of both populations and industrial and economic activities from the centre of cities to edge-of-town or out-of-town developments and, thereby, has demanded more travel intensive lifestyles (Hay and Trinder, 1991).

The UK National Travel Survey (DfT, 2001) illustrates that, in both urban and rural areas, people are having to travel further in order to access basic goods and services. There has been a significant decline in the proportion of households living close to a local food store, from 68% to 57% within six minutes walk; in 1998, 5% had to walk more than 26 minutes, an increase of 3% from 1989/91.

Traditional labour markets such as manufacturing, mining and farming have declined and there is now less overall employment in many parts of the UK, but especially low-skilled jobs. Technological developments have also served to change long-established working geographies, with new employment opportunities springing up in different locations, demanding different skills and providing more dispersed employment patterns than the more traditional industries.

Hospital services have also been rationalised into fewer and larger units serving wide areas, and are often located in places that are difficult to reach without a car (Murray, 1998). A recent UK Office for National Statistics (ONS) Omnibus Survey conducted on behalf of the Social Exclusion Unit (SEU) (SEU, 2002) identified that:

- 15% of respondents say they have difficulty getting to hospital;
- 6% say they have difficulty getting to their doctor's surgery;
- 5% have difficulty getting to the dentist.

Figure 2.2: Increased distance of local facilities in urban and rural areas in the UK (1989-99)

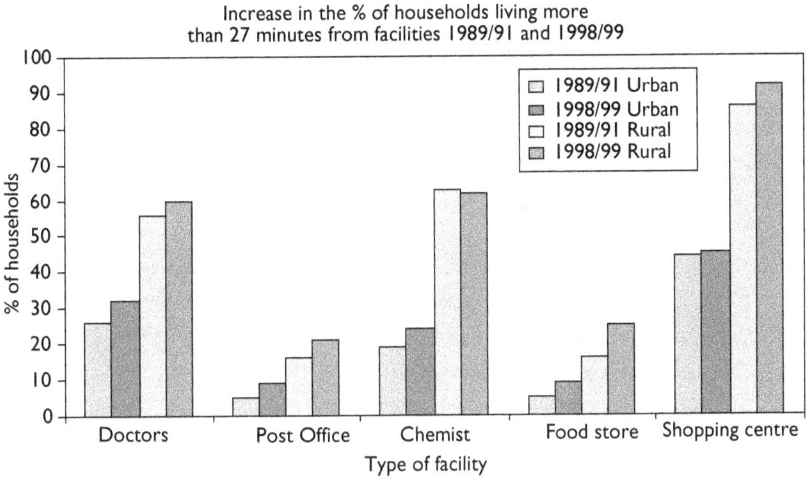

Increase in the % of households living more than 27 minutes from facilities 1989/91 and 1998/99

[Bar chart showing % of households by type of facility (Doctors, Post Office, Chemist, Food store, Shopping centre) comparing 1989/91 Urban, 1998/99 Urban, 1989/91 Rural, and 1998/99 Rural]

Source: National Travel Survey 1989/91 and 1998/99

In the UK, changes in food retailing practices have also resulted in the number of shops falling by about 50% in the last 20 years; the growth of large hypermarkets allow the benefits of cheaper food and the convenience of car-borne access but often result in less choice in price and quality to the already disadvantaged who cannot access them (Elkins et al, 1991).

This dispersal of activities has been exacerbated by the extreme 'flight' of local services from many areas of deprivation (Hutton, 1996). Many low-income communities in the UK now lack even basic amenities such as a general food store or a doctor's surgery (see Figure 2.2). The facilities that are available are often of poor quality and the goods they provide can be over-priced. High crime and fear of crime in these areas make them unattractive to businesses and customers alike and help to fuel the decline (SEU, 1998).

The UK government SEU's Policy Action Team on Jobs found a general lack of suitable local jobs within the deprived neighbourhoods it visited. However, there was rarely a lack of jobs within reasonable travelling distance of these areas, but unemployed people in the area did not necessarily take these up. A variety of reasons for this were offered, including a lack of skills among the resident population but also poor transport links and/or a reluctance to travel out of the area of residence.

The government's Neighbourhood Renewal Unit noted that the boroughs of Kingston and Richmond have 50% more doctors than Barnsley and Sunderland (adjusting for age and needs), yet Barnsley and Sunderland are likely to have far fewer people with access to a car given their income levels. This means that those in the greatest need of medical help are often least able to access it (SEU, 2002).

The majority of shops serving people living in deprived neighbourhoods and remote rural areas in the UK are small, independent convenience stores. The number of such stores declined by almost 40% between 1986 and 1997 and the Policy Action Team 13 (1999) report identifies that the three main reasons for the closure of these independent local stores are:

- falling local demand;
- competition;
- crime and the threat of crime.

High levels of crime in poor areas mean that people are reluctant to travel about in them, particularly at night. This, combined with higher insurance costs and regular break-ins, means that enterprise becomes unprofitable and risky. Crime not only encourages the closure of small businesses in many poor areas but also serves to deter new businesses and investment into these areas. Many smaller shops are run and owned by people from minority ethnic backgrounds who are often exposed to intolerable levels of racial abuse with little support from the police in these areas.

There is a similar trend towards disinvestment by the business community at the neighbourhood level and a reorientation to larger and regional markets in the US. The structural changes in retailing and the consequences for residents of urban neighbourhoods have been examined in a number of studies (for example, Bingham and Zhang, 1997). The loss of neighbourhood businesses has been more pronounced in low-income and minority ethnic communities in the central cities and inner suburbs. In many cases, the lower levels of competition have led to unfair pricing schemes that take advantage of the captive market. In other cases, gaps in key retail and service sectors, such as supermarkets and banks, have emerged leaving residents with the choice of travelling out of their neighbourhood to obtain items for their household, purchasing them at higher costs at convenience stores, or doing without (Troutt, 1993; Cotterill and Franklin, 1995).

Several US studies have documented the failures of the food retailers to meet the needs of residents in poor communities (Ashman et al, 1993; Sustainable Food Centre, 1995; Gottlieb et al, 1996). In the past 30 years, the supermarket industry has become increasingly more centralised; the total number of food stores has declined while at the same time the average store size has increased steadily (Public Voice for Food and Health Policy, 1995 and 1996). The movement of supermarkets to suburban locations paralleled trends in population shifts and new transportation corridors (Yim, 1993) and thus, larger chain grocery stores are disproportionately located in the suburbs than non-chain stores (Chung and Myers, 1999). The existing stores in urban areas located in or adjacent to poor neighbourhoods were closed or sold and the combined effect has been to create an urban grocery store gap as low-income areas have fewer and smaller stores per capita (Cotterill and Franklin, 1995).

As a result of the combination of these wider land-use patterns and service

Figure 2.3: Average distance travelled per person per annum in the UK by mode of transport and level of household income

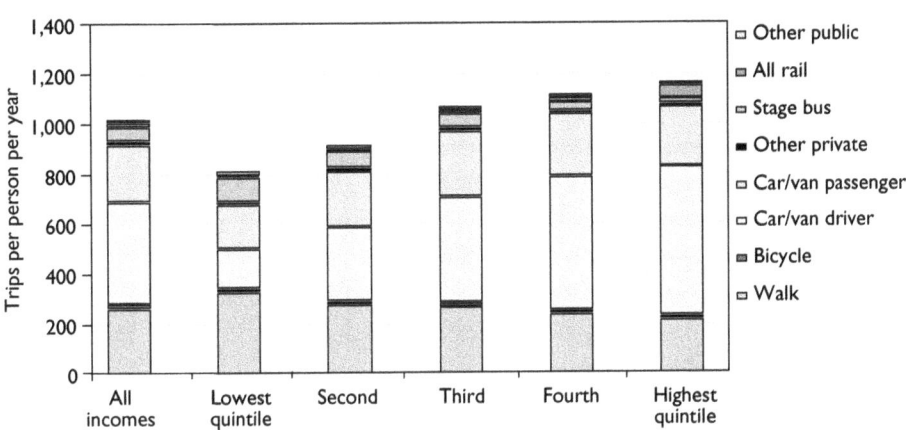

Source: UK National Travel Survey 1998/99

delivery trends in both the US and UK, people in deprived communities are increasingly forced to travel outside their local areas in order to access even basic facilities and amenities.

Declining public transport services

Meanwhile, public transport services have largely failed to adapt to new land-use and activity patterns on both sides of the Atlantic. This may explain why the car accounts for the vast majority of the travel of all income groups (see Figure 2.3). High car dependency, even among the lowest-income households, suggests that public transport is generally inadequate to the mobility and accessibility requirements of a modern society and that even those on a low income will go out of their way to own or gain access to a car.

People without cars usually take more time, expend greater effort, and pay a higher marginal costs to reach the same destinations as people with cars (see Figures 2.3 and 2.4). This may explain the shorter distances they travel and would suggest they are less able to access the full range of services and amenities available to car drivers.

In the US, there is an increase in the average journey distance with increasing income but this is less marked than in the UK; the average journey time hovers around 20 minutes for all income groups. The longer journey times for shorter distances is explained in part by their greater reliance on slower modes of travel such as transit and walking.

Analysis of the 2001 US Nationwide Personal Transportation Survey by Pucher and Renne (2003) shows the differences in trip rates and miles travelled per day across income groups in the US. The disparities are due in part to the lower rates of automobile ownership and resulting inability to access destinations. However,

Figure 2.4: Journey distances and travel time in the UK by income quintile

30
25
20
15
10
5
0
Average journey length (miles); average journey time (minutes)
Length
Time
All
Lowest
Second
Third
Fourth
Highest
Income quintile

Source: UK National Travel Survey 2001/02

Pucher and Renne (2003, p 55) note that the relationship between income and travel by the poor is confounded by:

> ... their higher rates of unemployment and retirement and thus fewer trips to work. Their shorter trip lengths might also result from the concentration of the poor in central cities, where things are closer together and do not require such long trips as in the suburbs.

As less people have used public transport services over time, the more frequency, reliability and quality has deteriorated, to the point where in many areas they no longer provide a viable transport alternative. Although approximately 87% of

Figure 2.5: Journey distances and travel time in the US by income quintile

25
20
15
10
5
0
Average journey length (miles); average journey time (minutes)
Length
Time
Lowest
Second
Third
Fourth
Highest
All
Income quintile

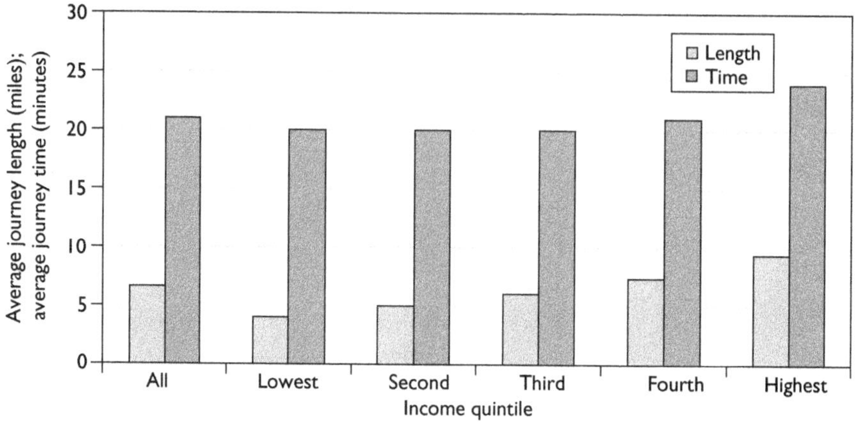

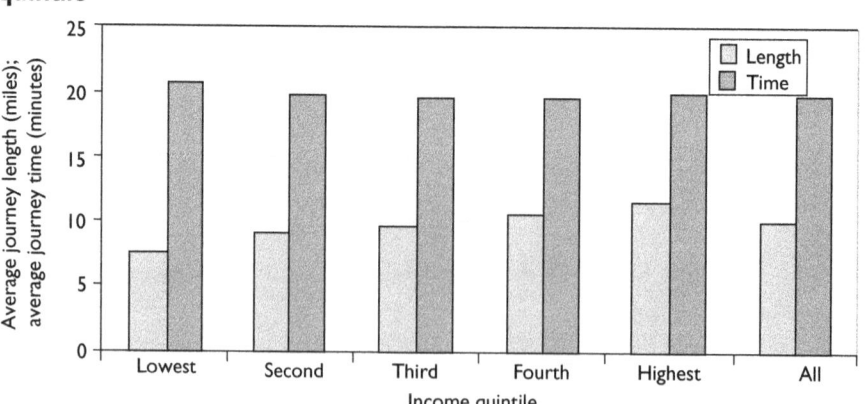

Source: US National Household Travel Survey 2001

Table 2.1: Trips and miles travelled per day by income in the US

Household income ($)	Trips per day, per person	Miles travelled per day, per person
Less than 20,000	3.2	17.9
20,000-39,999	3.9	26.4
40,000-74,999	4.2	30.2
75,000-99,000	4.3	30.7
100,000 and over	4.8	26.9
All	4.0	26.9

Note: In order to isolate urban travel, the sample was limited to residents of urban areas and trips of 75 miles or less.

Source: Calculated from the 2001 NHTS by Mary Ann Keyes, Federal Highway Administration, US Department of Transportation

people in the UK live within 13 minutes walk of an hourly daytime bus service, in some parts of rural England that figure is as low as 36%. Only 19% of the population live within 13 minutes walk of a local train station, although this also differs for different parts of the country, rising to 57% in London and falling to 6% for rural England. This information is unavailable for the US.

Even in urban areas, people often do not have access to regular bus services. Some deprived neighbourhoods have become effective 'no go' areas for public transport services; drivers refuse to operate routes because of fear for their personal safety and they are withdrawn.

Using crow-fly distances to public transport is anyway a very crude and flawed measure of accessibility, masking the reality of people's actual experiences. This is because it says nothing about whether the service connects with the right destination or about its frequency, reliability, safety or quality or whether routes match people's needs in terms of coverage and operating times. It also offers no indication of the cost of travel to the individual, both in terms of fares and journey times, or whether vehicles are accessible for people with disabilities, pushchairs, heavy shopping and so on. Many of the people experiencing or at risk of social exclusion are also over-represented in the section of the population that experience physical difficulties in accessing public transport, for example, older people and women escorting small children. Fear about personal safety can also serve to act as a mobility constraint, particularly for women, older people and, more surprisingly, teenagers. More generally, fear of accidents and mugging when walking, particularly at night, can serve to make some groups virtual prisoners in their own home (Lucas et al, 2001).

Low literacy rates and language difficulties, which have high prevalence among the poorest sectors of the population in both the UK and US, can also reduce people's ability to access information about the transport system, which has an impact on its use. There is also anecdotal evidence to suggest that some low-income groups would prefer to carry out their activities within their own neighbourhoods and are reluctant to travel to places further afield. This is not only based on choices about the cost of travel, but also lack of familiarity with the transport system and the wider area, as well as more deep-seated parochial attitudes in some instances (TRaC, 2000).

Car availability within households and among different social groups

The effect of mass car ownership on land use and activity patterns and failure of public transport (mass transit) to adequately adapt to these means that more and more people are choosing to own and drive cars. Car ownership is now the norm within most households in both the UK and US. In the US, approximately only 8% of households do not have regular access to a car, while in the UK this applies to approximately 27% of households. The differences in travel behaviour between non-car owning and car-owning households are stark, and it could be argued that, in car-dominant societies, lack of access to a car is in itself one of the key defining factors in people's disadvantage.

National statistics demonstrate that, in both the US and the UK, the overwhelming majority of households without a car are concentrated in the lowest income quintile (see Figures 2.6 and 2.7). In 2002, 63% of people in the

Figure 2.6: Car ownership in the UK by income quintile (2000)

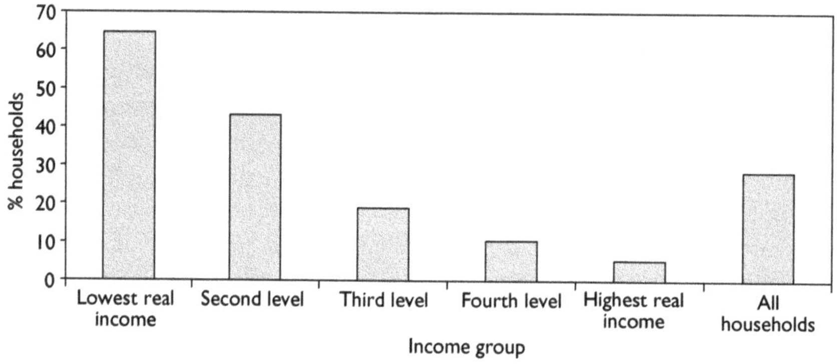

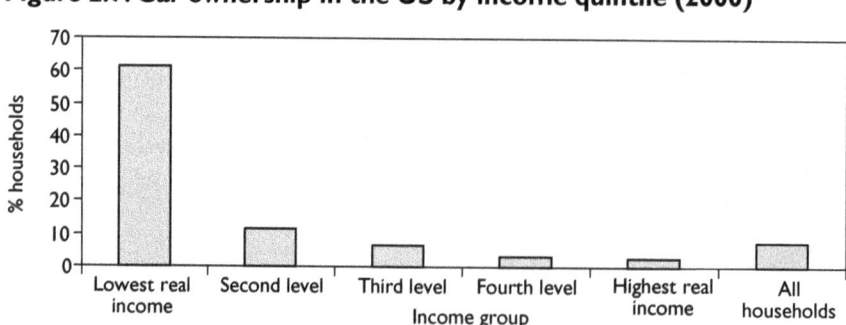

Source: UK National Travel Survey 2001

Figure 2.7: Car ownership in the US by income quintile (2000)

Source: US National Household Travel Survey 2001

lowest household income quintile in the UK did not have access to a car. The figures are similar to those for the US, although overall vehicle ownership is higher for all categories. In 2001, 61% of households in the lowest income category in the US did not have access to a vehicle. This would suggest that, in most instances, non-car ownership is usually not a choice but rather based upon affordability and/or an inability to drive.

Women, and in particular older women, are less likely to have access to a car or to be the main driver in one-car households (see Figures 2.8 and 2.9). Fewer women than men, across all age bands but most markedly over the age of 60,

Figure 2.8: People with driving licences in the UK by age and gender (1975-2001)

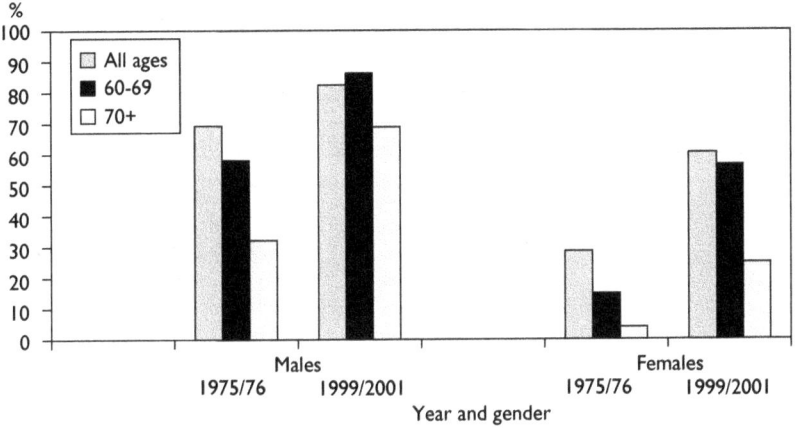

Source: UK National Travel Survey 2001

Figure 2.9: People with driving licences in the US by age and gender

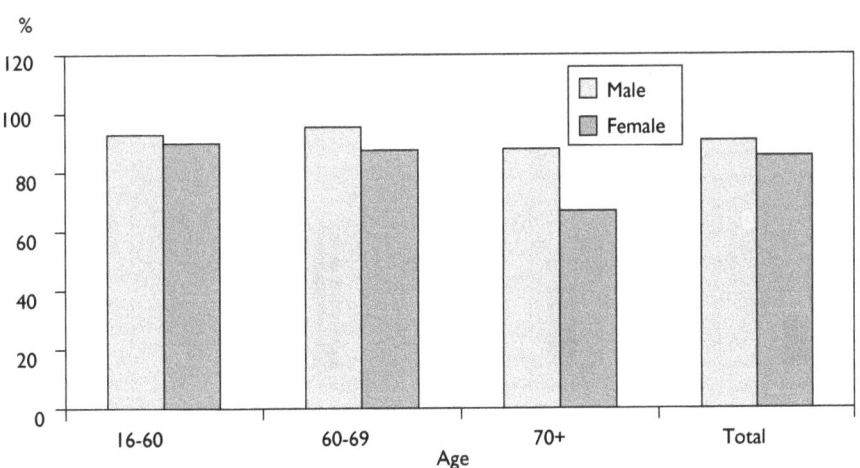

Source: US National Household Travel Survey 2001

Running on empty

hold driving licenses, although the level has continued to increase and is twice as high as in 1970. Partly because women tend to live longer than men, more experience mobility difficulties, making public transport use prohibitive and making them more reliant on lifts from friends and families.

There are also marked differences in car access across racial and ethnic groups. In the US, approximately 5% of white households are car-less, compared to over 20% of black, 15% of Native Hawaiians/Pacific Islander, and 14% of Hispanics of Mexican origin (see Figure 2.10).

The evidence for observing similar trends in the UK is not currently available. However, the UK Labour Force Survey data on main mode of transport to work by ethnic origin demonstrates that people from all minority ethnic groups in the UK, but particularly people from black and mixed ethnic origins, are less likely to drive to work than their white counterparts, suggesting a similar pattern of car ownership among minority populations in the UK (see Figure 2.11).

Figure 2.10: US households without a car by race/ethnicity

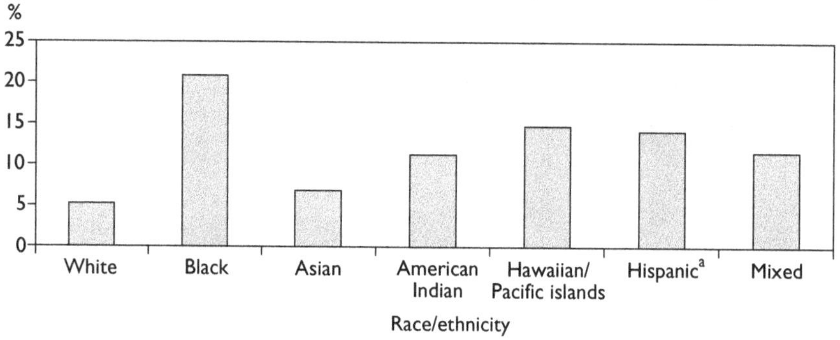

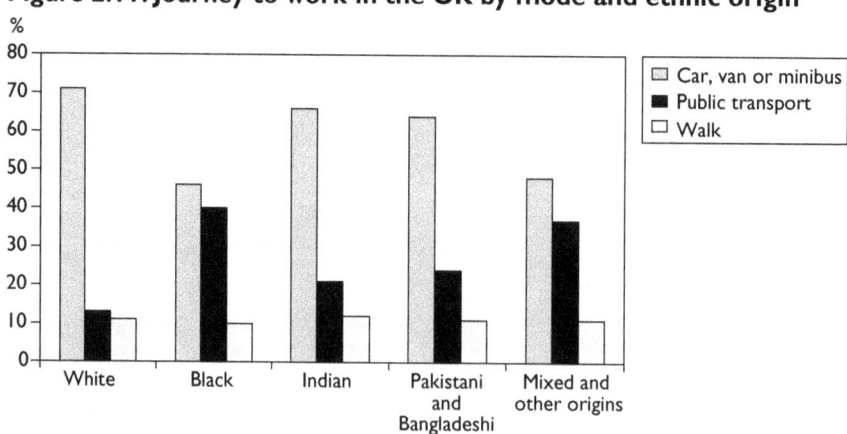

Note: [a] Mexican only.
Source: US National Household Travel Survey 2001

Figure 2.11: Journey to work in the UK by mode and ethnic origin

Source: UK Labour Force Survey 2001

Figure 2.12: Journey to work in the US by mode and ethnic origin

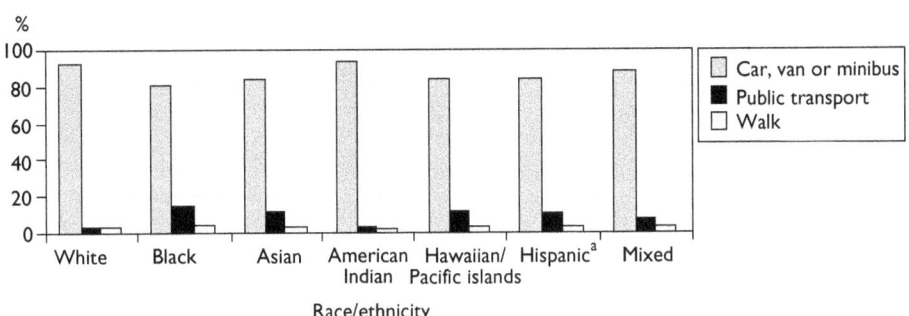

Note: [a] Mexican only.
Source: National Household Travel Survey 2001

In the US, the automobile is widely used for commuting across all racial and ethnic categories, testament to the auto-oriented nature of the urban structure. Consistent with data on automobile availability by race, racial and ethnic minorities are much more likely to take mass transit or walk to work than white workers (see Figure 2.12).

The cost of transport

The cost of travel is an overwhelming constraint for people on low incomes, dictating both the method and extent of their travel. Often it means people simply cannot afford to get to the places they need to go, whether this is to work, or to the hospital or the shops. At other times, it means that they have to walk unreasonably long distances, in unfavourable and stressful circumstances to carry out their daily activities. This can inhibit the geographical extent of job-search activities and work-travel patterns, while time constraints are identified as particularly important for women, given the 'double burden' of their domestic role and employment responsibilities (TRaC, 2000).

In the US, it has been identified that transportation expenditures pose the greatest burden for low-income families, who spend nearly 40% of their net income on transportation (nearly 10% of their income is used for the commute alone). A report by the Surface Transportation Policy Project (2001) shows that US families devoted 19.3 cents per dollar on transportation, second only to housing expenditures. The overwhelming majority (95%) of the funds spent on transportation by these poor households in the US are for private vehicles.

This may go a long way in explaining the disparity in automobile travel between the different income groups in the US. Figure 2.13 demonstrates that car drivers in the lowest income groups log the shortest annual distances at around 8,700 miles, compared to an overall average of approximate 13,800 miles for all drivers. A recent study for the Joseph Rowntree Foundation also found that car drivers in the lowest-income group in the UK spend 24% of the weekly household

Figure 2.13: Average miles driven per year by income quintile

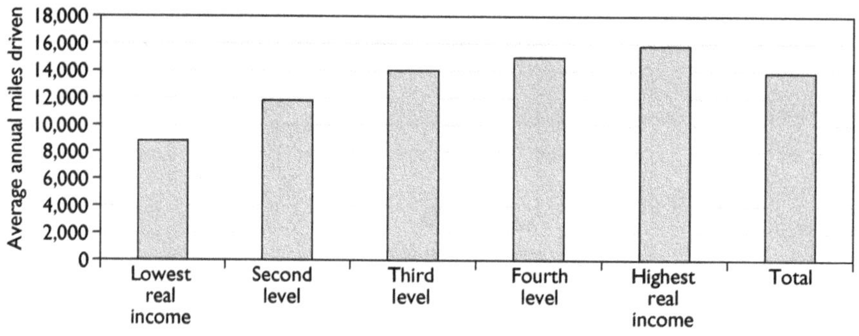

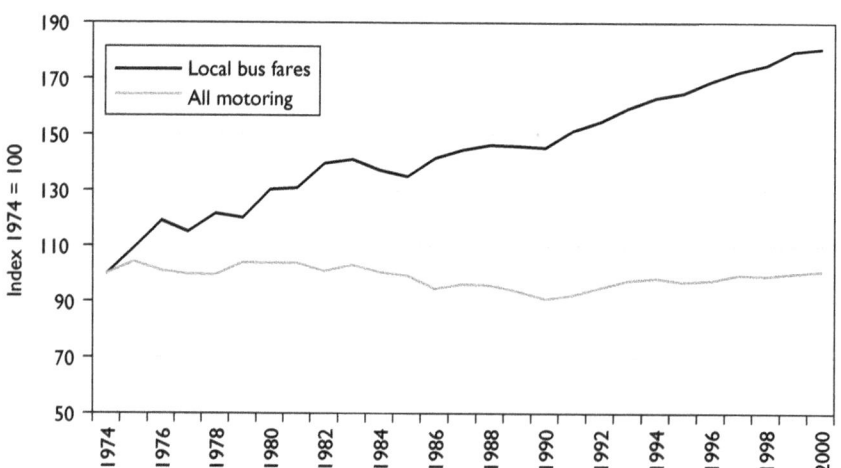

Source: US National Household Travel Survey 2001

budget on motoring, compared to 17% in the highest quintile (Lucas et al, 2001). However, the rising cost of public transport fares in the UK has also made travel by public transport even more prohibitive for many low-income households. Local bus fares in the UK have increased by 80% in real terms over the last 25 years, while motoring costs have remained broadly constant (see Figure 2.14). This means that the car is often the cheaper option for low-income households and is helping to fuel the trend for increased car ownership and use among even the lowest-income households.

Figure 2.14: Bus fares and motoring costs (1974-2000[a])

Note: [a] These data are not available for the US.
Source: SEU (2002)

Exposure to accidents, pollution and community severance

The previous sections of this chapter have predominantly been concerned with access to the transport system, but low-income groups are also disproportionately affected by the negative impacts arising from this. Poor people are much more likely to live in urban areas, in close proximity to busy roads and to undertake walking trips (on average, poor people in the UK undertake nearly double the walking trips of the rest of the population). As such, people on low incomes experience far higher levels of exposure to pedestrian accidents and traffic pollution.

Traffic is a major source of both noise and air pollution with subsequent increased health risks from nitrogen oxides, carbon monoxide, hydrocarbons and ground-level ozone (Holman, 1989)[1]. The rising volume and speed of traffic is also an area for concern. Road accidents are now the largest single cause of accidental death in the UK, while the pedestrian fatality rate for children is the highest in Europe (DETR, 1998). As a consequence, children suffer a dramatic loss in independence, as parents have increasingly felt obliged to impose restrictions on them. Pensioners too are at great risk as pedestrians; the fatality rate (both per head of population and per mile walked) is many times higher among older people, particularly among those aged 75+ (Hillman, 1989).

Transport infrastructure, especially large roads with heavy volumes of traffic, can also result in community severance. Hillman (Hillman et al, 1976) underlines the cost to community life:

> Wide roads and streams of motor vehicles destroy the function of the street as a locus for social interaction and break community ties ... the residential street used to be the traditional play space and social milieu for children and provided an introduction for them to the world beyond their family, without their needing to be accompanied to reach it.

Children in the lowest social class grouping in the UK are five times more likely to be involved in a road accident as pedestrians than those in social classes I and II. Evidence submitted to the SEU by the Centre for Transport Studies at Imperial College (SEU, 2002) demonstrated a clear link between areas of deprivation and pedestrian accident rates for children. The relationship holds even after controlling for factors such as housing density. Small-scale studies also suggest a disproportionately high rate of pedestrian accidents among minority ethnic children, over and above the effect of social class.

The Acheson report on health inequalities in the UK (Acheson, 1998) identified that poor people in the UK are also more likely to be exposed to air and noise pollution from traffic because of their proximity to busy roads (SEU, 2002). Smaller studies have also confirmed this relationship (for example, White et al, 2000). Pollution from traffic fumes can exacerbate the symptoms of people who are already at higher risk of suffering from respiratory diseases. Traffic noise can be a major factor in depression and stress-related illnesses, as well as more generally negatively affecting people's quality of life.

Past road building programmes have cut through some deprived areas and severed communities both through their physical infrastructure and the volume of traffic that passes along them. Busy roads can cut people off because of fear of accidents and reduce the level of social interaction within communities. Numerous local studies have demonstrated the relationship between high traffic volumes and reduced quality of life (SEU, 2002). There is anecdotal evidence to suggest that major roads are more likely to cut through poorer areas because these communities are less likely to raise objections to their construction due to their disenfranchisement.

These findings echo trends in the US. Low-income households and communities of colour share a disproportionate burden of the negative consequences of the transportation system and at the same time do not see the compensatory benefits in terms of access and mobility. These burdens take the form of increased exposure to pollutants, community disruption from transportation investments, and occurrence of injuries and fatalities.

For example, studies have shown that minority ethnic children in the US are at higher risk of pedestrian injury than white children (Braddock et al, 1991; Kim et al, 1992; Olson et al, 1993). These injuries are due in part to the fact that walking is more common among these populations than among the white population and thus they are exposed to threats more often. But these threats are also due to low levels of pedestrian investments, higher levels of traffic volumes, and fewer traffic calming measures in communities of colour.

The history of freeway building in the US has contributed to the severance – and in some cases razing – of urban neighbourhoods. These road investments primarily benefited higher-income groups at these communities' expense. Evidence of this type of disruption and dislocation comes from a case study in Nashville (TN), where an African American community was destroyed to build a freeway in the 1950s (Hodge, 1986). Although the practice of mass displacement and disruption has nearly ceased, the population and neighbourhoods affected by these highways are still suffering from the consequences of past decisions.

Do these transport inequalities matter?

Since non-drivers and people without regular access to a car tend to be concentrated among households in the lowest-income groups and in the most deprived neighbourhoods, they are already at risk of social exclusion. Women, lone parents, older people, people with disabilities, people from minority ethnic groups and young people are all less likely to live in households with a car. However, the people who are solely dependent on walking, cycling and public transport or mass transit services have not traditionally featured as significant factors in the development and implementation of mainstream transport policies (Bruton, 1993). Ironically, these are the very people that are more likely to need to use key public services, such as healthcare facilities, schools, colleges and welfare services.

In a highly mobile society, a lack of adequate transport provision means that individuals become cut off from employment, education and training and other opportunities. This in turn perpetuates their inability to secure a living wage and thus to fully participate in society. Poor access to healthy affordable food, primary and secondary healthcare and social services exacerbates the health inequalities that are already evident among low-income groups, further reducing their life chances. People can become housebound, isolated and cut off from friends, family and other social networks. This can seriously undermine their quality of life and, in extreme circumstances, may lead to social alienation, disengagement and, thus, undermine social cohesion.

Poor transport links and polluted and unsafe walking and waiting environments reduce social and economic activity within deprived communities. There can be knock-on effects in terms of crime and anti-social behaviour, with implications for personal safety and the more general desirability of these areas. Businesses suffer from the loss of custom and this encourages the flight of services from these areas and a reduced local employment base. Poor accessibility into and out of many deprived areas also discourages inward investment and leaves them abandoned and isolated.

In turn, this costs the state in terms of higher welfare payments and reduced tax contributions. It also serves to undermine the wider social policy agenda in terms of reducing unemployment, improving educational attainment and reducing health inequalities. The evidence for this is stark, although it remains under-researched and poorly examined by the welfare professionals charged with the task of addressing these social ills.

Welfare to work

In the UK, young men with driving licenses are twice as likely to get a job than those without (Stafford et al, 1999). The Audit Commission (1999) has identified that 38% of job seekers cited lack of a car and/or poor public transport as a barrier to getting work. In a recent ONS Omnibus survey carried out for the SEU (SEU, 2002), 13% of people said that they had not applied for a job in the past year because of poor transport. The figure rose to 18% in deprived areas (as identified by the Index of Multiple Deprivation 2000) and 25% for 16- to 18-year-olds.

The high cost of transport relative to wages also acts as a barrier to getting people from welfare into work in some cases. Evaluation of the UK Welfare to Work programme identified that 14% of lone parents were prevented from taking up employment because they could not afford the cost of transport to work (Green et al, 2000).

Transportation is also frequently cited as a barrier to employment by welfare recipients in the US (Waller and Blumenberg, 2003). Welfare recipients who face long commutes tend to earn less than those who find work close to home (Ong and Blumenberg, 1998). However, the suburbanisation of jobs and lack of housing opportunities for low-income and minority ethnic groups in these areas mean many are forced to commute longer distances without the reward of higher wages.

Later chapters of this volume demonstrate that considerable policy attention has been given to the problem of providing transportation for access to work at both the federal and state level in the US. Less attention is paid to access to other services, whereas the UK takes a broader focus to also consider the ways in which poor transport can undermine educational achievement and contribute to poor health and reduced quality of life.

Educational attainment

In 1999, only 24% of 16-year-olds in the most disadvantaged schools in the UK gained five or more GSCE A-C grades, compared with the national average of 46%. At Key Stage 2 (10-11 years), 54% of pupils in disadvantaged areas reached Level 4 in Maths and English, compared with 69% and 70% respectively for the national average (DfEE, 2000).

In the US, young adults living in families with incomes in the lowest 20% of all family incomes were five times as likely to drop out of high school as their peers in the top 20% of the income distribution. In 1999, approximately 3.8 million young adults were not enrolled in a high school programme and had not completed high school. These youths accounted for 11.2% of the 34.2 million 16- to 24-year-olds in 1999 (Kaufman et al, 2000).

Part of the problem in the UK is that children living in deprived areas usually attend the nearest school to their home because of a lack of available transport and a legacy of home-to-school transport policies. These only provide free school travel for journeys over three miles and only then providing the student attends the nearest suitable school. Parents on low incomes are unable to move house in order for their children to gain access to a better school and cannot afford the travel costs of sending them further afield. A survey of parents choosing secondary schools showed that those living in rented sector housing are one and a half times more likely to cite travel inconvenience as a reason for their selection than owner-occupiers (Sheffield Hallam University and ONS, 2001).

Adults in deprived areas are also likely to have low levels of qualifications and low basic skills and this can serve to undermine the educational achievement of their children, as they cannot support them in their learning. This is why good access to continuing and adult education facilities can be a crucial factor in enhancing the life chances and employability of both present and future generations. Further education facilities in the UK are usually situated in places that are difficult and expensive to reach by public transport, and many young people are unable to drive and do not usually receive assistance with the cost of their travel.

Callender (1999) identified travel costs as the biggest expenditure associated with post-16 education in the UK and found that one in every five students in the UK had considered dropping out of their studies because of the burden of these costs. Six per cent of students have missed college at some point during the academic year because they could not afford the cost of transport. Six per cent of 16- to 24-year-olds have turned down the offer of training or further education because they are unable to get to the educational establishment offering them a place.

The consolidation of secondary schools in the US poses problems of access as smaller neighbourhood-oriented schools are closed and larger sub-regional schools take their place. Meier et al (1991) have shown that the lack of urban access to educational facilities has placed barriers to participation in after-school activities and other special programs. In a study of the school location, access and achievement in rural schools, Talen (2001) found substantial variation in access to schools and that distance to school was inversely correlated with student achievement.

Barriers to educational attainment have not been a central focus in the transportation policy discussion in the US. However, as school choice and vouchers move from discourse to policy, the barriers that inadequate mobility present to children attending schools outside of their neighbourhood may be given more serious consideration.

Reducing health inequalities

Poor access to healthcare facilities, brought about by poor transport availability, a lack of primary healthcare facilities in deprived areas and the location of hospital facilities in places that are hard to reach by public transport, can result in missed appointments. This can mean that illnesses are not discovered or treated so quickly, with an adverse implication for the success rate and cost of certain treatments.

Poor access to healthy affordable food and a reduced ability to socialise and visit friends and family can also act to reinforce and perpetuate ill health. This, combined with the disproportionate impact of road traffic accidents and poor air quality on low-income groups, all contribute to continuing health inequalities in the UK and the US.

A recent ONS Omnibus Survey found that around 31% of people without access to cars in the UK found it difficult to travel to hospital – 7% of them had turned down appointments in the last year because of a lack of transport (SEU, 2002). A third of older people attending doctors and healthcare centres in London experienced difficulties getting there.

Public transit is not providing access to medical facilities for many poor in the US and may even discourage some from seeking care (McCray, 2000). Non-working poor in urban areas are particularly disadvantaged in that they are more likely to name transportation as a barrier to receiving healthcare than the working poor (Ahmed et al, 2001). These problems extend to rural areas where public transit is often not an option. Although lack of financial resources is by far the greatest constraint, the immobility to travel to healthcare providers contributes to differential health outcomes. The costs of treatment are increased for these patients in the long run as minor or treatable problems become more severe through neglect.

Historically, decision makers and providers of public services have not tended to recognise these problems in the delivery of their services and an assessment of whether their facilities are located in the places that are most accessible on foot or by public transport is rare. There is little academic and even less policy research on the inequitable outcomes of socioeconomic development predicated on private mobility or in-depth analysis of the particular travel behaviour of socially excluded groups. Most national travel datasets cannot be sufficiently disaggregated to identify localised travel patterns and transport evaluations tend to concern themselves with journey timesavings to users rather than test the ability of the system to link people to places.

Conclusion

This chapter has demonstrated that people without regular access to a car but living in car-dominant societies such Britain and the US are overwhelmingly concentrated among low-income households. The poorest sector of the population travel far less (both in terms of distance and number of trips) than the average population. They are also more likely to be exposed to road traffic accidents and traffic-related pollution. Non-car ownership is more prevalent among the UK population, but greater numbers of people are actually affected in the US. This is likely to have an influence on the type of policy responses and practical initiatives that can be employed to address their transport needs. Women, older people, lone parents and minority ethnic populations all tend to be over-represented among low-income groups and are also all more likely to be non-car owners; this is also important to bear in mind when policies are being developed.

The data also identify that a significant proportion of households on very low incomes in the US (approximately 29%), and to only slightly less of an extent in the UK (approximately 27%), do own and drive cars. Research evidence suggests that many more, given the choice, would do so: since 1989, the percentage of households without vehicles has significantly declined even among the poor. The data suggests that this increase in the level of car ownership among poor households does not speak to their overall levels of mobility nor the benefit that they receive. Indeed, it is suggested that poor households may be making financial sacrifices in order to purchase and operate these vehicles. The data show that car drivers from the lowest-income quintile are spending a far greater proportion of their income on travel-related costs. It suggests these households are prioritising travel expenditure over other items of essential household expenditure – a possible indication of its overall value to that household. However, the disparity in overall annual distances travelled between low-income car drivers and the average population suggests that their vehicle use is constrained by affordability factors.

It has not been possible to provide the evidence to directly correlate the effect of the transport inequalities that have been identified among the UK and US population with a reduced ability to access key services and activities. However, the available information suggests that a lack of adequate transport provision means that certain sectors of the population are experiencing a reduced ability to participate in employment, education and training, healthcare and other opportunities. This in turn undermines their life chances, with a cost to both the individual and the state.

Later chapters will demonstrate that, in the past, consideration of these issues has not played a part in either mainstream transport or land-use planning and service delivery decisions to the detriment of already disadvantaged sectors of the population. The statistical evidence suggests the need for more integrated policy decisions that specifically focus on reducing the gap in travel between the 'travel rich' and the 'travel poor'.

Note

[1] A high proportion of air pollution in industrialised countries is attributable to the transport sector, which is responsible for 50% or more of emissions (ECMT, 1993).

References

Acheson, D. (1998) *Independent Inquiry into Inequalities in Health Report*, London: The Stationery Office.

Ahmed, A., Syed, M., Lemkau, J.P., Nealeigh, N. and Mann, B. (2001) 'Barriers to healthcare access in a non-elderly urban poor American population', *Health and Social Care in the Community*, vol 9, no 6, pp 445-54.

Ashman, L., de la Vega, J., Dohan, M., Fisher, A., Hippler, R. and Romain, B. (1993) *Seeds of change: Strategies for food security for the inner city*, Los Angeles, CA: Department of Urban Planning, University of California.

Audit Commission (1999) *A life's work: Local authorities, economic development and economic regeneration*, London: Audit Commission.

Bingham, R. and Zhang, Z. (1997) 'Poverty and economic morphology of Ohio central city neighborhoods', *Urban Affairs Review*, vol 32, pp 766-96.

Braddock, M., Lapidus, G., Gregorio, D., Kapp, M. and Banco, L. (1991) 'Population, income, and ecological correlates of child pedestrian injury', *Pediatrics*, vol 88, no 6, pp 1242-7.

Bruton, M. (1993) *Introduction to transportation planning* (3rd edn), London: UCL Press Ltd.

Callender, C. (1999) *The hardship of learning*, London: South Bank University.

Chung, C. and Myers, S.L. Jr (1999) 'Do the poor pay more for food: an analysis of grocery store availability and food price disparities', *The Journal of Consumer Affairs*, vol 33, no 2, pp 276-96.

Cotterill, R. and Franklin, A. (1995) *The urban grocery store gap*, Storrs, CT: Food Marketing Policy Center, University of Connecticut.

DETR (Department for the Environment, Transport and the Regions) (1998) *A new deal for transport: Better for everyone*, London: The Stationery Office.

DfEE (Department for Education and Employment) (2000) *Policy Action Team on Jobs*, London: DfEE.

DfT (Department for Transport) (2001) *UK national travel survey 2001*, London: DfT.

ECMT (European Commission Ministers for Transport) (1993) 'Transport growth in question', 12th National Symposium on Theory and Practice in Transport Economics, Paris: OECD Publication Services.

Elkins, T., McLaren, D. and Hillman, M. (1991) *Reviving the city: Towards sustainable urban development*, London: Friends of the Earth.

Gottlieb, R., Fisher, A., Dohan, M., O'Connor, L. and Parks, V. (1996) *Homeward bound: Food-related strategies in low income and transit dependent communities*, Working Paper, UCTC no 336, Berkeley, CA: Transportation Centre, University of California.

Green, H., Smith, A., Lilley, R. and Marsh, A. (2000) *First effects of ONE*, DSS research report 126, Leeds: Corporate Document Services.

Hay, A. and Trinder, E. (1991) 'Concepts of equity, fairness and justice expressed by local transport policymakers', *Environment and Planning C: Government and Policy*, vol 9, pp 435-65.

Hillman, M. (1989) 'Neglect of walking in UK transport and planning policy', Paper presented to First Feet Symposium, 19 May, London.

Hillman, M., Henderson, I. and Whalley, A. (1976) 'Transport policies and planning realities', *Policy & Politics*, vol 10, no 2, pp 56-7, December.

Hodge, D. (1986) 'Social impacts of urban transportation decisions: equity impacts', in S. Hansen (ed) *The geography of urban transportation*, New York, NY: Guilford Press, p 302.

Holman, C. (1989) *Air pollution and health*, London: Friends of the Earth.

Hutton, W. (1996) *The state we're in*, London: Vintage.

Kaufman, P., Kwon, J., Klein, S. and Chapman, C.D. (2000) 'Dropout rates in the United States: 1999', *Education Statistics Quarterly*, vol 4, no 4, http://nces.ed.gov/programs/quarterly/vol_2/2_4/e_section3.asp

Kim, W.D. and Palmisano, P.A. (1992) 'Racial differences in childhood hospitalized pedestrian injuries', *Paediatric Emergency Care*, vol 8, no 4, pp 221-4.

Lucas, K., Grosvenor, T. and Simpson, R. (2001) *Transport, the environment and social exclusion*, York: York Publications Ltd.

McCray, T. (2000) 'Delivering healthy babies: transportation and health care access', *Planning Practice and Research*, vol 15, nos 1-2, pp 17-29.

Meier, K.J., Stewart, J. Jr. and England, R.E. (1991) 'The politics of bureaucratic discretion: educational access as an urban service', *American Journal of Political Science*, vol 35, pp 155-77.

Murray, S. (1998) 'Social exclusion and integrated transport', Paper presented to Transport Seminar, University of Manchester, 2 December.

Olson, L.M., Sklar, D.P., Cobb, L., Sapien, F. and Zumwalt, R. (1993) 'Analysis of childhood pedestrian deaths in New Mexico', *American Emergency Medicine*, vol 22, pp 512-16.

Ong, P. and Blumenberg, E. (1998) 'Job access, commute and travel burden among welfare recipients', *Urban Studies*, vol 35, no 1, pp 77-93.

Policy Action Team 13 (1999) *Improving shopping access for people living in deprived neighbourhoods*, London: DoH.

Public Voice for Food and Health Policy (1995) *No place to shop: The lack of supermarkets in low-income neighborhoods*, Washington DC: Public Voice for Food and Health Policy.

Public Voice for Food and Health Policy (1996) *No place to shop: Challenges and opportunities facing the development of supermarkets in urban America*, Washington DC: Public Voice for Food and Health Policy.

Pucher, J. and Renne, J.L. (2003) 'The socio-economics of urban travel: evidences from the 2001 NHTS', *Transportation Quarterly*, vol 57, pp 49-77.

SEU (Social Exclusion Unit) (1998) *National strategy for neighbourhood renewal*, London: The Stationery Office.

SEU (2002) *Making the connections: Transport and social exclusion. Interim report*, London: SEU.

Sheffield Hallam University and ONS (Office for National Statistics) (2001) *Parents' experience of choosing a secondary school*, ONS Report.

Stafford B. et al (1999) *Work and young men*, York: York Publications Ltd.

Surface Transportation Policy Project (2001) *Driven to spend: The impact of sprawl on transportation expenses*, Washington, DC: Surface Transportation Policy Project.

Sustainable Food Centre (1995) *Access denied*, Austin, TX: Sustainable Food Centre.

Talen, E. (2001) 'School, community, and spatial equity: an empirical investigation of access to elementary schools in West Virginia', *Annals of the Association of American Geographers*, vol 91, no 3, pp 465-86.

TRaC (Transport Research and Consultancy) at the University of North London (2000) *Social exclusion and the provision and availability of public transport*, London: DETR.

Troutt, D. (1993) *The thin red line: How the poor still pay more*, San Francisco, CA: Consumers Union of the United States, West Coast Regional Office.

Waller, M. and Blumenberg, E. (2003) 'The long journey to work: a federal transportation policy for working families', *The Brookings Institute Series on Transportation Reform*, Washington, DC, July (www.brookings.edu/es/urban/publications/20030801_Waller.htm).

White, D., Raeside, R. and Barker, D. (2000) *Road accidents and children living in disadvantaged areas: A literature review*, Edinburgh: Scottish Executive.

Yim, Y. (1993) *Shopping trips and the spatial distribution of food stores*, Working Paper, UCTC no 125, Berkeley, CA: Transportation Centre, University of California.

Part Two:
The UK perspective

THREE

Transport and social exclusion

Karen Lucas

This chapter presents a summary of recent developments in transport and social policy in England under the social exclusion policy agenda. These have emerged largely in response to increasing government recognition of the issues raised in the preceding chapters of this volume and the growing acceptance of both social and transport policy makers within central government that a 'social welfare approach' to transport decision making and policy delivery is needed in the UK. Similar policy strategies are also being developed in Wales and Scotland (less so in Northern Ireland) under their devolved Parliaments, but consideration of these is not included in this chapter, due to the author's lack of expertise and familiarity with the subject outside of England. For those interested in pursuing this line of enquiry, the Scottish Office and National Welsh Assembly websites provide a good starting point (see www.scotland.gov.uk; www.wales.gov.uk).

Understanding the concept of social exclusion

From about the mid-1990s onwards, the term 'social exclusion' increasingly emerged as a popular policy concept in the UK and other European countries. The concept is usually described as being initially derived from the 1980 French socialist policy agenda. This has long been concerned with a failure to secure the 'insertion' of certain groups on the periphery of French society into the mainstream agenda to avoid social fracture and preserve French economic competitiveness and national sovereignty (Mandanipour et al, 1998).

The focus of the social exclusion agenda is both practical and moral. From a practical point of view, governments must identify ways in which they can successfully intervene to ensure greater participation by and inclusion of socially disadvantaged groups within society. Morally, there are policy decisions to be made over the type of behaviour and values that should be promoted within that society and the extent to which individuals, groups and communities should be protected against certain prevalent negative values that could disadvantage them, such as racism, sexism and homophobia.

In 1993, the Commission of the European Communities published an action programme to tackle the problems of social exclusion in European member states. The programme places a strong emphasis on tackling the combined aspects of the problems that are manifest in areas where a high proportion of the population experiences a whole range of deprivations or social ills such as unemployment, poor health, poor housing conditions, low educational achievement and exposure to high levels of crime. Within the programme there is recognition that social exclusion is manifest in different ways between countries, in different cities and within cities. In some instances, social exclusion and physical segregation may be synonymous, whereas in others a more fine-grained pattern of differentiation between conditions in geographical areas may exist. The programmes instigated by the different European Community (EC) nation states to tackle social exclusion have therefore been varied, but the main policy focus has tended to concentrate on the same broad areas, namely employment, education, housing, health and public service delivery.

Addressing social exclusion became a central policy concern in the UK following the election of the New Labour government in May 1997, which has followed a two-pronged approach to tackling the linked problems the government associates with social exclusion. On the one hand, the policy focus has been on addressing the problems of individuals through a variety of mechanisms including:

- a revised and revitalised 'welfare-to-work' programme including New Deal for Employment, Sure Start and low-wage tax credit top-up incentives;
- policies to improve educational attainment in schools and encourage increased participation in post-16 education;
- programmes designed to address specific problems such as teenage pregnancy, rough sleeping and reoffending by ex-prisoners.

On the other hand, and designed to complement this approach, it has introduced an area-based programme to address the poor physical condition and service delivery problems of Britain's most deprived neighbourhoods, as identified by the Index of Local Deprivation 2000.

In August 1997, the Social Exclusion Unit (SEU) was established to assist in the development and delivery of this policy agenda. The main aims of the unit are to:

- improve understanding of the key characteristics of social exclusion and the impact of government policies on it;
- promote solutions to the problems associated with social exclusion by encouraging cooperation across departments, disseminating best practice and making recommendations for changes in policies, machinery or delivery mechanisms, where necessary.

Recognising transport as a social problem

The SEU's first report, *Bringing Britain together* (1998), announced a programme of investigation into the multiple problems facing people living on Britain's worst estates. The report recognised that many of the problems experienced by traditionally excluded groups and individuals are exacerbated by gaps in the policy and service delivery system at the local level. Among other problems (poor housing, ill-health, high unemployment and low educational attainment), the report noted the problem of poor transport and accessibility.

It found that physical isolation was a regular feature of many of Britain's poorest neighbourhoods and recognised that many deprived areas lack the basic public and private services that others take for granted, for example local food stores, health services and banks. Furthermore, it noted that, although car ownership is low in most deprived neighbourhoods, many are located in outlying areas in the urban periphery that are also poorly served by public transport provision. This effectively causes an 'accessibility deficit' in the resident population, which can contribute to their social exclusion.

Following this report, 18 policy action teams (PATs) were appointed with a remit to spend approximately 12 months examining practical ways to address the problems of deprived neighbourhoods. However, the problem of poor transport and accessibility was not a subject addressed by any of the teams, although some did note this problem at their reporting stage.

The earlier transport White Paper, *A new deal for transport: Better for everyone* (DETR, 1998), had picked up on the possibility of a differential impact of transport policies on people in different socioeconomic groups and geographical locations. To address the problem, it stated that it would set in motion a new national framework for producing a fairer and more inclusive system of transport by:

- providing better public transport and easier access to facilities;
- reducing community severance caused by transport;
- reducing the need to travel through better planning and technology;
- promoting better transport choice for disabled people;
- reducing the fear and level of crime on the transport system;
- promoting better conditions for those working in transport.

The White Paper recommended that, in future, indicators of transport trends would need to be broken down by income groups, geographic (rural/urban) area, and age and gender in order that the impact of policies of different groups in society could be monitored. It also recommended that providers of other key services should consider the transport implications of their policies for socially disadvantaged groups.

Several government and independently funded studies picked up on these issues. It was not necessarily a new area of inquiry in the UK: dating as far back as the early 1970s, numerous researchers had been drawing attention to social inequities arising from transport delivery in the UK (see, for example, Hillman, 1976; Goodwin, 1990; Grieco, 1995). Others had examined the problems and concerns of different disadvantaged groups (for example, Hamilton et al, 1991, on women; Cahill et al, 1996, on children; Noble, 2000, on older people) or of people living in disadvantaged communities (such as Stewart, 1999, women and children living in Deptford, London; Davis and Ridge, 1997, children living in rural communities).

Most of these earlier studies tended towards identification of the transport problems of different disadvantaged groups and areas, and the research was predominantly qualitative in nature. Thus, it did not attempt to identify the extent and severity of the problem within neighbourhoods or for the country as a whole. Nor did these studies make evident the effect of poor transport in terms of the wider welfare agenda – that is, people's inability to access work, learning, healthcare and other basic services and amenities – and the lifestyle consequences of this.

From about 1999, however, several studies began to directly examine the interactions between transport provision and social exclusion (for example, Church and Frost, 1999; TRaC, 2000; Lucas et al, 2001). Other studies were also making visible the links between transport policy and other areas of welfare delivery, such as health (Hamer, 1999) and employment (Institute of Employment Research, 1999).

In 2001, the SEU, in recognition of the growing body of evidence, picked up on this area of enquiry and initiated a study to make evident the links between transport and social exclusion. Its conclusions are as follows:

- *Work:* two out of five job seekers say that lack of transport is a barrier to getting a job.
- *Learning:* nearly half of 16- to 18-year-old students find their transport costs hard to meet.
- *Health:* over a 12-month period, 1.4 million people missed, turned down or chose not to seek medical help because of transport problems.
- *Food shopping:* 16% of people without cars find access to supermarkets difficult, compared with 6% of people with cars.
- *Social activities:* 18% of non-car owners find seeing friends and family difficult because of transport problems, compared with 8% of people with access to a car.
- *The impact of traffic:* children from households in the lowest socioeconomic group are five times more likely to die in road accidents than those from the highest. (SEU, 2003, p 9)

The study also found that these outcomes have clear implications for a number of other areas of government policy, most notably those encouraging welfare into work, reducing health inequalities, raising educational attainment and participation in post-16 education, crime reduction and neighbourhood renewal.

As Chapter Two identified, there are a variety of reasons why this situation has occurred. These include a whole series of prohibiting factors relating to the location of where activities take place, including issues of the timing of services, personal safety, journey distances and so on. Equally important are the circumstances of the person wishing to undertake that activity and any constraints they may experience according to this, such as the income that is available to them or their personal responsibilities. In most instances, transport will be a third key element in determining whether they are able to undertake that activity. Based on a multiplicity of such factors, an individual will decide whether it is possible to proceed with a planned activity; they may have to reschedule or relocate the activity, or abandon that activity entirely if other options are unavailable. In the case of social exclusion, people often abandon activities that are essential to their well-being, such as taking up job opportunities or visiting a doctor (see Figure 3.1).

Figure 3.1: Factors affecting accessibility

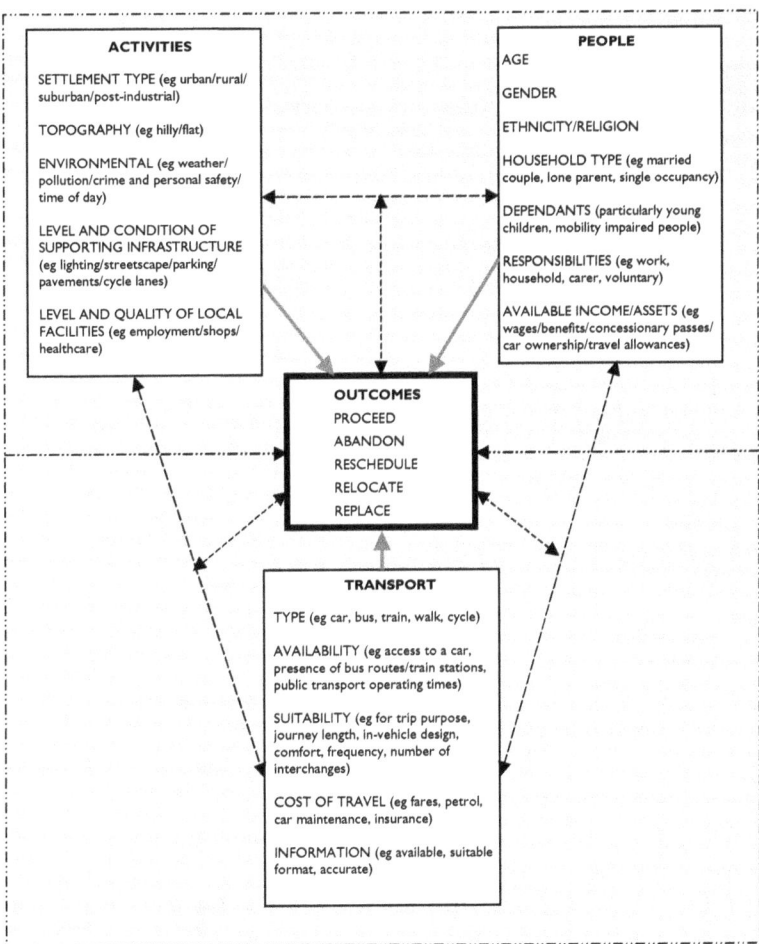

Research has shown that there are numerous reasons why people might be experiencing these difficulties (see, for example, TRaC, 2000; Lucas et al, 2001) and different people may be more or less affected by different circumstances and conditions. Table 3.1 summarises key concerns about transport according to different social groups. For those reliant on public transport services, there may be gaps in the network coverage and other factors such as the timing of services and the cost of fares, which prevent people from travelling. Other factors such as fear for personal security and physical disability can also act as significant barriers to travel.

Accessibility planning: a new local function

A key aim of the government's new strategy for addressing transport and social exclusion, as set out in the SEU report (SEU, 2003), is to ensure that people experiencing these problems can reach opportunities such as work, education and health treatment by improving access to these opportunities. The report recognises that this is not only about improving transport but cuts across many areas of policy delivery, for example changing where and how services are delivered, reducing fear of crime and providing better information and travel training. It introduces a new duty for local transport authorities in England to undertake Accessibility Planning as part of their next round of Local Transport Plans (LTPs), due for submission in 2005. The aim is to ensure a clear and consistent process for identifying groups and areas with accessibility problems, linked to an action plan for addressing these. The strategy is still in its developmental stages, but it is envisaged it will involve four key stages:

1. *An accessibility audit* to identify whether people can get to key activities within a reasonable time and cost, safely and reliably.
2. *A resources audit* to identify the existing resources and potential funding sources that are available to address the problems that are identified.
3. *An action plan* to develop and prioritise solutions and a cross-agency strategy for delivering these.
4. *Implementation and monitoring of this strategy.*

Local transport planners are to lead the process of accessibility planning in partnership with land-use planners and other local service providers and agencies influencing people's accessibility. The bodies that have been identified as needing to be involved in accessibility planning include JobCentre Plus, Primary Care Trusts, NHS Trusts, local education authorities, Learning and Skills Councils and Crime and Disorder Reduction Partnerships, New Deal, Health Action Zones, community transport organisations, and TravelWise partnerships. Success will also depend on the ways that these bodies can engage and interact with the commercial sector and communities that are the primary focus of this policy attention.

Transport and social exclusion

Table 3.1: Key concerns about transport by social group[a]

	Children	Younger people	Older people	Disabled people	Minority ethnic and faith groups	Women	Unemployed people and low-paid workers
High risk of pedestrian accident		Most vulnerable to crime on, and waiting for, public transport, but seen by others as perpetrators of crime	Fear of crime on, and waiting for, public transport	Physical access onto the public transport system may be difficult or impossible due to vehicle and infrastructure design	Fear of crime on, and waiting for, public transport	Fear of crime on, and waiting for, public transport	The cost of public transport particularly in connection with work and job-search activities
Vulnerable to exposure to air pollution		Cost of transport often prohibitive to travel and concessions often no longer generally available	High risk of pedestrian accidents	Vulnerable to exposure to air pollution	Certain faith groups forbid the use of public transport	Physical access on to the public transport system may be difficult or impossible due to vehicle and infrastructure design, in their role as the main carers of young children and responsible for household shopping	Absence of routes to areas of employment, particularly low-skilled work in urban periphery
Fear of crime on, and waiting for, public transport		Least likely to be catered for in terms of local service provision and activities	Vulnerable to exposure to air pollution	Higher risk of traffic-related accidents	Racism from service providers and decision makers both actual and institutional	Time burden of travel in light of the need to combine work- and home-based activities	Over-reliance on expensive taxis, particularly for journey to work

contd.../

Table 3.1: contd.../

	Children	Younger people	Older people	Disabled people	Minority ethnic and faith groups	Women	Unemployed people and low-paid workers
	Fear of exposure to 'stranger danger' when walking or travelling unaccompanied	Least likely to be consulted or considered in the decision-making process	High dependency on local services	Physical access to facilities and barriers to movement from infrastructure design	Often not catered for in terms of local service provision and activities and so must travel further to access appropriate goods and services	Over-reliance on expensive taxis, particularly for shopping	Absence of routes at times of the day for shift workers
		Service providers often actively discriminate against this group	High number of 'reluctant drivers', particularly in rural areas	Access to information in a suitable format (Braille/large print/audio)	Access to information in a suitable format (multi-lingual)		
			Access to information in a suitable format (Braille/large print/audio). Physical access on to the public transport system may be difficult due to vehicle and infrastructure design				
	Loss of freedom and restricted movement even in local area due to parents' fear for safety	Youth disaffection from lack of things to do and a tendency for blame to fall in this direction	Can lead to a 'prisoner in own home' effect, particularly at night	The 'prisoner in own home' extends to all times of the day	Increased dependency on private cars which may not be affordable and/or social isolation	Reluctant car dependency and/or stress arising from travel behaviour	Trade-off between cost of travel and ability to take up or continue employment. Car ownership becomes a key factor in ability to access work

Note: [a] It should be noted that membership of one or any combination of these groups does not automatically signify either social exclusion or transport poverty. An over-riding factor, in most cases, will be poverty interacting with the absence of choice about both personal and situational circumstances.

The need to develop the culture and practice of accessibility planning in transport and land-use decisions has been recognised for some time but, despite attempts by various authorities over the last 30 years or so, the necessary links between the policy aims of the different sectors and their differing administrative structures and delivery time scales, analytical techniques, data availability, technology and skills have proved elusive in most local authorities. Moreover, where these techniques have been previously applied, they have rarely been used to address instances of social inequity arising from the transport system.

How will accessibility planning work?

As Chapter One identified, transport analysis in the past has tended to focus on issues relating to the physical operation and maintenance of the transport system. This has led to a tendency to overlook whether people, particularly those without cars, can get to the places they need to go in order to carry out their daily activities. The difference with accessibility planning is that it is people-centred, location-specific and evidence-based, thereby catering for the actual activity needs of people, with a focus on prioritising the needs of socially excluded groups and communities in the transport planning and decision-making process. Another difference is that it requires a multi-agency approach to addressing these needs and looks beyond solely transport solutions to include land-use planning and service delivery solutions by other relevant sectors.

Accessibility auditing

Step One of the accessibility planning process as identified by the SEU report (SEU, 2003) requires that local transport authorities undertake accessibility audits in collaboration with other key stakeholders. Previous research undertaken for the Department for Transport (DfT) (Lucas, 2001) has identified that this can be as complex or simple a process as the assessor chooses to make it, with the potential to include use of models and Geographical Information Mapping Systems or hardcopy maps and a pen and paper. Essentially, however, assessment of accessibility requires consideration of three key elements (as identified in Figure 3.1):

1. The circumstances of the *people* under consideration, taking account of factors such as:
   - age (retired, adult, children and so on);
   - gender;
   - cultural factors (gender, ethnicity, faith and so on);
   - responsibilities (carer, lone parent and so on);
   - financial circumstance (wages, concessions and so on);
   - personal skills and abilities.

2. The *type of activity* they wish to undertake, defined in terms of:
   - the home location: physical isolation, local and mobile service availability;
   - the location and timing of a range of services and facilities in the wider area;
   - environmental factors such as crime levels, topography and so on.
3. Transport availability (or access without travel) including:
   - type of transport available;
   - physical design of vehicles (for example, disabled access);
   - cost of fares;
   - acceptability, comfort and so on;
   - information, timetables and so on.

A key aim at this stage is to identify 'hotspot' areas where people experiencing or at risk of social exclusion encounter difficulties in their attempts to access key activities such as employment sites, education facilities, healthcare services, leisure and shopping and cultural facilities. For this reason, accessibility audits need to reflect local understandings of access needs and local consultation forms an important part of the accessibility audit process. At one level, this will require consultation with service providers and other stakeholders that have developed perceptions of the problems faced by people accessing their services. It must also involve some means of refining and extending these perceptions through consultation with 'in-need' groups and communities.

By definition, socially excluded people are hard to reach and, inevitably, there is a significant resource issue in ensuring that such groups are consulted and listened to, as will be seen in a number of the case study chapters that follow. Most importantly, professionals need to build up relationships that foster trust with socially excluded groups and communities. To achieve this, the people consulted need evidence that their opinions are important in the decision-making process, that they are being listened to and that their needs are being recognised. As many of the areas that are likely to be identified will probably already be the focus of neighbourhood renewal programmes and other area-based initiatives, some will already have ongoing community forums – local people together with the delivery agencies working in their area – and it may be possible to tap into these and utilise other consultation exercises that have been carried out by these organisations.

Resource audits and action planning

It seems unlikely that large sums of additional government finance will be available to local transport authorities to address the problems they identify. The SEU report suggests that considerable resource savings can be realised if the existing funding that is available for subsidising public transport, non-emergency patient transport, home to schools transport, specialist social services transport and voluntary and community transport is integrated. Emphasis is also placed on securing resources from the non-transport sector such as Neighbourhood Renewal Funds.

In general it is usually easier to enter into resource negotiations with different agencies once a specific set of policy actions has been identified and agreed by the relevant partners. Clearly, the delivery of accessibility improvements can and should involve not only improvements to the transport system but also, where appropriate, the retiming and relocation of local facilities, home delivery, mobile and virtual services as well as improvements to the surrounding environment such as better street lighting or increased policing.

For this reason, resource audits should aim to be as broad as possible and identify:

- relevant agencies, their funding responsibilities and structures;
- staff time and availability;
- commercially operated transport networks (routes and timetables);
- vehicle pools (for example social services, schools and patient transport, community transport, voluntary schemes and so on);
- mobile, home delivery and teleservices;
- land, properties, rate structures and so on;
- scope for retiming and/or restructuring essential services (for example, GP surgeries in village halls);
- external funds, bidding options/arrangements;
- information, advertising, market research and so on.

One of the key barriers to the amalgamation of resources across delivery agencies in the past has been that each funding body has sought to demonstrate best value in terms of their own policy objectives. To overcome this problem, accessibility planning partnerships will need to demonstrate the contribution that improvements to local accessibility can make in the delivery of the policy objectives of the other sectors that are involved. For example, the SEU report identified that over a million people missed, turned down or chose not to seek medical help because of transport problems. Health professionals involved in the DfT accessibility planning pilot studies recognise that this has a serious implication for the reduction of health inequalities and are prepared to engage in resource negotiations on this basis.

In some cases, there may be no need for additional resources to be provided per se, as there will be scope for efficiency gains through better coordination of existing resources through institutional reform, or by enabling more effective exploitation of existing funding. Conversely, there may be instances where current policies and funding decisions are effectively reducing accessibility for people without access to a car, for example the centralisation of local services. In these circumstances discussions with decision makers may serve to reduce or reverse such practices, thus constituting an effective 'resource' for accessibility planning purposes.

It is clear, however, that many of the interventions that will be required to resolve the accessibility problems experienced by deprived groups and communities will require some form of additional public subsidy. The April 2002 UK budget announcement only identified a small amount of new funding to support accessibility planning and it is unclear at this time where the additional resources will be found by government in the 2004 Government Spending Review. Local authorities will need clear guidance from the different relevant central government departments (for example, Department for Work and Pensions, Department of Health and so on) on which resources can and should be drawn upon locally in the context of the national funding framework. Ideally this would include information on:

- the type of funding streams available;
- the order of magnitude of the fund;
- the allocation criteria;
- the local budget holder/bidding body.

Once this is established, the method for identifying options and the resources necessary to deliver them at the action planning stage is already one familiar to most local government agencies. The key stages in the process are as follows:

- *Agree policy objectives* through stakeholder involvement and local consultation.
- *Identify a set of locally appropriate options* (this may include options for immediate/short-term solutions with further options for future actions in the longer term).
- *Identify appropriate delivery agent(s)*.
- *Undertake discussions of feasibility* (costs/timeframe/responsibilities/staffing and so on) with relevant delivery agent(s).
- *Refine options*.
- *Submit bids to external funding bodies*.

The experience of the case studies in the following chapters of this volume shows the value of working across the various relevant sectors and institutions to improve accessibility, and the successes that can be achieved from this. However, it also highlights that staffing resources can be extremely limited, with personnel often combining multiple functions to fulfil their existing duties. Joint working across the various sectors identified for accessibility planning should help to alleviate some of these problems, by achieving maximum output in minimum time and cutting down duplicate efforts between the sectors.

The involvement of local people, not only in the identification of problems and needs but also in the delivery of local solutions, can sometimes help to reduce the burden and lead to 'quick wins'. It can also contribute to the longer-term sustainability of projects, and assist with the capacity-building process required to enable local communities to define their own needs. In addition, action plans need to be developed in close collaboration with the communities living in the areas they target, in order to ensure that they are addressing the actual problems experienced by people, rather than professional perceptions of their needs. Chapter Eleven of this volume discusses the process of community impact assessment and shows how this is helping to secure community involvement in transport decision making in the US.

Why will accessibility planning make a difference to social exclusion?

A key benefit of accessibility planning is that it allows consideration of the needs of minority groups whose demand for transport may be suppressed within the market due to a number of deterrence factors, such as inability to pay, fear for personal safety, and so on. Current policies in transport, land-use planning, employment, health and education suggest that accessibility planning has the potential to become a major influencing factor in the decision-making process both within central and local government in the UK.

At the national level, accessibility planning will allow the government to comprehensively and systematically assess the extent and severity of the problem of poor transport and may lead to a more fundamental review of transport spending in the UK. It is likely that a set of core national performance indicators for accessibility planning will be adopted and that these will effectively be 'co-owned' between the DfT and the other relevant departments (for example, Department for Work and Pensions, Department of Health, Department for Education and Skills, and so on). This will encourage these departments to think for the first time about the effects of their wider policies on transport and access.

At the local level, accessibility planning will provide transport planners with a robust tool to consider the effects of changes in the transport system on people's access to opportunities such as employment, shopping, health services, social support networks, recreation, countryside and so on. It will demonstrate how transport impacts are distributed across geographical areas, population groups, trip purposes and modes of travel, ensuring compatibility with equity objectives. This will allow gaps in the transport network to be identified and for the contribution of new services to overall equality of opportunity to be evaluated.

Perhaps more importantly, accessibility planning will ensure greater consistency between transport and other public policy objectives, including: land-use planning; housing; health; education; local regeneration; and regional development. It will help to make evident the transport implications of other areas of public policy decision making, service delivery (especially the opening, closure and relocation of public facilities such as hospitals, healthcare services, schools and colleges) and the scheduling of services. Accessibility planning will also provide land-use planners with a consistent approach for assessing the impacts of new developments and the needs for development control decisions to improve access to the transport system.

Finally, accessibility planning can be used with communities to explain transport and land-use proposals in terms that they can easily understand, such as journey times to shops, or travel time and cost to work. Equally, communities themselves can adopt the method to argue for new services and facilities in their areas.

Clearly, accessibility planning in the UK is still in its infancy and it will be some time before it will be possible to assess whether these aspirations for the method can be realised. In the first of the four UK case study chapters that follow, Murray Grant, Chief Policy Officer for Merseytravel, the Passenger Transport Authority (PTA) for Merseyside, explains how accessibility audits have been used to help plan the public transport network in regeneration areas in order to maximise access to employment for job seekers in Liverpool. In Chapter Six, Mike Preston describes how the Braunstone Community Association in Leicester used the concept of accessibility planning to win funding from the government's Urban Bus Challenge to support new bus services for local people. Both examples suggest a hopeful outlook, but all four case studies demonstrate that the devil is in the detail and that a great deal of political will within central government and commitment from local champions will be needed if the process is to really succeed.

References

Cahill, M., Ruben, T. and Winn, S. (1996) *Children and transport: Travel patterns, attitudes and leisure activities of children in the Brighton area*, Brighton: Health and Social Policy Research Centre, University of Brighton.

Church, A. and Frost, M. (1999) 'Transport and social exclusion in London', Unpublished, London: Transport for London.

Davis, J. and Ridge, T. (1997) *Same scenery, different lifestyle: Rural children on low-income*, London: The Children's Society.

DETR (Department for the Environment, Transport and the Regions) (1998) *A new deal for transport: Better for everyone*, London: The Stationery Office.

Goodwin, P. (1990) 'Demographic impacts, social consequences and the transport policy debate', *Oxford Review of Economic Policy*, vol 6, no 2, pp 76-90.

Green, H., Smith, A., Lilly, R. and Marsh, A. (2000) *First effects of ONE*, DSS Research Report no 126, Leeds: Corporate Document Services.

Grieco, M. (1995) 'Time pressures and low-income families: the implications for social transport policy in Europe', *Community Development Journal*, vol 30, no 4, pp 347-63.

Hamer, L. (1999) *Making T.H.E. links: Integrating sustainable transport, health and environment policies: A guide for local authorities and health authorities*, London: DoH and DETR.

Hamilton, K., Ryley Hoyle, S. and Jenkins, L. (1999) *The public transport gender audit: The research report*, London: University of East London.

Hillman, M. (1976) 'Social goals for transport policy', in *Transport for society*, London: Institute of Civil Engineers.

Institute of Employment Research (1999) *Minority ethnic groups and access to jobs*, Bulletin no 51, Warwick: University of Warwick.

Lucas, K. (ed) (2001) 'Factoring social exclusion into local transport planning', Unpublished report to Mobility and Inclusion Unit, DfT, UK.

Lucas, K., Grosvenor, T. and Simpson, R. (2001) *Transport, the environment and social exclusion*, York: York Publications Ltd.

Mandanipour, A., Cars, G. and Allen, J. (1998) *Social exclusion in European cities: Processes, experiences and responses*, London: Jessica Kingsley Publishers.

Noble, B. (2000) 'Travel characteristics of older people', in *Transport Trends 2000*, London: DETR, pp 9-25.

Parkinson, M. (1998) *Combating social exclusion: Lessons from area-based programmes in Europe*, Bristol: The Policy Press.

Rogers, B. (1979) *The study of social policy*, London: George Allen and Unwin.

Rogers, J.J. (2000) *From a welfare state to a welfare society: The changing context of social policy in a post-modern era*, London and New York, NY: Macmillan Press Ltd and St Martin's Press Inc.

SEU (Social Exclusion Unit) (1998) *Bringing Britain together*, London: The Stationery Office.

SEU (2002) *Making the connections: Transport and social exclusion*, London: SEU.

SEU (2003) *Making the connections: Final report on transport and social exclusion*, London: SEU.

Stewart, J. (1999) *Poor show*, Rochdale: Rochdale Alternative Press.

TRaC (2000) *Social exclusion and the provision of public transport*, London: DETR.

FOUR

Ensuring access and participation in the Liverpool city region

Murray Grant

Introduction

This is the first of four UK case study chapters in this volume that illustrate the way in which local policy practitioners are implementing policies and initiatives to improve accessibility for people experiencing 'transport poverty' in their administrative areas. This chapter describes how accessibility planning in the Merseyside region was used to support job creation as part of an integrated regeneration strategy.

Background to the Liverpool case study

Merseytravel is the Public Transport Authority (PTA) and Executive for the Merseyside region and is responsible for coordinating all public transport provision for the area. The organisation covers the five local authority areas of Merseyside and is controlled by 18 councillors from across the area. Commercial transport operators provide the majority of bus and rail services, which presents a number of problems in attempting to provide integrated transport in the UK outside London.

It has long been recognised by Merseytravel that transport does not exist for its own sake: to be truly effective it has to be at the centre of the demands and aspirations of people living and working in the Liverpool city region, meeting their needs in the most effective and sustainable manner. While improvements to public transport are essential for the sustainable development of our cities, very often 'conventional' public transport is not able to provide the optimum level of service to support the wide and varied patterns of dispersed activities. A new concept of public transport is required to ensure all members of a community have equal access to opportunities.

Merseyside is a large metropolitan area located in the north west of England. The region is dominated by the City of Liverpool, which is the historical centre with administrative and commercial services, vital to the economy of Merseyside. Liverpool accommodates the region's main higher educational, social and cultural institutions and substantial investment is taking place in the city centre in the construction of high-quality residential development. In addition to the City, there are four other local authorities in Merseyside: Knowsley, Sefton, St Helens and the Wirral. Excluding the Wirral, these areas are contained within a conurbation more than 20km in diameter. The River Mersey forms an important barrier between the two parts of the metropolitan area, which are connected by two road tunnels, a rail link and the Mersey Ferries.

Merseyside has suffered severe economic decline for many years, resulting in problems severe enough for it to remain an Objective One region under the European 2000-06 Structural Fund Programme. (It was first declared an Objective One region in 1994.) Merseyside has a population of 1.4 million and of this population, 450,000 live in Liverpool. It is one of the UK's most densely populated regions overall. However, the area has experienced large population decline in line with its economic decline. There is evidence that this decline may be stabilising in line with the improvements to the local economy that are now becoming evident. This trend is expected to continue in the wake of Liverpool being named European Capital of Culture in 2008. In this context, the region faces problems of managing a regenerating economy in a sustainable way, whereby economic growth can be enabled without placing undue strains on the transport network and without contributing to environmental decline. Equally, it is recognised as inevitable that rising prosperity will result in increased car ownership and usage. Projections indicate that growth in total traffic from 1996 have been calculated as 16% by 2006 and 24% by 2011.

This poses both short- and longer-term problems: first, to ensure that as economic and employment prospects improve, all residents have equal opportunity to access jobs and other opportunities; and second, to continue to ensure that those for whom use of a car, for whatever reason, is not possible are not prevented from continuing to have equal access. A range of initiatives are being implemented to address these emerging policy demands and it is recognised that public transport clearly has a role to play in assisting modal shift from the car. However, despite continuous and considerable investment in public transport in Merseyside, there has been a continuing decline in public transport usage.

It is also recognised that there remain large numbers of citizens across the region who, through economic circumstances, age, infirmity or choice, are not car users. Their economic opportunity and lifestyles are constrained because of society's increasing overall dependency upon the car. Employment opportunities are increasingly only available in dispersed locations, often with 24-hour shift working. Hospitals and other public facilities are centralised away from easily served public transport corridors. At the same time, many local shops and other facilities, such as post offices, are closed, adding to further demands to travel that can impose real barriers to those most dependent. As earlier chapters of this volume have demonstrated, 'transport poverty' is created and social exclusion based on the citizens' neighbourhood becomes likely.

The effects of this isolation are beginning to be quantified. Research in

Liverpool suggests that some residents 'save up' trips in order to incur less travel cost (Transport Studies Unit, 1998). By doing so, their access to good quality, fresh and cheaper food is limited. Unexpected trip requirements to healthcare services or a chemist may prove a financial burden and their travel horizons to search for jobs or training may become severely restricted, due to a lack of good travel information or lack of 'life experience' beyond the immediate environment. Such isolation can have other effects: research suggests increasing tendencies to antisocial behaviour against the public transport network (Crime Concern, 1994). In addition, the costs and time of using the public transport network may militate against taking up job training or other opportunities.

Faced with a multitude of problems that can bear down on people living in deprived communities (such as poor housing, educational and health facilities and fear of crime), poor transport may not be expected to feature as a serious problem area. However, poor transport provision runs across many of these other problem areas, exacerbating their effect and creating feelings of isolation.

Finding solutions

As we have seen in Chapter Three, policy makers are increasingly arguing that, if social exclusion is to be addressed, a multidisciplinary and multi-agency approach needs to be forged. This chapter demonstrates that local transport agencies need to be seen as key partners in order to find solutions and fund new initiatives to changing transport demands. Figure 4.1 shows how some issues currently being addressed as transport problems may have different starting points but could be addressed using similar policy responses to those being addressed by the social exclusion policy agenda.

It is clear, as the recent Social Exclusion Unit (SEU, 2003) report, *Making the connections: Final report on transport and social exclusion*, has shown, that the transport and wider social agendas must be drawn together, and that current national transport policies concentrating on the 'transport agenda' must be broadened out to provide better services for excluded communities. Equally, as the report stresses, such an approach makes it incumbent on a wide range of other government departments and agencies to pay proper regard to the transport implications of their service delivery.

Integrating transport policy and implementation with the wider social agenda has been a key element of Merseytravel's approach for the past 10 years. It has been driven largely by the realisation that the area's economic and social problems required a particular approach to transport provision. The introduction of the Community Links Team in 1995 was a natural progression from policies set out in the 1993 policy statement to ensure a better understanding, at a community level, of transport requirements. The new policies emerging from the SEU report have served to galvanise this approach.

Figure 4.1: Drawing together the transport and social exclusion agendas

The transport agenda	The social exclusion agenda
Rising car ownership	Increased cost of public transport Declining levels of public transport
Congestion Road traffic accidents	Community severance
Pollution and health effects	Poor health
Poor land use and transport integration	Centralising health and other public facilities
	Large supermarket development – Loss of local shopping and other Facilities
Costs to business and the community	Dispersed economic development and employment opportunity
Leads to:	
The requirement to reduce car travel and the need to travel	Social exclusion and increased travel opportunities

Possible common responses

- Better land use, regeneration, and transport integration
- Increased public transport provision
- Mobility management
- Car share/home delivery
- Localised facilities
- Multi-agency partnerships

Travel on Merseyside

The last countywide travel survey in 1996 showed that 41% of Merseyside households did not have access to a car. This figure is above the national average, and far higher in many deprived communities. Nevertheless, car travel accounted for 52% of total journeys in Merseyside (compared to 46% in 1988). Walking accounted for 25% (29% in 1988) of all journeys, with public transport (buses and trains) accounting for 17% (19% in 1988).

In common with the rest of the UK, the following trends have been identified across Merseyside:

- increasing car ownership;
- increasing dependence on the car;
- declining bus patronage;
- increasing relative costs of transport.

In addition to the increase in car use, the average trip rate per day has increased by 10% since 1988, to a 1996 level of 2.7 trips. While trip rates for walking and bus have fallen, they have increased for car driver and car passenger. The overall increase in trip rates has previously been seen as a positive improvement, reflecting increasing economic growth and prosperity. However, as Figure 4.2 illustrates, there is a wide disparity in trip rates across income bands, which shows that, for those on lowest incomes (who will generally be non-car owners), the ability to travel is limited compared to higher-income earners.

It has also been identified that those on the lowest incomes in the Merseyside region will also suffer most from the disproportionate rise in public transport costs compared to motoring and other cost of living indices (see Figure 4.3).

Figure 4.2: Differences in trip rates across income bands

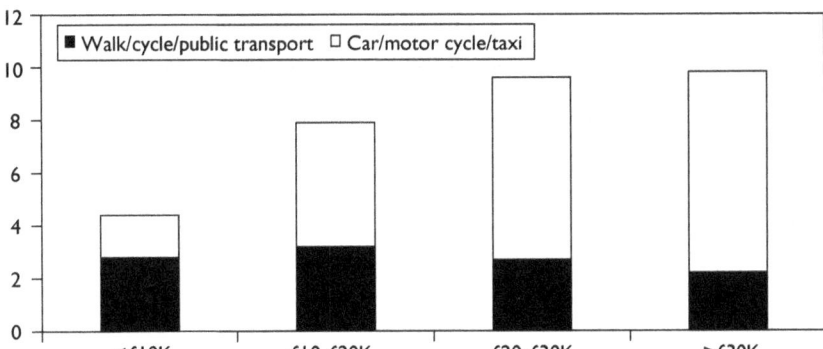

Figure 4.3: Trends in public transport fares, motoring costs and the Retail Price Index

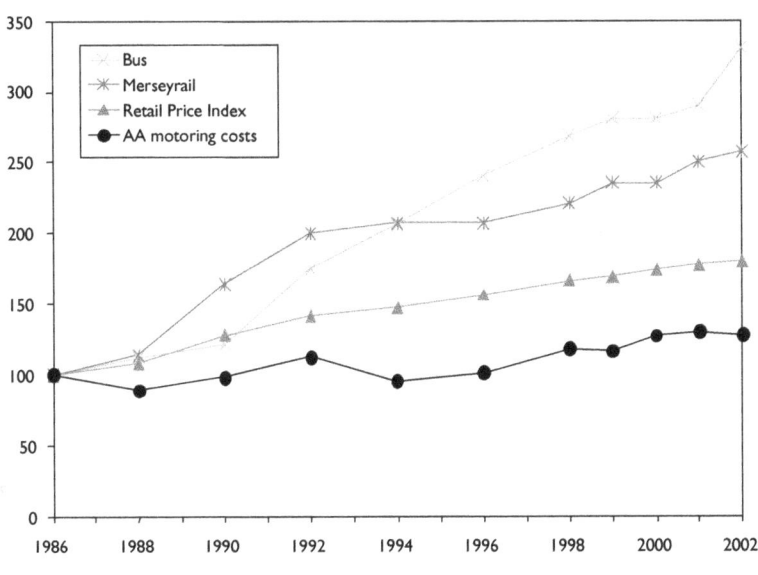

Sources: Merseytravel Annual Passenger Services Monitor, AA Technical Department

These rises in user costs can be attributed to the deregulated bus industry in the UK. As in other UK areas outside London, Merseytravel can exercise no control over fares, or other quality measures such as frequency, over the 85% of the local bus network that is provided on a commercial basis. It is clear, however, that those most reliant on the bus are constrained in their ability to make trips, compared to other groups, and that the success of the wider social and economic programme to increase employment, training and other opportunities may be hindered by failures in the transport system. Solutions need to be found within the existing framework.

Aligning the transport and wider social programmes

The overriding objective of the Merseyside region is to create jobs and full employment. This is set out in the Economic Action Plan for the region drawn up by The Mersey Partnership, a multi-agency partnership from across a broad spectrum of business, public sector and community and voluntary organisations. At the present time, the regeneration agenda is largely set within the context of the European Objective One programme. Given that this programme runs from 2001 until 2006, and the Local Transport Plan runs from 2001 until 2005, this provided an ideal opportunity to ensure the two programmes were aligned in order to maximise benefit to the region.

Local Transport Plans (LTPs) are drawn up by local transport authorities (LTAs) and passenger transport authorities (PTAs), such as Merseytravel, in order to set out integrated transport policy for their areas. They focus on the government's five overarching objectives: the environment, safety, the economy, accessibility and integration (DETR, 2000). The Merseyside LTP therefore provides the local response to these overarching government objectives by setting the plan in the context of the wider Merseyside regeneration agenda based on targeting improvements in a range of policy areas such as environmental improvements, job creation, training opportunities, and measures to address social exclusion.

The Merseyside LTP states that:

> ... the aim of the plan is to develop a fully integrated and sustainable transport network for Merseyside, which supports economic, social and environmental regeneration and ensures good access for all in the community. (Merseytravel, 2000)

Table 4.1 lists the four main objectives of the Merseyside LTP.

The aims of the Objective One programme are set out in a Single Programming Document; the Programme Complement provides a more detailed operational context. In agreeing these documents, great care was taken to ensure that improvements to (particularly public) transport was recognised as a major requirement of the programme. The success of this approach can be measured in the level of financial resources (in the region of £35 million) being made available

Table 4.1: LTP objectives for Merseyside

Policy Objective 1	To ensure transport supports sustainable economic development and regeneration.
Policy Objective 2	To moderate the upward trend in car use and secure a shift to more sustainable forms of transport such as walking, cycling and public transport.
Policy Objective 3	To secure the most efficient and effective use of the existing transport network.
Policy Objective 4	To enhance the quality of life of those who live and work in, and visit Merseyside.

for transport within the programme. This was matched in turn by increased Department for Transport (DfT) funding for complementary measures in support of the programme.

A particular feature of the Merseyside Objective One programme, from the inception of the first five-year programme in 1994, has been targeting funding towards 38 Pathways areas. These are designated areas of greatest social need within Merseyside, as identified by a range of measures including income and unemployment levels. At the time, national policy did not recognise the need for such targeting, which allowed the allocation of European funding to alleviate and address severe social problems in these areas. This was therefore a unique approach to identifying those geographic areas and communities most in need.

In the second programme, operating from 2001, eight Strategic Investment Areas (SIAs) have been created as the focal points for major investment that will create the best conditions for job creation. There is, therefore, a clear need to ensure that there are adequate transport linkages between the Pathways areas where unemployment is highest and those areas where new jobs will be created.

Figure 4.4 shows the Pathways areas and SIAs.

Policy responses

In its 1993 Public Transport Strategy, Merseytravel's goal was to "ensure quality of travel opportunity for all".

With the onset of the first Objective One programme in 1994, and the creation of the Pathways areas, Merseytravel's response was to establish the Community Links Team to provide a focus for ensuring that the particular transport needs of these communities would be addressed. The Community Links Team has as its mission statement the commitment to "work with the community on transport issues that affect their lives".

Within the first programme, there was a clear demand from the Pathways communities for community transport as the main solution to their transport demands (see Chapter Seven of this volume for an explanation of community transport in the UK). This was largely based on a belief that this form of transport provision could be owned and operated at a local level, and that the creation of

Figure 4.4: Pathways areas and Strategic Investment Areas (SIAs)

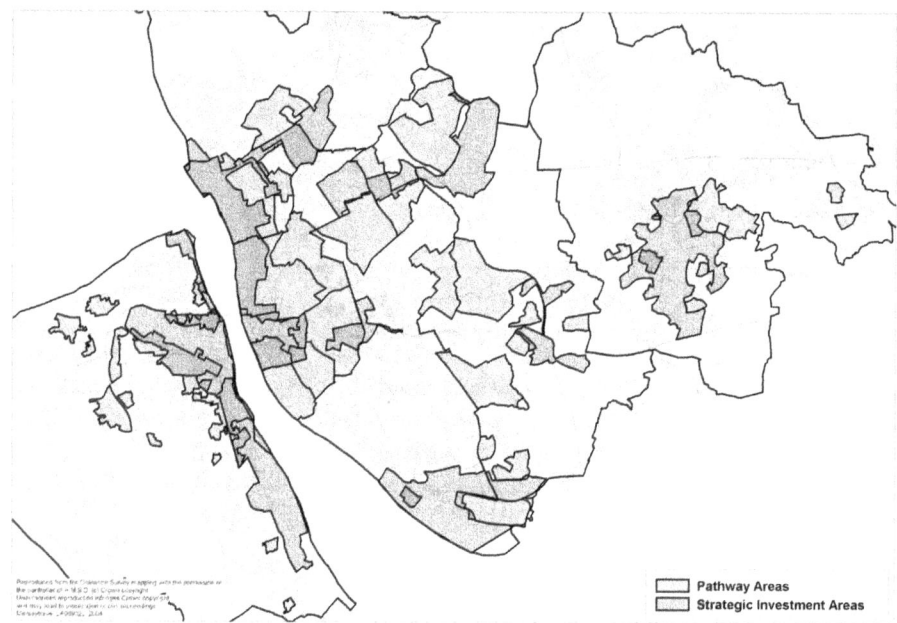

community transport providers would itself provide a source of employment and training. At this stage, in the mid-1990s, it was equally clear that there was neither the local capability to create this kind of resource nor support at national or European level.

Nevertheless, Merseytravel and Liverpool Housing Trust, along with a number of small community transport providers, succeeded in facilitating the creation of Merseyside Community Transport. This was established to provide a central resource to promote and lobby for additional resources for the sector and facilitate further development and training. Some core funding was provided by Merseytravel and the Housing Trust in recognition of the role of community transport as an important player in overall public transport provision in the area. Improved conditions had also been established for the operation of the community transport sector with the advent of the second Objective One programme in 2001. At national level, there was greater recognition of the role of the community transport sector, and integration of the LTP and Objective One transport programmes, described earlier in this chapter, provided a clear commitment to the provision of European funding.

As a specific measure, a £5 million fund was created to support local community-based schemes. To assist with this process, the Pathways Transport Group was established as a partnership between Merseytravel and the Pathways communities, to jointly decide on the most appropriate improvements that could be made at a community level. The funding available was outside the main transport programmes. The integration of the two programmes, coupled with new government policies, also allowed for a much firmer definition of transport improvements that would be required to support economic regeneration. These included commitments to provide revenue support for new bus services to ensure access to employment opportunities. This had not been available in the first programme. A final element in linking the transport and social and economic regeneration programmes was provided by the support given by many of the government-funded Single Regeneration Budget (SRB) partnerships, and initiatives such as the Merseyside Health Action Zone (HAZ).

The involvement of the HAZ took the form of support and recognition of the importance of public transport to health policy aims and objectives. It was largely the result of a very proactive programme by Merseytravel to 'sell' the need for collaborative working and the importance of transport to their programmes. In many cases, transport issues or the involvement of the transport sector had not been included in the HAZ programmes because of a belief that transport issues were the responsibility of the transport authorities, or that they were not important to the particular programme they were undertaking. Largely this attitude was a product of its time, although it remains prevalent in some new initiatives, or because transport 'problems' are often masked by other problems where transport is a potential solution. The 1997 Transport White Paper (DETR, 1998) guidance for the first LTPs (DETR, 2000) and, most significantly, the recent SEU (2003) report have provided a new framework for better cross-sector and partnership working. However, real success is likely to rest on organisations that adopt the most proactive approach to working with other agencies.

Support for transport from the HAZ could be either in kind (for example, by ensuring transport issues were written into action plans and so on), or in the form of direct financial assistance for new services or infrastructure. It was stipulated from the outset that continued support would only be forthcoming where clear evidence of need was established, and that this in turn had to be a jointly owned process. Consequently, Merseytravel, in partnership with other funding agencies such as the HAZ and SRB boards, provided the resources and support for the Pathways Transport Group to undertake a fundamental and wide-ranging review of the transport needs of residents living in the 38 Pathways areas, together with an assessment of requirements of the SIAs. This review was designed to:

- quantify the current and future demand for travel, and identify barriers preventing Pathways residents accessing new training, employment and other opportunities being created as part of the regeneration of the area;
- make appropriate recommendations for improvements.

Particular emphasis was placed on the following:

- to enable employers to recruit and retain a higher proportion of their workforce from Pathways areas;

- to enable post 16-year-old students to have access to the right training and education opportunities;
- to ensure the unemployed and those wishing to re-enter the labour market could do so with ease;
- once in employment, to ensure that employees have good access to continuing, high-quality and sustainable travel choices.

The results of this extensive research have been used to develop an action plan for Pathways areas, called *Breakthrough: A transport action plan for the Pathways communities* (Merseytravel, 2003), as a support to the LTP, and to support the Objective One programme. In particular, the plan aims to break down transport barriers for the following groups within each of the Pathways areas:

- young adults aged 16-19 years of age;
- adult job seekers (especially the long-term unemployed);
- lone parents;
- minority ethnic groups;
- people with physical or learning disabilities, poor short-term health or chronic health problems;
- older people.

Key issues that emerged from the research were as follows:

- Commercial bus fares within Pathways areas are too high and require a range of ticketing initiatives to ease the cost burden.
- Access to the current range of reduced rate tickets in Pathways areas is generally good but there are some areas where new outlets are needed.
- Information provision within Pathways areas is poor and requires attention.
- New bus services are required to ensure access to jobs, training and other job opportunities.
- Linked with this is the need for continuing support and cooperation with the community transport sector.
- Greater cooperation and integration between Merseytravel and community-based organisations is required to provide a focus to assess continuing transport demands.
- In this light, new and innovative solutions to providing better information or new bus services would have to be found.

These findings are fully in line with what has subsequently been reported in the 2003 SEU report. They also provide the framework within which bids for additional resources can be made and the context for persuading organisations such as Merseytravel to examine the possibility of 'bending' main programmes to target the Pathways communities. In terms of the problem of bus fares that

Ensuring access and participation in the Liverpool city region

are too high, the report also provides further evidence for changes to the way bus services are currently provided.

Practical applications

There are two good examples of how this approach is now beginning to provide some improvements to transport provision in the Pathways areas, both of which also provide evidence of the cross-sector partnership and funding which is crucial.

Job Link

As a result of the plan, Merseytravel was able to bid for the new government Urban Bus Challenge Fund, which was established in 2001. The challenge was specifically designed to provide new funding to address issues of social exclusion and particularly to create new journey opportunities for work and training[1]. The strength of the bid was helped by matched funding provided by JobCentre Plus[2], SRB partnerships and the Objective One programme. Figure 4.5 shows the first network of services designed to link Pathways areas and SIAs.

The buses operate on a number of fixed routes and are timetabled to meet specific shift start and end times. Over the remainder of the day, the vehicles are available on a demand-responsive basis. They provide transport for clients who are referred to the scheme to employment and training opportunities from JobCentre Plus and their specific area-based action teams, and other key agencies such as Job, Enterprise and Training Centres (JETs).

Figure 4.5: Job Link network December 2003-June 2004

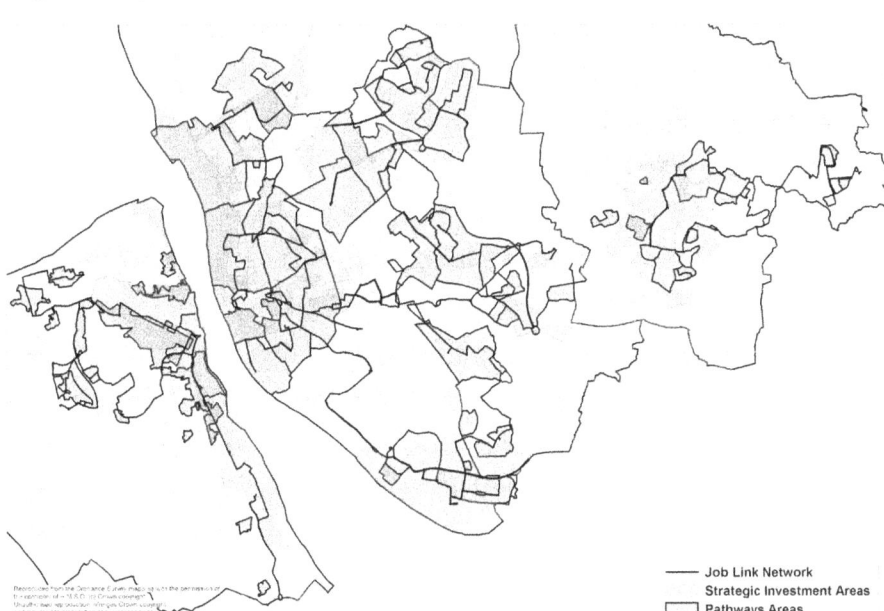

For the majority of respondents, bus services are the main means of getting to and from work and they are reliant on the times the services run and their reliability. The Job Link service has so far proven that it is reliable. The demand-responsive part of the service will give residents the chance to take up employment that is out of core working hours, at weekends and overtime opportunities. The employment agencies were also very aware of the demand-responsive service and have started making good use of the service to take people to interviews, and then to ensure people can get to the jobs they are being placed in, if there is no scheduled service available.

Regular monitoring has revealed that the service is recognised by users as having made their current jobs more secure. Users are now able to get to work on time. It has also provided the potential for some people to look for new jobs further afield.

Neighbourhood travel coordinators

A more recent initiative seeks to improve information about what public transport is available in the Pathways areas and bridge the gap with conventional provision, which was recognised as not being particularly good in many of the areas. It also recognises that many of the target communities find it difficult to use standard information.

Neighbourhood travel coordinators (NTCs) are being established in a number of pilot communities (see Chapter Five of this volume for an example of the work of NTCs). Their role is to be community-based, operating in a range of community facilities. Their role is not only to provide information, but also to explain it where necessary. They also mentor those who may well be nervous about making a journey to an area they do not know. This is part of a recognised problem of limited travel horizons. JobCentre Plus, the health authority and regeneration partnerships will provide funding and, if successful, it is likely to be extended to other areas.

Summary and conclusions

Job Link and NTCs are two examples of specific initiatives designed to improve access to jobs and training for deprived communities in Liverpool. Both initiatives have arisen from a commitment to ensure that public transport plays a full part in the social and economic regeneration of the region, and a positive response to meet the issues of social exclusion that can arise from poor public transport provision.

Provision of services such as Job Link, although clearly important, is essentially short-term intervention to alleviate immediate shortfalls in transportation for those most in need. Long-term solutions to ensure that local transport policy making and implementation are more equitably distributed across the population as a whole have to lie with better integration of land use, regeneration and transport planning, and with joint planning of service delivery across all public services. Equally, in the UK the integration of transport and delivery of the wider social equity policy agenda will remain extremely difficult by the continuation of a deregulated bus industry.

Until these long-term changes can be made and have an effect, public transport providers must adopt a proactive, innovative and flexible approach. This has to be based equally on a commitment to fully engage and consult with the local community and to attempt to meet their aspirations. This is not easy, and can be time consuming, resource intensive and subject to rebuffs and disappointments. It can also run against the grain of conventional transport planning and provision and staff training requirements to undertake such work should not be underestimated; neither should opposition from within an organisation to changes in the way services such as information are provided, particularly if these are seen as being a challenge to past custom and practice.

Working with communities for whom 'fighting' with authorities and providers of services is unfortunately seen as the only way to improve their condition is also a challenge, requiring a careful negotiation and often new engagement techniques. Merseytravel has found that honesty and transparency can go a long way to minimising possible conflict over priorities. Equally, it has to be accepted that not all schemes will succeed in the way that it was hoped. Merseyside Community Transport has so far failed to deliver the full extent of anticipated improvements to transport services in deprived areas, and the full potential of the sector to provide new and innovative services to Pathways areas has yet to be realised.

Nonetheless, the real success on Merseyside has been the mainstreaming and integration of transport policy with the wider social and economic agenda. This approach has been given added impetus with the 2003 SEU report and in the longer term will enable both better integration of service delivery, but also joint funding of initiatives such as Job Link.

Notes

[1] Subsequent Urban Bus Challenge funding, also matched by other agencies, was secured in 2002, taking total investment in the Job Link service to €6.7 million.
[2] JobCentre Plus is the government agency responsible for promoting job-search activities with unemployed people in the UK.

References

Crime Concern (1994) *Safety on public transport on Merseyside: Towards a strategy for Merseyside*, Swindon: Crime Concern.
DETR (Department for the Environment, Transport and the Regions) (1998) *A new deal for transport: Better for everyone*, London: The Stationery Office.
DETR (2000) *Guidance on full local transport plans*, London: DETR.

Merseyside Objective One Partnership (2000) 'Merseyside Objective One Programme 2000-2006', unpublished.

Merseytravel (1993) *A public transport strategy for Merseyside*, Liverpool: Merseytravel.

Merseytravel (2000) *Merseyside transport plan*, Liverpool: Merseytravel.

Merseytravel (2003) *Breakthrough: A transport action plan for the Pathways communities*, Liverpool: Merseytravel.

SEU (Social Exclusion Unit) (2003) *Making the connections: Final report on transport and social exclusion*, London: Office of the Deputy Prime Minister.

Transport Studies Unit (1998) *A study to examine the public transport needs of low income families, with reference to the impacts of the 1985 Transport Act on Merseyside*, Oxford: Transport Studies Unit, Oxford University.

FIVE

Halton Neighbourhood Travel Team

Julian Westwood

Introduction

This second UK case study details the work and ethos of an innovative project, the Halton Neighbourhood Travel Team (NTT), intended to address issues of social exclusion and transport. Located to the south of Liverpool, Halton is a unitary authority that has enduring issues of social exclusion but also a willingness to innovate in its response to these problems. This study covers the first 12 months of the project and consequently some of what is described is 'work in progress'. The principal actions of the NTT have been to introduce/manage:

- a Personalised Journey Planning service;
- student travel packs and college services;
- subsidised works services;
- a journey share website (www.haltonjourneyshare.com).

To understand what we have worked to achieve with the NTT, it is necessary to understand that each of these actions contributes to the others and to the overarching aim of the project: to overcome the transport barriers preventing people accessing opportunities in terms of training, education and employment. Throughout this work, there has been an emphasis on working with residents of those communities suffering the worst effects of social deprivation.

This study, unlike others, begins with an understanding of models for working with socially excluded communities and brings that to the transport arena, rather than the other way round. Being a newcomer to the transport arena, I have been aware that my perspective on the issue of social exclusion is sometimes very different to the received wisdom in this field. I have sought to convey that different approach in this case study and tried to explain why issues were approached in a particular way and where I feel that issues remain to be addressed by the sector in tackling transport and social exclusion.

Background

A summary glance at the statistics that surround the Halton area confirm that it is a place where the tipping point between exclusion and opportunity is finely balanced and might be influenced in the right direction. Comprising the two towns of Runcorn and Widnes at the lowest bridging point on the River Mersey, this is the 38th most deprived borough and the second smallest unitary authority in England (see Figure 5.1). Halton's health statistics can only be described as appalling, with the fourth highest Standardised Mortality Ratio (SMR) (the increased chance of premature death for residents of certain areas compared with the national average). For 1999-2001, Halton had the fourth worst SMR for all cancers and the 23rd worst SMR for all circulatory diseases. Employment fares little better, with 4.3% of the eligible population unemployed in 2001 compared to a national average of nearer 2.8%.

Now blighted by the legacy of the chemical industry that had once brought money through the towns, but never delivered any real sustainable local wealth, Halton has failed to attract significantly large employers. Consequently, travel-to-work patterns are fragmented both spatially and temporally, with people needing to travel to shift work typically at small- to medium-sized enterprises.

Similarly, educational achievement is low in the borough. In terms of education take up in 2001, 61% of 16-year-olds were in full-time education in Halton (compared to 71% in England). Seventy-four per cent of 16-year-olds in Halton were in education or training (compared to an England average of 82%). The problems faced by the borough are clear. Ten wards in Halton are within the top 10% of deprived wards in England. These 10 wards include 66,310 people; that is, 54% of the population of the borough. Evidently these areas meet the criteria of a pernicious synergy of deprivation across health, employment, education and housing. This constitutes social exclusion.

If Halton has its problems, then there are also indicators of growing opportunity. The strategically significant positioning of the borough between the growth hotspots of Manchester, Chester and Liverpool and as neighbour to Warrington has seen inward investment increasing in recent years. House prices too have begun to rise sharply in the past five years and now approach the national average. Local projects also promote the need for Halton businesses to employ local people with the argument that within the borough there are enough jobs for all of the residents.

The trick would seem, then, to be to connect these communities in need with areas of opportunity. What the NTT would strive to ensure was that this was a meaningful connection where skills and abilities were matched to requirement. This required an approach that concerned itself with detail – with individuals – rather than a broad brush approach.

Figure 5.1: Halton Borough Council geographical area

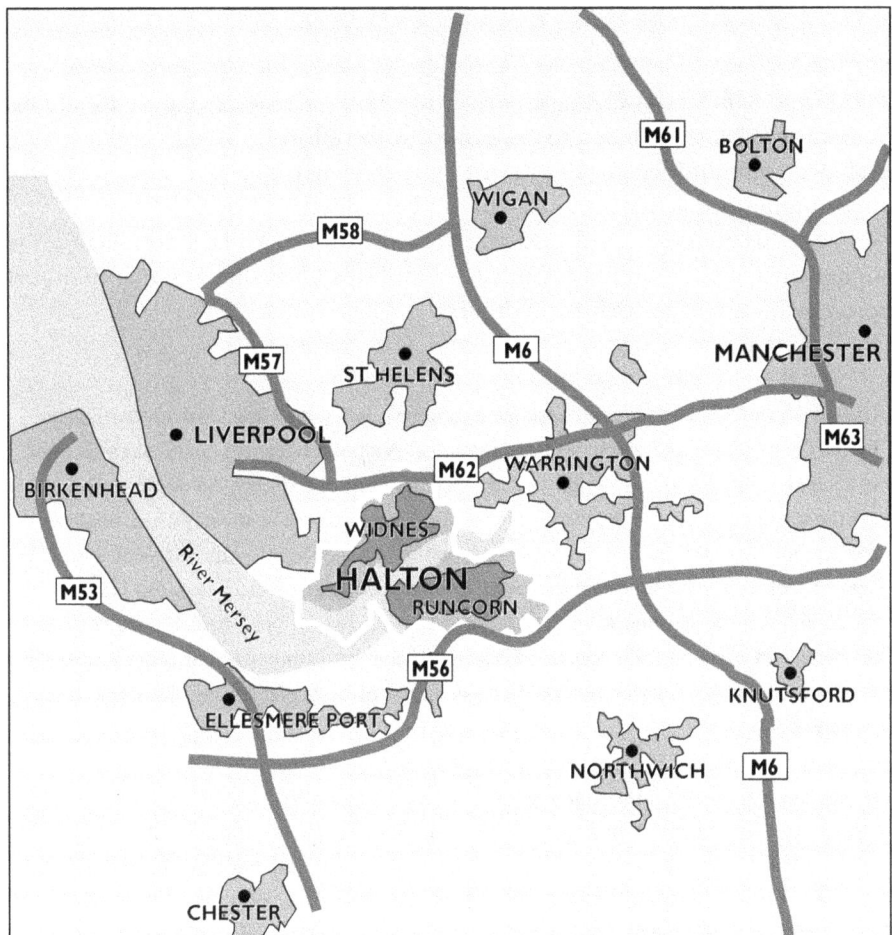

Source: Map supplied and reproduced by kind permission of Halton Borough Council

Seeking a fresh perspective on transport and how it relates to social exclusion

In his foreword to the Social Exclusion Unit (SEU) report, *Making the connections* (SEU, 2003, p v), Tony Blair makes the case for examining the ways in which transport problems can exclude people from services and opportunity:

> Imagine being offered a job and having to turn it down simply because there is no way for you to get there. Imagine being too afraid to walk to the bus stop after dark. Imagine an expectant mother having to take three buses to get to her nearest antenatal clinic. For all too many people, problems like these are still a part of everyday life. Solving them has the

potential to open up untold opportunities. However, if we do not do more, people and whole communities can be trapped in a spiral of social exclusion.

The Prime Minister's warning is well made, both in that the failure to address transport issues can do much to undermine other efforts to engage and revitalise excluded communities, but also in that by addressing transport issues a wealth of opportunities and actual achievement can be realised.

Now let us consider a real case study where you do not have to imagine the plight that transport can put people in – but instead have the way that transport becomes a solution for them and others.

Gary is 25 and had been unemployed for over a year when his New Deal advisor referred him to the NTT during a transport clinic session at Widnes Job Centre. Gary was interested in a job at a distribution facility on an industrial park in Runcorn but did not know how to get there from his home in the North of Widnes. The length of the journey was complicated still further by a difficult and irregular shift pattern. Following discussions with the NTT area coordinator, a Personalised Journey Plan was produced for Gary detailing his options for completing the journey. It was the 200 bus service that the NTT had recently rerouted to include an early morning journey between Widnes and Runcorn that proved to be of best use to Gary, a service he had been unaware of before receiving the Personalised Journey Plan.

It was several weeks later when we contacted Gary again to check how useful the intervention of the NTT had been. Gary told us that the transport options we had informed him of had allowed him to attend his interview and he has since been employed full time. Gary went on to use the 200 service to travel to work.

However, the story does not end there. Gary used his contacts in his new job to help his brother, who had also been unemployed, to gain employment there. Gary advised his brother of the 200 service which he also went on to use. After five weeks of employment, Gary bought his own car and now gives his brother a lift into work. Gary is keen to register with haltonjourneyshare.com (an Internet-based lift sharing service provided by the NTT) to offer other employees and job seekers the chance of transport to this difficult-to-reach site. When we asked Gary what he thought of the services, he told us, "The service and journey plan was a godsend. I couldn't have taken or even looked for employment here if those bus services didn't exist".

Gary's story is a real success and one that the NTT were delighted to discover. From being excluded from opportunity because of perceived transport barriers, Gary was not only included but went on to facilitate his brother's return to employment and now offers to help other job seekers overcome transport barriers.

This example goes a long way to demonstrate what it is that the NTT is trying to achieve. Some of the key lessons clear in this example are as follows:

- there is a need to join up initiatives;
- people have developing transport needs and progression routes should be anticipated and developed in a sustainable manner;
- sustainability can be on an individual level;
- transport barriers can become transport incentives.

What is not immediately evident from this example, but which I will seek to illustrate, is how an intelligence-led project can help to facilitate and replicate this kind of development from exclusion to inclusion, from transport poverty to transport wealth[1].

Researching the problem

At much the same time that the SEU began its research into transport and social exclusion, Halton Borough Council commissioned its own, not dissimilar, piece of work (Mott Macdonald/Richard Armitage Transport Consultancy, 2000). This comprehensive report engaged with over 80 community groups, individuals in target groups, training providers, employers and transport providers. A series of seminars was held that brought together these organisations for the first time to look at issues of transport as a significant barrier to achieving their shared aims. A synopsis of the findings of this process is as follows:

- a comprehensive bus network was available in only parts of the borough[2];
- little transport available for shift workers;
- no transport to childcare;
- personal security concerns;
- lack of buses to industrial sites;
- lack of specific/tailored travel advice;
- no innovative transport schemes[3].

The theoretical link had been made; but the report identified that lack of transport is a *real* barrier to accessing services and opportunities.

Moving from research to action, a Links and Access Strategy was developed to address the issues identified. The three elements to this strategy are:

1. To improve bus services for employment sites
2. To provide services for residents with a disability
3. To provide personal advice and innovative services through the NTT.

The original statement of purpose for the NTT, as stated in numerous funding applications, was:

> To implement carefully targeted improvements to the transport network at ground level by increasing use of existing services, redirecting resources for supported bus services and developing innovatory schemes with employers, community groups and transport providers.

The social aims of the NTT are to:

- help combat social exclusion in vulnerable groups;
- encourage community participation in transport and neighbourhood renewal;
- promote employment, education and lifelong learning.

Strategic positioning and funding

The original funding sought for all elements of the Links and Access Strategy was the Urban Bus Challenge (UBC). Unfortunately, as a revenue-based project, the NTT element was unsuccessful through this funding stream[4]. In attempts to address the numerous issues that confront the borough the local authority, Halton Borough Council, developed five priorities for all of its activities. These priorities were then adopted by the local strategic partnership (LSP) as the focus for its community plan – a requirement for receipt of Neighbourhood Renewal Funding[5]. In this community plan, under the priority of Combating Poverty and Deprivation were the themes of Income Maximisation and Affordable Public Transport. It was under the second of these themes that the NTT was identified as an action.

It was via this route that the NTT secured a funding package from a mixture of government regeneration budgets, including the Neighbourhood Renewal Fund, the Single Regeneration Budget (SRB) and the Department for Education and Skills (DfES), with Halton Borough Council providing accommodation and management support. This manner of mixed funding sources presented both advantages and difficulties for the project. The time-limited nature of funding proved to be a marvellous spur to activity: if we wanted to achieve something there could be very little 'lead-in' time. It also meant, however, that staff looking for long-term security could be 'poached' by other authorities looking to emulate the project but who had more substantial funding available. Similarly, the regime of quarterly monitoring and target setting provided a real focus for efforts and a measure of success, but also emphasised some areas of work to the detriment of others.

People, innovation, transport

To this point, the project had been driven forward by John Mooney, Halton's transport coordination manager. It was John's commitment to the principles of the project that meant he was willing to break with tradition and look to employ a team with 'people skills' rather than transport qualifications. Within his existing team, there was already a wealth of transport skills and effective working relationships. By blending this with people grounded in community development, capacity building and community project management, the necessary skills mix between transport and experience of addressing social exclusion would be in place. It was this step, perhaps more than any other, combined with the way in which the 'people' and 'transport' teams came together, that secured the success of this initiative. With the concept and makeup of the team itself innovatory, innovation became a central part of the team's ethos.

The original team had two area coordinators, Karen and Paula, who perhaps best reflected this mixed team approach. Karen had a great deal of experience of working in the public transport sector, a wealth of working relationships with transport operators, and an extensive knowledge of the local transport network. Paula, on the other hand, brought with her a great deal of experience of working with voluntary and community groups with her experience including work on a number of education and disability focused projects. As NTT team leader, my experience included project management in the voluntary and youth sectors and more recently in community development. This work had involved the development of a number of community-based projects designed to address a wide range of social exclusion issues. From the outset, this was seen as a leading team with regard to reducing social exclusion, but based within the transport section of the authority. The principles that informed the working of the team were not those usually to be found in the transport sector but clearly based on the principles of sustainable project delivery and management, community development and problem solving.

The basic concept: Personalised Journey Planning

Personalised Journey Plans (PJPs) are the cornerstone of the work of the NTT. In other parts of the country, PJPs are used as part of TravelWise initiatives as a way of encouraging modal shift. Car users are asked to complete the details of the journey that they currently make – days, times, origin, destination and so on – and a PJP is produced to present them with more environmentally sustainable alternative modes for making the same journey. One of the most interesting elements of the work of the NTT has been to manage the transformation of the PJP from a tool for addressing the excesses of transport-rich communities to meeting the needs of the transport poor.

The NTT wanted to use this technique of providing tailored travel advice as a way of helping people overcome the transport barriers preventing them from accessing opportunity. Having collected the details of the journey to be made, the area coordinators would begin to explore possible ways of completing the journey. The vision was to produce timely, accurate, accessible and free advice to residents seeking to access opportunity, with the emphasis placed on those residents seeking education, training and employment.

The attitude of the area coordinators and administrative support in preparing the PJPs was one of a 'can-do' attitude, and in all but a very few cases, a way to complete the identified journey within acceptable parameters was found. The information was presented in a style that we felt was clear and encouraging; the coordinators were able to add explanatory text where necessary. The information provided could include such elements as operator, departure point and time, the likely cost of the journey, its duration, the location of the return journey departure point, time and cost, health implications and environmental impacts for each of the modes suggested.

The emphasis was on providing as many options and as much information as possible in order to inform and empower the individual through choice. In addition, each PJP was accompanied by a full public transport timetable for the borough with the relevant options highlighted and, where appropriate, a map. What we were responding to was the recognition that there was both a 'perception gap' concerning the availability of transport, and also that transport poverty may also be a poverty of information. Personalised Journey Plans allowed us to address both of these issues in a way that also empowered the individual to address them for themselves in future.

How do you reach the 'hard to reach'? Marketing PJPs

For any project intended to address issues of social exclusion, how it overcomes the difficulty of engaging with its intended audience is key. The NTT had certain advantages in this area in so much that, by having so clearly defined a target group (that is, those seeking to access opportunity in education, training or employment), a clear network of agencies is already in place with whom to develop partnership working. With the NTT being such a small team (myself, two area coordinators and one administrative assistant), accessing the resources of other agencies was always going to be a crucial element in our service delivery. Around each 'type' of person that we were seeking to assist – the would-be student, trainee, or employee – we drew up a network of those agencies with which they would come into contact and who could be used to promote our service.

The challenge for the NTT in the first instance was to persuade partner agencies of the value to them and their clients of the service we provided and then to put in place the procedures and practices to ensure that this was done effectively. The first stage was relatively easy, as transport problems were a common and recurring issue for every one of those organisations. Seen as a barrier to their own work and an unwelcome burden on their organisation, the idea of a group dedicated to answering these problems was met with a great deal of enthusiasm. What took a little longer than expected to communicate to these partner agencies was the manner in which we worked and how that would benefit them and their clients. For many months, we would be met with puzzled expressions and the question, "So you don't have money for tickets and you don't have any buses – how can you help?".

An early success was using the recruitment days in local colleges as a way to promote our service to students and to collect requests for PJPs from them. Similarly, we held transport 'clinics' in the various job centres and also with the local JobCentre Plus outreach teams. The strategy, then, was one of selective promotion. While any resident in the borough could request a PJP for any journey, we actively sought those people engaged in the activities that we were tasked to support. The plan, of course, was to deliver much of the work ourselves in the first instance while demonstrating the value of it to our partner organisations, so that in time we could withdraw and allow them to take over the request element of the process.

The experience of this part of the project was mixed. The colleges provided large numbers of requests, but often failed to perceive that we were not catching people early enough. Providing PJPs to students on or soon after their induction day is a worthwhile endeavour but does not, perhaps, reach precisely the target group we were aiming for. A simple example was that, while the colleges had negotiated reduced rates for weekly and monthly bus tickets, the students were not given any advice regarding which operator provided the better service for them. Time and again, the PJP process revealed that one operator or another provided a significantly better service for individual students. Equally, we found a group of four students who thought they could not get a car park pass and so stopped car sharing and instead each bought a £9.00 weekly bus ticket. We advised them that they *could* get a car park pass and they returned to what was for them the more sustainable option.

What the colleges repeatedly failed to grasp was that, if students have already got to the point of induction, then they have most likely overcome the mental barrier that transport presents, even if they have yet to find how they will actually make the journey on a daily basis. What we required was for the colleges to promote the PJP service along with their first-line advertising. Students needed to be aware that there was assistance for them to make a journey from the moment they consider a course. In this way, we could make significant inroads into the limited transport horizons with which people exclude themselves from taking up opportunity.

The college's own outreach 'community' classes service would fail on this simple point. Since a course was offered 'in the community' at a school or community centre in the evening, no thought was given to the accessibility of these points to non-car users. Indeed, many of these locations at the periphery of towns, with course finishing times in the evening when much of the transport network has effectively shut down, are almost impossible to reach by public transport. If the required course was not offered in the immediate locality on the night a potential student wanted, then he/she was, in effect, excluded. Similarly, for those young people looking to take up a course, or for older people looking to enter training for employment or to enhance their skills, the lack of transport may well exclude them at the earliest of stages, stages that were still proving problematic for us to reach.

The job centres presented challenges of a different sort. Job centres are obvious candidates for partnership working for any project looking to engage with people seeking to access employment. The NTT was welcomed into these venues eagerly and although getting the joined-up working between ourselves and the job centres to an acceptable level was agonisingly slow at points, all could see the potential and the benefits that were realised. What did become apparent, however, was the need to have the frontline job centre staff act as referrers to the services of the NTT. The requirement of attendance at the job centre in order to receive some state benefits meant that not everyone there was looking to access opportunity. Consequently, having a member of the NTT attending the job centre on the busiest days (signing-on day) meant that, although a lot of people passed through, not as many of them as might be hoped were actively seeking employment. By having the job centre staff direct active job seekers to our service, we ensured that our limited resources were utilised to greatest effect.

An interesting area of development work was to offer the PJP service to the private employment agencies that handle so much of the recruitment into factories and offices. By informing these agencies of the services provided by the NTT and supplying them with PJP request forms to return to us, we began to gain much more effective access to people actively seeking employment. This is an area of work that the NTT looked to expand.

User satisfaction

An important part of any project is its ability to measure user satisfaction. For the NTT, this was especially important as our intervention had the potential to assist with life-changing opportunities. One element of our SRB funding required that we would follow up each PJP with a telephone call to track how successful we had been in assisting people with accessing opportunity. What had not been considered at the project-writing stage was the time that this would consume. Combined with the time taken to actually produce the PJP, this was beginning to hamper the ability of the team to actually produce PJPs and develop partnerships. The compromise was that we would make up to three attempts to contact each PJP recipient, one attempt in the morning, afternoon and evening. We would then consider those that we had managed to contact to be our sample for the whole group. Initial results were encouraging in the extreme. The results were:

- 100% of PJP recipients who responded said they would use the service again;
- 100% said they would recommend the service to a friend;
- 96.8% said the PJP was relevant to their needs;
- 40% had gone on to access education, training or employment opportunities using the plan.

While the high levels of satisfaction with the service is gratifying, it is the final figure – the level of success in helping people access opportunity – that is especially pleasing. If we remember that people have come to PJP because they do not think they can make this journey, then helping 40% to actually access opportunity is a strong endorsement for the work undertaken[6].

The hidden benefits

If the first tier of outcomes for the PJP process is extremely worthwhile, then it is not without some drawbacks. Without the benefit of having a computer-based timetable resource, the area coordinators literally had to work from paper timetables in order to complete the PJP (for a newcomer to the industry, this was a quite remarkable state of affairs). This was massively time-consuming with a complex plan easily taking up to an hour to complete. This work, then, could be laborious and frustrating, but there was a hidden benefit.

It is in the second tier of work with PJPs that what I have come to consider to be the real benefits of the project are to be found. The joy of PJPs is the wealth of information that is collected through the interview process. By developing a relatively simple database, we were able to remove some of the monotonous elements of producing each plan. Much more importantly, however, we captured data concerning the times, days, dates, origins and destinations of journeys that people were having difficulty making while trying to access employment, education or training.

The significance of this should not be underestimated. Numerous documents talk about the need to 'connect communities', to draw lines between where there are people who are unemployed and places where there are job vacancies. The question is, how do you match skills with employment opportunity? As has been discussed elsewhere in this study, the SEU's call for Accessibility Mapping is informed by the same question of whether people can get from these areas to those opportunities and services within acceptable parameters. Again there is no direction on how we test if people *want* to make that journey.

What a database of PJP requests offers you is real data, not theoretical accessibility issues. In effect, each PJP provides a mini-case study on accessibility between specific geographical points within certain types of journey, commute, education and so on. The real potential here is achieving the elusive meeting of qualitative and quantitative evidence in a format that can be manipulated in different ways.

Setting the parameters

One of the developments that we made in the PJP process was that each plan produced was given a primary and secondary effectiveness score by the area coordinator who produced it. (The criteria are given below.) Put simply, they test what is available, the current network and show where there is unmet demand.

The potential of the database, then, is massive. Searches can be performed to analyse any element of the request, the plan, or the effectiveness rating:

a) From which parts of the borough are people trying to get transport before 06:00?
b) Where are people having difficulty getting home to after a 22:00 shift finish?
c) What education destinations are women trying to get home from following a 21:00 lesson finish?
d) Can a route be identified between people seeking employment at a new factory?
e) How many times have we recommended the 200 service?
f) How many times have we referred people to women's safe transport?
g) Which residents from this factory with low wages are paying over £20 each week on transport?
h) Show me the location of people we were unable to help and their destinations.

Examples (a) and (b) provide a way of testing the existing network while (c) shows how it is possible to refine the groups that you are looking at. Example (d) illustrates the way that this technique could be used to develop the business case for a new or altered route. Monitoring the effectiveness of subsidised services can be seen in (e), while (f) combines this with issues of safety. With (g) we can really start to see the potential for looking into the problem and identifying groups within the 'socially excluded' who are being hit hardest by the disproportionately high cost of public transport. The chance to innovate is really provided through example (h). Continually working to identify those you have not been able to help yet is the entire purpose of working with hard-to-reach groups. Searches similar to those in examples (g) and (h) provide the opportunity for a project to be at its most innovative – what will work for them?

Combined with geographical information systems (GIS) mapping, this database would generate a powerful visual tool for seeing the times and the places where the existing transport network, including all those different avenues that the area coordinators would have exhausted, fails to meet actual need. Overlay indices of deprivation, incidents of crime on public transport and other indicators of social exclusion, and the power of this process in generating data for meaningful analysis of the travel needs of people, begins to become clear. From this the provision, routing, timing and costing of the subsidised network could be meaningfully informed. Where subsidised services have been provided because they have always been provided, new provision could be matched to actual need rather than perceived or 'best guess' need. Beyond the scope of the subsidised network, it may be that, if applied in larger areas, commercially viable routes might be identified from this data and the public transport system finally made to serve the people who need it most, rather than company shareholders. The experience of the NTT case study throws into relief the way in which the theoretical accessibility planning approach put forward by the SEU report needs to be adapted in order to identify real-life demand and difficulty.

The three-part model of People, Activity and Availability put forward in Chapter Three and the accessibility planning approach recommended by the SEU provide a first basis for addressing these issues. What the experience of the NTT has demonstrated, however, is the *degree* to which each of these three elements must be pursued. Most importantly, the 'people' must be engaged with directly. Bureaucratic organisations often have a notion of what it means to consult people that community-based workers/initiatives would find incredibly remote. An understanding of the 'activity' that is to be engaged in must again be as it is perceived by the people involved. Assumptions about which shopping centre people will use, for example, can be very misleading.

The 'availability' of transport is a question that the local and national authorities must address. Accessibility planning must be supported by a framework of funding that will encourage innovation in service provision rather than just repeat the old response of "let's put on a bus". I would suggest that the manner of personalised journey planning as I developed with the NTT begins to address, at least in part, each of these areas of concern. In effect, properly managed, it provides a point of direct contact between the authorities and the very people they are seeking to assist. Better still, it is the nature of that point of contact that it provides high-quality, timely information about the problems of accessibility.

An example will help to illustrate the point. In the new town areas of Runcorn served by the dedicated Busway, the SEU's accessibility planning method would appear to demonstrate that all residents of some of the most deprived wards in the country have exceptionally high levels of access to the neighbouring industrial estates. What the NTT method would reveals is that, of those residents of these wards looking to make journeys for employment, it is to the industrial parks in Widnes and neighbouring Warrington that they are looking. In this way, the NTT method refines the process of accessibility planning; it informs which journeys people should be looking to make rather than simply assuming that the largest areas of need should be linked to the largest area of job vacancies. (There must be an effort to ensure that, for example, skills of job seekers in certain areas are matched to the job vacancies in others.)

Spotting the gaps

By collating and managing the data generated from PJPs, we were better able to find solutions for people's needs in a sustainable way. Another example of where working around social exclusion is significantly different to market models for accessibility planning is the necessary and informative focus on failure. Where a commercial business will look to work with those people it has already been successful in serving – that is, its customer base – the definition of social exclusion means that the NTT was always looking to engage those it had failed to assist or had as yet failed to contact. The attitude was always that our efforts should be directed towards those individuals and groups of individuals who we had been unable to help.

By searching the database on a daily/weekly basis, areas of origin, destination and travel at particular times of the day that were especially problematic could be highlighted. In some instances, solutions such as the rerouting of subsidised services were appropriate; but more often it would be smaller-scale solutions that were best. For example, where one or two people were having trouble getting from a specific neighbourhood to an industrial area, car sharing as passengers or taxi sharing might well become a more viable option. By getting people to register their interest in the car-share/taxi-share database at the point of completing the PJP request, these options for further joining up services become that much more effective.

Realising the potential of a journey-sharing database as a tool for social inclusion

It has become clear through the NTT programme that the intelligent use of Journeyshare Database Systems offers huge potential for identifying travel needs. The idea behind these systems is simple and widely understood. A database manages the process whereby people offering to share their vehicle on a specific journey are matched with people looking for a lift to make the same or a similar journey. Usually people will have something else in common beyond the similarity of journey: they may well be employed at the same site, or live in the same community. In effect this is the formalisation and facilitation of something that has always happened.

Currently, car-share databases of one kind or another are being promoted to address the adverse effects of increasing car usage, road and parking congestion. Interestingly, the limitations of infrastructure in the road network or the provision of parking spaces has created this new market for managing the adverse consequences of the transport-rich elements of society. Database providers are keen to enter at the top of the market, promoting the number of blue chip companies using them to help manage their car parking crisis or equally to demonstrate their environmental credentials. As with PJPs, the task of the NTT has been to reconceive the function of the car-share database to become a tool that has social inclusion as its primary focus.

Much of the basic functionality of the database remains the same. The trick comes with how to put those people without vehicles, and perhaps without jobs, at the heart of the process rather than them once again being marginalised by it. This was something that the business-minded database providers who submitted tenders for this project had clear difficulty in grasping. When companies were invited to make presentations to the NTT, they were specifically required to demonstrate how they would use their product to address the needs of socially excluded communities. The results of those first meetings were not encouraging.

One company, which played very much on the personal security offered by its system, required a one-off payment so that identities could be checked against credit card details. The difficulty here of course was that many of our target audience might not even have a bank account, let alone a credit card.

Another company began to explain how their product worked by saying, "So, you've got everyone in their cars....". With households in the borough without access to a car running at levels in excess of 30%, we had to interrupt the presentation to make the point again. Still another company were delighted to show us the numerous graphs, maps and charts that they could produce for us to demonstrate levels of uptake, repeat sharers, miles shared, and so on. They could not, however, produce a map showing us who they had not matched, once again leaving the transport poor to sit by the side of the road.

Similarly, while these companies could show how they might tie in with the parking management of a busy industrial site, where all the employees earned enough to run their own car, none of them had experience of demonstrating how provision of a car-share database might help a company that paid low wages and was struggling with the recruitment and retention of its workforce. By using a car-share database as part of its recruitment package, a company offering low wages, or which is particularly isolated from its workforce by location or the timing of shifts, can achieve benefits for both itself and its employees. By offering this service on an industrial estate-wide basis, the small, not particularly profitable, companies that typified those in Halton could come together to resolve a common problem. This is not rocket science but it is joined-up thinking and service provision in the way that seems to confound so many initiatives and seemed to be remote from the business focus of the database providers.

For individuals, the way in which they were going to access the service was going to be key. For ease of administration on our part it was going to be necessary to utilise an online resource hosted separately from our organisation. For individuals and organisations with online access, it required little more than the provision of a link to give full access to the benefits of this service; for those without Internet access, the provision of a call centre on a freephone number that could also allow access to the full range of services was provided. Where possible, these routes of access are promoted and provided through our partner organisations. Due to the PJP service that we already offered, it was also possible for us to act as an intermediary and register online for people who sent paper-based requests through to us. In practice, this was already in place, as one of the questions on the PJP request form asked people if they wanted their details included on a car-share database.

As with the PJP service, beyond the obvious and important service of providing people with necessary transport, the car-share database could be utilised as a valuable source of information. Again it was those people who we had been unable to help, the enduringly transport poor, that were of real interest. What we required of the car-share companies was the means to access on a daily basis those people requesting lifts to access work, education or training who had not been matched successfully. For these people, the wider PJP process might still offer them a viable transport link. This connection could easily be part of the online process: a simple link redirecting people to an online PJP request form, or indeed one could be prepared using the journey data already provided.

Clusters of people, or those along the line of a route, could perhaps be served through a taxi share, again to be brokered through the car-share database. In effect, a taxi service is, after all, a flexible lift offer without restrictions on times or locations. Again, the application of car-share databases to companies required a radical rethink. Elsewhere in the country, they are utilised by companies where the provision of car parking for employees has become too great an expense. The impression given by the industry is that this is the preserve of the blue chip companies.

In Halton, where the local authority is the single biggest employer, the situation is quite different. There is no congestion and free car parking is provided throughout the borough in an attempt to encourage commerce[7]. Within car-share databases, it is possible to have discreet areas so that, for instance, employees of one company will only be matched to other employees of that company. Beyond that, it is possible for companies to collaborate with each other so that there is a shared pool of offers and requests for lifts. These elements to the service would, of course, still be included, but what we looked to do with the NTT was extend this collaborative working to attract and include those small enterprises for whom lift sharing might not seem practicable. With any matching database, there is a certain level (a 'critical mass') below which the rate of matching is ineffective. What we wanted to do was bring together businesses on an industrial estate, maybe 100 units where none employed more than 50 people, so that together they would cross the threshold for that critical mass.

For those people struggling to maintain a car for commuting, the sharing of costs would make their transport more sustainable, while people unable to make journeys would gain access to cheap and convenient transport. The arguments for the businesses to support this were equally strong. Divided between so many companies, the cost for a discreet area became negligible (and indeed may have been 'gifted' by the local authority). The ability to retain existing staff by reducing their transport costs would be a tangible benefit as would be the reduced pressure on car parking. With a little refinement, it would be possible to allow people seeking employment on that industrial site to find out how many prospective matches they might have if they were to take up work there. The potential for refining the service and targeting services goes on.

At the end of the first year, the partner company has been identified and the website purchased. Discussions had been started with regards to the refinements to the database that were required; there was still some way to progress on this initiative.

Improving access to education

As has already been described, the colleges were one of our principal partners in trying to reach people wanting to continue or return to education. Trying to manage the distinct peaks in demand from the colleges in September and again around Christmas when they looked to attract and enrol large numbers of students presented its own challenges. Just providing enough team members to sit in on each of the open nights at the different colleges and campuses proved to be a great strain. Consequently, we developed a different way of working with this group.

Student travel packs

It was decided that, in the case of students, we would provide them with as many resources for resolving their own transport problems as possible. What was developed, following a successful pilot the previous year, was a student travel pack containing campus-specific travel information and advice. In effect, this was a reverse route and timetable for those bus services serving the appropriate campus. The pack itself also included a complete timetable and leaflets detailing advice on the different sources of funding available to them. In addition, there were maps of how to reach each campus and a statement of the local authority's policy regarding post-16 transport. All of this was contained in a plastic wallet designed to be as attractive as possible. Some 4,000 of these packs were prepared and delivered to the colleges for distribution to the students. Of course, each pack also contained a PJP request form with freepost envelope and a credit card-sized card with the contact details for the NTT.

As described earlier in this chapter, the key issue in working with the colleges was always to try and emphasis the need to engage prospective students early enough in their deliberations about attending college. Those attending open days and induction courses had largely made their decisions and either resolved transport needs or would overcome them regardless. Again it was those people who excluded themselves from the process because of issues of transport that we needed to contact. Persuading the colleges to include something about the NTT in their promotional material proved to be a difficult task. This was not because of any unwillingness on their part but because, as often seems the case with transport, the moment we were not there reminding them that this was a big issue for them, it was forgotten or categorised as 'not my problem'.

In an attempt to catch prospective students 'further upstream' in the process, we began to contact all students finishing secondary education and asking them if they were considering college and would like us to outline their transport options and the likely costs/benefits available to them. This was reasonably successful, although we were restricted in what we could tell them so far in advance, perhaps too far upstream. The real benefit of this exercise, however, was capturing a database of their addresses so that we would be able to contact them again nearer the time when our intervention would be to greater effect. A relationship that we could have developed further in this area would have been working with the Connexions careers service.

College shuttle bus

During 2002/03 in work instigated and managed primarily by John Mooney, £180,000 was secured from the DfES to improve transport links and support for students. The Halton Pathfinders Post 16 Transport Partnership was formed with members from the local education providers, transport operators, and other allied agencies. The NTT became a mechanism for delivering improvements on behalf of this partnership.

The first year proved to be tremendously successful. A yearly increase of 32% of 16- to 18-year-olds participating in further education was certainly in part due to improved transport provision. Another great success for the partnership was securing funding from the LSP to continue much of this work beyond the life of the original funding stream.

The principal achievements of the partnership were:

- providing additional bus services to the three main college sites in Halton, generating in excess of 100,000 additional trips on public transport;
- establishing a door-to-door minibus service to ensure students with a disability can have improved access to education;
- working with Halton Community Transport to provide travel training to students with a disability in transition from high school to further education;
- providing the students, via the colleges, with additional support for travel costs;
- providing comprehensive travel packs for students and sixth-form schools;
- providing a PJP service for students;
- holding public transport surgeries at colleges and attending open days to offer travel advice;
- conducting research into unmet travel demand.

Improving access to employment

The 200 bus service: a case for being intelligence-led

An example of how the NTT worked to better utilise existing resources to the benefit of all is provided by the 200 bus service that was utilised by Gary in the example at the beginning of this chapter. Funded through the UBC as part of the Links and Access Strategy, this was originally a circular service linking estates in Runcorn with high unemployment to the neighbouring industrial areas with job vacancies[8]. After a few months of writing PJPs, one of the area coordinators noted that this was the sixth time she had not been able to help a resident of Hough Green in Widnes get to a job on one of the estates served by the 200 service. The result was that we could make the case for altering the first journey of the day to include Widnes and drop off at all employment sites in time for a 6am shift start. The result was increased patronage on the service (see Figure 5.2) and, more importantly, as detailed in the case study at the beginning of this chapter, Gary and his brother into employment.

Admittedly, this was achieved with human brainpower rather than by the database (not developed at that stage), but the principle is clear. Rather than using broad strokes across a map linking need with possible opportunity, PJPs can provide a very clear picture of the types of journeys that people want to make, rather than the journeys it is assumed they should make. In this way, you have a better indication that people in this community have skills that will get them employed at that factory or industrial estate.

The point here is a significant one. This valuable, but also expensive, subsidised bus service could be refined in its delivery by using intelligence gathered through another role. The rerouting was radical – but based on hard evidence. We knew that there was a history of people in the new area trying to gain employment at those sites. The skills match and the demand for the service were in place. Sure enough, the passenger usage figures reflected this and numbers on that first journey began to climb steadily and show a sustained increase in usage of about 25% (see Figure 5.3).

The example, hopefully, makes the point. By utilising the available intelligence, the network can become responsive to real need in the community. The positive

Figure 5.2: Alterations to 200 bus service following analysis of Personalised Journey Plan (PJP) requests

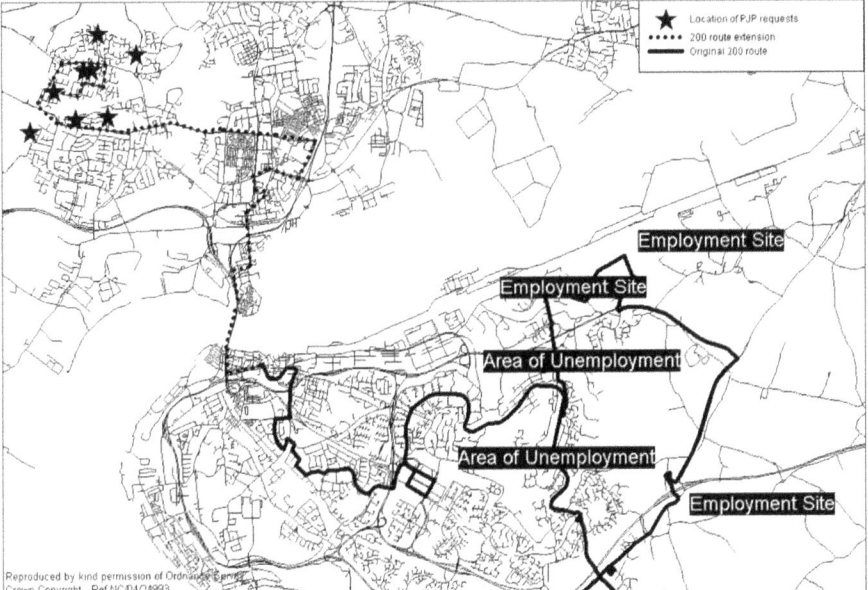

Note: This map was produced with the kind assistance of Merseytravel.

Figure 5.3: Patronage on route 200 (2003)

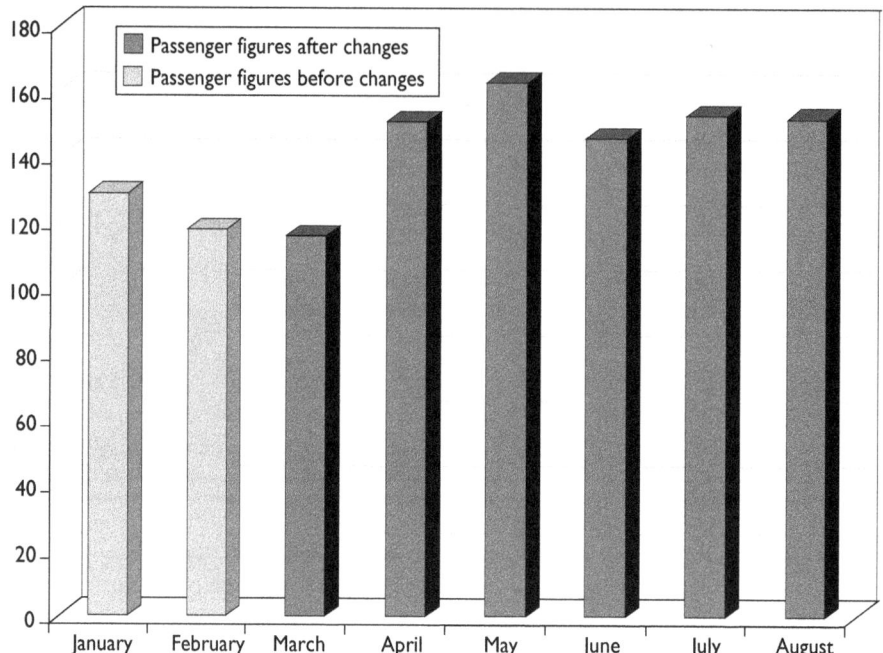

impact of amending this service has been acknowledged by the staff at JobCentre Plus, as demonstrated in this statement from the local Job Centre manager in Widnes:

> Having consulted all teams across the Job Centre, all feel the changes are already making a difference. The revised operating times have opened up vacancies to Widnes residents which they would previously have not considered due to transport limitations. Therefore the changes are clearly beneficial to our customers, ourselves as referring agents and the local community, and are much appreciated.

The 832/939 Job Link service

In partnership with Merseytravel, the NTT helped to develop a Joblink service intended to connect the most deprived of Halton's wards with emerging opportunities in South Liverpool. With UBC and European funding, this 832 service provided an extremely high-quality, accessible minibus with a flat fare of 50 pence. The service was timed to reach employment sites in time for shift changes and runs for 18 hours each day.

An important innovation with this service is that for those parts of the day when not committed to its fixed route, the bus becomes the 939 demand-responsive service. This 939 can be booked to take job seekers, students, and so on, to interview or workplace visits not readily accessible by the existing network. Only authorised partners, such as JobCentre Plus, can make these bookings and in our case this was handled through the NTT.

The Job Link service provides an example of best practice in what might be achieved with UBC funding. The service is of the highest quality, provides excellent value to users and seeks where possible to be responsive to unmet need through the demand-responsive element. At the time of putting the route together, the NTT database was not developed to the point of being able to inform route planning as described earlier. Instead, we worked closely with the job centres and council researchers to identify the areas most likely to benefit from the service. A useful review process would be to check the current routes against what could be identified through the database.

Snapshot table of achievements

Table 5.1 gives a 'snapshot' of achievements for the first year of the NTT. It gives an idea of the volume of work undertaken and the demonstrable impact it is

Table 5.1: Snapshot of achievements for the first year of the NTT

Output	Number	Outcomes
Additional trips to college on public transport	100,000+	Contribute towards 32% increase in 16- to 18-year-olds participating in further education
Trips to college by students with disabilities	3,200	12 students travelling to college each day
Travel packs issued	4,000+	Improved access and information for students
Public transport surgeries conducted in colleges	20+	Students receive personalised advice face-to-face
Transport surgeries held in job centres	50+	Job seekers able to access information and advice directly
Number of new jobs created directly	5	New posts created
Number of PJPs issued to Halton residents	606	More Halton residents into education, training and employment
Percentage increase in users of 200 service first journey since NTT instigated changes	25% and increasing	Residents from Widnes now able to access jobs in Runcorn in time for 6am shift start
Number of people in target group accessing education, training or employment as a result of receiving personalised journey advice	227 (figure extrapolated from sample)	People accessing opportunities as a result of NTT activity

having to the benefit of residents of Halton. These figures cover the first nine months of the project.

Towards a model of social sustainability: lessons learned

The underlying principles of community development are about empowerment, capacity building and personal or group progression. The idea is that the people who are enduring a difficulty are often the best placed to recognise and implement a solution. By working always with an exit strategy in mind, this leaves the recipient with the skills and confidence to effect their own change in future, thus the solutions that are provided are sustainable. Working in this way, the individual will move towards what is most appropriate for them in terms of cost, convenience, environmental impact, health benefits and so on.

For a community development practitioner coming into the transport field, familiar ways of working and the received wisdom of project development now seemed quite at odds with the norm. One of the key lessons learned from the NTT experience has been the need for the transport sector to clearly identify what its aims are in regards to social inclusion. Indeed, the entire area of 'socially necessary services' needs clarification of purpose because this will have implications for how services are monitored and evaluated. More sophisticated and apt measures of achievement need to be developed.

A multidisciplinary approach may well be the best way to approach these issues; restricting the people involved to only those with a transport background will stunt the debate and the scope for real innovation. Involvement at the grassroots, concerning yourself with the real problems faced by people, and often the answers that they find, produces a wealth of real intelligence about the transport needs of the communities you serve.

An effective monitoring system for socially necessary services should provide a cost/benefit analysis that places a value on the movement of people from exclusion to inclusion. Put simply, is the value of the intervention of the 200 service to be measured by the fare Gary placed in the box or as a proportion of the reduction of benefits paid to Gary while he was unemployed *and* the money that he now contributes through tax? If we must put a figure on the impact of subsidised services in order to determine their effectiveness, then let us remember that this is an initiative to achieve social change that happens to be delivered through a bus service. Social criteria should be used to monitor effectiveness, not the standards of the commercial bus operators.

The transport business seems peculiar in the degree to which it is content for its users to remain anonymous. The reason why the PJP service has been so key to developing the wider interventions of the NTT has been that it allows for the effective tracking of the people you seek to work with. By knowing your clients and understanding their developing transport needs, it is possible not only to achieve a better service for them but also the better use of costly resources.

When trying to achieve social sustainability, it is the through-flow of beneficiaries that is important rather than the static and impersonal number of bums on seats or fare box revenue. For example, services such as the 832 or 200 could be pump-primed in the sense that each user referred is time limited for how long they can use it; say, four months. During this time, all the resources of the NTT are brought to bear on their situation – PJPs, the commercial network, journey share, taxi share, advice on saving to buy a car through a credit union and then registering with the journey share, and so on. All these could be used to help identify progression routes. The result would be a constant renewal of capacity in the original service to provide transport for more people.

From a market model that relies on maintaining a captive market of bus users we arrive at a situation where we look to move people on from what is an expensive service to other parts of the network or to other sustainable forms of transport, for example, walking or cycling. In this way, by having the original set up and running costs benefit as many people as possible, the cost/benefit analysis can swing in the favour of social sustainability[9]. The final evaluation/exit strategy for such a service should be a function of this kind of evaluation. This is not a soft option: the criteria can be every bit as rigorous and robust as profit-driven systems.

The SEU (2003) report mentions the need to overcome restricted travel horizons among excluded communities. The degree to which the complexities of making a journey, working out timetables, making connections or travelling somewhere new can act as the final barrier or handy excuse for people to not access opportunity, should not be underestimated. The term agoraphobia, literally 'fear of the market place', is particularly apt when we consider the reluctance of some members of socially excluded communities to take up opportunity, to put themselves into the market place. To be the first in three generations of your family to have a job, or to be the only person you know going to college next year, requires reserves of courage and commitment that few of us in mainstream comfort can truly understand. For some, transport truly is the barrier; these people would like to take up opportunity but have no means to access it in a sustainable way. One of the great benefits of the PJP technique is that, through a combination of personal contact, encouragement and advice that is specifically relevant to needs, these restricted travel horizons can be overcome.

The true benefits to be derived from the PJP process go far beyond helping individuals, as the information gathered can inform strategic decisions about transport provision and the future planning process. By linking real need for transport with accurately identified areas of opportunity, the accessibility planning process can be tied directly into the real world, taking it beyond theoretical need to actual present requirements. This work is only just beginning to be explored by the NTT, but the potential is clear and the argument, I think, persuasive. Once populated with enough case studies this database will allow a meaningful analysis of transport needs to be made.

Without doubt an important element in the success of the NTT was the reasonably compact area in which we worked. As a unitary authority it is possible, on occasion, to move quickly and to have good communication across different agencies. This is not to suggest that such a model could not be replicated across a larger organisation, but that the importance of working close to the ground is a significant lesson[10]. Even less subject to doubt, however, is the clear demonstration that by engaging with the people you seek to assist, your intervention will be that much more effective and sustainable to the very real benefit of all.

Notes

[1] Private car ownership is in no way assumed to be the only outcome for this kind of intervention. I do respect, however, the right of individuals to determine what best suits them and what is sustainable in their terms, be that a private car, bus pass or bicycle.

[2] As part of its development as a new town, Runcorn has a dedicated Busway that penetrates all of the new town housing estates and much of the old town.

[3] At the time this research was undertaken and following its completion, Halton Community Transport, under new management, introduced a number of schemes to address some of these issues.

[4] It remains a problem with funding streams, such as the UBC, that they stifle innovation. In place of a creative dialogue, the conversation goes, 'The answer is a bus; now what's the problem?'.

[5] Local strategic partnerships have been set up in the 88 most deprived areas of the UK to help bend mainstream policies and programmes towards the reduction of social exclusion.

[6] Because of the method of collecting this data these results should only be considered a 'snapshot' of what had been happening. A more scientific follow-up study of the technique would be both welcome and worthwhile.

[7] The exception is the pinch point at the crossing of the Mersey River by the Silver Jubilee Bridge – the provision of a second crossing for the Mersey (costed at in excess of £300 million) was felt to be beyond the remit of the NTT.

[8] There was an additional leg to the first journey of the day from the depot in Widnes through Runcorn to those areas covered by the circular element of the route. The revisions to the route extended this first leg to take in more of Widnes.

[9] Social auditing may prove a useful mechanism for this kind of evaluation. Halton Community Transport is currently undertaking such a review and I await the results with interest.

[10] Some elements of the project such as the Journeyshare database would of course work more effectively when drawing from a larger population base.

References

Mott Macdonald/Richard Armitage Transport Consultancy (2000) 'Halton Links to Employment', unpublished report for Halton Borough Council.

SEU (Social Exclusion Unit) (2003) *Making the connections: Final report on transport and social exclusion*, London: SEU.

SIX

BraunstoneBus: a link with the future

Mike Preston

Introduction

This third UK case study looks at how officers from the Braunstone Community Association (BCA) and Leicester City Council secured two new local bus routes to enable the people living in Braunstone to access key services in the wider area. The scheme was borne out of a series of government-funded case studies, which identified that commercially run and tendered bus services were severely inadequate in addressing the transport needs of the resident community. Local people were actively involved in identifying the type of services they would like to see for their area.

In particular, this chapter shows how dreams must often be tempered to match legislation, funding and institutional realities. It offers some powerful lessons for any organisation aspiring to secure and manage their own transport service.

Background

Based on the south western edge of Leicester, Braunstone is a New Deal for Communities (NDC) Pathfinder area which, along with 17 other deprived neighbourhoods across Britain, received central government funding in 2000 to help the community tackle a range of issues associated with social deprivation. Braunstone received £49.5 million.

Braunstone is a 70-year-old estate, which is home to some 15,000 people, the vast majority of whom live either in council housing or houses they have bought from the council. The rest of the housing is mostly owned by housing associations to which, like council tenants, residents pay less than a market rent. Half of the estate, South Braunstone, was built as a garden suburb with high ideals and design specification; this part of the estate still retains a distinct feel of its former glory. The second half, built slightly later and to a much lower specification, was built to facilitate inner-city slum clearance and still retains the feel of a community apart, that has long since given up asking for an equal slice of the pie.

Braunstone Community Association was formed as the company to deliver the New Deal programme. It is important to be aware that the evolution of BCA and the delivery of the Braunstone New Deal programme since that time has been a troubled one. Perhaps more energy has been expended on politics and recrimination than on getting the job done and solving the very real problems the people of Braunstone face. Nevertheless, through all of this, strong, positive projects have emerged which have truly tackled the issues of Braunstone. A beacon among these is the BraunstoneBus project.

Braunstone connected: the dream

Unlike the majority of transport initiatives in the UK, BraunstoneBus emerged as a response to a need expressed by Braunstone residents in the major community consultation leading up to the NDC government award. This clearly showed that local residents saw a lack of transport as a key cause of the isolation of Braunstone from the wider area. An outcome of the consultation was a published aim to achieve "total coverage of public transport in the area" (Braunstone Community Association, 1999, p 42), not an easily measurable objective or even realistic target, but one which left no doubt that a very significant improvement in public transport was being called for by the people of Braunstone.

In 2001, the Transport Studies Group at the University of Westminster carried out a study funded by the UK Department for Transport's Mobility and Social Inclusion Unit. Braunstone was chosen for a case study because of its position as an NDC area and the problems of poor transport that had been identified through community consultation. The case study developed a broad idea of the type of service Braunstone people were asking for through close collaboration with NDC officers and local residents. The case study also involved parallel work with several members of the Leicester City Council transport team. In particular, the city's public transport coordinator demonstrated a highly supportive approach and a commitment to enhancing bus services for Braunstone.

In 2002, the government, pleased with the success of the Rural Bus Challenge initiative aimed at reconnecting rural communities through innovative community/public transport initiatives, launched the Urban Bus Challenge (UBC) fund to seek similar community-based innovative solutions to the needs of deprived urban communities. With the close support of the Transport Studies Group, I drafted Braunstone's UBC bid. However, BCA was informed that successful UBC bids could only be awarded to local authorities, not community bodies such as the BCA. Although the bid could be written by BCA, it was clear it would need the support of Leicester City Council. However, the council was initially concerned about submission of a bid, feeling that it did not have the time resource to undertake this work itself and, as the opportunity to bid for UBC would last for three years, a more cautious approach was recommended to develop the bid for a further year before submitting it.

The BCA offered a counter argument that no one had a great deal of time to prepare bids in the first year and an early bid may just provide the 'edge' which could be lost the following year. Besides, a failed bid would still leave us with 12 months to develop it for the next bidding round. An additional selling point for our bid would be the ability of Braunstone to utilise NDC money to provide match funding.

Following the outcome of the earlier research and community consultation exercises, the Braunstone bid was based primarily on small vehicles weaving through and linking key points (shops and community centres for example) within the estate. It was envisaged that no home in Braunstone should be more than a three-minute walk from the bus route. There would be the additional possibility of routing links to the city centre and the nearby out-of-town shopping and commercial areas situated near Junction 21 of the M1 motorway. This would meet the purpose of improving access to better shopping, health facilities, employment opportunities and leisure facilities. The initial concept was to run the service as an offshoot of BCA. It would be a social enterprise that would, in time, provide the first opportunity, born of NDC, to grow a company for the long-term financial gain of the community.

In order to provide a further attractive element to our bid, it was proposed to address issues of air pollution by using electric vehicles. Leicester has Environment City status for its policy efforts in the field of environmental protection and enhancement. The documented respiratory health of Braunstone people indicates that any activity to reduce harmful airborne emissions could only help to alleviate this issue.

The additional cost of electric vehicles to the project would be £300,000 – primarily the price of the vehicles and the cost of the battery charging equipment. The vehicles would restrict the range of journeys to the amount of charge capable of being stored in the batteries. The size and design of buses would be limited to the few vehicles of this type in production and the ongoing maintenance would present a range of specialist mechanical issues. With this in mind, it is perhaps fortunate that the UBC assessors, with a need to trim our bid, felt that the winning element of our bid was about community-based public transport and the opportunities this would bring. They clearly felt that electric buses could be dispensed with.

To our surprise and delight, the BCA was awarded £1.13 million of UBC funding to deliver a diesel-powered bus service, to which we added £334,000 NDC funds. This was to be one of the largest UBC projects in the country and would require of BCA a level of professional experience and expertise that it clearly did not possess. A first step, therefore, was to appoint a bus professional to develop the service. We were very fortunate to recruit Mark Carrara, a person with more than 30 years experience in the field, who also possessed tenacity and focus that was to prove invaluable. It was on his appointment that BCA finally awoke to the realisation that this was a project of major potential, which required and merited significant commitment.

BraunstoneBus: the reality

The BCA began working towards the initial aim of creating our own bus service, which would involve purchasing vehicles, employing staff and developing the necessary infrastructure. Since this would be a major departure for BCA, our ideas quickly evolved into thinking about setting up a separate bus company which would have its own board and a remit to plough any surplus back into the service or 'gift it' to support other Braunstone community projects. The vision was for the company to grow, to develop further profitable routes and to tender for services. As this would be a not-for-profit social enterprise, all of the financial benefit would be for the people of Braunstone. But, try as we might, we could not achieve this dream.

The New Deal for Communities has been devised by central government to explore new ways of regenerating communities that have been failed by the old ways. Braunstone Community Association was set up to provide this new way for Braunstone. Leicester City Council, as owner and landlord of over 90% of the area, in many respects represents the old way. Therefore, there is an inherent tension in the relationship, and in the short history of BCA, the interaction between the two organisations has, consequently, been testing. Additionally, as a new organisation, striving to embrace the concepts of community inclusion, leadership and democracy, BCA has experienced many internal issues that it has struggled to resolve. This has understandably caused other organisations, including Leicester City Council, to exercise due caution in their working relationship with BCA.

As the official recipient of the UBC grant and, therefore BCA's accountable body for the project, Leicester City Council necessarily held a view about the wisdom of following the bus company approach. At the regular project board meetings between the two organisations, the council repeatedly expressed its caution about the ability of BCA to set up and run a bus company. The Government Office for the East Midlands administers the NDC funds and, in the context of the £340,000 NDC grant awarded for the project, also expressed some concern over BCA setting up and running their own bus company. The BCA had no history of running anything commercially and had a staff base that broadly lacked the experience and expertise to do so. Even with the stand-alone company, the bureaucracy and conflict inherent in BCA was causing a painfully slow progress, which at times stagnated altogether and, as fresh problems tripped into view, the day the buses would begin to run drifted way out of sight. Issues around registration for VAT, tendering for vehicles (new and second hand), storage of vehicles, weekly payment, cash handling and banking were proving very difficult and time-consuming to overcome. There was a reason, it seemed, why each and every problem was insurmountable.

All of these BCA-centred issues were set against a backdrop of spiralling insurance costs, which would hugely inflate the cost of running the service, and prevent BraunstoneBus from achieving one of its goals: to train and employ

Braunstone bus drivers. Insurers were either dropping out of the bus market or inflating their premiums to a prohibitive level. Those who were prepared to offer insurance would not permit drivers with fewer than two years commercial experience. Larger bus companies provide their own insurance cover and so are able to waive this restriction to give employment opportunities to freshly trained, inexperienced drivers.

Bus driving is a challenging and highly responsible job, which is operated on a shift basis and is not well paid. Consequently, there is a national shortage of bus drivers. We were concerned that we could have insufficient drivers to run the service, so the provision of driver training for Braunstone people was an important element of our preparation. Consequently, we had commenced a partnership with a national bus operator to recruit and train Braunstone people to drive buses. Braunstone Working, the BCA employment project, coordinated and funded this programme, which has now produced 12 qualified bus drivers. However, the insurance issue appeared to have forced these new drivers to go and work for another operator for two years before joining the staff of BraunstoneBus.

In spite of the array of seemingly insurmountable problems, we produced a thorough business plan. However, the process of receiving the support of the BCA board and the council became increasingly complex, hugely bureaucratic and particularly fraught. For one month, the BCA had nothing to do but wait. The initial intention had been to launch the service in August 2002; the earliest possible date was now June 2003. Clearly, we were failing to provide the community with the service they had requested and deserved and which, by this time, they were fully entitled to expect.

The business plan was developed and refined to meet the requirements of both the BCA board and the council cabinet. The BCA board was content but cabinet after cabinet passed without the document being approved. No sooner had one draft been completed than additional information and council officers on the project board required assurance. The councillors, their views of BCA in this context understood by their officers, were not even invited to make a decision. Quite simply, the council, as the accountable body, was very reluctant to expose itself to the risk of BCA setting up a bus company.

The disappointment was that the council had signed up to the initial bid, which described the setting up and running of the service by BCA. The company was to be a more focused and streamlined way of achieving this aim. The loss of the company would also mean the loss of the opportunity for Braunstone to develop a business that, if successful, would bring income back to the community.

The greatest proponent of the bus company was the then chief executive of BCA, for whom it was now becoming a battle he was determined to win. Other team members were losing the will to fight on through the morass and had quietly begun to explore an alternative solution, which involved putting the service out to commercial tender. Soundings indicated that this would immediately meet with the approval of the project board and council cabinet.

Inviting professional bus companies to run the service would eliminate all infrastructure issues, therefore bringing the launch date for the service forward five months, from June to January 2003. The day after the departure of the chief executive of BCA, the council welcomed with open arms the proposal by BCA to tender out the service. The Government Office of the East Midlands, also, was relieved by the decision, UBC agreed to the change and the BCA board, accepting that the overriding issue now was to get the show on the road, also supported the proposal.

Making it happen

The challenge was to devise a sustainable bus service, with a chance of meeting sufficient demand to survive beyond the period of UBC and NDC funding. Any bus service, other than those that are deemed to be of social necessity, ultimately has to be self-financing. The possibility of the service ceasing once the subsidy ran out would mean, for us, that we had failed. The central element of the original concept for BraunstoneBus was to develop a service, using small buses, which would weave through Braunstone and make all parts of it accessible to its residents. This assumed that Braunstone people had sufficient reasons to take these journeys and in sufficient number to make it viable. Mark immediately questioned the original intention to purchase the 15- to 18-seat vehicles necessary to navigate the tight roads. This, he rightly pointed out, would seriously undermine any prospect of commercial success and sustainability. We needed the ability to carry larger numbers of passengers on each journey.

The problem, therefore, became one of introducing a full-time bus service that would be of use to a significant number of residents. It was evident that the potential for success lay in the secondary element of the original concept, which was to depart from the Braunstone circuit and offshoot to the nearby retail and business parks, along with the additional possibility of linking into Leicester city centre. Although Braunstone has 15,000 residents, it consists of mainly semi-detached 1920s council housing which covers a large area with no high density flats or blocks and few focal points where large numbers of people might want to catch a bus to or from. The vehicles would have to complete a great deal of mileage to collect their fares.

The conclusion was inescapable: the service would be unsustainable without taking in other areas and meeting the needs of people in the wider area. This would have two significant effects: the expansion of the route would provide an increase in destinations to Braunstone people and the anticipated extra income received would offer the chance of the holy grail for a sustainable bus service – commercial viability. People from outside the area would be using the BraunstoneBus, adding to the social integration which is a key aim of the NDC programme; plus, the wider usage would give Braunstone a chance of a commercial service. The grant funding would offer a period to explore possibilities and tune the service to meet demand before commerciality became an imperative.

We chose to go through a consultation exercise to get a more detailed idea about what residents wanted. A note of caution should perhaps be sounded, that many people, when questioned, describe the nature of the service they would like to see operating. This does not mean that they have any need to use that service or would choose to do so should it commence. It is at least as important to watch what people actually do rather than ask them what they might wish to do in the future. As anticipated, the consultation results were mixed and did not give a clear direction. However, to our relief, the comments did confirm demand for the areas of employment, schools, shopping, hospitals and leisure facilities that we had identified.

Traditionally, urban bus services travel to the urban centre from the outskirts, taking people from their homes to their places of work, shopping areas and leisure facilities. As people increasingly have the choice of out-of-town facilities, it is perhaps the case that public transport has not kept up with this shift. Braunstone is positioned on the Leicester outer ring road between two major retail parks, business and industrial areas and close to a hospital and schools all situated on the ring road. It was felt that residents could benefit from – and want to use – a service linking each part of Braunstone with these nearby facilities currently only accessible by private transport. This aim would also help to support the Braunstone Working Project, which is helping to increase the numbers of Braunstone residents in work. The bus service was seen as a crucial resource to make jobs in the wider area more accessible. In this respect, the provision of this service would be a leap of faith in the efficacy of the work of NDC and Braunstone Working in particular. Initial on-board surveys of the bus service show passengers have taken up employment because the service enables them to access a new place of work. More still are using the service because it provides an easier route to work.

Much time was spent establishing a route that opens up access to real employment opportunities for the people of Braunstone. As a bus service survives on volume, judgements had to be taken about the greatest demand, which would be borne out or otherwise once the service commenced. Information was taken from the Braunstone Working Skills Audit and the interest shown by Braunstone people to seek particular types of work. It was evident that, perhaps because many Braunstone people have existed outside the mainstream of opportunity and education, the greatest employment opportunities for residents may be in service and manual industries. The nearest industrial estate is the home of the main post office sorting depot for the city. Additionally, it supports a number of warehouses and offices including some of national organisations. It was felt that the employment opportunities offered were insufficient to generate the kind of work that would fill buses from Braunstone.

Also within this estate is an Aldi supermarket that appeared to be popular with residents, but without reasonable access for public transport. As this store is in a very isolated location, the consequence of missing a bus for a shopper could be a long stand until the next bus arrived. It would be far better to take shoppers to

ASDA, which is part of the much larger Fosse Park complex with many other shops, cafes and toilet facilities to visit between buses. Ruling out serving this area of employment and low-cost shopping opportunities was a difficult decision but, once taken, afforded the opportunity to take the service along Narborough Road, a traditional shopping street with many adjacent streets of housing. It was believed that this route would attract more passengers and offer a more attractive service.

A further aim was to route the bus past as many schools as feasibly possible. This would contribute to improving the area's poor school attendance, especially at senior school where there is no longer an estate-based facility. It would also help to meet the aims of our NDC delivery plan in achieving safer routes to school.

We also wanted to provide a service to one of Leicester's three hospitals on the way to the main outer shopping areas. This would also provide a further employment opportunity for residents. Beyond the hospital is the major out-of-town shopping centre, Beaumont Leys, which has a wide range of shops, a market, a flea market/car boot and a bingo. Additionally, this part of the route would serve a large population in two other deprived areas of Leicester, Beaumont Leys and Braunstone Frith. Mark, the BraunstoneBus Manager, believed this part of the route would carry more passengers than the Fosse Park end and thus help to support its commercial viability.

Also taken into consideration when deciding the initial route and, importantly, its flexibility for the future, were planned developments within the area. As part of the NDC programme, a burgeoning development programme is already underway including the refurbishment of previously unwanted housing, a new health centre to meet the needs of 50,000 local people, a leisure centre which will attract people to Braunstone, a library and community resource centre. Throughout this process, it was fully understood that the desire to provide a service for Braunstone people to access key facilities to tackle issues of social deprivation – unemployment, ill-health and so on – would only achieve a sustainable service for Braunstone if it were *used*. Ultimately the community would decide where they want to travel. Their aspirations may change as facilities and opportunities shape their lives and travelling habits; this would be reflected in the on-bus demand for each part of the route and in the results of surveys requesting additions to the route.

Thankfully, however, a responsive service is actually defined by the demand the community has for it. But it is not quite that simple! We are aware that the service cannot be sustained by revenue from Braunstone passengers alone: we have to take people from outside Braunstone where they want to go. Their demand patterns can and probably do differ from those of Braunstone residents. A very delicate balancing act is needed to generate demand along the route while establishing that the demand in Braunstone is the paramount aim of the service. On an ongoing basis, analysis of the route and survey work can be used to maintain the proper emphasis; the start of any new route can be informed by experienced practitioners but can only be conjecture. Ultimately, the route was more finely tuned by taking into consideration some nitty-gritty yet important operational issues, such as the avoidance of roads with road humps. This was especially important, as we had decided to use the new disabled access, low-floor vehicles which could easily sustain damage from road humps. Narrow roads with cars parked on either side were also keenly avoided.

It was decided that buses would run within walking distance of each home in Braunstone every 30 minutes during the day and hourly at evenings and weekends. This level of service required four buses. The proposed route was timed over and again throughout the day, evening and at weekends to ensure that the timetable would reflect the real duration of the journey. Given that the expectation of passengers is for a prompt service, an early bus can wait but a late one can rarely catch up.

Testing the service

Grant funding to support what would otherwise be forced to operate as a commercial service offers the flexibility of testing demand through offering a wide-ranging timetable. It was decided to take full advantage of this opportunity in the first few months of the service. To achieve the best service coverage possible, it was proposed to draw up a timetable for a full seven-day operation, with a good evening and weekend service. Clearly, there would be a significant cost attached to such a high level of service. However, it was felt that it was better to start at a high level of service and, if necessary, reduce where demand did not materialise rather than failing to provide a service and never knowing the level of demand – which could well justify service provision.

This approach has subsequently been shown to be effective by the success of the 301 service to the Beaumont Leys market on Sundays and, in contrast, the little-used weekday services between 10am and midday. Such practical testing over a period of six months has enabled passengers to show us the services they want to use at any given time or day, but also the growth in demand over time.

Next we had to decide how to pitch the fares. Should we charge Braunstone residents less than passengers from outside the area? Should all fares undercut the competition, and, if so, by how much? Should we have an introductory fare? A balance had to be drawn, in common with all pricing policies, to maximise both demand and income. The additional factor in this equation was the potential for use of the grant to subsidise fares. It was decided that we should keep fares low in Braunstone for the residents, the beneficiaries of the grant and the people we most want to use the buses to enhance their quality of life and life opportunities. It was also decided that we should offer an introductory fare that undercut other similar local services. It was felt that it is important, initially, to maximise passenger numbers to transfer travelling habits to our service. After this had been achieved, it would be possible to introduce some increases which would, if carefully applied and monitored, help to move the service towards sustainability after the funding had gone. The general aim was to ensure fares at least 5p cheaper per journey than similar local services.

An unexpected opportunity

Shortly before we had hoped to launch the 301 service, a decision made by one of the commercial operators in the area forced a dramatic rethink that would have a significant impact on the future of BraunstoneBus. A commercial operator had approached BCA some months earlier to ask if we would subsidise their loss-making 17 route from Braunstone to the city centre via the Royal Hospital. The advent of a bus lane along an adjacent route into the city had made the 17 relatively slow and unattractive. Hospital visitors, staff and outpatients were in insufficient numbers to make it commercial. Due to the lack of profitability in the route, old, unattractive and uncomfortable vehicles were being used which, bearing in mind it was a hospital route, did not provide for disabled access.

Leicester City Council, believing there was an ongoing social imperative to maintain a service to the Royal Hospital, suggested a dial-a-ride service. The BCA, keeping an eye firmly on the target of long-term sustainability, believed that this would be a drain on UBC and NDC resources. Our plan was to develop this service as a two-vehicle route with new disabled access buses, taking it past the hospital, the new Leicester City football ground, the Leicester Tigers rugby ground and make it work. Additionally, there are over 300 new student apartments being built along the route as well as a new waterside residential development. The new Braunstone Leisure Centre also would be accessible from the city centre by this service and the nearby Narborough Road, teeming with travellers to and from the city centre at rush hours, could be incorporated into the route. Finally, the service would go to the railway station, which would create significant additional mobility for Braunstone residents and all travellers in between. Through careful planning of the route, in conjunction with the 301, it would be possible for a traveller to use a combination of both services to travel from the centre of the city to either of the city's two largest edge-of-town shopping and leisure facilities.

Although we remained hopeful of the money lasting six or more years, market research indicated that the UBC fund would perhaps only give us the 301 route for a period of five years. The two routes would, of course, spread the money more thinly and therefore we would only be likely to get three years for our money if running the two services. There was a clear decision to be made: diversity or longevity? It was felt that the diversity offered tremendous advantages to Braunstone people, who had clearly indicated in community consultation that they felt the public transport service to and from Braunstone was inadequate. This is a situation exacerbated by the level of vehicle ownership in Braunstone, which is markedly below the city average. That the services would have only three years rather than five to achieve commercial sustainability, or possible additional funding, would add greater urgency to the tuning of the route and perhaps add sharpness to the thought and decision-making processes which would move us toward our goal. We decided to take a chance and have two bus services operating from Braunstone. The 317 would become our second service. The chance paid off: within six months the 317 was taking almost twice the income of the old 17 service while charging lower fares.

That the service is under continual review – matching fares and routes with usage – is certainly no bad thing and commensurate with both a commercial and a customer/community-focused approach. Clearly passengers require some continuity and assurance that the service, which, for example, takes them to their new job today, will be there to do the same in a month's time. For this reason, adjustments to the timetable have to date been carefully controlled and widely publicised; bus stops have timetable frames, which are kept in good condition and up to date; buses carry copies of the current timetable; the hospitals give out timetables with their appointments, and each home in Braunstone is delivered a new timetable in advance of changes (see Figure 6.1).

The tendering process

The time saved in tendering was immediately and wonderfully apparent. The months of attempting, without success, to set up the BraunstoneBus Company and the envisaged months of continued preparation would be replaced by a two-month period during which professional operators would tender and the winner would commence operation. However, a further problem emerged almost straight away: the city council is not the tendering authority for bus services. The city uses the tendering services of Leicestershire County Council. In this case, the service being managed by BCA and run through funding from UBC, for which the city are accountable, appeared to worry the county council which indicated that it did not wish to carry out the tendering process. At this stage, it began to seem that there might be no mechanism to get the service started. Perhaps bureaucracy had finally achieved victory over the hope and optimism with which the idea of a bus service had commenced.

Fortunately, careful negotiation and a creative approach to solving the problem brought about a refreshing solution. The county council lent their expertise and paperwork, which was amended to enable the city council to become the tendering authority for this service. The experts at the county council oversaw the administration, but the city council remained the official body for the process at all times.

With all of the problems out of the way at last, the services went out to tender during November 2002, with a given start date of 4 January 2003. The way this service was tendered required operators to offer a price for running a clearly identified timetabled route, with vehicles of a defined specification, for a given duration. The successful company would then run that service at that fixed price. The passenger income would be collected and administered by the company and deducted from the amount the company is paid by the tender. As passenger

Running on empty

Figure 6.1: Defining the routes

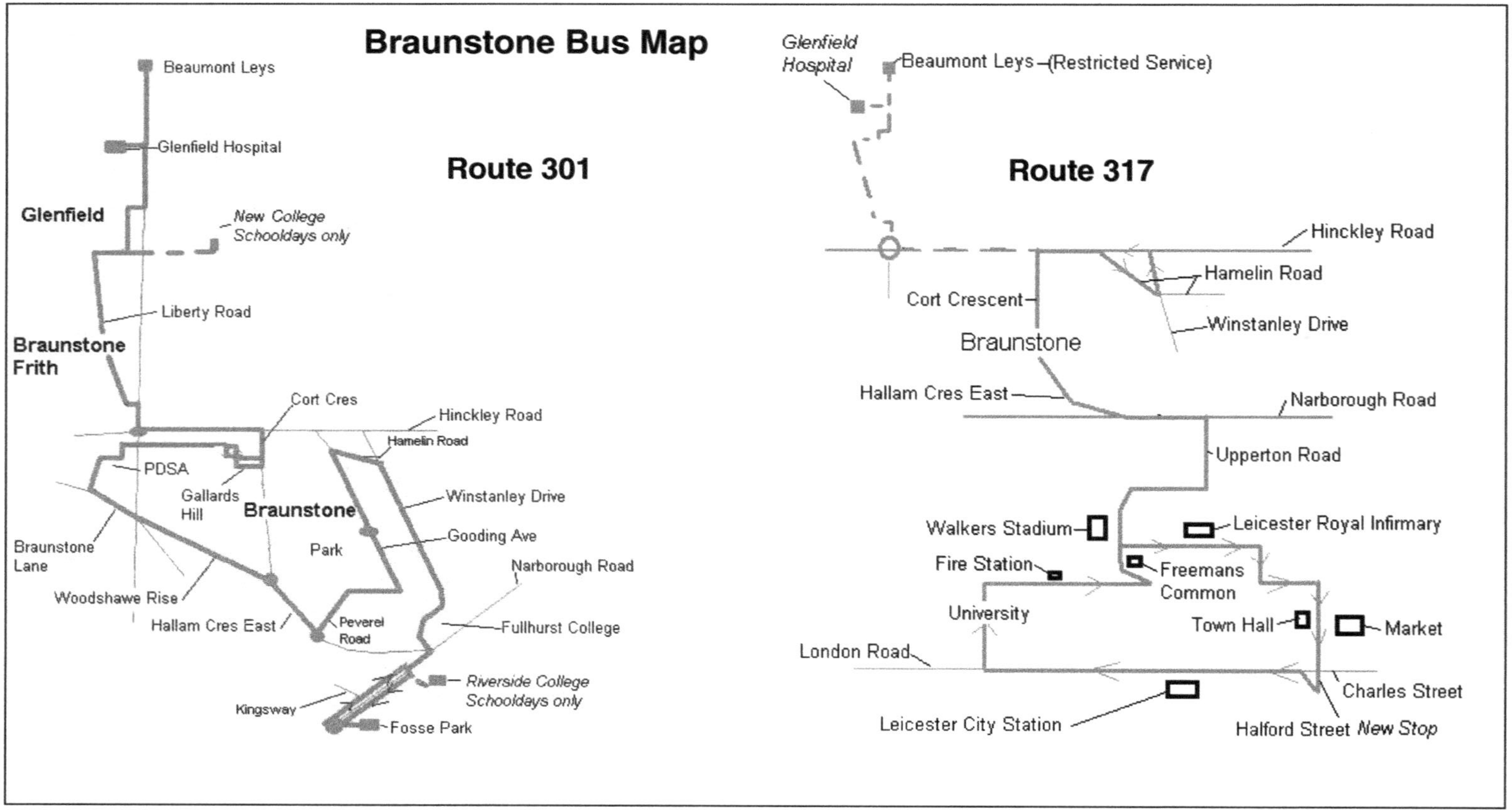

Braunstone Bus Map

Route 317

Route 301

106

income grows, so the drain on UBC resources would decrease until, hopefully, there would be no grant funding required at all and the service becomes commercially sustainable.

In all, 65 bus and coach operators are active in the East Midlands. Each was invited to tender for the 301 and the 317 service. Six companies tendered, for both services. The tenders were largely clustered within a small range, with only a very few highly speculative prices entered. Supported by reassurances from the county council experts, we felt confident that we had received competitive tenders. Our predictions were accurate: both services would run for three years. A large national company won the 301 service, and the 317 by a much smaller local company. This would provide an interesting comparison as the services developed.

The contract, which was immediately sent to the successful companies, contained important clauses for the community:

- wherever possible, the operator would employ local residents as drivers;
- the buses would be of low-floor design with wheelchair accessibility;
- the buses would be route branded and carry the Braunstone logo, which would give the service the desired community feel and a sense of ownership to the people of Braunstone.

To define the working relationship between the city council and BCA in relation to the UBC, a legal agreement was drawn up. As though to underline the extent to which such documents are removed from the day-to-day operational reality, the agreement was finally concluded six months after the commencement of the service and a good year after the UBC grant was awarded. It numbers some 30 pages and, in the event of a disagreement, it may again see daylight and justify the £15,000 that was paid to the legal professionals who wrote it.

On the road

In the dark of a very cold morning on 4 January 2003, many people still emerging from the aftermath of their New Year's celebrations, the 301 and the 317 services began (see Figure 6.2).

Timetables had been distributed across Braunstone and along the rest of the routes. The services had also been advertised in the free BCA paper, *The Braunstone Alert*. The *Leicester Mercury*, too, had been very helpful in running positive and informative articles. Yet still the dream of buses overflowing with passengers was far from reality. In those early weeks, many journeys ran empty or with just a handful of passengers on board.

Leicester City Council contributed to the infrastructure of the route by replacing old bus stops with new signs displaying the new service. They also accelerated their programme of raising curbs at stops to create a level access onto low-floor vehicles.

Running on empty

Figure 6.2: A cartoon highlighting the arrival of the two new bus services

AND THEN TWO TURN UP AT THE SAME TIME!

Source: Braunstone Community Association (drawn by Paddy McCullough, BCA Inclusion Manager)

The different nature of the two routes makes direct comparison of the services difficult. One company was contracted to run a traditional two-bus service from Braunstone into town and the other a far more experimental four-bus service around the perimeter and between new satellite shopping and business centres which have primarily been designed to facilitate the aspirations of private car users. However, from the first day of the service, our exit strategy was underway. Each service has its break-even point and must achieve this within the three-year duration of the contract to ensure commerciality and therefore long-term viability. Each service understandably began operation considerably below this point and continues to do so. However, the 317 (see Figure 6.3) showed very early signs of popularity, which has increased by a healthy amount in each month of operation. The operator ordered and purchased new low-floor buses immediately after winning the contract, which were liveried with the BCA logo and destinations and put into service from the start of the service on 4 January 2003. The service was operated by a small pool of regular and committed drivers who achieved a high standard of reliability from the outset, getting to know customers and developing a strong customer base who not only found the service convenient but also pleasant to use.

The 301 route is more complex, requiring competent, experienced and committed drivers to achieve the reliability that encourages passengers to change their travelling habits. This did not happen: vehicles left the garage late; they took wrong turns, missing out parts of the route and, on occasion, failing to pick up passengers as they sped past stops. Drivers did not know the fare structure and seldom worked on the route long enough to develop a rapport with passengers. There were reports of drivers being rude to passengers and, on one occasion, two 301 drivers, at the point where two buses cross, getting stuck with neither

Figure 6.3: A bus used on the 317 route

driver being prepared to reverse, followed by a loud argument which Braunstone residents had to defuse.

The BCA felt the need to write a letter to each 301 driver to explain the purpose of its efforts and to encourage them to feel part of the regeneration of Braunstone and development of an excellent bus service. The vehicles used were old and the display signs, wooden boards placed inside the windscreen, were often incorrect. The new vehicles arrived six months into the contract, immediately increasing passengers by 10%. To date, the livery has not been completed; consequently the link between BCA and this service remains unpublicised.

The 301 service experienced a number of incidents of stones being thrown at the bus windscreen from the street by Braunstone children. There was also trouble for the service on the school run when teenagers refused to pay and were abusive to drivers when demanding the fare. Although the police are yet to apprehend anyone over the vandalism, the school attended by the teenagers took decisive action and excluded one of those responsible.

The 317 service, although improving, runs at approximately half of its break-even point. The 301, now improving at a faster rate than the 317, runs at approximately a third of its break-even point. The bus team, mindful from the outset of the exit strategy for the project, has conducted a factually-based six-month review. Each service has its strengths and weaknesses. The review has identified them and made a series of proposals for the future of the BraunstoneBus service, proposals that, of themselves, could bring the service to break-even point.

However, an exciting development involving a new partnership looked set to make these proposals insignificant in comparison.

Taking stock: the six-month review

Once the service was underway, the project board agreed to meet less frequently and to hand over responsibility for the day-to-day running of the service to a project team consisting of a BCA resident director, a council accountant, Leicester City Council public transport coordinator, the BCA's BraunstoneBus coordinator and myself. The team meets monthly. A major review of the service was carried out after it had been operating for six months that proposed a significant change to the service. However, before this time, journeys showing no demand and fine-tuning of the service to meet specific needs resulted in two timetable changes that more closely aligned need with service provision and reduced the cost of the contracts by £13,000.

Detailed information about passenger numbers is available to the operator from the Wayfarer computerised ticketing machines, which were specified as part of the tender requirements. Numbers had increased to 7,200 passengers by July. The team further analysed the information on a zonal basis for each journey. There was also a great deal of softer information collected through the on-bus surveys conducted by the BCA Community Inclusion Team. Examples of the comments made are summarised in Figure 6.4.

During the first week of operation, beginning 4 January 2003, both the services carried 2,614 passenger journeys over six buses. Figures at 4 January 2004 showed 9,204 weekly passenger journeys were made, an increase of 252%. This is still not enough for the services to be commercially viable. The sustainability figure is 15,517 passenger journeys being undertaken across all six buses over a

Figure 6.4: Customer feedback from on-board surveys

"We have a great laugh on this bus service."
"I use it to get around Braunstone and see my family."
"I work as a classroom assistant at Bendbow rise school – this bus helps me take my son to Queensmead School and then get to work."
"It's cheaper – this is the first time I've tried it today."
"There has been some trouble with the kids shouting at the driver – they get off at Caldecote School."
"I like the fact it's hail and ride, it drops me right outside the doctor's."
"I go to the Gala Bingo on this bus and visit my sister and Glenfield Hospital."
"The drivers on a weekend get stones thrown at the bus as standard."
"I've just applied for a job at Tesco because of this service."
"We go swimming at Beaumont Leys because of this service, it's great."

period of seven days, with the average fare of 58p being paid. Cost increases, fuel, insurance, wages, maintenance, overheads and all the rest, mean the passenger numbers would have to increase over time to above the 15,517 figure or the fares would have to increase to a prohibitive level, which could reverse any growth.

Research has also provided some data on usage and customer satisfaction – a small sample showing combined figures for the 301/317 services appears in Table 6.1.

The 317 service has shown a better-than-expected performance throughout the route and across the timetable. However, it was evident that it was carrying three times more passengers into town than out. To bring the outward journey up to the level of the inward journey would, in itself, bring the service close to breaking even. On-board surveys had shown that the city centre stop was not sufficiently close to the main shopping area. While it was 'OK' when not carrying shopping, it was too far to walk with heavy bags. Furthermore, the stops adjacent to the central shopping area are served by several other bus services that compete with the 317 service on the critical part of the route close to the city. On its inward journey, the 317 competes on an equal basis for passengers. However, on the way out, competing services are picking up nearly all of the potential 317 passengers. The effect of this situation for Braunstone residents is that they either have to walk to the inconvenient 317 stop or walk a distance into Braunstone from the nearest stop used by competing services.

The bus service received its first petition from passengers living in Braunstone who wished to see a more central city stop. The council, mindful of the surfeit of buses using the city centre and the potential for other operators to object to a subsidised service competing with them, initially resisted the proposal. However, at the review, the debate was fully aired and the council subsequently worked hard with the Braunstone bus manager to achieve a city centre stop, which would best address the competing aspects of this issue. A city centre stop is now in use as part of the revised route.

The 301 service clearly showed that the Fosse Park end of the route, the one for which there were high hopes, was not being well used by Braunstone residents

Table 6.1: Data on usage and customer satisfaction (by number)

Satisfaction	Yes	No	No answer
Routes	82	6	3
Timetables	77	2	14
Use			
Work	32	5	44
For visiting	50	8	33
Shopping	93	0	3
Leisure	78	3	14
Cross the park	65	12	14
Sunday travel	72	3	19

or those along other parts of the route. In contrast, the Beaumont Leys end, incorporating the Glenfield Hospital, which was a late addition to the route shortly before it went into service, was carrying over twice as many passengers. The project team, led by the vision and experience of the bus manager, began to form the view that the 317 service could be enhanced by taking it out onto the Beaumont Leys part of the 301 route. At the same time, the unsuccessful Fosse Park portion of the 301 could be reduced to a far less frequent service, which would, nevertheless, provide a genuine opportunity for Braunstone people wishing to get to these shopping facilities and employment opportunities.

The team initially decided on a new, four-bus 317 service from the city centre to Beaumont Leys to replace the 301, and a limited service to Fosse Park called the 303. This would reduce the overall need for vehicles from six to four. A concerning aspect of this proposal would be breaking the news to the bus companies. This worry was soon heightened when information in a BCA board paper about the proposal came to the attention of the bus companies. The company operating the 301 understandably believed that the investment they had made in vehicles merited their continued operation of the service. That their poor performance had potentially impacted on the lack of popularity of the 301 was, for them, a separate issue. As a significant deliverer of bus services in Leicester and Leicestershire, it was of understandable importance to the council that a disagreement over this service would create a wider issue for their many other services. This was, of course, of far less importance to BCA for whom the 301 and the 317 and the service to Braunstone residents were its key interests.

It was extremely encouraging, therefore, when the combined knowledge of the city's and the BCA's public transport coordinators brought about a further significant opportunity. For some time, the NHS has understood that it has severe and increasing car-parking problems at each of their three Leicester hospitals. Their preferred solution has been to deliver a bus service connecting the three hospitals to enable the transfer of patients, staff and possibly documents while alleviating the parking difficulties being faced at each of these sites. Unfortunately, an earlier invitation for bus companies to tender a price for this service had proved too expensive for the health service budget. This information was passed on to Mark, the BraunstoneBus Manager, by the city council, which had been involved in the earlier tendering process.

The proposed new 317 service already connected two of the three hospitals. By retaining all of the six buses used for the combined 301/317 service, it would be possible to extend the service to the third hospital, the Leicester General in the east of the city. The cost of this extension of the 317 service would, of course, be less than for the provision of the entirely new service the bus companies had previously tendered for. Working together, Leicester City and the BCA made a timetabled and costed proposal to the NHS that would, if accepted, provide an additional funding source, which could increase the duration of the service from three to five years. The existing elements of the new 317 service would not be affected so there would be no dilution of the service for Braunstone residents. However, those with an appointment at Glenfield Hospital or those wishing to travel to the east side of the city would have the opportunity to do so.

This proposal coincided with the discontinuation of another service, the 70, from connecting with the Royal Hospital. The 317 is now the only service from the west of Leicester connecting with the Royal Hospital. Passenger numbers have begun to increase further as a consequence of this.

The new service required the two companies to work together in cooperation, not in competition, as is the case elsewhere in the city. Both companies, when invited to comment, expressed concern over the feasibility of this arrangement. In light of the differential levels of performance of the two companies and the proposed merger of the routes, the project team felt that the bus companies should be invited to the meetings. Here they could discuss issues, agree solutions and plan together for the future. The NHS would have a place on the project team and the project board.

Sadly, following protracted discussions and due to other financial commitments, the NHS has had to delay a commitment to this proposal for the foreseeable future. In the meantime, other avenues of funding are currently being explored, alongside work being carried out to ensure Braunstone benefits from a sustainable bus service. We are certainly not yet at the stage where 'we all lived happily ever after'; indeed, this position can never be reached amid the shifting demands of passengers of a bus service.

It is currently most likely that we will return to the original plan to extend the 317 and reduce the 301 (rebranded as the 302) (see Figure 6.5). This would, of course, require a reduction in the number of vehicles being used. The bullet will, after all, have to be bitten.

At the cutting edge of new technology

As part of the NDC grant, which complements the UBC grant, funds are included to develop two interesting aspects of modern public transport – green issues and the use of technology. Working with the locally-based environmental charity, Environ, we explored the possibility of operating the vehicles on bio-diesel. This is fuel made from vegetable oil, either first-use (directly from harvested plants such as flax and rape seed) or second-use (from recycled oil retrieved from restaurant outlets or from larger-scale industrial uses such as crisp manufacturers). The oil must undergo a chemical process to remove the glycerine content, which can then be used for the production of soap or a range of other products.

This initiative proved even more timely, as the foot and mouth outbreak of 2001 brought about tighter regulation which has made the disposal of all food produce, including oils, more tightly controlled and therefore more expensive. Subsequently, the Chancellor of the Exchequer reduced fuel duty on bio-diesel. Our work came to the attention of the Leicester media which ran a series of articles about the 'Braunstone Fryer'. Along with local radio stations, national BBC Radio 5 Live wanted an interview. All the media covered it as a humorous

Running on empty

Figure 6.5: Braunstone bus map route 302

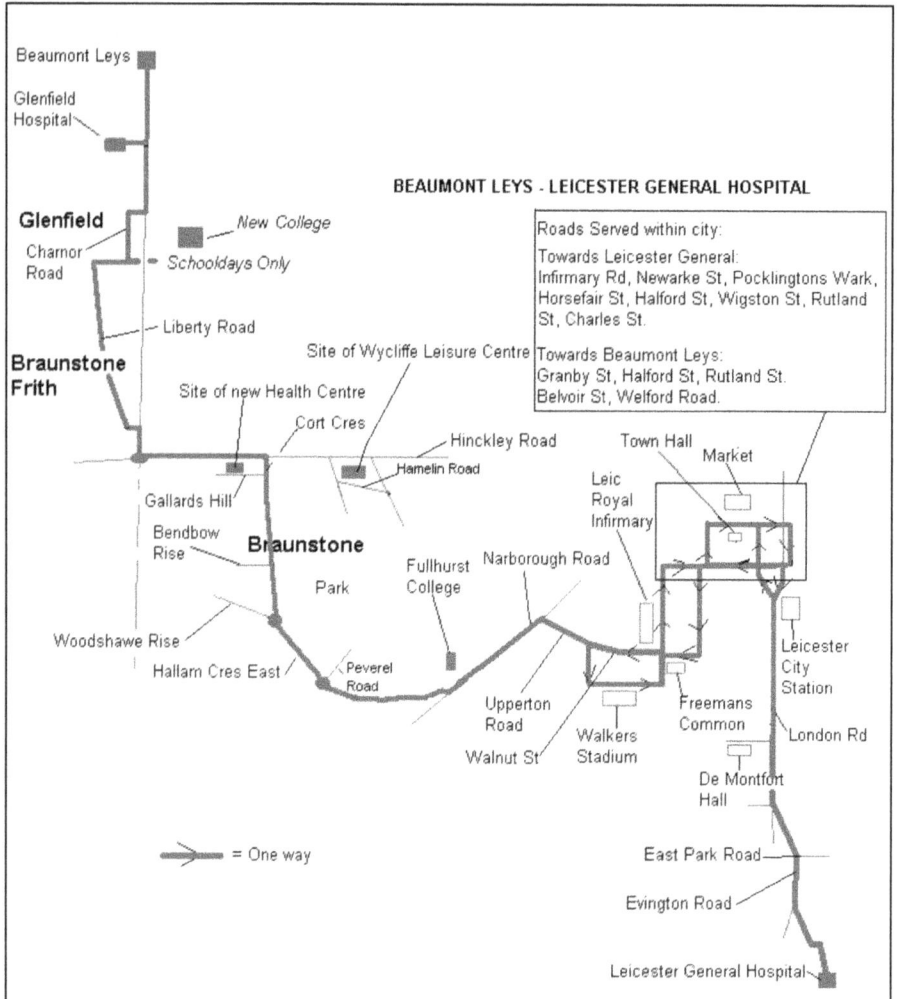

story suggesting that a group of cranks and boffins were getting together to run buses smelling of fish and chips. The view that any publicity is good publicity was seriously tested by this particular piece of media interest. Vindication was near at hand when ASDA among others began to recycle their own oil waste to use bio-diesel in their vehicle fleet.

At this stage, typical usage of bio-diesel is in the form of a 5% blend in normal mineral diesel. It is expected that this percentage will increase as bio-diesel production increases and engine manufacturers, having already approved the 5% blend, confirm that unmodified engines can run without reduced performance or long-term engine damage on blends with a higher vegetable content. This work appeared to have come to fruition when one of the two bus companies agreed to share the cost of a fuel storage facility to enable a bio-diesel blend to be used in their 317 vehicles. This would have had the added benefit of enabling the company to fuel all of its fleet with the same blend. The positive publicity for BCA throughout Leicester would have been considerable. However, when this proposal was taken to BCA board members, they rejected it, feeling that giving Braunstone money to a private company that would then use it to benefit its whole fleet would not be a good use of Braunstone's money. Consequently, the result of a considerable amount of work to address issues of pollution in Braunstone has, for now, come to nothing.

StarTrak is the early warning information system (see Figure 6.6), becoming a regular fixture at urban bus stops, which displays the time of arrival of the next bus. This is a satellite tracking system that also enables a central traffic controlling system to automatically change traffic lights to green to enable a late bus to make up time. Braunstone Community Association was approached by the city council, which intended putting six StarTrak signs in Braunstone to display information about the popular 16 service between Braunstone and the city centre. Additional funding from BCA would increase this number to nine, covering each city-bound stop on the estate. Funds would also enable the 301 service to fit the necessary equipment on the vehicles, which would enable StarTrak to signal the arrival of this service at the few stops where it coincides with the 16 service. New technology also enables information from StarTrak to be accessed by passengers using their mobile phones.

Figure 6.6: StarTrak early warning information system

The nine signs are now up and running with the BCA logo visible on each. However, the uncertainty over the 301 route and the limited portion of the existing, or any likely alternative, route which would be served by the signs has caused us to delay spending on the on-vehicle equipment. The money saved, if spent on subsidising the route, could extend the duration of the contract by another valuable month.

The impact of BraunstoneBus on social inclusion and lessons for the future

BraunstoneBus is one of the more visible demonstrations of the difference NDC is making in Braunstone. It is proving to be an increasingly popular service for Braunstone people. The sight of buses around the area and beyond is also something about which Braunstone people voice their pride. The service has arrived before some of the other key Braunstone projects. Consequently, the full impact of the service on the use of, for example, the leisure centre, the health centre, new housing developments and employment initiatives on the route have yet to be felt.

The journey from concept to fruition has not been that long in the grand scheme of things, but it has been hard and fraught with unnecessary bureaucratic obstacles. Clearly planning socially inclusive transport in the context of a commercially led market requires a judgement call that can only be made through experience and observation. It is not easy to find the correct solution, as there will always be resistance to change and/or demand for a service that could never achieve commercial success.

Unless there is a continual funding stream to support community bus services, insufficient use will cause them to fail, even though they are of vast benefit to the people who do use them. Perhaps, as Julian Westwood suggests in Chapter Five, there is a need to reconsider how we evaluate such transport initiatives and a need to rethink funding mechanisms to recognise their real worth to transport poor communities.

In its first year of operation, the service has already encouraged numerous people back into work; it has broadened people's horizons for leisure pursuits and it has given residents a greater choice of affordable shopping. As NDC projects in Braunstone create a greater number of skilled people and a consequent greater number of employed people earning a higher average salary, so will the expectations of residents grow in line with their ability to pay. The suitability of the route and the quality of the service in meeting these expectations will have a direct effect on the popularity of the service. If it meets demand, the use will rise in line with increasing income. Should it fail to meet people's real travel needs, they will use cars in order to secure and maintain their social inclusion. Nevertheless, a word of caution is in order. The BraunstoneBus experience has taught us that, while it is important to listen to people telling us where they want to go in planning transport services, it is equally important to trial ideas. At the

BCA, we have learnt that the trial is the only way of learning whether the voices heard are those of genuine passengers. The lesson is perhaps to listen to people, but not to believe them until they are actually on the bus!

References

Braunstone Community Association (1999) 'New Deal for Braunstone Delivery Plan', unpublished document.

SEVEN

A road less travelled: case studies from community transport

Martin Jones

Introduction

This is the final UK case-study chapter. It describes the wide variety of community and voluntary-run and owned transport services that are provided in the UK under the broad umbrella of community transport. In January 1999, Glenda Jackson MP (1999, p 18), then a British transport minister, noted that:

> ... long before anyone in the mainstream transport world would have considered that disabled people were part of their business and their responsibility, community transport was providing wide ranging door to door services tailored to meet the needs both of individuals and groups.... For many years and in many areas they have been the only people recognising and working to meet the needs of communities and individuals excluded from other transport provision – and so from much of everyday life.

The provision of inclusive transport services has always been the goal of the community transport movement. For three decades now, long before terms like 'social exclusion' were on everybody's lips, community transport groups up and down the country were identifying individuals or groups of people who were being excluded from many areas of life, which most others would take for granted, because of a lack of transport. However, community transport was never an academic or campaigning movement; the purpose of spotting these gaps was to set about finding ways to fill them and that is something that community transport has done very successfully and in a variety of interesting and often innovative ways.

Community transport is important in two ways. It is important because it shows that things can be done differently and better by the devolved voluntary sector. Community transport has pioneered the development of accessible transport for disabled people in this country. It created the concept of demand-responsive transport. It identified the problem of transport deprivation and at the same time demonstrated methods of overcoming it. Second, but no less importantly, it has made a huge difference to the lives of vast numbers of people who were previously being prevented from playing a full part in society. This matters.

The following case studies are all based on visits made by myself to community transport projects between April 2001 and April 2003. They illustrate, in particular, services that have been provided to increase access to health, education and training, and employment. Almost all the organisations highlighted, however, also either provide additional services to enable socially isolated people to access leisure, cultural and other opportunities or build these objectives into the services the case studies describe. The one exception to this is perhaps Transport Access Patients in Cornwall (see later in this chapter), which has a very specific access to health services remit; wider access needs in the county continue to be met by individual voluntary car schemes.

I have chosen only six examples of community transport projects, each offering a different approach to the problems of social exclusion, but there is considerable regret about the myriad other projects up and down country that I might easily have also included as examples of good practice. There are, for example, projects in the West Midlands doing extremely interesting (and worthwhile) work with pregnant schoolgirls, and with prisoners and their families (keeping families together while one member serves a term of imprisonment is considered a key factor in reducing reoffending rates).

The limitations of space have meant relatively few references to 'quality of life' services, but these are a major feature of almost every community transport organisation in the UK. Indeed, some community transport projects particularly specialise in this type of provision. For example, TraVol, based in Pontypridd in South Wales, has an extensive programme of excursions covering a large part of Wales and the west of England and designed to give disabled people the opportunity to visit sites of historical interest, museums, old market towns and other places of interest. Meanwhile, in East Anglia, the National Trust has recently set up a community bus service to enable people living in the towns and villages of Suffolk to visit not only Trust sites such as Sutton Hoo but other places of interest too.

On the access to work and training front, I would have liked the time to properly describe the work of Hackney Community Transport (HCT), based in East London. This has established a highly successful Passenger Carrying Vehicle training project that specifically aims to recruit people onto its courses from the areas of greatest deprivation in the surrounding area. This involves a great deal of proactive marketing and a firm commitment to providing support to trainees once recruited. It also works closely with local employers to ensure they have a good understanding of the quality of training that is being provided. Many, in fact, contact HCT whenever they have a driving vacancy, to see if there are newly qualified people available they can consider. So far, of the 43 people who have achieved the full qualification (33 more are still in training), 32 have secured jobs as professional drivers and the remaining 11 have gone on to further education. In most cases, it is not just 43 people: it is 43 *families* who have benefited (and now add to that the impact on local shopkeepers of 43 more people earning, and spending, money). As is so often true with community transport, although the base numbers appear fairly small, the impact can be enormous.

So what this chapter provides is not a comprehensive study of all the many different forms of community transport project, but rather snapshots of a movement that is constantly changing, constantly adapting their services to meet new, or newly discovered, areas of need.

Wheels to work (Liverpool)

> "Don't tell me what you do. Tell me what you could do."

These were the words of John Duvall, describing the ethos behind LIFT, the Netherley and Valley Local Initiative for Transport – a wheels-to-work project in Liverpool. Netherley and Valley describes two wards on the south-eastern fringe of Liverpool. The area consists of six linked housing estates; that is, about 7,500 properties with a combined population of just under 15,000 people. John is the Development Officer for the scheme and insists that:

> "The objectives are at the forefront. What we provide is determined by what we are trying to achieve. We are solution-led."

The population of Netherley and the Valley is on the decline, especially among the young. This is not surprising. The official average unemployment rate is 10.23% but the rates on some of the estates rise to as much as 40%. Youth unemployment across the two wards is 22.8%. Education and skills attainment is low; there is less than average participation in training; there are few leisure facilities and high levels of crime. It might be on the edge of the green belt, but it is not 'well-to-do'.

It is tempting to describe Netherley and the Valley as a forgotten area of Liverpool, but this is not wholly true. In 1995, it was designated as a Pathways area under the European Objective One, Round One Programme. The Netherley and Valley Partnership was established under this programme, and in 1997 secured £5.1 million of funding under the government's Single Regeneration Budget (SRB). This enabled the partnership with the local communities to be developed and a six-year regeneration programme using SRB money and other funding sources to address some of the local economic needs to be created.

One of the projects established by the partnership, in conjunction with Merseyside Community Transport, was LIFT. The aim of the scheme was to ensure that Pathways communities in the Netherley and Valley area benefited from improved access to employment, training, education, essential services and other key facilities.

John explains how the focus of the scheme came about:

> "Towards the beginning of 2000, the Partnership commissioned a skills audit for the area and this clearly demonstrated a major shortfall in the skills needed to enter the job market. The skills deficit was particularly pronounced among the 16-24 age group.... However, although bus services into the city centre were pretty good, services to those areas where jobs were being created and indeed to the places where colleges and education centres were located were dire. In some cases, this involved journeys of an hour in each direction and if you were trying to attend a course where the timings did not complement the bus timetable, you needed to allow at least two or three hours travelling time for each day."

Although LIFT did not intend to concentrate exclusively on young people, it was clear that their needs were going to become one of the project's driving forces. It acquired early on a minibus and a van, which were made available to local residents for a variety of community activities. Towards the end of last year, they applied for and received a grant of £20,000 to support the purchase and first year's running costs of 10 scooters. The Valley Wheels initiative was born. John explained:

> "Going to college by bus was obviously extremely difficult. Many of these kids did not yet have a full driving license and even if they did, you've really got to be earning before you can afford to put a car on the road. We started to hire out the scooters for a fiver a week (much less than it costs us to keep the scooters on the road – insurance alone is £7 a week) and suddenly a 2.5-hour round trip took only half an hour each way. College became feasible. So did New Deal placements and proper, paid employment."

The young adults using the scooters also received compulsory bike training, all the necessary equipment to keep them safe, insurance, 24-hour roadside recovery and free servicing. The beneficiaries had to live in the Netherley and Valley Partnership area (the scheme has expanded since and now takes people from Speke-Garston and Dingle-Granby as well), had to be attending work or college for at least three days a week and had to sign a hire agreement guaranteeing they would not abuse their scooters (workers on the scheme have been generally pleased with the responses they have had; nevertheless they have taken scooters from one or two people who breached the agreement).

I spoke to three members – Chris, John, and Shaun – to find out what difference the scooters had really made to their lives. Chris attends Riverside College, which used to involve two bus trips and a journey of between 60 and 80 minutes each way. That journey now takes 20 minutes. John has recently secured a job with a jeweller in Chester, 35 miles away. The journey takes 2.5 hours by bus but an hour by scooter, whereas Shaun has seen his journeys cut in half by getting access to the scooter. All three are also able to use the scooter for social activities and it is plain, talking to them about their future plans and current lifestyle, that the provision of independent transport has made a significant difference both to their confidence and to their prospects.

Chris told me:

> "On some days, you might have just the one class which lasts maybe an hour. If it is going to take you over an hour to get there and the same again to get back, it is not exactly easy to summon up the motivation. The scooter has transformed things for me, to be honest."

During my visit to LIFT in 2001, I was also introduced to two young men, Paul and Terry, who had managed, with the support of LIFT, to secure New Deal placements at the Jaguar (formerly Ford) plant at Halewood, 10 miles away. These placements had recently been turned into proper full-time paid jobs and both Paul and Terry were clearly delighted:

> "We couldn't have kept up with even the placement without LIFT. Some of the shifts start at 6.30am and there are simply no buses around at that time – even later on it takes an hour, two buses and a long walk."

They explained that LIFT provides a minibus service to get them there and back (the direct journey taking only 20 minutes). The minibus is extensively used to take people to jobs, training and job interviews. Its journeys are tailored to the individual needs of its users, which can vary from the regular ten-mile trip to Halewood for people like Paul and Terry to transporting people 35 miles to Wigan for a job interview. The LIFT has developed close working relations with the local employment services to ensure that what it is able to offer becomes known to people looking for jobs or placements.

Now that Paul and Terry are established at Jaguar, they expect to move over to using the scooters shortly, which will give them even more independence. In the longer run, however, once they have started to earn a bit of money, they anticipate taking driving lessons and eventually getting their own vehicles.

In addition to getting people to training opportunities, LIFT also offers training itself. Its bus driver training programme (supported by the European Social Fund) puts trainees through an NVQ Level 2 qualification in transporting passengers by road, customer care, disability awareness and basic skills such as numeracy and literacy. Arriva North West has committed itself to providing an interview and the very real prospect of a job for anyone who successfully completes the LIFT course.

While much is done to get them on the road to employment and greater independence, LIFT's Valley Wheels users are encouraged to put something of their own back into the community as well. First of all, part of the hire agreement means that most of them contribute at least four hours a week voluntary work to LIFT. This may involve valeting the van and minibus or helping out with work on the office database. They get paid £5 for four hours work, so the money they pay out to use the scooter each week is returned to them when they contribute their own time to the project.

Some of the users now also do voluntary work for other local organisations. Chris, for example, coaches disabled children to play football, something he would not be able to do if the independent transport provided by the scooter was not available to him.

"It is all a form of recycling," says John:

> "We are trying to help them realise their own potential through training and jobs while at the same time giving them the opportunity to contribute to their local community. A lot of young people have bags of energy and goodwill to spread around but they need to be given the chance to get their own lives going first. Helping them reach training and jobs is part of that process.... Although the core services we offer have arisen from detailed research that was commissioned by the Partnership, we want LIFT to be able to adapt and shift to the needs of the community. We are not about buses or bikes or vans – we are about people and we must be led by what they need, not what we want to offer."

John is acutely aware of the many different forms that community transport can take and does not advocate one form as being any more, or any less, valuable than another. He is clear, however, that perceptions of what community transport is, and is for, need to change among some funders and politicians:

> "Community transport is not about filling the gaps left behind by so-called 'mainstream' and statutory passenger transport. We are mainstream transport; we just provide a more personal and flexible service that works with the communities, which is governed not by the need to generate profit but by the desire to meet the needs of a community."

Auto Response (South Wales)

In 1994, Jeff Edwards was looking forward to returning to Merthyr Tydfil. After many years working in the City of London, he was finally returning to the Welsh Valleys. His optimism was soon dented. Merthyr Tydfil, a town with a population of 58,000, had, he discovered, extremely high levels of youth crime. Illiteracy rates were well above the national average. Drug and alcohol abuse was rampant. Although unemployment was nominally running at about 8%, researchers from Sheffield Hallam University estimated the underlying rate to be 28.7%. Jeff remembers:

Case studies from community transport

Auto Response South Wales

> "A vicious circle was beginning to develop. Many of these kids were under-educated, had no jobs, no self-esteem and were turning to drugs and alcohol to fill the gaps in their lives. Cars would be stolen to fund their habits. Many of them knew, or learnt, enough about cars to steal them, strip them down, and sell off the parts for cash. At one point, as many as 12 cars were going every night."

He felt that something had to be done, and while the country's politicians argued about who was toughest on crime, Jeff and his colleagues at the Aberfan and Merthyr Vale Youth and Community Project, which he chairs, started to get tough on the causes of crime. He explained:

> "A lot of the people involved in this circle of crime, or considered to be at risk of getting involved, were either unemployed and with little or no qualifications, or else serial absconders from school. We therefore set out at first to provide an alternative source of education, focusing primarily on the acquisition of basic skills. However, it soon became clear that many of the youths involved in the project were very interested in cars and so we decided to take advantage of that both to provide training in motor maintenance that could possibly lead to work but also to show them the importance of taking a responsible attitude to cars. We didn't want just to teach skills, although that was important; we also wanted to challenge behaviour."

Running on empty

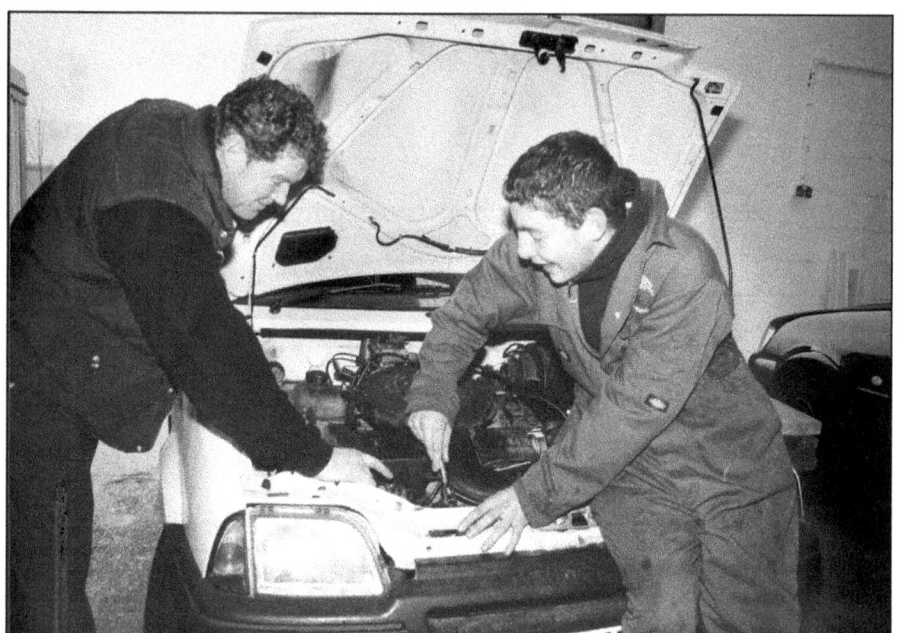

Auto Response South Wales

The Diversion Auto Project was born. Old vehicles were bought and the teams of young people would learn to strip and rebuild them. They also went through courses in basic skills, health and safety and IT. Many of the youths on the programme were referred to the project by the courts, by social services or by the local education authority in the case of long-term truants. By 2001, the project has outgrown their original premises in Merthyr Vale and moved to the outskirts of Merthyr Tydfil. At this point, there was growing concern at the role transport was playing in restricting access to jobs. North–south public transport links are not bad during the day, but they only tend to run from about 6am to 6pm and east–west links are simply non-existent.

The Youth and Community Project, therefore, entered into a partnership with Working Links, itself a public–private partnership between the Department for Work and Pensions (DWP) and accountancy firm Cap Gemini, to set up a wheels-to-work scheme. Whereas most wheels-to-work schemes are based on mopeds, scooters or mountain bikes (see earlier in this chapter, Wheels to Work [Liverpool]), the Merthyr project aimed from the start to go for four wheels, as Jeff explains:

> "Working Links provided the capital to buy the cars, and we hire them out to people to whom it could make a difference. They get the car for £15 per week for a maximum of 15 weeks, by which time they are expected to make their own arrangements. If they have been working for three months, they should have been able to put aside a little money but also if a bank sees three months' worth of pay slips and a reference

Case studies from community transport

Jeff Edwards (left) and Rob Williams, Diversion Auto Project Manager, Auto Response South Wales

from an employer, chances are they will look kindly on a request for a loan to buy a car of their own."

Most of the people who benefit from the project are referred by the job centre to Working Links and from there to Wheels to Work. The scheme is also able to help out people who it identifies. However, if it hears about people who are having trouble breaking into work, then it can take them on directly.

Having started out with just two vehicles, the Wheels to Work project now has 40. It has been a vital element in the regeneration of the Merthyr Tydfil area. In recent years, many derelict sites were converted to call centres, shopping malls or light industrial developments. Employment opportunities were being created but the means to reach them was often not there. The bus network was not up to the task. Journeys could take up to two hours by bus (but only 20 minutes by car) and stopped altogether at 6pm.

Wheels to Work also provides its own bus services from the local area to places of employment where this makes better sense, such as when several people all get jobs in the same place. The project also encourages car sharing. Should four people aim to work in the one location, Working Links might recommend one of them to Wheels to Work, but only on the condition they offer lifts to the other three.

The project also occasionally takes advantage of their workshop facilities to fix the cars of local residents. Jeff explains:

"We don't generally do commercial maintenance, but if someone's car breaks down and they can't afford to fix it but also they cannot get to work without it, we might take it in, sort it out and just charge for parts. Keeping people mobile is as important as getting them mobile in the first place."

With well over a 100 people having been loaned cars so far, and perhaps 400 others helped into work through car-sharing or the bus services, Jeff believes that the scheme can expand still further:

"Now that the road infrastructure serving Merthyr and the surrounding district has improved, we are only 20 minutes from Cardiff, 30 from Swansea and we already have one client who does the 60-minute journey by car to Bristol. People's employment horizons are being stretched and this is important. Our statistics are quite good, but it is the human examples that prove the worth of the project. We have persistent truants who now attend the project or school five days a week. We have put about 500 people into work. One man got his first-ever job through us – he was 28 years old!"

The example of Merthyr Tydfil demonstrates how critical poor transport links can be in creating high levels of unemployment and how that can itself lead to drug and alcohol abuse and to crime. The Wheels to Work and Auto Diversions project, however, also demonstrates that, with imagination, commitment, and sustainable financial support, vicious circles can be broken.

Sure Start (West London)

When I arrived on the South Northolt estate, I knew there was something peculiar about it but I could not put my finger on what. It was Anna Whitty, from Ealing Community Transport, who pointed it out to me:

"Just look around you, it's 11 o'clock in the morning, it's bright and sunny, school's out for the summer. What do you see?"

The answer was 'nothing', or rather 'no one'. The estate was made up of perhaps a dozen streets of houses and flats but it was deserted. Even the playground was empty. There was virtually no sound apart from a throb of traffic in the background from the main road. Even if you took the burnt-out car as a one-off (it was parked rather neatly in a marked bay), this did look like a pretty depressing area to have to live in. You got the feeling it was an area that needed help.

Just over two years ago, it started getting it; South Northolt, on the western edge of the borough of Ealing in West London, has been designated a Sure Start area by the government and will receive over £4.5 million over 10 years. The

Sure Start, South Northolt, Ealing

Sure Start initiative has a number of key objectives that include improving the social and emotional development of children; improving children's health; improving children's ability to learn; and strengthening families and communities. These national objectives are backed up by a series of specific targets (for example, a 10% reduction in children reregistered on their area child protection register; a 5% reduction in the proportion of low-weight babies; at least 90% of children with normal speech and language development at 18 months and three years). It is a strategy of early intervention that aims to break the intergenerational cycle of particularly disadvantaged children's underachievement and poverty of aspiration.

Kate Saunders is the Project Manager for Sure Start in South Northolt. She told me that, after the need for affordable childcare, transport had emerged as the number one concern for most people:

> "Parents describe feeling trapped on the estates. In the mornings, the five major roads that encase the area are gridlocked and buses have a reputation locally for not stopping for passengers encumbered with buggies and shopping bags. Parents around here are known to be low attenders at healthcare appointments, there are very limited opportunities for young children to learn to play and socialise in groups. People don't feel that comfortable walking around their estate and yet feel it is virtually impossible to go beyond the streets where they live if they have the kids in tow."

The priority for most parents is to just manage their day-to-day existence and to get out more often than they have previously been able to. However, South

Northolt Sure Start also has national objectives to meet, so it tries to put on activities that will benefit the health and development of the children while at the same time giving the parents some relief from the pressures of their daily lives. For example, it has already started to fund: health visitors; speech therapy; a dietician; a Homestart volunteering programme, to offer parents some practical support in raising their families; a counselling service for local homeless families; and regular crèches and toddlers groups. They also run a community chest grant scheme to help existing groups expand their services by buying new equipment or extending staff hours. Classes on IT (for parents and for children) and cookery are also advertised.

However, even with a relatively large amount of money to play with and close local consultation, it is not that easy to make the changes that are needed. There is a national shortage of healthcare professionals so recruitment is difficult; there is also a chronic lack of suitable community premises in the area and that makes establishing new toddler groups and crèches very tough going. With all these obstacles, it is not surprising to learn that take-up of the services offered by Sure Start was slow:

> "We needed to develop ways of bringing wary parents into the fold. We like to think that the services we are offering are supportive rather than judgmental but you cannot demonstrate that until someone has at least given it a try. We needed to find some way of offering something that would be very attractive and completely unthreatening. Something that would allow them to find out more about Sure Start without committing them to anything until they were sure it was OK."

That 'something' proved to be the PlusBus – "the best investment we ever made", says Kate:

> "Anyone who has ever tried to use a bus while also maintaining a grip on two toddlers, three bags of shopping and pushing a buggy with a baby in it will appreciate how impossible it often is to get around without your own car. We were getting a lot of feedback that suggested that not only were people not getting out of the estates to the shopping centres in Uxbridge and elsewhere, but that even travelling the relatively short distance to our own local base was a major chore. One woman told me how she was once trapped on a bus that moved off with herself and one of her children inside the vehicle and her remaining child left on the pavement. Until PlusBus came along, this woman had turned into a virtual recluse, leaving her house perhaps as little as once a month."

When Kate realised how fundamental the transport problem was, she contacted Anna Whitty at Ealing Community Transport (ECT) and said, "We need a minibus!". To her credit, Anna turned round and said, "No you don't, what you need is a professionally managed and operated service".

This emerged as the Ealing PlusBus, dedicated to the Sure Start programme. It started up in April 2001 and operates throughout the day, five days a week. Apart from sickness and holidays, the same person, Shaun Byrne, always drives the vehicle and a bookings administrator, Irene Turvey, is also employed by ECT but is based at the Sure Start office. Ridership has increased quickly, with just over 200 passengers carried in the first month rising to about 650 in July. Anna said:

> "People have had such difficulties with buses in the past that we expected getting people onto the service would be a gradual process. However, Shaun is just brilliant and his attitude and in particular his terrific way with the children has done a lot to quickly build a sense of trust. Parents know they will get a safe ride, their kids will be safely strapped into their seats and that they will get help with unloading the shopping, bringing their children down off the bus and so on. I think the knowledge that ECT is a community-based organisation rather than a commercial venture helps as well."

The PlusBus service offers a door-to-door service within the area but is not greatly restricted in the purposes of journeys people wish to make, other than giving priority to health-related journeys. Many do use it to participate in Sure Start-sponsored activities, but they might just as likely use it to finally undergo hassle-free trips to the shops.

"It's been a bit of a foot in the door as far as Sure Start is concerned," said Anna:

> "People hear about the bus service, go on it and Shaun is very good about encouraging them to learn about the other things Sure Start has to offer and to gently encourage them to try them out as well. We are particularly pleased that the PlusBus has managed to greatly increase the proportion of families from ethnic minorities that have become engaged with Sure Start."

In fact, both Shaun and Anna told me that, in some blocks of flats, individual parents have been despatched to try out the new service and then report back to their neighbours. "Passenger numbers had trebled within four months of starting up, so they were obviously giving PlusBus the thumbs up," Anna commented.

The parents I spoke to were certainly delighted with the new service: "It's fantastic," said Heather, whose little boy Karim loves travelling on the bus and is particularly fond of Shaun:

> "How many years have women had to struggle to use public transport? And now this service comes along and everything is so much better. It's safe, it's reliable, being door to door is great. It is like a dream come true, honestly."

Irene also reports a lot of enthusiasm:

> "We get no end of people commenting, 'I don't know what I did before this service started up'. They are all very grateful for the service although in some cases you have to nurture an understanding of how it works. If we are full with bookings for the whole morning, a woman who rings up at ten expecting to be picked up in time to make her doctor's appointment at 10.15 is going to be disappointed. It takes a while with people who do not have fluency in English but everyone, staff and passengers alike, are very supportive of each other and people learn quickly enough how to make best use of what we can offer."

Shaun concurs. He introduced me to another mum, Jacqui, who has four children including one who is four years old and a new baby girl. The four-year-old was in nursery in one direction, his older sister in school in the other direction and the baby girl had to be taken around on the journeys too. Jacqui frequently used to miss appointments with the doctor or other healthcare professionals and told me she was not sure how she would have managed once her baby daughter had arrived on the scene were it not for the PlusBus.

"Ealing CT has proved they are not just a contracted service provider," says Kate. "They are playing a full and vital role in the partnership and have done a great job of increasing the involvement of local people in Sure Start".

Anna Whitty says that the experience of Ealing demonstrates the crucial role community transport can have in combating social exclusion:

> "ECT is quite large as community transport projects go, delivering services to a range of people across the entire borough. The PlusBus is just one vehicle – yet look at the difference it is making to the lives of the people on those estates."

Kate agrees:

> "Our survey of local families last summer made it clear that transport was very much part of the problem. What the ECT PlusBus has done is shown that, managed right, transport can actually be part of the solution."

Car scheme cooperation (Cornwall)

Research conducted by the Department for Transport (DfT) (Steer Davies Gleave, 1999) identified about 5,000 community transport schemes across the UK. The Community Transport Association has always believed the number to be much higher because of the number of tiny, village-based community car schemes in virtually every county that were just not showing up on anybody's radar. Many of these are fiercely independent and often have no interest in anything other than simply providing trips for local people who are not able to use public transport.

These schemes are a very valuable part of the community transport network, but how is it possible, with the way many of them operate, to make better use of available resources and, therefore, to increase capacity? An experimental project in Cornwall, run by Age Concern but with the full involvement of almost all the known car schemes in the county as well as several health agencies, may be showing the way.

The story begins in 1997 when Age Concern in Cornwall and the Isles of Scilly took the decision to centralise their transport operation. At the time, they were running 13 minibuses and eight car schemes across Cornwall. Although providing vital services, there was a growing feeling within Age Concern that their buses were being under-used and the car schemes lacked coordination. Age Concern did not always have complete details about the drivers on their books at a time when proper vetting was become an important issue and there were also insurance implications for what seemed a rather ad hoc approach.

Running in parallel to Age Concern's initiative, Pam Price, the Specialist Commissioning Manager at West Cornwall Primary Care Trust, was exploring ways of improving patient transport. She organised a survey in the north east of the county to find out what people did in order to get to hospital, both for appointments and for visiting. She found that use of public transport was virtually non-existent (1%) but that, although many people had not heard about community car schemes, a surprisingly high proportion of those that had were using them.

This led to Pam convening a meeting of the 18 known car schemes in Cornwall (including Age Concern) to see how things might be better organised. The overwhelming conclusion was that patients needed a single number for community car schemes. Did this mean that all the 18 schemes needed to merge?

"Not at all," explains Ann Lewis, Head of Transport at Age Concern:

> "First of all, this meeting was just about patient transport and all the county's schemes offered trips for a variety of reasons, including but not exclusively for health. The meeting determined that a one-stop shop was needed for health transport and Age Concern agreed to set one up."

The result was Transport Access Patients (TAP). The idea is simple; you would think it to be obvious except that no one appears to have done it before. All but one of the 18 groups present at Pam's original meeting agreed to join a consortium for the booking of non-urgent health-related journeys. Each scheme retained its own identity and continued to take bookings for other journeys through their own phone lines. What was developed, however, was a booking system that meant people resident anywhere in Cornwall could phone a single number and be booked onto a journey with their closest or most appropriate car scheme. If a caller lived some distance from the nearest scheme, a trip would still be arranged but the caller would be told if it might be cheaper to use a local minicab firm.

The scheme has been in operation since February 2002 and is already able to guarantee to meet all trip requests; these currently total between 300 and 400 per month. The existence of a single telephone number has made it much easier to market the information to patients. A single leaflet can be used by doctor's surgeries across the whole county while the Royal Cornwall Hospital in Truro automatically includes TAP details in the information they send out to patients when appointments are made.

The TAP concept has already been extended to provide additional back up to the non-emergency patient transport service and this is beginning to bring enormous benefits in areas such as bed blocking and community transfers. Pam explains:

> "Too often, patients were ready to go home but were not able to do so because there was no ambulance available for them. With the involvement of the car schemes, via TAP, we have been able to speed things up considerably. This helps the hospital release beds more quickly and so reduce waiting times for treatment but is also greatly appreciated by the patients themselves who are usually anxious to return home and get very frustrated when the doctor says they can go but there is no transport available to take them."

In recent months, the social services department at Cornwall County Council has also started to negotiate with TAP to use the scheme to benefit both their adult clients and children. Ann Lewis puts the success of TAP down to simplicity:

> "There's no great bureaucracy involved here and we are not trying to take over any car schemes or tell them how to run their affairs. This is just a way of maximising the benefits of the multitude of voluntary car schemes that have supported community life in Cornwall for many years."

Some of the agencies with whom TAP liaise have also shown an imaginative approach to the building of links with local MPs. In April 2000, the Cornwall Community Health Council invited five Cornish MPs to take part in an experiment to illustrate the difficulties of getting to hospital without a private car. They were each placed in a Cornish village and given an appointment for the Royal Cornwall Hospital in Truro or Derriford Hospital in Plymouth and had to find their way there by using public transport.

> "Four of the MPs took between five and eight hours to do the return journey," says Ann, "while the fifth MP never made it at all – the journey proved impossible to do in one day. Ever since then we have had tremendous support from our MPs. When, for example, we were experiencing problems over our funding, the MPs intervened on their behalf with great success."

Health and social exclusion (Norfolk)

North-east Norfolk as a whole is popularly regarded as an area of outstanding natural beauty and rightly so, but looking beyond this, the area is characterised by a largely rural economy, with few employment and training opportunities outside the main towns in the district and the city of Norwich, situated 15 miles to the south of North Walsham. Generally wages for those in employment are notably below the national average. The area also has one of the highest percentages of retired people, per head of total population in England.

North Walsham Area Community Transport Association (NWACTA) was established in 1999 to develop community transport services in the mainly rural eastern end of the North Norfolk district and the market towns of North Walsham and Stalham. The project's operating area contains 44 parishes, with a total population of about 50,000 in a combined area approaching 100 square miles.

Public transport between the major towns and the city of Norwich is good, but services directly benefiting the rural parishes are patchy or non-existent, with only a few parishes having a bus service into North Walsham, Cromer or Great Yarmouth. In addition, an extensive transport needs survey revealed that 25% of the people above retirement age in North Walsham had no car. The challenge was to deal with transport problems both within the town itself and, in particular, in the network of villages and hamlets surrounding it.

Paul Gray is the founding Coordinator of the NWACTA. He explained why the scheme was so badly needed:

> "Transport is regarded as a significant barrier by many wishing to access education, training, employment, childcare, medical and social facilities within the district. Against a general background of low income, many families spend a much higher-than-average percentage of their income on owning and running one or more cars in order to achieve an acceptable level of social inclusion."

It is against this backdrop that NWACTA came into existence. A variety of funding sources enabled the development of regular Dial-a-Ride services into market towns and shopping centres; a volunteer car service, Medi-Ride, to take people to primary healthcare facilities, including GPs, dentists and a range of facilities offered in the two small hospitals in the locality; and transport for older people who otherwise would not be able to attend social and group activities, such as lunch clubs, meetings and day care.

Medi-Ride was developed as a result of feedback received through NWACTA drivers, who reported that passengers were timing all their medical appointments to coincide with the once-a-week Dial-a-Ride service in their area. This effectively gave them just a two-hour window in which any health appointments could be made. This discovery led Paul to set up a community car service specifically to deal with visits to local hospitals, GPs, opticians and so on. It has been enormously successful and one has to wonder as to the number of people who had previously put off making medical appointments because of the difficulty of getting to them.

Most recently, with the relocation of the major regional hospital, the Norfolk and Norwich University Hospital, to the south western outskirts of Norwich, NWACTA is running a highly successful pilot project offering door-to-door, flexible transport for patients, their escorts and visitors to this hospital. With the increasing difficulty in qualifying for NHS transport, many local people are coming to regard NWACTA's Hospital Bus as an attractive alternative to a difficult journey by public transport or one that is prohibitively expensive by taxi. Even people who do have access to a car have preferred to leave it at home when challenged by ill-health, the effects of treatment or the prospect of an unfamiliar journey through the congested city of Norwich. Since it started in November 2002, the Hospital Bus has carried 300 patients, escorts and visitors – 70 in one month alone.

A series of regular excursions is also provided for shopping in Great Yarmouth and Norwich, and young people too are not forgotten, with evening excursions to leisure activities in the area. While the Hospital Bus and Medi-Ride have particularly attracted attention, the Dial-a-Ride service is also worthy of note, not least because it is not restricted to older people or those with disabilities.

Paul says:

> "The Dial-a-Ride operates under Section 19 and we have four criteria for membership. The Traffic Commissioner accepted our request that people meeting any one of them should be deemed eligible to join the scheme."

The criteria include disability and being unable to walk to the nearest bus stop but also included are the phrases, 'No bus service available to where I want to go', and, 'No bus service at all'. Although the DfT has recently reinterpreted Section 19 (of the 1985 Transport Act) to incorporate car-less people living in areas without a bus service, Paul accepts they were fortunate to have received such a liberal view of their membership criteria:

> "The Commissioner was right to allow us to operate like this. We go to many areas where there is simply no public transport at all. In such places, it would be harsh indeed to suggest we couldn't offer a service in case it threatened the interests of the commercial bus industry."

One such area is Eccles by the Sea. The houses in Eccles were built as holiday homes following the Second World War, after the original village of Eccles Juxta Mare fell into the sea as a result of coastal erosion. The nearest shop is five miles away; there is no bus service; and the county council have so far refused to accept responsibility for maintaining the road, which is therefore technically 'unadopted'. Although Eccles has over 200 households in permanent residence, they have no gas, no street lighting, no public transport – and no road! "Eccles is an example of the sort of problems we have to deal with," said Paul. "Without our service, the people living here would be totally isolated."

Support for the project is strong. During my visit, I travelled on two different Dial-a-Ride services as well as the Hospital Bus. All three buses were full and the passengers were insistent that the NWACTA was a vital component of their lives. Mrs Gathergood from Honing said:

> "I did wonder at the start what Dial-a-Ride would be like, but having used it, it is perfect because you don't have to worry about a thing. Without it, I would be stuck at home and have to sell up and move into town. For me, it is an absolute lifeline."

Bill and Sylvia Blackman from East Ruston told me:

> "We don't drive. If it wasn't for the Dial-a-Ride, we could not get out of East Ruston. It's made a world of difference to us."

Another passenger, Katie Richards, is 82 years old and partially sighted. She talked in particular of the importance of Medi-Ride:

> "If Medi-Ride did not exist, I would be unable to get to my appointments. There is no alternative. It is vital to my well-being."

Many others also praised the care and attention of the drivers.

Although it is a truth universally acknowledged that NWACTA has provided vitally needed services, and provided them efficiently and professionally, the future for the scheme is uncertain. Paul tells me that they have a current shortfall of about £18,000 per annum:

> "The sums just don't work. If no one is prepared to come in with long-term funding, this project, relied upon by so many people, will fold. Over time, the physical and mental well-being of our current passengers

> may be compromised, their opportunities for exercising their independence will be curtailed and the need to migrate into the urban areas will become increasingly necessary. The hidden cost of permitting social exclusion is surely greater than the investment in preventing it."

Paul is concerned that so many potential funding sources are looking to fund the new, exciting, sexy projects and shy away from services that are established, have been proven to be needed and have been proven to be efficient.

Regeneration (East Ayrshire)

> "In today's modern age of holidays in space and the Internet, it's hard to believe that there are young people in this area who have never been outside of East Ayrshire. We also have an older generation who are trapped in their homes that have never been further than Ayr."

This is what Sheila White, Coordinator of Coalfield Community Transport (CCT) in East Ayrshire, told me when I met her. The Coalfields area covers 345 square miles of diverse country. The total population is about 46,000, with about 7,000 in the town of Cumnock, then about three small towns of about 4,000 people each and a plethora of villages with populations ranging from 2,000 down to 100 or even less. For people who can get to Glasgow, 38 miles to the north east, or Ayr, 16 miles west, there are certainly jobs. However, East Ayrshire itself suffers from low employment, low pay, poor health, a lot of youth crime and significant drug use. Public transport is poor and, even where it does exist, there are other obstacles such as concerns about personal security that make it not always an acceptable option.

Cumnock was built to house people recruited to work in the mines. Until the mid-1980s, deep shaft mining was the main source of employment, directly or indirectly, for the entire area. Now that is gone and what is left is a string of social problems and the haemorrhaging of the youngest sections of the population to the more certain prospects in Glasgow and elsewhere. If the Coalfields area is to become a place to work, live and play once more, then something needs to be done to increase access to employment, to healthcare, to social activities and to other services and activities.

Sheila White, originally from the coalfields area in South Wales, so no stranger to the problems that occur when the coalfields die, thinks that East Ayrshire is a great place to live providing you are well off. She notes:

> "The trouble with that, of course, is that it means house prices are going up all the time and that makes it harder for people coming onto the house market for the first time to afford anywhere to live locally. This only exacerbates the problem of youth exodus."

If the problems of people living in the Coalfields area were interconnected, as suggested by the Scottish Executive (1999)[1] – high unemployment, high crime rates, fear of going out alone or at night and vandalism – then it was clear to Sheila and her colleagues at CCT that the solutions must be too.

The benefit of Scotland's strategic approach to combating social exclusion can be seen from the funding position of CCT. The project was only established in autumn 2001, becoming operational in spring 2002, yet it has already received nearly £300,000 in grants with more expected later in 2003. About a third of this money has come directly from the local Social Inclusion Partnership (SIP). SIPs are one of the main local manifestations of the Scottish social justice policy agenda and, although money is also meant to be generated locally, they bring access to significant grants from the Scottish Executive, grants which do not have to be match-funded. Sheila believes the scale of Scottish Executive Funding can be justified:

> "This may seem like generous funding, compared to how some community transport projects start off life, but every penny is vital. We have a massive job to do in this area and, to be honest, you can't 'half-regenerate' an area. You either spend the money, wisely of course, or you don't get the results. We've got the money, the challenge now is to get the results."

Local consultation procedures identified that many local people found public transport to be unsafe and expensive. Using public transport to get to work, training, healthcare and social activities was fraught with difficulty because of the number of areas with no or only skeleton services and specific reference was made to the issue of safety when old, young or otherwise vulnerable people were needing to travel in the evenings. It was thought that community transport might offer a way around many of these problems.

Coalfield Community Transport decided to start with group transport, in order to quickly provide some practical assistance to the many self-help organisations struggling to provide services and organise activities for their members. It has been very successful so far. The funding target for the current financial year was to have 25 groups, but CCT has recruited over 100 groups and many are reporting dramatic increases in their activity levels.

For example, the osteoporosis group has doubled its membership while the Cumnock and Doon Valley Blind Club are now organising regular theatre trips. Many other groups are developing too, although I feel a fair few are still limited by their own aspirations. The group transport service has also enabled a primary school in Muirkirk to transport 32 children into Auchinleck for swimming lessons. It is a round trip of nearly 30 miles and is the first time in its history that the school has been able to offer swimming lessons to its pupils. Even churches are benefiting, with one local kirk reporting that Sunday morning congregations are regularly full now that worshippers from neighbouring villages can get to it.

The churchgoers have nicknamed their service 'Wheels to God', somewhat irreverently, one feels.

From April to December 2002, CCT carried over 4,000 passengers, and with group membership still rising it is confident of equally good figures this year. It has over 130 drivers, many of whom will drive for a variety of organisations and all of whom will undertake MiDAS training: "We've a lot of things we want to do, but we don't believe we can afford to cut corners on quality standards," said Sheila:

> "We joined MiDAS [the CTA's driver training and assessment programme for the voluntary sector] because we want our users to know safety matters. We bought Optare Aleros because we wanted our disabled passengers to use the same entrance as everyone else. Sometimes, the way you do things is as important as the things you actually do."

However, although group transport has been their first project, CCT do not want to let the grass grow under their feet. Sheila told me:

> "This year we will be starting the Dayhopper service and a Wheels to Work project. We may also get a community bus service off the ground, but if that doesn't start this year then it certainly will by spring 2004."

The Dayhopper will be their first foray into providing for individual transport needs. The target-user base is people who are geographically, economically or socially disadvantaged. The core activity of the Dayhopper will be shopper services into various shopping centres in Ayr, Glasgow, Kilmarnock and Irvine. However, they are also planning to offer excursions, and Sheila anticipates this is likely to take the form of trips to cinemas (some villages are more than 15 miles from one), leisure centres and other social centres. The service is expected to be heavily used at weekends and in the evenings.

The Wheels to Work scheme is expected to start on a small scale initially, with about six or so scooters. When the scheme has taken shape, and the local community understands how it works, CCT will look to expand it. The lease life for each scooter will be about a year, so there is plenty of time for people who have got jobs as a result of finding independent transport to save up for their own vehicle or even perhaps to take driving lessons. The community bus is also a firm plan but CCT continues to think beyond the next year. "Another idea we have had, and intend to pursue, is something called Cinemobile," Sheila told me:

> "Many settlements in Scotland, including most of East Ayrshire, are miles and miles from the nearest cinema. We are already planning to offer Dayhopper trips to these cinemas. But wouldn't it be so much nicer if we could bring the cinema to this area instead?"

Highlands and Islands Arts run a mobile cinema that does just that. Their Screen Machine is a large lorry containing a 110-seat cinema and does indeed tour remote areas, bringing the latest movies. Move over mobile libraries, your time is up! Sheila explains:

> "Some might say that taking people to the cinema is community transport but that bringing the cinema to the people is not, but the value of a really integrated approach to social inclusion is that such silly demarcations are not necessary. Everyone in the SIP is working together to meet fairly large-scale objectives. If we are the best-positioned to bring Screen Machine to East Ayrshire, then it will indeed be us who does so."

Conclusion

In the last 20 years, community transport has had a very significant impact. The transport options open to many of the most marginalised people in British society have been extended. The provision of appropriate forms of transport for, among others, disabled people, people on low incomes and teenagers has improved the access of these groups to work and training opportunities, to health facilities and to sporting, cultural and other leisure activities. One question remains: if community transport provides such a valuable service, why is there not more of it?

Despite the acknowledged quality of the services community transport can provide, and despite the high priority given by the present government to combating social exclusion, the fact remains that the vast majority of community transport projects in the UK exist on marginal funding. Demand for services almost always outstrips supply, sometimes to a frightening degree. Community transport projects are constantly in a state of financial crisis and their long-term future almost always in doubt.

In recent years, community transport organisations have become quite adept at drawing down funding from a wide variety of sources. This has become a necessity with core funding from local authorities always vulnerable. However, many of the alternative sources of finance – trusts, the Community Fund, various rural funding streams from the Countryside Agency – are for limited periods of time, typically three years. These bodies also tend to want to support new initiatives rather than existing services. As a consequence, the financial base of many community transport organisations can be very weak. If most of their income is project-related and if those projects are anyway of a limited duration, then the organisation is still at risk.

Some community transport projects have begun to explore the 'social enterprise' model. This involves a mixture of transport or related services, some of which require grant funding but some of which may actually produce a surplus which can then be ploughed back into the organisation and allow other important services to be subsidised. The problem with this approach is that it is often only when an organisation reaches a certain size – that is, achieves 'critical mass' – that it can be confident of its long-term financial future. There has to be enough surplus money in the system that the loss of one large contract or grant is not going to cause the whole project to fail.

Research into the cross-sector benefits that can be associated with community transport provision is depressingly thin, but it does not take a tremendous amount of thought to appreciate. In general terms, it represents the cost to both health and social services budgets of thousands of mostly older people *not* getting out of their homes on a regular basis. On top of the direct impact of having to provide services to people's homes, rather than having them visit the surgery, chiropodist and so on themselves, can be added the likely drop in general health of anyone who is unable to lead a reasonably active social life. Similarly, having many young people unemployed with all the financial and social costs that entails suggests that money spent on a transport service that helps such people into work is money that will be matched by a reduction in public spending elsewhere.

Voluntary organisations always want more money and government, both local and national, always insists it is doing as much as it can. It is important, however, to understand just how many aspects of modern life can be affected by the provision of good transport links – or by the lack of such provision. Financial support for community transport should represent a wise investment for any public body concerned with keeping both the economy and its people healthy, concerned about the marginalisation of many in society; concerned, indeed, about the wider consequences of that marginalisation particularly among young people.

If one of the strengths of community transport is that it is a grassroots movement with no direct ties to any part of government, it is true too that this is also one of its weaknesses. Nobody has an obligation to fund it, although there can be sharp social consequences if a project collapses or is unable to operate to full capacity through lack of money. To fully benefit from what community transport has to offer, society has to find a way to help the community transport movement achieve financial sustainability without taking away the independence that has been crucial to its development.

Note

[1] In 1999, the Scottish Executive set out its long-term strategy for tackling poverty and injustice in the document *Social justice: A Scotland where everyone matters*. The strategy acknowledged that the reasons some people suffer poverty, inequality and discrimination are complex and interrelated. Housing, health, education and employment opportunities, fear of crime and poor environment are not issues that can be tackled in isolation. A coordinated approach is necessary if we are to tackle poverty, promote equality and close the existing opportunity gaps.

References

Jackson, G. (1999) 'Better for everyone', *Community Transport*, Jan/Feb, p 18.
Scottish Executive (1999) *Social justice: A Scotland where everyone matters*, Edinburgh: Scottish Executive.
Steer Davies Gleave (SDG) (1999) *Review of voluntary transport*, London: Department of the Environment, Transport and the Regions.

EIGHT

Conclusions from the UK experience

Karen Lucas

For some time, researchers have been highlighting inequalities in the transport system for certain groups and communities. Equally, some local transport authorities have attempted to address social equity issues in their delivery of public transport services and where mainstream public transport has failed, community and voluntary transport organisations have been working to meet the transport needs of minority and marginalised groups. Until the advent of the 2003 Social Exclusion Unit (SEU) report and its new policies for accessibility planning, however, these efforts have been fragmented and piecemeal.

For the first time, the UK government is openly acknowledging that people's inability to access key services because of poor transport is a factor in their social exclusion. More than this, it has put in place a comprehensive cross-departmental policy framework to address this problem. This requires not only that transport policy makers consider the impact of their decisions on the social welfare of citizens, but also that those concerned with the delivery of the welfare agenda consider transport and accessibility as a vital element in encouraging people from welfare to work, reducing health inequalities, improving educational attainment and achieving neighbourhood renewal.

The UK case studies (Chapters Four to Seven) demonstrate that there is already a lot of good practice happening 'on the ground' and, for transport authorities like Merseytravel that have been championing a social equity agenda in transport for more than ten years, the SEU policies will simply help to reinforce the good work that is already going on. It should also make it easier for non-transport professionals such as Mike Preston in Braunstone and Julian Westwood in Halton to gain the support of the transport sector in the delivery transport projects to encourage neighbourhood renewal. Clearly, there is also an important role for the community transport sector, which already has a huge amount of experience and knowledge to impart in relation to the successful delivery of practical projects and initiatives aimed at improving transport for socially excluded groups and communities.

Despite these promising signs, however, there are still some significant barriers and risks that could undermine the delivery of the new agenda. Most notably these include:

- short termism and over-simplification of the problem;
- under-resourcing and competing funding priorities;
- legislative and institutional barriers;
- reconciling social concerns about transport.

Short termism and over-simplification of the problem

As Grant points out in the Liverpool case study (Chapter Four), provision of bespoke services such as those provided through the Job Link programme, although clearly important, are essentially short-term interventions to alleviate immediate shortfalls in transportation for those most in need. Clearly, long-term and financially sustainable solutions are needed if we are to ensure that local transport policy making and implementation are more equitably distributed across the population as a whole. These have to lie with better integration of land use, regeneration and transport planning, and with joint planning of service delivery across all public services. Until these long-term changes can be made and have an effect, public transport providers will need to adopt a proactive, innovative and flexible approach. This is time-consuming, resource intensive and subject to rebuffs and disappointments as the Braunstone case study (Chapter Six) highlights.

Furthermore, as with all aspects of the social inclusion agenda, the level of complexity involved in getting the individuals that are the target of the accessibility agenda to change their current practices, attitudes and perceptions should not be underestimated. In his chapter (Five), Westwood uses the term agoraphobia to describe the reluctance he has encountered when working with some members of socially excluded communities to encourage them to take up new opportunities. Long-standing (sometimes intergenerational) and inculcated activity patterns, illiteracy and language barriers, limited travel horizons, low expectations and reduced aspirations are incredibly difficult to reverse. For some, lack of transport is a real barrier to taking up new employment or other opportunities, but it must be recognised that for others it can be used as a convenient excuse for remaining in familiar and comfortable 'home' territory. Simply providing new transport links will not solve these problems and longer-term education and travel-training programmes will clearly be needed in some instances. These are labour intensive, micro initiatives, which need to be planned and delivered to individuals often over very long, even intergenerational, time periods if they are to have a significant effect in terms of behavioural changes.

Under-resourcing and competing funding priorities

Many of the interventions that are required to resolve the local transport problems experienced by deprived groups and communities will require public subsidies of public transport or other local services. The escalating cost of providing these services is already significant and increased demand for tendered services will tend to encourage even greater price increases in an oversubscribed market. The

April 2002 UK Budget announcement only identified a small amount of new funding to support the new strategy and, although the 2004 Spending Review may identify some additional monies, in essence, most of the funding for accessibility planning is expected to come from existing (redefined) budgets, via Local Transport Plans (LTPs) and special challenge funds. The SEU itself identifies that this will be insufficient to bring about the step-change that is needed to reverse current trends in service-level provision.

The Treasury is currently undertaking a bus subsidy review, which aims to ensure that public subsidies for local bus services are refocused on increasing passenger numbers, while also meeting the needs of people on low incomes. In the present financial climate, however, the public purse clearly cannot (or is reluctant to) extend itself much further than what has already been committed to transport over the next 10 years. The greatest proportion of this spending will go to projects which realise very small journey-time savings for large numbers of people who already have good access to transport (for example, by-passes, other road building, high-speed rail links, commuter routes and so on). Current policies to improve public transport services primarily do so with the aim of encouraging modal shift from cars. This not only fails to benefit the travel poor but also has the perverse effect of encouraging the travel rich to travel further and/or faster, with dubious 'benefits' to the economy, the environment and social inclusion.

The SEU vision for accessibility planning also relies heavily on non-transport sector agencies recognising the value of transport in the delivery of their own policy aims and objectives and thereby the worth of making a financial or resource contribution to transport services. Unless improved accessibility becomes a stated performance target for these other sectors, however, it is unlikely that they will bend valuable resources in this direction, particularly in the light of their own constrained budgets. As was pointed out in Chapter One of this book, the UK is currently witnessing a re-evaluation of welfare spending with a view to reducing rather than increasing its expenditure.

Legislative and institutional barriers

There are a number of legislative barriers that will also need to be addressed if accessibility planning is to be effective. Planning comprehensive bus services in a deregulated market is problematic. The 1998 UK Competition Act prevents bus operators from agreeing timetables, leading to inefficiencies in services frequencies and routing. Introducing new 'community-owned' service providers into the market is virtually impossible under the present insurance system for drivers. This often leads to effect monopolies within areas, an issue that the Office of Fair Trading seems reluctant to engage with. Integrated ticketing is still experiencing problems in the UK, despite revised guidance from the Office of Fair Trading, which introduced a block exemption for this for bus operators and provisions in the 2000 Transport Act giving local authorities the power to promote operator cooperation on joint-ticketing. There are also issues with the legislation surrounding the registration and operation of flexibly routed and community transport, although this is currently under review by the Department for Transport (DfT).

The institutional arrangements for accessibility planning are equally fraught with difficulties. In the first place, local transport authorities are not, strictly speaking, very 'local'. Most cover large areas embracing several metropolitan or district councils within them. This means that they must engage with numerous layers of more local administration if they are to be truly responsive to local needs. In addition, the type of multi-agency working that is envisaged by the SEU report is time-consuming and organisationally difficult. Previous efforts by transport authorities to secure the interests of other sectors in transport planning have met with mixed success. A recent study of local authorities' progress in this respect recommended that authorities are at very different stages in this process, with some far advanced in the delivery of jointly-funded and managed projects, while others are still considering how they should approach partnership working.

The SEU report rightly identifies that accessibility planning will not work if it is seen as a problem of transport and that non-transport solutions should be a key component of the action strategies that are developed. Despite the increasing policy rhetoric of integrated transport and land-use planning in the UK, major land-use developments continue to be located in places that people without cars find difficult to reach. While the problem is one of land-use planning, these decisions are often out of the hands of planners themselves, who are regularly forced to bow to the pressures of other more powerful interests, such as private profit, job creation and cost-efficiency savings. Many local land-use decisions in the UK are in fact made by other decision makers within both the central and local government, who may not hold the interests of transport and accessibility at the forefront of their decision making.

Even if this issue is resolved, land-use planning alone cannot improve local accessibility in isolation from local public service planning and other policy decisions. In practice, concerted and integrated action is needed between the providers of services, both within the private and public sector, who are the main drivers of new developments and land-use patterns, and land-use planners, who have the responsibility of regulating and controlling development activity. In areas where this approach has already been attempted, however, local transport planners are reporting difficulties in linking up with decision makers in some sectors and convincing them of the importance of transport and accessibility to their own delivery agendas.

Finally, the SEU recommends that effective public consultation and participation in transport decisions will be vital to the successful delivery of their proposals. As Westwood points out in Chapter Five, familiar ways of working and the received wisdom of project development among community development workers are not seen as the norm in transport planning circles. In fact, transport authorities have been required to consult with local people in the preparation of their LTPs since 1999, but public involvement in transport decisions is still not common in local transport planning and delivery.

Many transport planners do not have the expertise and skills necessary to fully respond to this emerging agenda. This is in part a legacy of the prevailing engineering culture within transport as a discipline. It can also run against the grain of conventional transport planning and provision and staff training requirements. The efforts needed to bring about changes in this prevailing culture and undertake such work should not be underestimated, neither should opposition from within an organisation to changes in the way services such as information are provided, particularly if these are seen as being a challenge to past custom and practice. Westwood suggests that a multidisciplinary approach may well be the best way to approach these issues and that restricting the people involved to only those with a transport background will stunt the debate and the scope for real innovation.

Reconciling environmental and social concerns about transport

Since 1994, transport and land-use policies in the UK have increasingly moved away from providing the infrastructure necessary to maintain high growth in personal travel and towards a demand management approach. Academics, policy professionals and the public would now generally agree that it would not be beneficial to encourage further growth in the number of cars on our roads.

It is reasonable to suggest that some sectors of the population have reached saturation point both in terms of the number of cars they own and the distances that they are prepared to travel. Clearly, however, other sectors, and in particular those households and individuals who do not currently own cars, offer the greatest potential to increase their car ownership and, more importantly, use.

On the basis of current trends, it would be reasonable to anticipate that car ownership will continue to grow at the same rate in low-income households over the next 10 years as it has over the last 10. This amounts to approximately an eight percentage-point increase (more than 40% growth). It is interesting to note that dramatic growth in car ownership among low-income households over the last 10 years has occurred despite a period of increased poverty among this sector of the population from 1979 to 1994 and no significant improvements in their income levels from 1994 to 2000. This would suggest that car ownership is increasingly considered as a basic need by even the very poorest in society. Future growth at this level is problematic for a number of reasons. As most poor people live in urban environments, increased car use among this sector of the population will lead to significant increased congestion on already busy roads. Another problem is that, although poorer car-owning households tend to use their cars less, they are more likely to own older and thus less energy-efficient and more polluting vehicles.

On the other hand, unless there are significant improvements to the public transport network and road safety in deprived areas, many people will need to own and drive cars in order to secure social inclusion. This represents a fundamental dilemma for future transport policy in the UK, namely, how to control traffic growth, without denying people on low incomes the right to own and drive cars.

New cars cost much more money and are usually out of the price range of most low-income households. This means that fleet replacement will be slower than it ideally could be and that some of the environmental benefits that could be realised from recent technological advancements will be undermined by the retention of more polluting second-hand cars by this sector. New cars also require more advanced technology to maintain them, which is often not available to smaller garages and the DIY mechanic. This not only raises the cost of running a car, pricing many people out of the market, but also undermines sources of gainful manual employment.

It is, of course, possible to simply price poor people and their undesirable vehicles off the road, by raising petrol prices or introducing parking levies, tolls and other mechanisms to reduce demand. These measures always hit those on the margins of car ownership the hardest. Not only is this inequitable but also could force people into inactivity and disengagement from society. This will not only have negative consequences for the economy, but could also lead to unregistered car use. Advocates of pricing policies suggest that, in the long run, equity is not an issue, as the money from charging will go towards improving public transport and thus benefit those on the lowest incomes. It is necessary to properly interrogate this assumption within the local context and fully evaluate the real effect of proposed measures on vulnerable groups and deprived areas. In particular:

- planned 'flagship' improvements are unlikely to serve the mobility needs of low-income travellers (for example, rapid transit commuter routes);
- some people could be priced out of the travel market altogether because they cannot afford the alternatives;
- pricing first and improving later means that many people who cannot afford to pay the charge will be left stranded in the interim;
- many people on low incomes are unable to use public transport because of physical impairment, or cultural and religious reasons, or their shift work patterns or the multi-purpose nature of their trip;
- road tolling can serve to divert traffic onto uncharged local roads and increase the problem of road safety and pollution in these areas;
- hypothecated revenues targeted at improving public transport often most benefits those who are most vocally disgruntled by the introduction of such measures, who are well able to pay the additional cost or find an alternative means of getting from A to B.

None of these problems are insurmountable, but they require forethought, commitment and considerable and concerted effort not only on the part of government but also the commercial sector if they are to be resolved.

Accessibility planning provides the hope of a more equitable future for transport and social policy in the UK, but it is only the first step on a long and bumpy road. In this respect, some valuable lessons can be drawn from other countries where similar policy problems are being addressed and in particular the experiences of the US in relation to its environmental justice agenda, to which the remaining chapters of this book now turn.

Part Three:
The US perspective

NINE

Transportation and environmental justice

Lori G. Kennedy

Introduction

Having examined the emergent policy agenda for transport and social exclusion in the UK, we now turn our attention to the environmental justice movement as it relates to transportation policies in the US. As a starting point, it is important to note that the term environmental justice has its roots in the US civil rights movement dating back to the 1960s, where there was a realization that racial discrimination was being compounded by environmental injustices. Many of the legal case histories surrounding environmental justice, including landmark US Supreme Court cases, started with issues of land development; that is, hazardous waste sites, landfills, zoning and so on. Over the last decade, however, there has been a movement towards recognition of environmental justice in the transportation arena. Although both the concept of environmental justice and the policy framework in which it is delivered in the US differ significantly from the UK social exclusion agenda, in the field of transport at least, there are some striking similarities between the two.

This chapter briefly outlines what environmental justice means to various entities and individuals in the US, tracing its origins in the 1964 Civil Rights Act (Senate and House of Representatives, 1964). It describes how transportation inequalities have moved to the forefront of US policy agendas in recent years under the banner of the environmental justice movement. It identifies the mechanisms by which concerns about transportation inequality have increasingly influenced this agenda and have been challenged by US law, the legal framework supporting environmental justice being one of the fundamental differences with the UK social exclusion agenda for transport. Finally, the chapter presents the different national approaches the US has taken on the issue and how local transportation policies have recognized and/or alleviated the problem of environmental injustice.

Executive Order human service transportation coordination

This year, President George W. Bush issued an Executive Order (Office of the Press Secretary, 2004) explicitly aimed at enhancing access to transportation for people who are transportation disadvantaged in the US. The Order formally recognizes that transportation plays a crucial role in providing access to employment, healthcare, education and other community services and amenities.

In fact, the importance of this role in the active participation of citizens has long been recognized in the US. A broad range of federally and state-assisted transportation programs has been created, in conjunction with health and human services programs, over the last 10 years, specifically to support people experiencing transportation disadvantage. However, the Order finds that the resources that are available are often fragmented, unused or simply unavailable. Furthermore, it is often difficult for citizens in need to understand and access the help that is available.

The Order establishes an Interagency Transportation Coordinating Council (ITCC) within the Department of Transportation, comprising the Secretaries of Transportation, Health and Human Resources, Education, Labor, Veteran Affairs, Agriculture, Housing and Urban Development, and the Interior, the Attorney General and the Commissioner of Social Security, as well as any other appropriate federal officials the chairperson of the council may designate. A key aim of the ITCC is to promote interagency cooperation to establish the mechanisms to ensure that transportation-disadvantaged people have access to more transportation services. The function of the ITCC is to:

a) promote interagency cooperation and the establishment of appropriate mechanisms to minimize duplication and overlap of federal programs and services so that transportation-disadvantaged people have access to more services;
b) facilitate access to the most appropriate, cost-effective transportation services within existing resources;
c) encourage enhanced customer access to the variety of transportation and resources available;
d) formulate and implement administrative, policy and procedural mechanisms that enhance transportation services at all levels;
e) develop and implement a method for monitoring progress on achieving the goals of this order. (Office of the Press Secretary, 2004, p 2)

The ITCC is charged with reporting its findings to the President by February 2005, identifying:

i) those federal, state, tribal and local laws, regulations, procedures and actions that have proven to be most helpful and appropriate in coordinating transportation services for the targeted populations;

ii) the substantive and procedural requirements of transportation-related federal laws and regulations or restrict the laws and regulations that are most efficient in terms of operation;
iii) its key findings and recommendations on an agency and program by program basis. (Office of the Press Secretary, 2004, p 2)

Interestingly in the light of the legal history of environmental justice in transportation, which is explored later in this chapter, the order explicitly states that its intention is only to improve the internal management of the executive branch and does not create any right or benefit, enforceable by law or in equity, by a party against the US government. This clause largely arises in response to the way in which transport inequity has emerged as an issue of environmental justice to be pursued through US civil rights law.

It is also worth noting, from the point of view of the transatlantic comparison that follows in Chapter Fifteen of this volume, that for the purposes of the Order, the persons who are considered to be *transportation disadvantaged* are only those people who qualify for federally conducted or federally assisted transport-related programs or services due to disability, income or advanced age.

The Order emerges from a long-standing recognition in the US that poor transportation and, in particular the lack of access to gainful employment resulting from this, is a major denial of civil and human rights. As Chapter Two of this volume demonstrated, in the US this most adversely affects people of color and other minority and low-income populations. As such, over the years it has been taken up as an issue for concern and, in some cases, legal action by the environmental justice movement.

What is 'environmental justice' in the eyes of US citizens, professionals and activists?

The term 'environmental justice' has evolved over the decades and is a term many professionals in the transportation field have struggled with, for lack of familiarity. It appears to mean many things to many individuals, including those citizens who are most affected by governmental policy or lack thereof. Most usually, the term has been used to embrace notions of discrimination, equity, denial of benefits, adverse effects, initially to people of color and other minority populations, but more recently to low-income populations. In relation to transportation issues, this would include consideration of the effects from road building and other transportation infrastructure, transportation-related air and noise pollution, congestion, denial of access to transportation and community severance.

Environmental justice and transportation: A citizen's handbook (Cairns et al, 2003, p 1) explains the definition of environmental justice in transportation as follows:

To parents living in a neighborhood with a lot of bus services, environmental justice might mean converting buses from diesel to natural gas, reducing their children's exposure to air pollution. A security guard working the night shift might feel that environmental justice has been served if the bus she takes deviates from its regular route to drop her off closer to home. Environmental justice to a non-English speaking neighborhood might mean having bilingual staff and community leaders running a public meeting. To low-income workers relying on bus service in a large downtown, environmental justice might mean that a city increases the frequency of buses instead of building a new light rail line that would serve upper-income commuters. In short, there is no single definition of environmental justice: its meaning depends on context, perspective and timeframe.

The concept stems from Title VI of the Civil Rights Act of 1964: 'Non-discrimination in federally assisted programs', which requires each federal agency to ensure that no person is denied the benefits of or subjected to discrimination under any program or activity receiving federal financial assistance.

Section 601 of the Civil Rights Act specifically states that:

> ... no person in the US shall, on the ground of race, color, or national origin, be excluded from participation in, be denied the benefits of, or be subjected to discrimination under any program or activity receiving Federal financial assistance.

Section 602 of the Act requires each federal agency empowered to administer a federal program to draw on the provisions of Section 601 by issuing rules, regulations or orders that will be consistent with the objects of the statute (1964 Civil Rights Act). The Legislative History of Title VI of the Civil Rights Act states that it was enacted because of the many examples cited where people of color in the US were denied equal protection and equal benefits under federal assistance programs related to vocational and technical assistance, public employment services, manpower development and training, and vocational rehabilitation.

Specifically, the history states that in every essential of life, US citizens are affected by programs of federal financial assistance. Through these programs, medical care, food, employment, education, and welfare are supplied to those in need. For the government, then, to permit the extension of such assistance to be carried on in a racially discriminatory manner is to violate the precepts of democracy and undermine the foundations of government.

Transportation and public transit services funding falls under the conditions of Title VI of the Act. However, over the past decade, civil rights activists and lawyers have increasingly brought into question the balance between protection of the 'human' versus 'environmental' rights in relation to the planning of federally assisted transportation projects and transport spending (see Chapter Twelve of this volume for an example of this).

The 1969 National Environmental Policy Act (NEPA), which governs such decisions, encourages productive and enjoyable harmony between *man* and his *environment*; to promote efforts which will prevent or eliminate damage to the *environment* and biosphere and stimulate the health and welfare of *man*; to enrich the understanding of the ecological systems and natural resources important to the nation; and to establish a Council on Environmental Quality (CEQ) (Section 2, National Environmental Protection Act, 1969) (Senate and House of Representatives, 1969). However, many feel that, in the past, transportation policies' 'human rights' have tended to be ignored in favor of economic efficiency and environmental protection.

Who are the transportation disadvantaged?

Poverty, disability, race and English-limited speaking all play a role in transportation inequality (Chapter Two of this volume). The 1999 Census data demonstrates a large percentage of the US population to be in poverty (see Table 9.1).

Female lone-parent families living below the poverty level are also seen to be a growing percentage of the US population within the Census data. Roughly 64% of the total civilian labor force is employed, but only 54% of the female labor force. Transportation is a problem for all women (see Chapter Thirteen) but is a particular problem for lone parents living on low incomes, the majority of whom are women of color (see Chapters Ten and Eleven). This means that the lack of adequate transportation arising from past transportation policies in the US can be taken up as a racial issue within the US legal system, and whether these inequalities arise from intentional discrimination or are a result of

Table 9.1: Percentage and number of households by income

Income ($)	Number of households	% of total households in the US
Less than 10,000	10,067,027	9.5
10,000-14,999	6,657,228	6.3
15,000-24,999	13,536,965	12.8
25,000-34,999	13,519,242	12.8
35,000-49,000	17,446,272	16.5
50,000-74,999	20,540,604	19.5
75,000-99,999	10,799,245	10.2
100,000-149,999	8,147,826	7.7
150,000-199,999	2,322,038	2.2
200,000 or more	2,502,675	2.4

Source: US Census Bureau (2000)

unintentional but disproportionate impact has become an increasingly important issue within US law.

Twenty-five percent of US citizens are classed as non-white, representing a sizeable proportion of the total US population (US Census Bureau, 2000). Hispanic or Latino (of any race) make up the second largest percent of the total population at 12.5%, while 12.3% of the non-white population is black or African American. Asians represent 3.6% and American Indian and Alaska Native represent almost 1% of the population.

Individuals with disabilities are also seen as a highly disadvantaged sector of the US population. The figures for people with disabilities in the US are set out in Table 9.2.

Finally, approximately 260 million individuals in the US do not speak English when conversing in their own home and this is also considered an issue in terms of their disadvantage. Eighty-two percent of the population speak English only and close to 20% speak a second language other than English (US Census Bureau, 2000).

While it is not certain exactly what proportion of this disadvantaged population actually experience a problem with transportation, it is clear that lack of personal transportation is a major barrier to employment. Approximately 130 million individuals commute to work in the US (almost half the total population). Modes of transportation to work are by car, truck, van, public transportation, walking, bicycling and telecommuting. Public transportation is used approximately only 5% of the time (US Census Bureau, 2000). This would suggest that, in most instances, public transit is not considered an adequate mode of transportation for the commute journey.

In 1960, when most transit companies were private and not subsidized, the cost of transit averaged 18 cents per passenger mile (1997 dollar), a little less than the cost of driving. By 1975, when almost all transit agencies were publicly owned and heavily subsidized, the cost per passenger mile reached 44 cents (paid mostly by taxpayers – non-transit riders). Today in the US, transit costs exceed 50 cents per passenger mile, three times the cost of driving (Thoreau Institute, 2003a).

Table 9.2: People with disabilities

Disability status	Number	%
Population aged 5-20	64,689,357	100.0
with a disability	5,214,334	8.1
Population aged 21-64	159,131,544	100.0
with a disability	30,553,796	19.2
% employed		56.6
Population aged 65+	33,346,626	100.0
with a disability	13,978,118	41.9

Source: US Census Bureau (2000)

Certainly lack of funding for public transit is not the answer. From 1991 through 2000, transit agencies spent more than $70 billion on capital expenses (two thirds going to rail projects) (Thoreau Institute, 2003b). However, most of this investment has been in urban areas to accommodate those in the wealthy suburban areas traveling to and from work, while inner-city public transportation systems (that is, bus systems, transit and so on) have remained untouched from an upgrade, operational, and maintenance standpoint since their inception of use. The majority of low-income and minority populations live in the center of cities and depend on this very intercity public transportation system to access family, friends and, most importantly, jobs. Transit agencies have also doubled the investment they have made in rail compared to buses, while buses carry 60% of all transit rides and 45% of passenger miles (see Chapter Twelve of this volume for an expansion of this discussion).

The precise effect of these transportation spending decisions on low-income, disabled, minority and older people has not been conclusively proven. However, the evidence suggests that, while everyone suffers from the lack of a decent public transit system, those already experiencing poverty and hardship suffer first and worst. Significant federal investment in accessible transportation systems and a broad range of federal program funding to allow the purchase or provision of transportation services and resources for persons who are transport disadvantaged in the US would suggest that it is a problem which has also been recognized by the US government.

Welfare to Work initiatives to address environmental justice

Welfare to Work (WtoW) recipients, a large percentage of whom come from low-income and minority populations, often experience a lack of adequate transportation as a barrier to work. There are many factors that contribute to these transportation barriers, including not being able to afford their own vehicle; lack of public transportation to and from work or other means of transportation; public transportation not being offered on the weekends or evenings, the only time when they can get a job; lack of childcare; no public transportation in rural areas and the job market locating further distances from the centers of cities (sprawl).

Transportation is often the largest challenge for people transitioning from the welfare program to work. While two thirds of new jobs are in the suburbs, a large percentage of welfare recipients live in rural or central cities. Existing public transit services often fail to provide adequate linkage to job opportunities. Data from the Urban Institute's *National survey of American families* show that twice as many welfare recipients with cars were working than those without cars (cited in FTA, 2000).

Historically, federal transportation funds were used to reimburse clients for transportation costs rather than provide transportation services. Welfare reform requires better use of transit services and a more systemic approach to link these to existing and proposed transportation infrastructure. Employers also need to be included in providing transportation services.

Presently there are three federal funding sources that can be utilized in assisting individuals from WtoW:

1. the Temporary Assistance for Needy Families (TANF) program administered by the Department of Health and Human Services;
2. the Welfare to Work Grants administered by the US Department of Labor;
3. the Job Access and Reverse Commute (JARC) grant program administered by the US Federal Transit Administration (FTA).

Temporary Assistance for Needy Families (TANF) program

Under the 1996 Personal Responsibility and Work Opportunity Reconciliation Act (PRWORA), a comprehensive welfare reform program established the TANF program. This created block grants to states, changing the nature and provision of federal welfare benefits in the US. This legislation dramatically changed the nation's welfare system into one that requires work in exchange for time-limited assistance and provides limited support for families moving from welfare to work. The legislation provides a limit on the amount of time an individual can receive welfare benefits and, with limited exceptions, welfare recipients are expected to engage in work activities to move from welfare assistance to permanent employment. This creates 'reverse' transportation commutes, often unmet by public transit, imposing additional transport burdens on people in WtoW programs. Many former welfare recipients are women with young children who live in older inner cities. Public transit often does not go to airport industrial parks and outer suburbs. When it does, the trip is often long, requires several transfers between buses, and is costly. These difficulties create disincentives to make the move to work and impose hardships on women.

As of March 2001, there were 5,488,616 people receiving TANF benefits. Since TANF money is 'block granted' to the states, each state is allowed to design and implement its own TANF program including setting benefit levels and determining who receives assistance. There are over 50 different TANF programs across the US, with some plans varying from county to county. The types of provided assistance varies and is directed at ongoing basic needs. States decide what services and assistance they will provide. The levels of assistance also vary from state to state. States can use TANF funds to provide services other than cash assistance to people as they make the transition from welfare to work and these services often include bus passes or other means of transportation to work.

WtoW grants program

The $3 billion WtoW grants program established by Congress as part of the Balanced Budget Act of 1997, provided funds to over 700 state and local grantees.

The purpose of the program is to supplement the welfare reform funds included in the TANF block grants to states. The WtoW funds were intended to support programs, especially in high-poverty communities, to assist the least employable, most disadvantaged welfare recipients and non-custodial parents make the transition from welfare to work. The long-term goal of the WtoW grants program is to promote long-term economic self-sufficiency of individuals who have serious difficulty with employment. A great deal of the WtoW program is spent on preparing participants for employment which includes assessment of service needs, job readiness skills, help finding a job and also developmental skills that include education, training, and transitional employment. Welfare to Work participants follow four different 'Pathways to Employment':

1. *Basic Employment Preparation Pathway*: individuals enter employment after receiving only general job search assistance or attending job readiness training. In this pathway they usually receive support services for childcare and/or transportation.
2. *Transitional Employment Pathway*: individuals enter employment after having participated in some intermediate type of work activity (that is, occupational internship).
3. *Education or Training Pathway*: individuals enter employment after enrolling in an education or occupational training program.
4. *Mixed Activities Pathway*: individuals enter employment after engaging in some intermediate type of work activity and education and/or training program.

Job Access and Reverse Commute (JARC) grant program

The FTA's intention with the JARC grant program is to assist states and localities in developing transportation services aimed at linking welfare recipients to job access and other related services. These transportation services through this grant program often include car and van pooling, new bus routes, connector services to mass transit, employer-provided transportation and transportation services to suburban employment centers and is intended to establish an 'all inclusive' and regional approach to job access. Under the last federal transportation Bill, the 1998 Transportation Equity Act for the 21st Century, $750 million over five years was authorized for the JARC grant program. In 1999, the first $150 million was authorized for JARC. In 2000, over 200 transit projects were funded in 39 states under the JARC grant program. (Examples of the JARC program in California are described further in Chapter Ten of this volume.)

Community impact assessment

Community impact assessment (CIA) analysis has been a recent approach many agencies have taken to ensure the community voice or voices are heard during the transportation planning and implementation phases of projects. It includes such approaches as community profiling, meaningful community involvement, consensus building, decision making, education, training and implementation. (An example of a CIA analysis can be seen in Chapter Eleven of this volume.)

Public involvement exercises

Public involvement and its role in transportation in the US has been an evolving process for more than three decades. The Federal Highway Administration (FHWA) and Federal Transit Administration's (FTA's) *Interim policy on public involvement and questions and answers* (FHWA/FTA, 1994, pp 3-4) defines the public as follows:

> ... citizens, affected public agencies, representatives of transportation agency employees, other affected employee representatives, private providers of transportation and other interested parties (eg 23 USC 134 (h)). The FHWA and FTA define the public broadly as including all individuals or groups who are potentially affected by transportation decisions. This includes anyone who resides in, has interest in, or does business in a given area, which may be affected by transportation decisions. The public includes both individuals and organized groups. In addition, it is important to provide similar opportunities for the participation of all private and public providers of transportation services, including, but not limited to, the trucking and rail freight industries, rail passenger industry, taxi cab operators, and all conventional and unconventional transit service operators. Finally, those persons traditionally underserved by existing transportation systems such as low income or minority households and the elderly should be explicitly encouraged to participate in the public involvement process.

Since the passage of Intermodal Surface Transportation Efficiency Act (ISTEA) in 1991, there has been much more of an emphasis on early, proactive and continual citizen/public input into transportation decision making with an emphasis placed on outreach to traditionally underserved populations. The passage of TEA-21 also reinforced these efforts. Subsequent to signing Executive Order 12898 in 1994, in 1997 the Secretary of Transportation signed the US Department of Transportation (DOT) order on environmental justice, *DOT final order on environmental justice: DOT actions to address environmental justice in minority populations and low-income populations*. In 1998, the FHWA issued its order on environmental justice, *FHWA actions to address environmental justice in minority populations and low-income populations* (FHWA, 1998). (Both the US DOT and the FHWA orders are discussed below in further detail.) All of these efforts by Congress and the federal government were derived from a growing concern and grassroots movement by the public, communities and the traditionally underserved to ensure that the power of decision making no longer rests solely with the government alone and that all individuals and groups have a voice from inception of transportation decisions that affect them and their communities.

Meaningful involvement of the public is the link between CIA, environmental justice analyses and public involvement processes. How we involve the public and citizens, how we define their communities, and how they are treated in a fair and equitable manner (perceived or actual) is the intent of environmental justice, CIA and public involvement as they relate to transportation needs and solutions and how the people of the US are treated individually and collectively in the spirit of the law, regulations and guidance.

Addressing the indirect effects and cumulative impacts of transportation

One of the most widely debated areas of transportation today is air quality and the health effects the transportation system is having on society. Since a large percentage of low-income and minority populations live in city centers, the effects of increased mobile source air toxics has had visible increasing adverse health effects to these populations.

The Council on Environmental Quality (CEQ) regulations (40 CFR § 1500-1508) define the impacts and effects that must be addressed and considered by federal agencies in satisfying the National Environmental Policy Act (NEPA) process as discussed above. According to the regulations, direct effects are caused by the action and occur at the same place and time. Indirect effects are caused by the action and are later in time or farther removed in distance, but are still reasonably foreseeable; for example, growth-inducing effects, induced land-use pattern changes, changes in population density or growth rate, or effects on air and water.

A cumulative impact is defined as an impact on the environment, which results from the incremental impact of the action when added to other past, present and reasonably foreseeable future actions regardless of what agency (federal or non-federal) or person undertakes such other actions. Cumulative impacts can result from individually minor but collectively significant actions taking place over a period of time. Cumulative impacts are the total effects on a natural resource or human resource (that is, community) due to the past, present and future activities of federal, non-federal, public, and private entities.

Agencies like the FHWA have taken a harder look in recent times at cumulative impacts in the approval of environmental documents under the NEPA process. Professionals are realizing that cumulative impacts are often the most damaging affects to low-income and minority communities due to past, present and proposed transportation projects that have taken place on their communities over a long period of time, often decades. It is often easy and apparent to the professional preparing these NEPA documents to visualize, quantify and document the direct and indirect effects of a proposed transportation facility and specifically those direct and indirect effects on the underserved. It is much more of a challenge to quantify the cumulative impacts of these transportation facilities such as traffic impacts, air quality impacts and/or water quality impacts to both the human and natural environments and from past, present and future perspectives.

Federal policies and legislation governing environmental justice

It can be seen from this brief overview that the US environmental justice agenda, as it relates to transportation disadvantage, although slightly predating the UK agenda in the delivery of a program of federally funded initiatives, is now adopting a similar brief. The current focus of US policy is on ensuring the greater availability and affordability of transportation services and delivering a seamless, comprehensive and coordinated community transportation system. One of the key differences between the US and UK model up to the US President's announcement this year has been the legislative and legal frameworks underpinning the concept of environmental justice in transportation as a human right.

Legal authorities

Legal authorities governing individuals challenging human rights have evolved over the past four decades, with more of a direct focus on transportation from the mid-1990s. These key authorities are as follows:

- Title VI of the 1964 Civil Rights Act;
- NEPA, 23 USC 109(h): the Federal-Aid Highway Act of 1970;
- DOT Title VI regulations;
- DOT and CEQ NEPA regulations;
- Transportation Equity Act for the 21st Century (TEA-21) – Section 1203;
- DOT Planning Regulations;
- Executive Order 12898: *Federal actions to address environmental justice in minority populations and low-income populations*;
- DOT Environmental Justice Strategy 1995;
- FHWA (1998) *Final Order on Environmental Justice: Department of Transportation actions to address environmental justice in minority populations and low-income populations*;
- FHWA Final Order on Environmental Justice: *FHWA actions to address environmental justice in minority populations and low-income populations*.

The following sections explain some of these and their relevance to the adoption of environmental justice policies for transportation in the US.

Title VI of the 1964 Civil Rights Act

Title VI of the 1964 Civil Rights Act as described in the beginning of this chapter is the main venue where individuals and groups have brought charges of discrimination against various entities receiving federal funding. These lawsuits over the decades have shaped the way the local, state and the federal governments have interpreted their laws and regulations and provided guidance. Specifically, those having a great effect on the way the federal government has provided guidance are described below, including the most recent US Supreme Court cases that will probably have the most lasting effect.

NEPA 23 USC 109(h)

Federal regulation 23 USC 109(h) of the Federal-Aid Highway Act of 1970, requires that:

> ... possible adverse economic, social, and environmental effects relating to any proposed project on any Federal-Aid system have been fully considered in developing such project, and that the final decisions on the project are made in the *best overall public interest*, taking into consideration the need for fast, safe and efficient transportation, public services, and the costs of eliminating or minimizing such adverse effects and the following: 1) air, noise, and water pollution; 2) destruction or disruption of man-made and natural resources, aesthetic values, *community cohesion* and the availability of public facilities and services; 3) adverse employment effects, and tax and property values losses; 4) *injurious displacement of people*, businesses and farms; and 5) *disruption of desirable community* and regional growth. (23 USC 109 (h); emphasis added)

DOT Title VI regulations

The regulations state that:

> A recipient, in determining the types of services, financial aid, or other benefits, or facilities which will be provided under any such program ... may not, directly or through contractual or other arrangements, utilize criteria or methods of administration which have the *effect* of subjecting persons to discrimination because of their race, color or national origin.... In determining the site or location of facilities, a recipient or applicant may not make selections with the purpose or *effect* of excluding persons from, denying them the benefits of, or subjecting them to discrimination under any program to which this regulation applies, on the grounds of race, color, or national origin.... (49 CFR 21.5(b)(2); emphasis added)

DOT and CEQ NEPA regulations

Section 101(b) of NEPA requires that:

> ... the Federal Government use all practicable means, consistent with other essential considerations of national policy, to improve and coordinate Federal plans, functions, programs, and resources to: fulfill the responsibilities of each generation as *trustee of the environment* ...; assure for all Americans ... an aesthetically and culturally *pleasing surroundings*; attain the widest range of beneficial uses of the *environment* without degradation ...; *preserve important historic, cultural, and natural aspects* of our national heritage ...; achieve a balance between population and *resource use* ...; and *enhance the quality of renewable resources*.... (23 USC 101(b); emphasis added)

Section 102(2) of NEPA requires policies, regulations, and public laws of the US and all agencies of the federal government to

> ... insure the integrated use of the natural and *social sciences* and the environment design arts in planning and in decision making which may have an *impact on man's environment*; identify and develop methods and procedures, ... which will insure that presently un-quantified environmental amenities and values be given appropriate consideration ...; include in every recommendation or report affecting the quality of the *human environment*, a detailed statement by the responsible official on – (i) the environmental impact of the proposed action, (ii) any adverse environmental effects which cannot be avoided, (iii) alternatives to the proposed action, (iv) the relationship between local short-term uses of man's environment and the maintenance and enhancement of long-term productivity, and (v) any irreversible and irretrievable commitments of resources. (23 USC 102(2); emphasis added)

So one can see, there were laws and regulations in place as early as the 1960s and 1970s to protect not only the natural environment but also the rights of human beings living in the US in relation to this. The US laws, regulations and executive orders described next were established in the mid-1990s and beginning of the 21st century to address these, as they relate to transportation.

Transportation Equity Act for the 21st Century (TEA-21) – 23 USC 1203 (f)(1)

The Federal-Aid Highway Bill is re-authorized by Congress in the US every six years. Transportation Equity Act for the 21st Century (TEA-21) is the most recent Bill enacted that disperses federal funding to each state and was also the only Bill in the history of the US to place so much focus on the 'human' environment and its effects from transportation. Section 1203, Metropolitan Planning, of TEA-21 states that:

> The metropolitan transportation planning process for a metropolitan area shall provide for consideration of projects and strategies that will:
>
> (A) support the economic vitality of the metropolitan area, especially by enabling global competitiveness, productivity, and efficiency;
> (B) increase the *safety and security* of the transportation system for motorized and *non-motorized users*;
> (C) increase the *accessibility and mobility options available to people* and for freight;
> (D) protect and enhance the environment, promote energy conservation, and *improve quality of life*;
> (E) enhance the integration and connectivity of the transportation system, across and between modes, for people and freight;
> (F) promote efficient system management and operation;
> (G) emphasize the preservation of the existing transportation system.
> (22 USC 1203 (f) (1); emphasis added)

DOT Planning Regulations – 450 USC 334(a)(3)

Section 450.334, Metropolitan transportation planning process:

> Certification, requires that the State and Metropolitan Planning Organization (MPO) shall annually certify to the FHWA and the FTA that the planning process is addressing the major issues facing the area and is being conducted in accordance with all applicable requirements of: …(3) Title VI of the Civil Rights Act of 1964…. (23 CFR 450)

In essence, MPOs under the certification of the federal government have to ensure that Title VI of the Civil Rights Act is being complied with annually.

Executive Order 12898

Executive Order 12898 was the first order of its kind in the US to specifically address environmental justice. Although not law, it was the first of its kind to require all federal agencies to address environmental justice. Executive Order 12898 (1994), *Federal actions to address environmental justice in minority populations and low-income populations*, required the creation of an interagency working group on environmental justice by the Environmental Protection Agency which includes the DOT.

The working group is required to:

(1) provide guidance to Federal agencies on criteria for identifying disproportionately high and adverse human health or environmental effects on minority populations and low-income populations;
(2) coordinate with, provide guidance to, and serve as a clearinghouse for, each Federal agency as it develops an environmental justice strategy in order to ensure that the administration, interpretation and enforcement of programs, activities and policies are undertaken in a consistent manner;
(3) assist in coordinating research by, and stimulating cooperation among, the Environmental Protection Agency, the Department of Health and Human Services, the Department of Housing and Urban Development, and other agencies conducting research or other activities in accordance with the Order;
(4) assist in coordinating data collection, required by this order;
(5) examine data and studies on environmental justice;
(6) hold public meetings; and
(7) develop interagency model projects on environmental justice that evidence cooperating among Federal agencies. (Executive Order 12898, 1994)

Since the Executive Order was signed in 1994, the majority of these items were completed and are on-going by the working group. Additionally, Executive Order 12898 required that each federal agency develop an agency-wide environmental justice strategy that identifies and addresses disproportionately high and adverse human health and environmental effects of its programs, policies, and activities on minority populations and low-income populations.

DOT Environmental Justice Strategy 1995

The US DOT issued its final environmental justice strategy on 29 June 1995. Elements of this strategy include:

1. Public Outreach on Implementation of the Environmental Justice Strategy – a review with environmental justice stakeholders, DOT's plans for the following activities: (1) grass roots meetings to better understand the environmental justice concerns and provide training on the transportation processes; (2) a secretarial level meeting of experts, traditional DOT stakeholders and environmental justice representatives to recommend specific policies and actions to implement Executive Order 12898 and the Department's Environmental Justice

>   Strategy; and (3) regional workshops for state and local officials on implementing the Strategy.
> 2. DOT Order on Environmental Justice – ensure DOT managers are fully aware of their responsibilities under Executive Order 12898 and pre-existing statutory mandates through information seminars. (Executive Order 12898, 1994)

Public outreach has taken place by the US DOT subsequent to the issuing of their final environmental justice strategy. Regional and national conferences have been held by DOT and have included grassroot activists, environmental justice stakeholders, DOT employees and practitioner professionals in 1995 and several years to follow to stress the importance of Executive Order 12898.

DOT Final Order on Environmental Justice

On 3 February 1997, the Secretary of Transportation for the US DOT signed the *DOT Final Order on Environmental Justice: DOT actions to address environmental justice in minority populations and low-income populations*. This order requires that each operating administration within the US DOT and respective responsible officials determine whether programs, policies, and activities for which they are responsible will have an adverse impact on minority and low-income populations and whether that adverse impact will be disproportionately high. In making determinations regarding disproportionately high and adverse effects on minority and low-income populations, mitigation and enhancement measures that will be taken and all offsetting benefits to the affected minority and low-income populations may be taken into account, as well as the design, comparative impacts, and the relevant number of similar existing system elements in non-minority and non-low-income areas.

The operating administrators and responsible DOT officials will ensure that any of their respective programs, policies or activities that will have a disproportionately high and adverse effect on minority populations or low-income populations will only be carried out if further mitigation measures or alternatives that would avoid or reduce the disproportionately high and adverse effect are 'not practicable'. In determining whether a mitigation measure or an alternative is 'practicable', the social, economic (including costs) and environmental effects of avoiding or mitigating the adverse effects will be taken into account (US DOT, 1997). Those respective programs, policies or activities that will have a disproportionately high and adverse effect on populations protected by Title VI ('protected populations') will only be carried out if:

1. a substantial need for the program, policy or activity exists, based on the overall interest; and
2. alternatives that would have less adverse effects on protected populations (and that still satisfy the need identified in

subparagraph (1) above, either (i) would have other adverse social, economic, environmental or human health impacts that are more severe, or (ii) would involve increased costs of extraordinary magnitude. (US DOT, 1997)

FHWA Final Order on Environmental Justice

On December 2 1998, FHWA issued its Final Order on Environmental Justice: *FHWA actions to address environmental justice in minority populations and low-income populations.* This order provides for the same information as the DOT Final Order.

Legal case history is where the governmental officials and practitioner professionals have turned to determine what constitutes a disproportionately high and adverse effect.

US case law history of environmental justice

The strong legislative framework surrounding transportation spending and delivery in the US suggests that a relatively longstanding and firm legal basis exists for citizens and communities to pursue any injustices that accrue to them through legal means. A look at history reveals that, in the 1950s, urban renewal and freeway locations in parks and inner cities impacted minority communities, yet hardly any litigation resulted.

Once NEPA was enacted, however, it was frequently used as a vehicle to stop undesirable development in the 1970s and 1980s.

Key US Supreme Court cases relating to environmental justice

Four Supreme Court cases have played a precedenting role in decisions surrounding environmental justice over the years. Although these cases do not directly relate to discriminatory practices concerning transportation, they have shaped other transportation discrimination cases and transportation policy in general at the local, state and federal levels and are vital to an understanding of legal precedent. These are as follows:

1. Washington v Davis, 96 SCt 2040 (1976)
2. Village of Arlington Heights v Metropolitan Housing Development Corporation, 97 SCt 555 (1977)
3. Guardians Association v Civil Service Commission, NYC, 463 US 582 (1983)
4. Alexander v Choate, 469 US 287 (1985)

All four cases challenged the Equal Protection Clause under the Fourteenth Amendment of the US Constitution. The first of these two cases served to define the difference between 'intentional discrimination' and 'disproportionate impact'. The second two answered whether Title VI reaches both *intentional* discrimination and *disparate impact* discrimination. In all four cases, the US Supreme Court concluded that:

> Official action will not be held unconstitutional solely because it results in a racially disproportionate impact; proof of racially *discriminatory intent or purpose* is required to show violation of the Equal Protection Clause. (97 SCt 555, 1977; emphasis added)

In Washington v Davis, 96 SCt 2040 (1976), the US Supreme Court held that the law is not unconstitutional solely because the plaintiffs proved a disproportionate impact, regardless of whether it reflects intentional discrimination. However, in this case the US Supreme Court went on to emphasize that:

> ... this is not to say that the necessary discriminatory racial intent must be express or appear on the face of the statute, or that a law's disproportionate impact is irrelevant in cases involving Constitution-based claims of racial discrimination.

And that:

> ... an invidious discriminatory intent may often be inferred from the totality of the relevant facts, including the fact, if it is true, that the law bears more heavily on one race than another. Nevertheless, we have not held that laws, neutral on its face and serving ends otherwise within the power of government pursue, are invalid under the Equal Protection Clause simply because it may affect a greater proportion of one race than of another. Disproportionate impact is not irrelevant, but is not the sole touchstone of an invidious racial discriminator forbidden by the Constitution. (96 SCt 2040, 1976)

In Village of Arlington Heights v Metropolitan Housing Development Corporation, 97 SCt 555 (1977), the US Supreme Court took the Davis case one step further in identifying specific factors to be present when a disproportionate impact has been identified in determining discriminatory intent. In this case, the US Supreme Court emphasized several factors that must be evident in deciding 'discriminatory intent' when a disproportionate impact has been identified. These factors are as follows:

1. the impact of the official action;
2. the historical background of the decision;
3. the specific sequence of events leading up to the challenged decision;
4. departure from the normal procedural sequence;
5. substantive departures;

6. legislative or administrative history.

In both the Davis and the Village of Arlington Heights cases, the burden of proof is on the plaintiff to demonstrate intentional discrimination or disproportionate impact that rises to the level of intentional discrimination.

In Guardians Association v Civil Service Commission of New York, 463 US 582 (1983), the justices were faced with this question of whether Title VI of the Civil Rights Act of 1964 reaches both intentional *and* disparate impact discrimination. There was not a majority by the justices on the answer and opinions on the interpretation of Title VI varied widely. However, the justices did proscribe a two-prong holding on discrimination under Title VI. First, Title VI itself (the statute) reaches only situations of 'intentional discrimination'. And second, actions having a disproportionate impact on minorities could be addressed through agency regulations that implement the statute of Title VI.

In Alexander v Choate, 469 US 287 (1985), the court again upheld an 'effects'-based regulation, finding that agencies were delegated:

> ... the complex determination of what sorts of disparate impacts upon minorities constituted sufficiently significant social problems, and were readily enough remedial, to warrant altering the practices of the federal grantees that had produced those impacts. (469 SCt 287, 1985)

Land-use cases

The following three land-use cases are also often considered to be at the core of the environmental justice movement:

1. East Bibb Twiggs Neighborhood Association v Macon-Bibb County Planning and Zoning Commission, 706 F. Supp. 880 (M.D. GA, 1989)
2. Margaret BEAN v Southwestern Waste Management Corporation, 482 F. Supp. 673 (S.D. Texas, 1979)
3. R.I.S.E., Inc. v Robert A. Kay, Jr., 768 F. Supp. 1141 (E.D. VA, 1991)

All required the burden of proof for the plaintiff and held in favor of the defendants based on the six factors used in the US Supreme Court case Village of Arlington Heights v Metropolitan Housing Development Corporation (see earlier in this chapter). In each of these cases, although the plaintiffs showed a disproportionate impact, discriminatory intention was not established by the factors. Case law has rallied around the term 'disparate impact' (discrimination) ever since, in order to further evolve case law and subsequently policy at the local, state and federal level surrounding the movement of environmental justice.

Transportation cases

Two transportation cases – Ralph W. Keith v Volpe, 858 F2d 467 (9th Cir. 1988) and Coalition of Concerned Citizens Against I-670 v Damian, 608 F. Supp. 110 (S.D. Ohio, 1984) – surrounded the disproportionate impact of low income and minority communities because of the proposed construction of transportation facilities. In the Ralph case, charges were brought under Title VIII of the Civil Rights Act of 1968 (The Fair Housing Act) and it was the one case where the ruling was in favor of the plaintiff.

In this case, the court pointed out that, under the Fair Housing Act, the circuits that have addressed the issue have agreed that the phrase 'because of race' does not require proof of discriminatory intent; rather, proof of discriminatory effect may be sufficient to demonstrate a violation of Title VIII (858 F2d 467, 9th Cir., 1988).

In the case of Coalition of Concerned Citizens, the court was quick to point out that the defendants are not prohibited from locating a highway where disproportionate impacts upon minorities will occur; Title VI only prohibits officials taking actions with disproportionate impacts without adequate justification.

Most recent US Supreme Court cases

Although Section 601 of the Civil Rights Act of 1964 prohibits discrimination on the basis of race, color or national origin with federally funded programs, Section 602 of the Act authorizes federal agencies to *issue* regulations to effectuate the requirements. In the case of Alexander v Sandoval, 121 SCt 1511 (2001), Spanish-speaking residents of the State of Alabama challenged the Alabama Department of Public Safety, claiming the state department's offer of the drivers' license exams only in English had a discriminatory effect, based on their national origin. However, the court ruled five to four that there is *no private right of action* (an individual's right to go to court to enforce a federal statute – applying to all public and private recipient of Federal funds) to enforce the disparate impact regulations under Title VI.

In essence, the Sandoval decision accepted the *validity* of discriminatory effects but set a precedent to stop private individuals from bringing suits under Title VI's regulatory *disparate impact* standard (Section 602). Private individuals can still bring suit under Title VI for *intentional discrimination* and this can still be shown by or inferred from the *totality of the facts* (that is, documented history of past discriminatory acts, legislative or administrative history to include statements by the decision makers, continued discriminatory effects over time, events leading up to the challenged decision, and other relevant facts). When considering the impact of this ruling, it is important to note that, in all the environmental justice cases cited above, the *totality of the facts*, although showing in many cases discriminatory impacts and effects, did not rise to the level that discriminatory *intent* was shown in the eyes of the law.

The precedent was reinforced in the case of South Camden Citizens in Action v New Jersey Department of Environmental Protection, 274 F3d 771 (3rd Cir., 2001), held subsequent to Sandoval, an African American and Hispanic community in Camden, New Jersey, did not want a cement plant located in their community because of negative cumulative environmental effects (air pollution) over the years and expected to continue. The city of Camden is one of the poorest cities in the county and is home to hundreds of contaminated sites. Their drinking water has been contaminated for years. Since the Sandoval case above had been ruled on, the judge in the Camden case invoked 42 USC Section 1983 (a federal law enacted after the Civil War to prevent states from revoking the federal rights of freed slaves) as adequate legal justification for their suit.

On 17 December 2001, the 3rd Circuit Court of Appeals ruled that 42 USC 1983 cannot be used to enforce a federal regulation unless the interest already is implicit in the statute authorizing the regulation. The 3rd Circuit reached its conclusion because the statutory authority for the Environmental Protection Agency (EPA) regulation in this case was Title VI, the same governing statutory authority for the regulation in Sandoval. Therefore, the 3rd Circuit followed the Sandoval case in deciding Title VI's prohibition on intentional discrimination would not support a private right to sue to enforce a discriminatory effect. A rehearing by the Court of Appeals was denied and the US Supreme Court refused to hear the case.

Section 1983 of 42 USC specifically states:

> Every person who, under color of any statute, ordinance, regulation, custom, or usage, of any State or Territory or the District of Columbia, subjects, or causes to be subject, any citizen of the US or other person within the jurisdiction thereof to the deprivation of any rights, privileges, or immunities secured by the Constitution and laws, shall be liable to the party injured in an action at law, suit in equity, or other proper proceeding for redress.... (42 USC, 1983)

Some believe that the use of 42 USC 1983 claims can get around the Supreme Court's ruling in Sandoval where there is no longer a private right of disparate impact suits under Title VI. Others feel that in order to seek redress through Section 1983, a plaintiff must show a violation of a federal right, not merely a violation of a federal law. The Circuit Court's view of the applicability and use of Section 1983 will be interesting to watch over the next several years in light of Camden. Federal agencies are, however, still required to enforce Title VI, both intentional discrimination (Section 601) and disparate impact discrimination (Section 602).

Conclusion

Environmental injustice is a longstanding problem in the US. The question to be asked is whether, in recognizing this, through both formal legislation and the purchasing and provision of transportation services and resources, we have been able to make any progress in resolving its impacts on low-income and other disadvantaged groups. The evidence of this chapter suggests that, in many ways, we have. The government and practitioners have perfected the NEPA process as it relates to transportation over the past several decades and we have made great strides in incorporating environmental justice into the NEPA and other planning processes over the past 10 years. The recently announced Executive Order for Human Service Transportation Coordination suggests that the issue is set to remain on the US political agenda, at least in the immediate term, although there is a strong emphasis on delivering improvements to current programs within the existing resources.

The legal case history described above has certainly played an important role in challenging discrimination in general in the US since the passage of the Civil Rights Act in 1964. In the early years, this did not have a large impact on the transportation industry as far as 'losers' and 'winners' are concerned. However, a stronger movement of legal cases with an impact (direct and indirect) on the transportation industry has emerged since the signing of Executive Order 12898 in 1994, with some success. (Further evidence of what legal success has meant in real terms is discussed further by the Metropolitan Transportation Authority case study presented in Chapter Twelve of this volume.) It is difficult to say if this movement will continue to be successful with the rulings heard with Sandoval and Camden, but strength of feeling and commitment among communities themselves and the activists and lawyers that represent them suggests that grassroots initiatives will continue to try and break down these barriers in the courts of law if they are allowed.

Evidently, there is no one solution to the transportation problems underserved populations face in relation to transportation. It requires a multi-faceted approach and relies heavily on the government's ability to manage many smaller systems of targeted delivery within the overall large transportation system we already have in place in the US. Perfecting and expanding these smaller systems (that is, WtoW, transit costs, use of public transportation and so on) to improve the overall transportation system will be the key.

The case study chapters that follow demonstrate how innovative transportation and non-transportation policy initiatives have been developed in the US over the last 10 years to help contribute to a more socially inclusive transportation system. Chapter Fourteen draws together some of the key messages from the US experience, to inform the final chapter on lessons learnt (Chapter Fifteen).

References

96 SCt 2040 (1976) Washington v Davis.

97 SCt 555 (1977) Village of Arlington Heights v Metropolitan Housing Development Corporation.

121 SCt 1511 (2001) Aleaxander v Sandoval.

274 F3d 771 (3rd Circuit, 2001) South Camden Citizens in Action v New Jersey Department of Environmental Protection.

463 US 582 (1983) Guardians Association v Civil Service Commission, NYC.

469 US 287 (1985) Alexander v Choate.

482 F Supp 673 (SD Texas, 1979) Margaret BEAN v Southwestern Waste Management Corporation.

608 F Supp 110 (SD Ohio, 1984) Coalition of Concerned Citizens Against I-670 v Damian.

706 F Supp 880 (MD GA, 1989) East Bibb Twiggs Neighborhood Association v Macon-Bibb County Planning and Zoning Commission.

768 F Supp 1141 (ED VA, 1991) RISE, Inc v Robert A. Kay, Jr.

858 F2d 467 (9th Circuit, 1988) Ralph W. Keith v Volpe.

Cairns, S., Greig, J. and Wachs, M. (2003) *Environmental justice and transportation: A citizen's handbook*, Berkeley, CA: Institute of Transportation Studies.

Executive Order 12898 (1994) *Federal actions to address environmental justice in minority populations and low-income populations*, Washington, DC: The White House.

FHWA/FTA (Federal Highway Administration/Federal Transit Administration) (1994) *Interim policy on public involvement and questions and answers on public involvement in transportation decision-making*, Washington, DC: FHWA/FTA.

FHWA (1998) *FHWA final order on environmental justice: FHWA actions to address environmental justice in minority populations and low-income populations*, Washington, DC: FHWA.

FTA (2000) *Use of TANF, WtoW, and job access funds for transportation*, memo, 1 June.

Office of the Press Secretary (2004) *Executive order human service transportation coordination 2004*, Press Release 24 February, Washington, DC: The White House.

Senate and House of Representatives of the US of America in Congress assembled (1964) *Civil Rights Act of 1964*, Title VI, § 601, Public Llaw (PL) 88-352.

Senate and House of Representatives of the US of America in Congress assembled (1969) *The National Environmental Policy Act of 1969*, PL 91-190, 42 USC 4321-4347, 1 January 1970; as amended by PL 94-52, 3 July 1975, PL 94-83, 9 August 1975.

Thoreau Institute (2003a) 'The falling cost of transportation', *Vanishing automobile update #4* (www.ti.org/index.html).

Thoreau Institute (2003b) 'The good news and the (mostly) bad news about transit', *Vanishing automobile update #4* (www.ti.org/index.html).

Title 23, US Code: *Highways*, chapter 1, subchapter 1, section 101.b, US Department of Transportation, Federal Highway Administration.

Title 23, US Code: *Highways*, Chapter 1, subchapter 1, section 102.2, US Department of Transportation, Federal Highway Administration.

Title 23, US Code: *Highways*, chapter 1, subchapter 1, section 109.h, US Department of Transportation, Federal Highway Administration.

Title 23, US Code: *Highways*, chapter 1, subchapter 1, section 1203.f.1, US Department of Transportation, Federal Highway Administration.

Title 23, Code of Federal Regulations: *Highways*, chapter 1, Federal Highway Administration, Department of Transportation, subchapter E: Planning and Research, part 450: Planning Assistance and Standards, subpart C: Metropolitan Transportation Planning and Programming, US Department of Transportation, Federal Highway Administration.

Title 42, US Code: *The public health and welfare*, chapter 21: 'Civil rights', subchapter 1, section 1983: 'Civil action for deprivation of rights'.

Title 49, Code of Federal Regulations: *Transportation*, subtitle A, Office of the Secretary of Transportation, part 21: 'Non discrimination in federally-assisted programs of the Department of Transportation: effectuation of Title VI of the Civil Rights Act of 1964', US Department of Transportation, Federal Highway Administration.

US Census Bureau (2000) *Census*.

US DOT (Department of Transportation) (1997) *DOT final order on environmental justice: DOT actions to address environmental justice in minority populations and low-income populations*, Washington, DC: DOT.

TEN

Job isolation in the US: narrowing the gap through job access and reverse-commute programs

Robert Cervero

Introduction

A significant and troublesome form of environmental injustice in the US is the physical isolation of the inner-city poor to rising suburban job opportunities. Unlike many parts of the developed and developing world, the poor and 'have nots' are principally concentrated in and near the urban centers of many US metropolitan areas, occupying working-class neighborhoods long abandoned by the middle class for 'greener pastures' (accelerated by the US's massive freeway building programs of the post-Second World War period). The concentration of jobless individuals in the center and explosion of jobs on the fringe has given rise to 'reverse commutes', both in terms of actual work trips for those fortunate enough to have a job and latent demand for those who cannot find work, whether for reasons of poor mobility options or structural employment problems.

In the US, reverse commutes have increased steadily over the past two decades and continue to capture a growing share of the total journey-to-work 'travel pie'. In 1990, reverse commutes made up over 10% of metropolitan trips nationwide and preliminary data from the 2000 census suggest that this percentage has risen since then (Pisarksi, 1996). Reverse commute has been especially pronounced in large, heavily urbanized states like California. Between 1980 and 1990, Southern California recorded the second-largest relative increase in share of reverse commuting nationwide (Rossetti and Eversole, 1993).

The location-liberating effects of cyberspace and telematics, along with rising affluence, have conspired to create a new geomorphology for economic production across the US; sprawling corporate enclaves, business parks, power centers, and other 'non-nodal' forms of development. Today, all US metropolitan areas (with the exception of New York and Chicago) have the majority of office space outside of traditional city centers. While 38% of all office space in US metropolitan areas was located in primary downtowns in 1999, nearly the same amount (37%) was found in highly dispersed clusters with less than five million square feet of space (Lang, 2003). Decentralisation of office-sector work, along with residences, has further prompted more and more retail and service jobs to shift to the suburbs, the kind of jobs that low-skilled individuals most often secure. It has been the rapid suburbanization of employment that has isolated increasing numbers of inner-city residents from outlying job sites. The problem has been made worse by the poor quality of public transport services from the central city to the suburbs. Many inner-city residents with suburban jobs work late-hour shifts and weekends, periods when many buses and trains do not operate. In addition, because large numbers of low-skilled inner-city residents have part-time jobs, contingency employment and irregular, odd-hour work schedules, matching services with demand can be an immense challenge.

Reverse commute public transport services have over the years been viewed as important means of enhancing the mobility and job prospects for inner-city residents. Yet, relatively little empirical research has been carried out that examines the reverse-commute marketplace.

Reverse commuting in the US

Reverse-commuting programs first arose as a policy concern in the wake of urban riots in the late 1960s. The McCone Commission, formed to advise the Johnson Administration on the cause of race riots, identified inadequate public transportation as one of several contributors to high unemployment rates among central-city black people (Cervero et al, 2003). Various reverse-commute demonstration bus services were introduced in the late 1960s and early 1970s; however, because of disappointing ridership results, policy support for specialized transit runs waned.

The 1980s were marked by a period of transit subsidy cuts and campaigns to privatize services. By the early 1990s, interest in reverse commuting regained momentum, in part due to expanding welfare rolls, continuing inner-city unrest, and worsening suburban traffic congestion. Heightened interest was also spawned by public policy directives that sought to introduce work incentives and set limits on welfare dependence, notably the federal government's setting of a five-year lifetime limit on cash assistance. 'Workfare' programs, like the federal government's Personal Responsibility and Work Opportunity Reconciliation Act of 1996 (PRWORA) and California's CalWORKs (California Work Opportunity and Responsibilities to Kids), fully embraced the notion that access to suburban jobs, and in particular improved public transportation services, are crucial toward reducing inner-city joblessness. Federal programs like Access to Jobs under the 1998 Transportation Equity Act (TEA-21) and multi-agency Bridges to Work provided tens of millions of dollars for expanding transit connections between inner-city areas and suburban jobs.

The national context

The post-Second World War period saw rapid population growth in US suburbs. While the US population grew by 56.1% from 1950 to 1990, central cities grew by 49.9% and suburbs by over 200% (Rosenbloom, 1992). During the 1990s, 83.7% of total population growth in the US's 50 largest metropolitan areas took place outside of central cities (US DOT Statistics, 1998). Today, suburban residents outnumber city dwellers. Suburbanization has been far from uniform – minorities and low-income individuals have migrated to the suburbs at a far slower rate than white people (as reflected among 12 large US metropolitan areas, wherein the percentages of urban residents who are African Americans is two to four times as high as in the suburbs).

Although minorities predominantly reside in cities, as noted earlier in this chapter, the fastest rates of job growth have been in the suburbs. The spatial gap between where many low-income Americans live (inner city) and where more and more jobs are being created (the suburbs) has been labeled spatial mismatch. Today, more than half of households receiving financial assistance live in central cities (Taylor and Ong, 1993).

Not all analysts agree that spatial mismatch is a root cause of inner-city unemployment, however. Taylor and Ong found that average commute times of minority residents in 10 large US cities did not increase between 1977 and 1985, either in absolute terms or relative to white people (Blumenberg and Ong, 1997). Instances of longer commute times by minorities were explained by their greater reliance on public transit; discrepancies between minority and white commute-times were thus mainly due to modal speeds, not distance of trips. For Los Angeles County, Blumenberg and Ong (1997) found that average commute times for former Aid for Families with Dependent Children (AFDC) recipients were about half those of the general employed population in that city, casting doubt, in their view, over the saliency of the spatial mismatch hypothesis in California's largest urban setting (Orski, 1998).

Several studies have attempted to gauge the prevalence of reverse commuting nationally. A study by Pisarski (1996) found reverse commute trips increased nationally from 9% in 1980 to 12% in 1990. The largest increases occurred in Milwaukee (2.8%) and Los Angeles (2.5%). In 1990, 3.1% of Southern California's journeys to work were from central to suburban counties – that is, from Los Angeles County to Orange, San Bernardino, Riverside, or Ventura Counties.

Impacts of the reverse-commuting phenomenon

Past studies on reverse commuting have generally focused on defining the scope of the problem as opposed to rigorously evaluating impacts. On the surface, transit service gaps appear to be huge. One estimate places the share of suburban entry-level jobs in the US that are not on public transit routes at 40% (Bania et al, 1999). A study of Cleveland, Ohio welfare recipients living in disadvantaged neighborhoods found a 40-minute commute by transit would bring only 8 to 15% of metropolitan jobs within reach, increasing to only 44% if the commute time was doubled to 80 minutes (Coughlin, 1998). Studies in Atlanta and Boston similarly found existing public transit services were not up to the task of connecting most inner-city residents to job opportunities within a reasonable travel time (Crain, 1970; Lacombe, 1998; Rich, 1999).

Results of specialized bus services targeted at poor inner-city areas underscore the limitations of transit in bridging the welfare-to-work (WtoW) gap. A series of federal and state reverse-commute experiments (mainly special bus runs between minority neighborhoods and the suburbs) that were mounted in the late 1960s and early 1970s to help abate poverty met with minimal success. An evaluation of these programs concluded that the number of developable reverse-commute routes was limited, large shares of users were not from the ranks of targeted inner-city residents, institutional constraints hampered performance and attrition rates were high. In most cases, ridership levels declined steadily with time as workers withdrew from the labor force or purchased cars and began solo commuting. One study of reverse-commute services targeted at residents of Los Angeles' Watts community found little evidence that they got people jobs or even better jobs (Crain, 1970).

A number of specialized services involving private entrepreneurs, such as door-to-door van connections, that were initiated in the 1980s met a similar fate. In 1985, the Urban Mass Transportation Administration (UMTA) sought to revive reverse-commute demonstrations, awarding 53 projects across 40 US cities to promote competitive transit services that linked the inner-city poor to suburban work sites (Rosenbloom, 1992). The most successful experience was Route 201 serving the Philadelphia area, wherein daily ridership was twice that predicted. Also, Route 201 covered operating costs through fare-box receipts. There was no evidence, however, that the route helped to reduce inner-city unemployment. Other reverse-commute services introduced by South Eastern Pennsylvania Transportation Authority that operated in conjunction with light-rail transit services were less successful due to declining ridership, resulting in the reduction and even the elimination of services (American Public Transit Association, 1999). One evaluation of UMTA's experiments found private carriers performed best at linking new job seekers to employment opportunities whereas public transit operators were most successful at serving those already employed. The study concluded that there were few opportunities for free-market provision of profitable reverse-commute services (Rosenbloom, 1992).

Notwithstanding these and other failed reverse-commute experiments, there have nonetheless been some notable successes. For example, in the early 1980s, the Metropolitan Suburban Bus Authority in the New York City area noticed feeder bus services from Nassau County to the subways connecting to Queens were filling up in the reverse direction. By 1988, the number of reverse commuters outnumbered inbound commuters (Rosenbloom, 1992).

Similarly, demand in the reverse-commute direction for Route 150 in San

Diego was so great that within two years of service initiation, extra-long articulated buses were introduced in the reverse direction. Most reverse-commute programs have been conscientiously designed, with public entities introducing new reverse-direction services in hopes of triggering ridership increases. For instance, in the mid-1990s, Yuba-Sutter Transit in California extended their Americans with the 1990 Disabilities Act (ADA) paratransit services into the late evenings and permitted the general public to use the service during this period, which provided much-valued access to many late-night entry-level jobs in the suburbs.

The success or failure of a reverse-commute service depends largely on project objectives and those who initiated it. For transit agencies, the primary aim is to increase ridership at reasonable fare-box recovery levels. From a broader public-policy perspective, the aim is not so much to fill buses as to move the unemployed off welfare rolls and into gainful employment. Accordingly, recent research has focused on employment outcomes rather than transit ridership levels. Studies have attached varying degrees of importance to public transit in successfully spurring inner-city employment (Blumenberg and Ong, 1998; Sanchez, 1999; Cervero et al, 2002). A recent panel study of Alameda County residents receiving AFDC in the early 1990s found transit accessibility was positively associated with successful WtoW transitions; however, owning and having access to a car was even more important (Cervero, et al, 2002).

While many low-skilled central-city residents face serious mobility challenges, the unmet mobility needs of others, for example semi-skilled, working-class individuals as well as the middle class, who regularly make reverse commutes should not be overlooked. While most car-owning residents with suburban jobs drive to work, transit could potentially fulfill the mobility needs of 'choice commuters' as well, helping to relieve traffic congestion and reduce tailpipe emissions. Importantly, attracting more middle-income riders to transit could form a critical mass of users that allow the kinds of services that meet the mobility needs of the inner-city poor to be sustained. To date, little research has been conducted on the reverse-commute needs of the broader traveling public.

The reverse-commute marketplace

In California's four largest metropolitan areas – greater Los Angeles, the San Francisco Bay Area, San Diego County, and metropolitan Sacramento – reverse commutes constituted only 7-11% of all journeys to work in the 1990s. Some reverse-commute trips are no doubt suppressed because poor or non-existent public transit connections prevent needy inner-city residents from securing suburban jobs in the first place. With the exception of the Bay Area, 19 out of 20 reverse-commute trips are estimated to be by private car. In fact, more reverse commutes in California are by carpools than mass transit. For low-income reverse commuters, public transport plays a much larger role, handling more than 10% of journeys to work in the case of San Diego County (Figure 10.1).

Empirical data revealed that two thirds or more of reverse commuters in large

Figure 10.1: Percentage of reverse commuters who patronize public transport: low versus non-low-income households across four Californian metropolitan areas

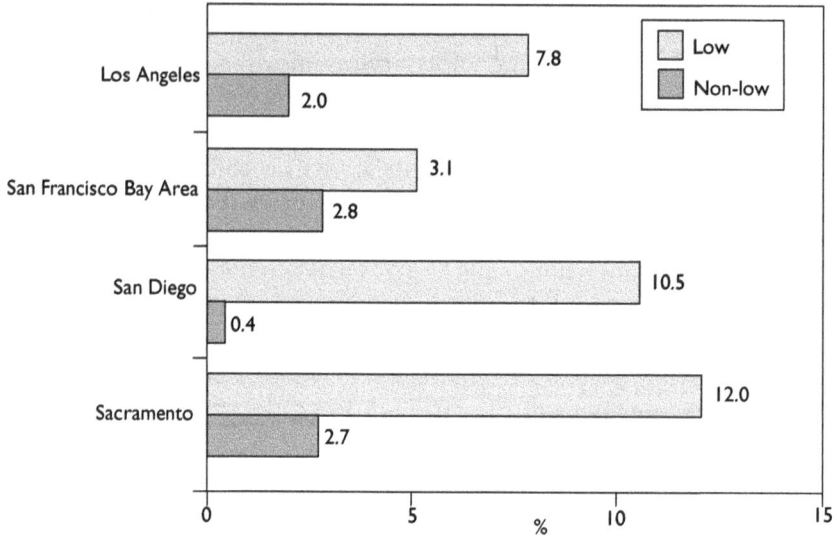

metropolitan areas occur during peak hours. Based on interviews of unemployed CalWORKs clients, there appears to be a sizable pent-up latent demand for off-peak travel. Limited public transport services during non-traditional work periods suppress this demand. Also, most reverse commutes are made in less than 30 minutes, generally less time than that spent making traditional radial (that is, suburb-to-downtown) commutes but more time than that devoted to most intra-urban and intra-suburban commutes.

Geographically, reverse commutes in California's big metropolitan areas are highly spread out. The diffusion of trip origins and destinations render fixed-route transit services impractical for many reverse commuters.

Reverse-commute profiles

Around one out of five reverse commuters in California's large metropolitan areas are from low-income households. Many are minorities, in particular Hispanic women. More than one out of five low-income reverse commuters are from households with one or no cars. Almost all of these individuals are transit dependent. From an estimated mode-choice model, the odds of a low-income reverse commuter taking transit was found to be five times greater than that of a middle-income person traveling in the opposite-flow direction. Appreciable numbers of California's reverse commuters match the stereotype often portrayed – many are low-income, car-less, minority workers who have no choice but to take transit to reach outlying job sites.

The hardships many of California's low-income reverse commuters face in using transit are underscored by comparing travel times and costs with those of private cars. For documented reverse-commute trips made by low-income workers in three of the large metropolitan areas, peak period travel times by bus were three to four times longer than those by private cars. While taking transit saves money, this benefit is often overshadowed by the quantum increases in travel times faced in trying to get from the inner city to suburban job sites via conventional bus transit.

Job-access and reverse-commute initiatives

In an effort to respond to California's reverse-commute and job-access needs, numerous initiatives have been taken around the state in recent years. Some have been prompted by the availability of federal grants like the Job Access and Reverse Commute (JARC) program administered by the Federal Transit Administration (FTA). In California, county social service agencies and local transit operators have received most JARC grants, in cooperation with state and regional agencies. Other funding sources, including grants from private foundations and the WtoW program (under the federal PRWORA of 1996), have also jump-started mobility initiatives aimed at transportation-disadvantaged individuals.

The state's CalWORKs regulation has furthered spawned job access and reverse-commute initiatives among county social services and welfare agencies. California Work Opportunity and Responsibilities to Kids requires all county welfare departments to provide supportive services, including transportation, that are necessary for a welfare recipient to obtain and retain employment or to participate in other WtoW activities (like job searches and job training). Public transport agencies have also had a presence through the introduction of reverse-commute bus services targeted at the inner-city poor.

As of 2002, 36 transportation programs aimed at serving the job-access and reverse-commute needs of CalWORKs clients had been introduced in California. Transit agencies and county welfare departments launched the vast majority of these programs. In most instances, these initiatives were products of sustained and collaborative efforts among multiple organizations.

To date, the lion's share of CalWORKs transportation programs have focused on modifying traditional fixed-route bus services, either by adding new routes or extending the hours of operations of existing ones (Figure 10.2). Nearly one out of four job-access and reverse-commute initiatives have involved some form of assistance targeted at individual beneficiaries, like child-transportation services, guaranteed-ride home allowances, or the initiation of carpool-vanpool services. Other improvements introduced throughout the state include the initiation of shuttle connections to job centers, low-interest loan assistance for purchasing or upgrading cars, and the extension of bus routes farther out to connect job centers and community college campuses.

The case studies reviewed below highlight 'best practice' experiences and

Figure 10.2: Relative frequency of job access and reverse commute in California (2002)

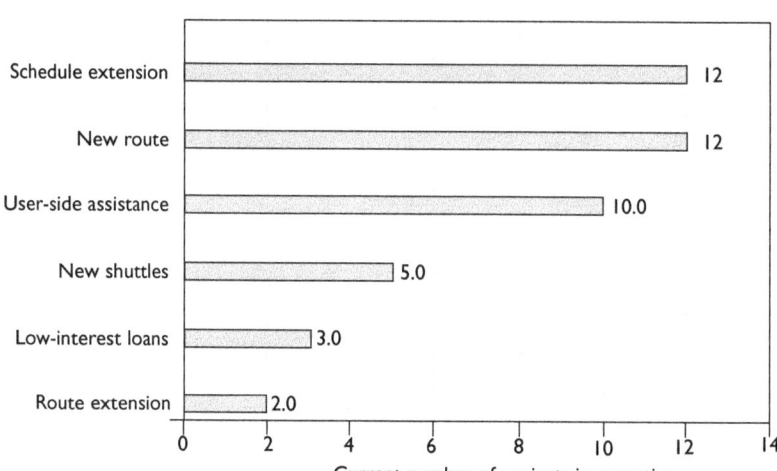

provided insight into impacts and outcomes. It is difficult to pass judgment on the many job-access and reverse-commute initiatives to date, however, because systematic evaluation has never been a high priority. What little evaluation exists has generally been in the form of qualitative information (for example, interview commentary) and has been more of an afterthought than a product of careful ex-post/ex-ante assessments. Many of the state's CalWORKs programs are also still in their infancy, making impact assessment all the more difficult.

Transit-based strategies

The most common transit-based strategy introduced by California counties has been purchases of bus passes for CalWORKs clients. By itself, bus pass assistance is a passive strategy, for, while it deals with affordability concerns, it fails to modify how transit services are delivered in ways that might enhance job access. With the support of federal and state grant awards, however, a number of transit service modifications have been introduced in California in recent years. In larger areas like San Diego and Los Angeles counties, brand new reverse-commute services targeted at inner-city, low-income communities have been mounted. In other areas, like Alameda County, the focus has been on extending the hours of bus operations. Some areas have opted to introduce door-to-door van services. So far, the near-term costs of these initiatives have been high. In most cases where door-to-door van services or late-night 'graveyard shift' operations have been introduced, costs have exceeded $10 per trip and in a few cases more than double this amount. Such figures begin to match what it would cost to hire private taxicabs to directly serve individual clients.

Small and rural counties have struggled the most to introduce consumer-responsive, fixed-route transit services. Often, densities are too low and travel distances are too far to operate cost-effective bus services. The most successful programs to date in small and rural settings have involved active employer support and co-sponsorship. Of particular note have been several successful reverse-commute bus shuttles that serve gaming casinos at California Indian Reservations (see Figure 10.3).

Besides employer involvement, these shuttle services been successful because of:

- high employment densities (that is, concentrated work sites);
- limited numbers of work shifts that allow effective co-scheduling of bus runs;
- high-speed, limited-stop services that make transit time-competitive with the private car;
- aggressive marketing by operators and employers.

In the case of Yolo County's casino shuttle run, ridership jumped 333% the first year of service. On-board surveys reveal most customers are very satisfied with the quality and price of service. Given that many were unemployed a year or so earlier, this employer-supported long-haul bus route is a bona fide reverse-commute success story.

Figure 10.3: Clean natural gas bus picking up employees at front door of Cache Creek Casino in Yolo County, California

Note: This special reverse-commute service is partly supported by the casino owner to ensure low-skilled custodial workers have convenient and reliable access to outlying employment centers.

While it is difficult to generalize given the state's limited experiences with transit service innovations to date, some inferences regarding specific transit services strategies can be drawn:

New targeted bus routes

There have been a few successes to date, with brand new reverse-commute bus routes introduced in California. Most notable has been a long-distance, limited-stop service – Route 422 – which connects several low-income, inner-city neighborhoods in the city of Los Angeles with suburban jobs in the San Fernando Valley. To date, Route 422 has been a productive, well-performing express bus service, covering relatively high shares of costs through fare receipts, experiencing steady ridership gains, and serving needy, transit-dependent populations. Customers, many of whom are Latino women from low-income households and who have no access to cars, are very satisfied with the service and most expect to continue patronizing in coming years. Many users have to make transfers to and from Route 422, however, meaning the service functions mainly as a mainline trunk route and suggesting that complementary feeder-distributor connections would be much-valued enhancements.

In San Diego County, three new reverse-commute bus routes have been introduced in recent years, with each enjoying steady ridership growth. Still, the costs per rider of these targeted services exceed those of all other fixed-route bus runs in the system, although compared to dial-a-ride vans and exclusive-ride taxis, they cost between 60% and 85% less per trip. While on-board surveys revealed passengers greatly value these new bus services, a common complaint was the absence of late-night and weekend services.

Schedule extensions

In several San Diego and Alameda counties, many CalWORKs clients and their caseworkers consider the absence of late-night and weekend bus services to be the most serious obstacle to job access. To date, most WtoW transit services have focused on introducing new routes or lengthening existing ones as opposed to extending service hours. A universal problem with running late-night transit is the high cost relative to patronage levels. Double-digit costs per passenger are not uncommon. Owl services and late-night bus runs in Alameda County have provided much-valued access to jobs at major employment hubs, like the Oakland International Airport and the Port of Oakland. However, some runs incur costs as high as $24 per trip. Such outlays are unsustainable and a clear sign that localities should enter into contractual arrangements with local taxicab companies to provide late-night services, ideally in the form of shared-ride taxis funded through user vouchers.

A limitation of these transit case studies is that they overlook unmet needs or 'latent demand'. Surveys of CalWORKs clients in Yolo and San Diego Counties suggested a considerable pent-up demand for transit and job-access services tailored to individual mobility needs. In the case of San Diego County, many jobless CalWORKs clients expressed a need for new routes and extended schedules to assist with job searching, making interview appointments, and eventually commuting to work. Since most clients live and work in fairly urbanized settings, respondents from San Diego County were most interested in seeing traditional bus services expanded. In more sparsely populated Yolo County, the majority of unemployed CalWORKs recipients wanted help with purchasing and maintaining private cars. If they get jobs and make commutes, many of Yolo County's survey respondents indicated they would be making chained, multi-legged trips to drop off and pick-up kids and attend job training.

Joblessness and complex travel patterns reinforce each other in places like Yolo County. Many of the county's jobless clients are women with children, and low-paying jobs make childcare too expensive. If they were to work, many would have to invest several hours a day aboard buses between home, day care, and work, a scenario that prompts quite a few to stay unemployed. Many single parents living in semi-rural and non-urbanized settings strongly feel that car ownership provides the only realistic alternative for getting off welfare and into full-time employment.

Car access and automobility

The working poor often need access to cars for the same reasons the non-poor do: public transit is unable to adequately serve multi-legged trips or late-night work schedules. In remote locations and even semi-rural settings like Yolo County, private cars can be the only viable means of mobility.

Statistical evidence from Alameda, Los Angeles, San Joaquin, and San Bernardino Counties shows that owning cars is more strongly associated with WtoW transitions than any transportation variable. Experiences in San Mateo County demonstrated that car ownership reduces the amount of work time missed and increases job-training participation among CalWORKs clients. Surveys conducted of transit passengers as well as CalWORKs clients revealed a strong preference for car ownership among those living in rural and remote areas as well as among those making chained trips, such as between home, childcare, and work.

Car-based strategies have not been without controversy. Buying, insuring, maintaining and operating a car can be beyond the means of many low-income households. Many donated cars are gross-polluters and are only a year or so away from expensive repair bills. Since vehicles owned by CalWORKs recipients are often aged and undependable, some have argued that interim transportation, like paratransit, should be made available until participants make enough money to purchase and maintain reliable cars. Another remedy might be to relax the $4,650 ceiling on the value of cars that CalWORKs participants are allowed to own. Tax credits for donating cars in good running order, such as introduced in several other states, might also be considered.

Car-based strategies should not be viewed as substitutes or replacements for transit. They can enrich the palette of mobility options available to the poor. For example, car ownership has been known to spawn informal jitney services in inner-city areas, providing shared-ride, door-to-door connections to job sites and retail centers at affordable yet market-clearing prices. In rural and remote settings, car-based strategies can also relieve financially strapped counties of high-cost transit services.

Paratransit

So far, there have been few instances in which shared-ride taxis, flexible-route jitneys, and other forms of small-vehicle, door-to-door paratransit services have been mounted to serve CalWORKs clients or reverse commuters. Of course, ADA paratransit services thrive in many parts of the state; however, these are limited mainly to older people and physically disabled people, groups to which most CalWORKs recipients do not belong. To date, the focus of WtoW transportation has been on traditional fixed-route bus services. The absence of paratransit is in part due to local ordinances that ban shared-ride taxis, jitney services, and other more personalized forms of mass transportation.

Several California counties have made headway in designing and implementing door-to-door paratransit services. Butte and Santa Cruz Counties have purchased vehicles and trained CalWORKs clients to drive shuttles as work experience or on-the-job-training. Contra Costa County uses vans to carry children of CalWORKs recipients to and from school and day-care centers each workday.

Providing a menu of mobility options

Two areas in California that have gone the farthest in crafting menus of transportation options for meeting the mobility needs of welfare clients are Santa Cruz and Contra Costa Country. In both instances, professionally trained social workers meet with clients to select the right mix of transportation services that best meet personal travel needs. While a buffet of options adds costs, the ability to custom-tailor transportation services to meet the individual mobility needs of each client is a huge benefit.

Santa Cruz's client-based approach toward job-access planning has given rise to a rich mix of mobility options, including door-to-door van services, emergency ride home provisions, carpool incentives, low-interest loans for car purchases, and work-related emergency payments. The county's van service 'kills two birds with one stone', since CalWORKs recipients not only ride but also drive vans, enabling a number of previously unemployed individuals to find permanent jobs in the transportation business.

As previously mentioned, Contra Costa County's client-based approach resulted in the introduction of a door-to-door shuttle service that takes children of CalWORKs adults who have recently found jobs to and from day-care centers and schools. The service is oversubscribed, suggesting there is a large pent-up demand for children's transportation in other parts of the state. As in Santa Cruz County, Contra Costa County also offers door-to-door van services to adults, ridesharing incentives, and various bus-route expansions. Through a partnership of transit operators, the regional planning agency, and several large employers, the county's Employment and Human Services Department saw to it that traditional bus services were better aligned to meet the mobility needs of low-income residents.

Implementation and coordination

Experiences clearly show that successful job-access and reverse-commute programs depend on successful collaborations. The many stakeholders – county welfare departments, transit service providers, regional planning entities, faith-based and charitable organizations, among others – must build partnerships that coordinate efforts in ways that deliver suitable and cost-effective transportation services to clients. Partnerships can increase productivity by tapping into scale economies. Teaming multiple service providers across multiple human-service agencies, for example, can create opportunities for centralized driver training, vehicle maintenance and inspection, vehicle scheduling, and insurance coverage.

Collaborations are sometimes easier said than done, however. Disagreements and 'turf problems' between California's county welfare offices and local transit agencies have thwarted progress in some instances. In small and rural counties, a lack of institutional capacity and staff training to do short-term needs assessments and long-range transportation planning have also been impediments. Additionally, funding programs can pose barriers. While many one-year grant sources are available, the absence of sustained multi-year funding discourages many localities from pursuing ambitious job-access strategies. Restrictions also prevent a van purchased to provide mobility for older people from being used to transport a CalWORKs client to a job interview.

Institutional problems also create contradictions that make it difficult to rationalize job-access programs. Surveys of low-income and jobless CalWORKs participants in California underscored the need to keep transit fares affordable. One way to do this is to competitively contract out services so as to lower operating costs. Most private vendors hire non-unionized, low-wage drivers to keep costs down. However, this can also end up lowering service quality. Experiences show that contracted services can compromise reliability and on-time performance. Sometimes contracted buses do not show up or are well behind schedule. Reliability is of utmost importance to many CalWORKs clients in that, if they arrive to work late more than once, they are usually let go, especially those who make a living serving customers in the restaurant, retail, and lodging industries. Additionally, efforts to introduce some door-to-door van services in the state have been stonewalled by organized labor out of fear that low-wage shuttle drivers will take away jobs from unionized workers or eventually depress salary levels. Enlarging partnerships to include union interests, private vendors, and others with a vested stake in job-access programs might avert such problems. Expanded partnerships can bring new people with fresh ideas and different perspectives to the table.

An action agenda

Although not everyone agrees how job-access and reverse-commute needs are best met, one finds virtual unanimity among local interests on one thing: more money is needed. Many of the state's transit providers and county welfare departments are financially stretched to the limit and thus incapable of mounting ambitious transportation programs targeted at the mobility needs of disadvantaged populations. More funding assistance, they contend, would allow them to be proactive rather than reactive. In truth, more money does not always translate into better transportation for needy individuals. The transportation field is littered with examples where provider-side subsidies and generous financial aid conferred few end-result benefits to consumers. On the other hand, aid that promotes and rewards efficiencies and goes to materially enhance services to intended beneficiaries – that is, transportation-disadvantaged California – can be money well invested.

It is important that funds meant to enhance job-access and reverse-commute services are earmarked. If provided in the form of general transportation block grants or transfer payments, few dollars will likely end up going to van services, late-night transit schedule extensions, car-access loan programs, or other initiatives that enhance job access. With today's backlog of unfunded highway projects and the struggles many transit agencies face in keeping existing bus routes running, job-access and reverse-commute programs would inevitably lose in the heated competition for scarce financial resources. In a competitive environment, transportation programs that reach a broad constituency invariably win out over ones that serve a small set of beneficiaries, especially those with little political clout.

In light of the state's unmet job-access needs and empirical evidence demonstrating that well-designed transportation services can stimulate WtoW transitions, California policy makers should seriously consider introducing a statewide version of the federal JARC program. Monies could go to supplement as well as provide local matches to federal JARC funding. Block-grant awards spanning at least three to five years should be provided. Longer-term funding guarantees would prompt county welfare departments and local transit agencies to pursue transportation programs that are more ambitious and creative than those introduced to date. State JARC grants should encourage localities to form the kinds of partnerships that increase the odds of job-access programs being custom-tailored to local needs.

To further encourage creative job-access and reverse-commute programs, a pilot demonstration program should also be considered. This program would fund well-conceived, cutting-edge initiatives, such as the combining of smart paratransit with user-side subsidies and local paratransit deregulation or the formation of community-based mobility enterprises that get inner-city neighborhoods into the business of designing, operating, managing, and maintaining job-access services. Set asides should also go for evaluation. Only through controlled experimental studies will it be possible to ferret out the value and roles of different transportation programs in inducing WtoW transitions. Ideally, evaluations should be based on outcome-based measures of performance (for example, job creation) as opposed to output-based measures (for example, transit service deployment).

Slow but steady headway is being made in California and other parts of the US in reducing job isolation and the journey-to-work mobility gaps as a form of social exclusion. Special job-access and reverse-commute programs, when well designed and targeted at specific mobility markets, have shown promise at reducing joblessness and helping the inner-city poor make the WtoW transition. While California has been a leader in this regard, other states can be expected to follow suit in coming years.

References

American Public Transit Association (1999) *Access-to-work best practices survey: Summary report*, Washington, DC (www.apta.com/govt/other/99wtwnet.htm).

Bania, N., Coulton, C. and Leete, L. (1999) 'Welfare reform and access to job opportunities in the Cleveland Metropolitan Area', Washington, DC, Paper presented at the Annual Fall Research Conference of the Association for Public Policy Analysis and Management, Washington, DC, November.

Blumenberg, E. and Ong, P. (1997) 'Can welfare recipients afford to work far from home?', *Access*, no 10, pp 15-19.

Blumenberg, E. and Ong, P. (1998) 'Job accessibility and welfare usage: evidence from Los Angeles', *Journal of Policy Analysis and Management*, vol 17, pp 639-65.

Cervero, R., Sandoval, O. and Landis, J (2002) 'Transportation as a stimulus to welfare-to-work: private versus public mobility', *Journal of Planning Education and Research*, vol 22, pp 50-63.

Cervero, R., Tsai, Y., Wachs, M., Deakin, E., Dibb, J., Kluter, A., Nuworsoo, C., Petrova, I. and Pohan, R. (2003) *Reverse commuting and job access in California: Markets, needs, and policy prospects*, Sacramento, CA: California Department of Transportation.

Coughlin, J. (1998) *Access to work and welfare reform: Demographics, jobs and transportation challenges*, Cambridge, MA: Volpe National Transportation Center.

Crain, J. (1970) *The reverse commute experiment: A $7 million demonstration program*, Washington, DC: Urban Mass Transportation Administration, US Department of Transportation.

Lacombe, A. (1998) *Welfare reform and access to jobs in Boston*, Washington, DC: Bureau of Transportation Statistics, US Department of Transportation, BTS98-A-02.

Lang, R. (2003) *Edgeless cities: Exploring the elusive metropolis*, Washington, DC: Brookings Institution Press.

Orski, K. (1998) *Welfare to Work, innovation briefs*, vol 2/3, pp 1-2.

Pisarski, A. (1996) *Commuting in America II: The second national report on commuting patterns and trends*, Washington, DC: Eno Transportation Foundation.

Rich, M. (1999) 'Access to opportunities: the Welfare to Work challenge in metropolitan Atlanta', Paper presented at the 1999 Annual Fall Research Conference of the Association for Public Policy Analysis and Management, Washington, DC, November.

Rosenbloom, S. (1992) *Reverse commute transportation: Emerging provider roles*, Washington, DC: Urban Mass Transportation Administration, US Department of Transportation.

Rossetti, M. and Eversole, B. (1993) *Journey to work trends in the United States and its major metropolitan areas, 1960-1990*, Washington, DC: US Department of Transportation, Federal Highway Administration.

Sanchez, T. (1999) 'The connection between public transit and employment: the cases of Portland and Atlanta', *Journal of the American Planning Association*, vol 65, pp 284-96.

Taylor, B. and Ong, P. (1993) *Racial and ethnic variations in employment access: An examination of residential location and commuting in metropolitan areas*, Berkeley, CA: University of California Transportation Center, UCTC Working Paper 17.

US DOT Bureau of Transportation Statistics (1998) *Welfare reform and access to jobs in Boston*, January, Washington, DC: US DOT Bureau of Transportation Statistics.

ELEVEN

Community impact assessment for US17

Anne Morris

Introduction

Since the passage of the US Intermodal Surface Transportation Efficiency Act of 1991 (ISTEA), there has been much more of an emphasis on proactive and continual citizen involvement in transportation decision making, with an explicit emphasis placed on outreach to traditionally underserved and disadvantaged populations. The Federal Highway Administration (FHWA)/Federal Transit Administration (FTA) *Interim policy on public involvement and questions and answers on public involvement in transportation decision-making* (FHWA/FTA, 1994) defines the public broadly as including all individuals or groups who are potentially affected by transportation decisions. This includes both individuals and organized groups who reside, have an interest, or do business in the given area affected by a transportation decision.

Community impact assessment (CIA) broadly describes an approach that a number of agencies in the US have adopted in recent years to ensure the voices of local people are heard during the transportation planning and implementation phases of projects. It includes such approaches as community profiling, meaningful community involvement, consensus building, decision making, education, training and implementation. The FHWA (1996, p 7) defines a community in part as:

> ... behavior patterns which individuals or groups of individuals hold in common. These behavior patterns are expressed through daily social interactions, the use of local facilities, participation in local organizations, and involvement in activities that satisfy the population's economic and social needs. A community is also defined by shared perceptions or attitudes, typically expressed through individuals' identification with, commitment to, and attitude toward a particular identifiable area. In addition, there are other concepts of community, which are not based on spatial relationships. Communities may be based on a common characteristic or interest, such as religion, ethnicity, income strata, or

concern for the economic viability of a region, which provides a psychological unity among members.

This chapter describes the CIA that was prepared to identify the impacts of widening a section of Route US17, one of the oldest transportation routes in the US, on nine communities located in the surrounding area.

Background

From the early 1700s until the late 1980s, when construction of Interstate 95 was completed, the King's Highway, or US17 as it became known, has served as the primary north-south route along the Atlantic coast from New England to Florida. In the late 1960s, studies were undertaken to address both the regional transportation needs and the potential economic impacts of improving the transportation system in the coastal corridor from Norfolk, Virginia through North Carolina and South Carolina to Savannah, Georgia. In order to address the issues identified in these and later studies, the North Carolina Department of Transportation (NCDOT) divided US17 within its borders into 18 independent projects. By the late 1990s, 10 of these projects were completed, under construction or being designed. The remaining eight projects, including the subject of this case study, were still in the planning or environmental stages.

The focus of this project is the US17 segment between the cities of New Bern and Jacksonville in rural Jones and Onslow Counties.

The project corridor surrounding US17 is approximately 16.1 miles (25.8 km) long and approximately 500–3,000ft (152.4–914.4 metres) wide. Within this segment, NCDOT determined that US17 should be widened from a two-lane roadway to a four-lane divided roadway on new location and/or a five-lane roadway on existing location. Since the inception of the project, a variety of alternative alignments and combinations of alignments had been explored, but no preferred alternative alignment had been selected.

Several of the remaining alternative alignments had the potential to impact on one or more African American communities. As a result of its sensitivity to the Executive Order 12898 on Environmental Justice (1994), the NCDOT authorized the preparation of a CIA for this project. This authorization occurred almost five years after the project began and almost six years after President Bill Clinton had signed Executive Order 12898. Under normal circumstances, the initiation of a CIA should have occurred much earlier in the project and been used as one of the decision-making tools for initial alignment locations, refinement and elimination, and identification of the preferred alternative.

Executive Order 12898 Section 1-1-101 states that federal programs, policies and activities should not have a "disproportionately high and adverse human health or environmental effect on minority and low-income populations". A minority is defined as an Alaskan Native, Native American, African American, Hispanic or Asian American. Low-income is defined as a person whose household

Community impact assessment for US17

Figure 11.1: Project area

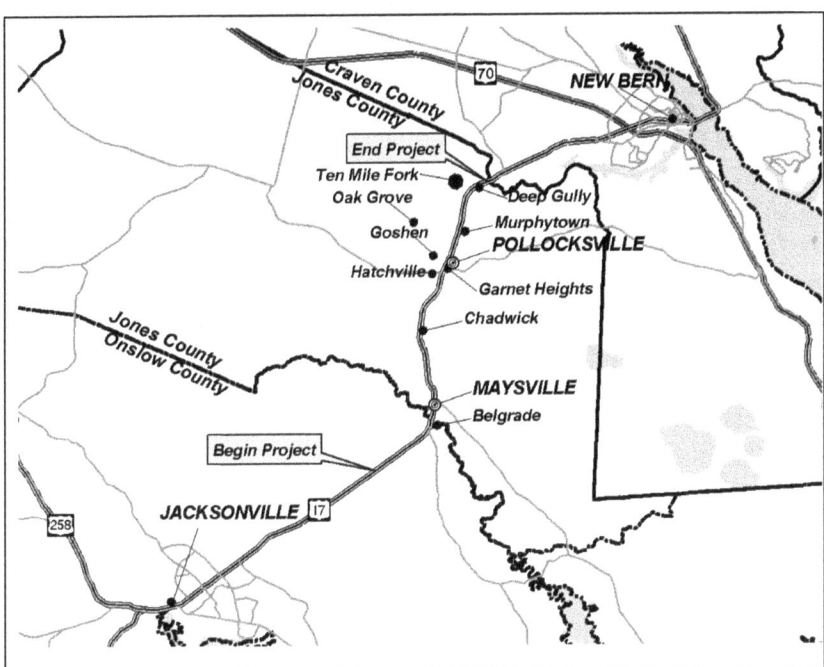

income is at or below the poverty guidelines set by the US Department of Health and Human Services. The poverty guidelines are used as a threshold for eligibility to federal income-sensitive programs such as the Food Stamps Program (a food subsidy), Free and Reduced Price Meal Program (a school lunch subsidy), Section 8 Housing (a housing subsidy), and so on.

As described in previous chapters, the Environmental Justice Executive Order is a process based on Title VI of the Civil Rights Act of 1964, a law that addresses the illegality of racial and other types of discrimination, and the 1988 Stafford Act, a law that addresses the illegality of income discrimination. Since executive orders are a process and not a law, they cannot be the basis of a lawsuit. Instead, they tend to serve as an early warning that, unless acknowledged, may lead to the basis of a lawsuit. The NCDOT was sensitive to this because several of their projects had been the subject of lawsuits filed under Title VI of the Civil Rights Act of 1964. Wishing to avoid a lawsuit that could temporarily or permanently stop the US17 project, the NCDOT initiated a CIA.

Scope of the CIA

The original scope of the CIA was to examine the impacts of alignment alternatives on four African American communities (Chadwick, Hatchville, Garnet Heights and Goshen). The CIA was initiated in 1999 and submitted to the NCDOT for their review in mid-2000. Following their review, the NCDOT decided to broaden the scope of the CIA to include two additional African American communities (Oak Grove and Murphytown), three predominantly white communities (Belgrade, Ten Mile Fork and Deep Gully), an integrated town (Maysville) and a predominantly white town (Pollocksville). All nine communities were located in unincorporated areas adjacent to or near the towns of Maysville and Pollocksville. This expanded CIA was submitted to the NCDOT in August 2001 for review and the final CIA was approved in January 2002.

The CIA was modeled on the Federal Highway Administration guidance (FHWA, 1996). It was divided into three chapters: US17; the project area; and the communities and their citizens. The first chapter provided a chronology of the efforts to improve US17, a description of existing US17, the purpose and need for the project, and the proposed improvements associated with the project. The second chapter provided a comparison of demographic characteristics between the state of North Carolina, Onslow and Jones Counties, and the census areas (tracts and blocks) within which the project was located. These characteristics included population changes, age, race, sex, educational attainment, housing owners and types, tenure, poverty, employment, employment sectors, commuting times and vehicle ownership. The third chapter provided a detailed discussion of each of the nine communities and two towns. Each community/town was described separately in order to address issues that were unique to it. The information presented about each community/town included its location within the project area, history, description of its geographic boundaries, community profile, concerns of the community's residents, potential beneficial and adverse impacts associated with improving US17, and possible ways to mitigate adverse impact and enhance existing conditions. This information was obtained from published and Internet sources, citizen meetings and 208 one-to-one interviews with the residents.

The evidence of previous research

In the five years prior to the initiation of the CIA, the project's public involvement efforts had consisted of two citizen involvement workshops, sporadic newsletters and a toll-free telephone number. The first citizen involvement meeting was held four years prior to the initiation of the CIA in October 1995 at Maysville Elementary School in Maysville within the project area. The second citizen involvement meeting was held two years prior to the initiation of the CIA in February 1997 at the Jones County Civic Centre located in Trenton, approximately 15 miles (24.1km) outside the project area.

The project newsletters had been mailed to those who had attended a citizen involvement meeting, used the toll-free telephone number, or expressed interest in the project through another medium. Of the approximately 2,600 residents in the project area, approximately 500 were on the project's mailing list and had received at least one or more newsletters. The toll-free telephone number had been used frequently at the beginning of the project, but as the project aged its use had diminished. By the time the CIA was initiated, only a few residents called for monthly updates.

Undertaking the CIA

Little detailed knowledge about the communities and their residents had been collected during the five years previous to the CIA. Therefore, extensive data collection had to be undertaken. The first step in beginning the CIA was to create a profile of the population within the project area: who was the public that could be beneficially or adversely impacted by the proposed alternative alignments? Data collection involved utilizing information obtained from the Internet and published sources. These sources included federal and state data depositories including the US Census and NC state data center. Since information from the 2000 US Census was not yet available, the majority of the information was obtained from the 1990 US Census. This was supplemented with mid-Census information and projections that had been undertaken by the NC State Data Center. This information helped identify a variety of demographic characteristics including the actual and relative size of the environmental justice populations. In addition, topographic mapping, mapping without contour information, aerial photographs and county property maps were also collected and utilized.

After studying the available demographic and cartographic information, the CIA team was ready to do primary-source data collection in the communities. The primary tool for this was a three-page questionnaire that could be independently filled out by a resident or administered by an interviewer. The format of the interview allowed for both open-ended and yes/no responses, depending on the question being asked. On average, the interviews took approximately 15 minutes to complete. Information collected using the questionnaire would be relevant not only to the CIA but also to the environmental document that would be written by others later in the process.

The questionnaire asked the following questions:

- What is your name, address (both physical and mailing) and phone number?
- What is the best way and time to contact you (phone, mail, email)?
- If you subscribe to a newspaper, which one (where should legal ads be placed)?
- How many years have you lived in the community and in your present home (tenure, stability)?
- Do you own or rent your home?
- Do you have relatives in close proximity (community cohesiveness)?
- Do you keep children in your home for relatives and unrelated individuals (social fabric)?
- How do you define your community (physical boundaries, social ties, and so on)?
- What is your main mode of transportation (car, bicycle, walking, carpool, other)?

- Do you depend on someone else for your transportation (social fabric)?
- If you work, where do you work and how do you get there?
- If you have children, where do they go to school and how do they get there?
- If they ride the school bus, where is the bus stop?
- Where do you go to the doctor/hospital, shopping, church, community facilities, work, and so on?
- If you know of any local family cemeteries or landfills, where are they?
- What utility services do you have (telephone, natural gas, propane gas, electricity, water, sewer, cable)?
- If you have a septic system or are on well water, where are they located?
- Have you attended any of the citizen workshops, if so which one(s)?
- Do you receive the project newsletter?
- Do you have an opinion on any of the alternatives?
- What do you like most about your community (possible enhancement opportunities)?
- What do you like least about your community (possible mitigation opportunities)?
- What would make your community a better place to live?
- Why did you move to your present location?
- If you did not live here where would you live?
- Do you have any general concerns or opinions?

The CIA team took the questionnaires into each community/town and to all community meetings. By the end of the project, a total of 208 residents had been interviewed. This figure represented approximately 8% of the approximately 2,600 residents within the project area. The vast majority of the questionnaires were administered by a CIA team member so potential problems associated with literacy were avoided. As a result of the interviews and other public involvement techniques employed during the project, the mailing list increased from approximately 500 to approximately 900 names. Approximately 250 of those names represented low-income and minority residents who were, for the most part, unaware or unfamiliar with the five-year-old project.

Lessons learned in preparing the US17 CIA

In February 2002, following the completion of the US17 CIA, a report was produced by the CIA team (NCDOT, 2002). The aim was to record the variety of non-traditional public involvement techniques that had been used and the results that had been obtained from using them. The object of this endeavor was to share not only what knowledge had been gained but also how that knowledge had been gained. Whether things worked as planned or not, a lesson was learned from each attempt and that knowledge was reinvested in the next attempt. It is important to note that, in this evaluation, the CIA team did not have a fear of failing and was willing to try untested ideas.

It was concluded that two major lessons had been learned in preparing the US17 CIA:

- traditional public involvement techniques do not work for every segment of the population;
- flexibility is the key to success when dealing with people.

Why traditional public involvement techniques do not work for every segment of the population

The traditional public involvement techniques used today are a product of the early 1950s when the 1956 Federal Aid Highway Act became law and the interstate highway system was in its infancy. This law mandated that the public be given an opportunity for involvement. Generally speaking, this meant that the public would be notified in an advertisement in the legal section of the newspaper that a public hearing would be held at a specific location, on a specific date and at a specific time. At the public hearing, the preferred alternative or the alternatives still under consideration would be presented and the public would be given the opportunity to comment. Their comments were supposedly analyzed and considered by the state departments of transportation. While the opportunities for public involvement were reaffirmed by the passage of the National Environmental Policy Act of 1969, the actual change from one-way public information to actual two-way public involvement has only recently occurred.

What is important to realize is that, in the early 1950s, the employees of the Bureaus of Public Roads, as many Departments of Transportation were then known, were almost totally white. White males filled the professional roles and white women were the clerical staffs. As a result, the traditional public involvement techniques used today reflect the financial, social and racial backgrounds of these individuals. That is not to say there is anything wrong with these techniques; rather, it is simply to define the public that they were designed by and for a public that was middle to upper income, predominantly white, literate, English speaking, that worked a first-shift job (8am to 5pm), had personal transportation and did not need childcare because their wives did not attend the public hearing. In many instances, other segments of the population were not expected to participate and, in some cases, were not encouraged to participate.

These traditional techniques do not work well with other segments of the public, specifically the public that is minority and/or low-income. Just as in many other instances, one size does not fit all. Since many of the practitioners do not come from minority and low-income backgrounds, there is little or no realization that these traditional public involvement techniques include barriers to participation by the minority and low-income populations. As a result, sole utilization of the traditional public involvement techniques often served to minimize or exclude the participation of minority and low-income populations. In some cases, this omission has probably been intentional and in others it has been out of ignorance. In addition, few practitioners tend to understand the basic principles of marketing: identify your audience(s), create a demographic profile and design a plan around their abilities and constraints.

Today, websites, newspapers and newsletters are the most commonly used public involvement tools and they generally work very well for those with disposable incomes who are literate and can speak English. A low-income person cannot afford a computer or a subscription to a newspaper; therefore, they do not have financial access to these tools and the information presented by these tools. In addition, websites, newspapers and newsletters all require that the user be able to read. Since most practitioners do not make the connection between low income, low educational attainment and low literacy levels, no consideration is given to the fact that segments of population may not be able to read; or, if they can read, may not be able to read English. Therefore, these written tools should not be relied on as the sole source of news dissemination.

In addition to financial and literacy barriers to participation, the traditional techniques do not address the demographic constraints of the low-income and minority populations to participation. Many of the environmental justice populations work second or third-shift jobs, or they work two jobs. Traditionally, citizen meetings have been held in the evenings, when many low-income persons are at work. In addition, many environmental justice households have only a single female parent who may be unable to attend a meeting because she does not have a babysitter, or cannot afford a babysitter. Often, environmental justice households do not have their own personal means of transportation and must rely on neighbors or employers for transportation. If meetings are not held in a location that is within walking distance of their homes, they are unable to attend. One of the most unrealized barriers to participation is concern for personal safety. Often meetings are held in a neighborhood where it is unsafe for persons of another race to attend. While residents may want to participate, they are unwilling to put their lives at risk to do so.

When citizen meetings are poorly attended, the assumption has often been 'the citizens did not show up because they either don't think their opinions will be heard, or they liked the project and didn't think it was necessary to attend', when in fact citizens may have been very concerned about the project but were unaware of the meeting, at work during the meeting, had no babysitter, did not have access to transportation or were afraid to attend the meeting in the planned location. The traditional public involvement techniques do not recognize the demographic constraints of the environmental justice populations and, thus, have worked against their abilities to participate.

As a result of not having 'meaningful access to decision-making information', the environmental justice populations may not find out about the project until late in the process. When they do express their concerns, these comments are often unwelcome because they may require a reexamination of alternatives, or reevaluation of a portion of the process that had been completed. The response in some cases has been "you should have made your comments earlier when it was appropriate". In extreme cases, a lawsuit will be filed against the state Department of Transportation (DOT) and the FHWA under Title VI of the Civil Rights Act of 1964. At present, there are approximately 50 active lawsuits that have been filed nationwide. Under the best of circumstances, this will slow the project down by several years. Under the worst of circumstances, this will stop the project altogether.

Why flexibility is the key to success in engaging with people

One of the lesser-known beatitudes is 'blessed are the flexible for they shall not be bent out of shape'. Whenever attempting to engage the public, always expect surprises, be ready to back up and be willing to try a new approach. What might have looked like it would work at 9am might be dead in the water by 9:15am. Be selective in choosing team members because not everyone deals well with people who are not like them.

The *Lessons learned* report (NCDOT, 2002) highlighted 10 techniques that were used to obtain information from primary and secondary sources. These included non-traditional public involvement techniques that were used to engage the environmental justice populations. Using a diary approach that chronicled the preparation of the CIA, each technique was described in terms of:

- What was done?
- What was learned?
- What should be done differently the next time?

A summary of the key recommendations of this report is presented in this format in the following sections.

Utilizing information of record

Before going into the field, it was necessary to have some sense of what the project area was like. While numbers alone would not provide a feel for the human element, they did provide a good starting point and showed where holes existed in the data.

What was done?

Initially, the Internet was used to obtain demographic information from the US Census, the NC Department of Commerce and the NC State Data Center websites. Although the majority of the information available was from 1990, these websites did provide some mid-Census information and projections. These sources provided a feel for the size and magnitude of the low-income and minority populations. They were supplemented with US Geological Survey maps, aerial photography, county tax maps and project mapping compiled from aerial photography flown in 1995.

Once in the field, local libraries were visited to research the history of each community. Little if any information was found about the African American communities for two reasons: much of the history of the US was written by and about the traditional white male power structure; and, the high level of illiteracy within the low-income and minority communities meant that there had been few in the communities that could read or write their own history. As a result, the majority of the history of the African American communities came from oral history provided by the community elders.

What was learned?

All data was helpful in one way or another. The different sources and layers provided a good patchwork and method to double check accuracy. In addition, the following was learned:

- information of record in rural counties was difficult and time consuming to obtain;
- a variety of sources were necessary in order to get a comprehensive picture of the area;
- historic information found at local libraries provided local flavor, but was not detailed;
- tax maps and tax assessor information could be out of date in rural areas because it was usually not computerized and updates were undertaken infrequently;
- utility customer lists provided up-to-date information because billing occurred every month;
- a copy of the local telephone book was essential.

What should be done differently the next time?

The team concluded that more time should have been spent searching the Internet. Every day more and more information is being added at all levels. Websites were found that had been created by local residents about their family histories. The local websites provided spin-offs to other sites and information, and stimulated new ideas for possible resources.

Generating new information

While much of the 'broad brush' demographic information found in the CIA could be obtained from existing Internet sites, US Census and state databases and other sources, information relative to individual community residents could be obtained only by sitting down and talking with them one-to-one.

Community impact assessment for US17

What was done?

The initial objective in interviewing the community residents was to obtain information about themselves and their communities. The residents were interviewed during several field trips to the project area. Two or three-member interview teams went door-to-door and identified themselves as representatives of the NCDOT. Interviews were conducted on weekdays and on Saturday morning. Team members carried interview forms at all times in order to take advantage of any situation where an interview could occur. When residents did not have the time to be interviewed, they were given interview forms and encouraged to fill them out and return them by mail.

Interviews took place at two multi-community meetings held at two African American churches, three voter-polling places, a public involvement workshop at a non-minority church, an elementary school, a grocery store, Parent Teacher Association/Parent Teacher Organization meetings at schools, in front yards, in living rooms, under clotheslines in back yards, under carports and so on.

The date and time of the public involvement workshops were announced in a newsletter mailed to residents, handed out during interviews and given out at the voting polls.

What was learned?

One-to-one interviews administered by a CIA team member eliminated the barrier of illiteracy and enabled the residents to be engaged in conversations. These conversations provided information not only requested on the interview form, but also volunteered by the residents. They voiced problems, provided community history and detailed past injustices to African Americans in the project area. Feedback received during interviews with residents that attended one or both of the citizen involvement workshops held prior to the initiation of the CIA suggested that the consultant's project mapping did not define their communities correctly. These personal interviews also helped develop a sense of trust between the CIA team and the community and revealed the deep-seated distrust that existed between the African American community residents and white public officials from Pollocksville.

The short time it took to complete an interview was helpful in getting citizens to agree to be interviewed. The most successful situations occurred when residents were voting or in their own home. It was more difficult to get interviews with residents when they were trying to get home quickly, such as at the grocery store or after a Parent Teacher Association/Parent Teacher Organization meeting. By conducting the interviews, rather than leaving the interview forms with residents, this did not embarrass anyone who could not read or write and it ensured that the interview would be completed. Had interview forms been left with a resident that could neither read nor write, the probability that the interview form would have been returned would have been minimal. Once the interview began, residents opened up and provided wonderful oral histories, told why their children had moved away and made referrals for other residents who should be interviewed.

Information learned during the interviews was helpful in other ways. The locations of small family cemeteries that could not be seen from the road and landfills that were never on a database were things that probably would not have been discovered until they were stumbled upon during construction.

What should be done differently the next time?

Some of the interview questions could be rewritten so that the residents could better understand them. While a copy of the latest newsletter was left with residents, it would have been better to include a project area map with the alternatives. Due to the uncertainty about when the project was going to be built, many residents were anxious about their future. Having specifics as to a funding or construction date would have done much to allay the fears of many of the older residents.

Holding workshops

Prior to beginning the CIA, two community meetings were held. The first meeting was held in October 1995 at the Maysville Elementary School in Maysville. The second meeting was held in February 1997 at the Jones County Civic Center near Trenton, approximately 15 miles (24.1km) west of the project area. Other than these two meetings, information had been sent to the residents through sporadic newsletters.

As a result of the one-to-one interviews conducted in the African American communities, it became apparent that most of the minority residents had not attended these earlier workshops and were not on the newsletter mailing list. In fact, some had not heard anything about the project and those that had heard about the project were not always well informed.

What was done?

In order to bring the project to the residents, four public involvement meetings were held. Two of these were held in minority churches, one was held in a white church and one was held in an elementary school. Everyone was given a copy of the latest newsletter and interviews were conducted as people were seated. The design team gave an oral presentation and used maps to display the project area and alternatives. Following the presentation, there was a lengthy question-and-answer period. This enabled rumors to be dispelled and everyone to be brought up to date. After the presentation, more residents expressed a desire to fill out an interview form.

What was learned?

The first and second church meetings were held in African American churches. These were comfortable familiar settings located within the African American communities. In these non-threatening environments, the residents asked questions and provided community histories and explained family relationships that existed within and among the African American communities.

The third church meeting was held at a white church in Pollocksville soon after an extensive effort to let residents know about the workshop. Newsletters had been passed out at the three voter-polling places only two days before the meeting and had been sent to everyone on the Pollocksville mailing list the week before the meeting. As a result, there was an unexpectedly high attendance. There was a good turnout from the white community, but few African Americans attended. The poor turnout among minorities could have been a result of the setting: a white church located in the middle of a predominantly white town after dark, or because recent meetings had been held in the African American communities. In addition, there were few older people in attendance. Having the meeting after dark could have contributed to their reluctance to attend, as many do not see as well after dark. They are afraid of falling and are often reluctant to drive at night.

The meeting at the elementary school in Maysville, an integrated town, was well attended by white people, but few minorities attended. The location was well known to everyone, easily accessible and it appeared that residents felt comfortable in the school setting. This meeting was started in the afternoon during the daylight hours and a good number of older people were present. They provided extensive community histories and suggested other residents that could provide additional history. Since the meeting was earlier in the day, parents who had children at Maysville Elementary School attended the meeting and then collected their children.

A comparison between the mailing list and the sign-in sheets showed that a number of attendees were not on the mailing list. Their attendance could have been a result of additional public involvement and their names were added to the mailing list.

What should be done differently the next time?

Having meetings that started earlier in the day and lasted longer could have increased the number of older participants, parents of school children and second-shift workers. At least one industry had first and second shifts and longer meetings covering both shifts could have allowed second-shift workers the opportunity to attend. The school seemed an excellent location for a meeting because parents who came to pick up their children also were able to attend the meeting.

Although large maps were prominently displayed at the meetings, smaller maps should have been inserted in the newsletters and available for the attendees to

Running on empty

take home and review. Based on the number of new names on the sign-in sheets, this was the first time many of the attendees had seen the project and the alternatives under consideration. More familiarity with the maps could have provoked more questions and more comments.

Using churches

Churches were considered as possible meeting places in the minority communities because they were in locations that were familiar to residents and safe for the residents to attend. These meetings were open to all residents from the Chadwick, Garnet Heights and Goshen communities and were held to communicate information about the project and to conduct interviews.

One of the local women, who knew everyone, stood at the front door of the church and recorded citizen names as they entered the church. This eliminated any embarrassment for those who were not able to read or write. Another meeting was held at a white Presbyterian church in Pollocksville. A sign-in sheet was utilized for this meeting.

What was done?

The project area was surveyed and the names of churches and their pastors were obtained. In the African American communities, it proved difficult to get in touch with the pastors. Many of the signs in front of the churches did not provide the pastor's telephone number and even when telephone numbers were provided it was often difficult to get any response. The churches were small and

Conducting one-on-one interviews at a local church

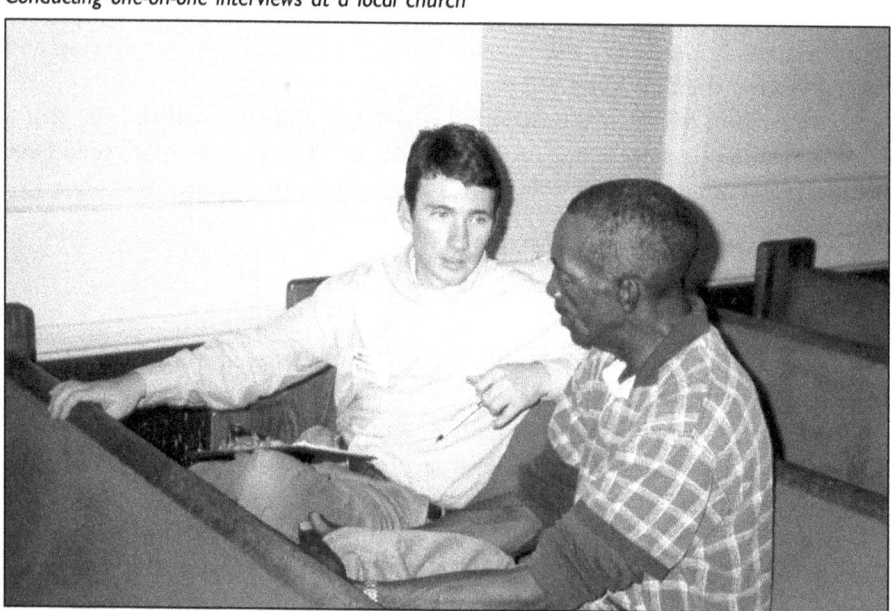

most did not have day staff. Even when the church signs provided the pastor's telephone number, it was difficult to get in touch with the pastor because they had non-church-related full-time jobs. Through the help of the local community leaders, meetings were held in two minority churches. Locating the pastor of the white church was easier because he was a full-time minister and the church had full-time day staff.

What was learned?

In the minority communities, many of the churches could not afford pastors and used rotating pastors who would preach at one church one week and another church the next week. Congregations might follow a pastor from one church to the next, or simply not attend church unless the church in their area was holding services. This presented a challenge in identifying and contacting pastors to request permission to have a meeting in their churches. It also said that the concept of the 'church as a center of the community' did not exist in many cases in the project area. The larger white churches had regular Sunday worship services, Wednesday prayer meetings and full-time pastors who were easier to contact.

What should be done differently the next time?

Additional attempts should be made to find out when churches hold worship services. Pastors should be asked if their churches have covered dish lunches after Sunday services or covered dish suppers after Wednesday night prayer services. Each of these would provide an opportunity for the CIA team to offer and bring soft drinks and make a presentation to the congregation.

A membership roll from each church should be requested so that all members could be added to the mailing list. If pastors did not want to share this information, they should be asked to make an announcement from the pulpit about an upcoming meeting. A packet of project information including newsletters, meeting flyers and maps should be sent to each church for distribution. In addition, large maps could be sent to each church so that they could display them.

Taking advantage of special events

The CIA team took advantage of special events, such as national Election Day.

A field trip had originally been planned in October 2000, but a conflict forced a postponement until the week of 5-10 November 2000. The rescheduled week included the national Election Day (7 November 2002). Initially, this was seen as a negative because many citizens would not be home, but at the voting polls or other places. Instead, this turned out to be a very positive occurrence.

What was done?

A call to the County election board revealed that there were voter-polling places in the Belgrade community (on US17) and in the towns of Maysville (on US17) and Pollocksville (within a few blocks of US17). As a result, one CIA team member was located at each polling place with table, chairs, a sign identifying the project, maps, newsletters, comment sheets and interview forms. Each table was also equipped with refreshments that proved to be a magnet for getting residents to come over and talk. In addition, a floating CIA team member was assigned to provide the other team members with food and periodic relief. These tables were occupied while the polls were open from 6:00am until 6:00pm.

A member of the Black Caucus, a nationwide African American group that stressed voting registration and participation from the minority communities, was also at the polling places. Impact assessment team members introduced themselves and explained the US17 project and their purpose. At one of the polling places, the Black Caucus instructed minority voters to participate in one-to-one interviews.

During the day, a representative of a local African American radio station stopped and asked to interview someone on the air regarding the project. A telephone conference was arranged between the radio station and the NCDOT project manager who talked about the project and answered questions that were telephoned in by the radio audience. Utilizing an African American radio station helped to target the minority audience and provide them with information without asking them to leave their homes and cars.

What was learned?

The event provided immediate feedback about what the residents knew about the project and an opportunity to dispel rumors about the project. This special event presented an excellent opportunity to access a large group of residents with only four CIA team members. The county election board later reported that 62% of the registered voters in the two-county project area had voted – a very high turnout.

What should be done differently the next time?

Contact with the voter registrar should be made earlier. They could provide information relative to the level of past voter turnout at each of the three polling places. If one polling place had a history of higher voter turnout, more team members might have been needed there. Bigger signs should have been used to identify the CIA team and the US17 project. Once the voters realized that the CIA team was not promoting a political candidate, they willingly spoke to team members. A larger display map should have been used and been laminated since it was displayed outside. Once voters saw people sitting and being interviewed, they came over and wanted to know what was happening. More chairs would have been helpful to allow older people a place to sit.

Organizations like the Black Caucus should have been identified earlier so that a meeting could be held to discuss the project with them and encourage their help. Local radio stations that target specific audiences should be identified and call-in opportunities with the NCDOT project manager arranged throughout the life of the project.

Taking advantage of regularly scheduled events

Each public school holds regularly scheduled Parent Teacher Organization/Parent Teacher Association (PTO/PTA) meetings. These are generally held in the evening and are fairly well attended. The principal and the president of the PTO/PTA at each school are responsible for setting the meeting agenda.

What was done?

Maysville Elementary School had a PTO and Pollocksville Elementary School had a PTA that met several times during the school year. Each school's principal allowed a CIA team member to make a five-minute presentation on the US17 project at their annual Christmas meeting. At the Christmas meeting, each grade performed specific Christmas carols; therefore, all children took part in the program and their parents and other members of the family came to see them perform. This presented an opportunity to introduce the project to the single head of household mothers who did not get out to meetings because they could not afford or did not have a baby sitter. After the meeting was over, a CIA team member stood next to the project maps which had been taped to the wall, answered questions and took names and addresses that would be added to the newsletter mailing list.

What was learned?

The principals identified the first meeting of the year and the Christmas meeting as the two best-attended meetings of the year. Since each child has a part in the Christmas pageant, their whole family came to see them. This presented opportunities to pass out newsletters, and collect names and addresses for the mailing list. However, it did not present many opportunities to conduct interviews: the parents were anxious to get their children home and in bed.

What should be done differently the next time?

These events presented opportunities to increase awareness of the project, pass out newsletters and talk to those who did not rush home to put their children to bed. It should not be thought of as an occasion to conduct interviews.

Using newsletters

Newsletters are one of the easiest ways to get information to a community if the mailing list is complete and if the community is literate. Names were constantly added to the mailing list as the CIA team went through the communities. Other names were taken from the Pollocksville water authority's customer billing list. This list included customers who lived not only in Pollocksville and Maysville, but also in the surrounding unincorporated areas within the project area where most of the low-income and minority populations lived. A comparison of the existing newsletter mailing list and the water authority's customer list showed that few of the residents in the surrounding minority communities had been included on the newsletter mailing list.

What was done?

Newsletters had been sent out over the previous two years in ever increasing numbers as the mailing list was expanded. While some on the mailing list may not have been able to read, the majority of the citizens could read at some level. In addition to being mailed, newsletters were handed out at public involvement meetings, at special events, regularly scheduled events, grocery stores, restaurants and when interviews were conducted.

What was learned?

Newsletters were not effective with those who could not read and their distribution was only as good as the mailing list. The extensive public involvement activities added many new names to the mailing list and many of these residents were African Americans who lived in communities that would be directly affected by the proposed alternatives. The absence of their names on the mailing list suggested that the earlier mailings had reached only a limited number of African Americans and low-income residents and that the sole use of newsletters could not be relied on to reach these populations.

What should be done differently the next time?

Newsletters could be written at the fifth-grade level so that school students could take them home and read them to their parents who may be unable to read. More colors, photographs and graphics needed to be used in the newsletters to make them more appealing and easier to understand. A self-addressed, stamped postcard should be included with the newsletter. The postcard could be used to solicit information from the residents such as where (place) and when (day of the week and hour of the day or night) would be convenient for them to go to a meeting; do they need transportation; do they need childcare at the meeting; and are they aware of any unsafe conditions?

Identifying programs that are income sensitive

Identifying federal income-sensitive programs that use the US Department of Health and Human Services definition of low income as their eligibility threshold was important. These programs could provide realistic information as to the number of low-income families in the project area that was more current than US Census information and generally within boundaries smaller than the US Census.

What was done?

Agencies that administered federal income-sensitive programs were contacted. Staff members were asked if their agencies administered other income-sensitive programs and if they knew of any other agencies that administered income-sensitive programs. While there are many income-sensitive programs, three of the most widely used programs were the Food Stamp Program, the Free and Reduced Price Meal Program and the Section 8 Housing Program.

What was learned?

While the US Department of Health and Human Services has defined low income, the agency does not know what federal programs or agencies use its threshold of eligibility. It took an incredible amount of time to locate these programs because no one agency knew what other agencies did. While each state administers these programs, the location and name of the agencies within each state that administer these programs vary. Finding out which state agency administers what program is challenging.

What should be done differently the next time?

The income-sensitive programs and their sponsoring agencies should have been identified earlier and alliances with their local representatives should have been formed.

Involving elementary school students

As part of data collection, the CIA team visited the Maysville and Pollocksville elementary schools and spoke with the principals. Each was asked to identify how many of their students were eligible for the Free and Reduced Meal Program, a school lunch subsidy program administered by the US Department of Agriculture. In order to be eligible for this program, a family's income must not exceed a certain level. Those families that do not exceed this income level are considered to be a low-income and an environmental justice population. Both principals said that approximately 65% of their students were eligible for this program. As a result of this high percentage, the CIA team asked the principals how many of the parents did they think were illiterate. The responses varied from 30% to 40%. This response meant that the sole use of written material would not be effective in reaching this portion of the population. During the conversation, the principal of Pollocksville elementary school asked that the CIA team provide her fourth and fifth-grade students with a civics lesson about the US17 project.

What was done?

A presentation called 'Where Do Roads Come From?' was created and shown to the fourth and fifth-grade students. As part of the presentation, environmentally sensitive overlays showing wetlands, floodplains, historic structures, archaeological sites, hazardous materials sites, communities and so on were superimposed on a map of Pollocksville. At the end of the presentation, each student was given a copy of the Pollocksville map with all the overlays. As a homework assignment, each student was asked to take the map home, talk with their parents about what they had learned and locate where they thought the road should go. Each student and their parents were to sign the map and return it to their teacher the next day. In return, each student was given a certificate as a 'Jr Environmentalist'. Almost all the students returned their map the next day.

What was learned?

Identifying the high rate of participation in the Free and Reduced Meal Program and potential level of parent illiteracy alerted the CIA team to the need to use other than written material to communicate with the public.

The 'Where Do Roads Come From?' presentation revealed that fourth and fifth-grade students are aware of many of the environmental issues addressed in the transportation process. The students proved to be an eager and dependable audience. This suggested that they could be used as a conduit to get information to and from their parents who might be illiterate.

What should be done differently the next time?

The 'Jr Environmentalist' program should be instituted earlier in the project and designed for not only elementary students, but also middle and high-school students. A newsletter written at the fourth/fifth-grade level could be written for the students to take home and read to their parents should their parents be unable to read. Students could help design the public involvement plan. They could interview their parents and ask where would be a convenient/safe place to have a meeting; what day of the week would be convenient to attend a meeting; what time of the day or night would be convenient to attend a meeting; do they need transportation to get to and from the meeting; and, do they need childcare at the meeting? Armed with this information, the CIA team could tailor meeting times and places to fit the schedules of the different publics.

Using grocery stores

Information obtained from residents identified the Independent Grocers Association (IGA) grocery store in Maysville as the only grocery store in the project area. The next closest grocery store was located approximately five miles (8km) outside the project area. The residents explained that the IGA grocery store took food stamps, a food subsidy program administered by the US Department of Agriculture. In order to be eligible for this program, a family's income must not exceed a certain level. Those families who do not exceed this income level are considered to be a low-income and an environmental justice population. Since the IGA grocery store took food stamps and was the only grocery store in the project area, it was assumed that many of the low-income residents would shop at this grocery store. Every month, each recipient's account receives an electronic benefits transfer from the US Department of Agriculture. Once this transfer occurs, the recipients can use their food stamp credit card to purchase certain food products.

What was done?

The CIA team went to the manager of the IGA grocery store, explained the project and asked for permission to staff a table outside the front door of the grocery store. The manager said he would provide a table and chairs inside the store in front of the produce section. As the produce aisle was where everyone entering the store started through the aisles, this location forced every shopper to pass the US17 table.

The manager was able to tell the CIA team the days of the month when the electronic benefits transfer occurred and the time of the day when most of the food stamps recipients shopped. In addition, the manager offered to put a copy of the newsletter in the shoppers' grocery bag and display a large map of the project area on a wall in the store near the exit.

The CIA team set up a table in the store and stopped shoppers as they came in the store. The residents were asked if they were familiar with the project, had time to talk about the project and were on the newsletter mailing list. Project maps and newsletters were passed out to everyone. If they had time to fill out an interview, one was conducted. If they did not have time for an interview, their names and addresses were taken and added to the mailing list.

What was learned?

The majority of shoppers came to the grocery store for a specific purpose and did not have time to speak at length or give interviews. Most of the shoppers were in a hurry to get what they needed and get home to prepare a meal or get back to their spouses and children in the car. Older shoppers were observed to be casual shoppers and did have the time to stop and fill out interview forms. It provided an opportunity to interact with low-income and other residents and obtain their names and addresses for the mailing list.

What should be done differently the next time?

In order to cover shift workers, older people, the low-income and other segments of the public, a full day in the store would be necessary. Incentives like free soft drinks or gift certificates could be used to attract shoppers and be a way to show appreciation to the store manager for his cooperation. On Saturday, giving away products in the store parking lot would be more visible than being in the store and have the potential to attract more shoppers.

Providing the public with project maps

One of the most frequent comments voiced by the residents was that they were not sure where the alternatives were located. Prior to the CIA, project maps were only displayed at public involvement meetings and then rolled up and taken away.

What was done?

Maps showing the proposed alternatives and several environmental considerations were shown at the public involvement workshops and voting polls. In addition, they were left at banks, the grocery store, the Pollocksville elementary school, the town hall and the water authority billing office.

What was learned?

For many residents, this was the first time they had seen the proposed alternatives. Many were anxious to know if any of the alternatives were close to their homes, businesses or churches and wanted to take maps home with them or stay longer and look at the maps.

It was obvious that many of the residents found the maps confusing. Using a larger type size would have been helpful for older people and the use of symbols would have helped those who could not read. The use of colors, rather than words, to differentiate the alternatives would also have helped those who could not read. For example, while they may not have been able to read the word 'red', they did know the color red. More attention should have been paid to the colors used to identify the alternatives in order not to confuse those who may have been colorblind. The maps used outside should have been laminated so the color would not run if it rained or something was spilled on them.

What should be done differently the next time?

The maps should have larger type sizes, be laminated, have the alternatives in different colors and utilize symbols where possible. The residents should be provided with 'take home'-size maps so that they could study them at their leisure.

Recording the project area visually

Even on projects that are shorter and smaller than this project, it is impossible to remember everything that was located in the project area.

What was done?

Each of the CIA team members was given a still camera and encouraged to take photographs of everything and everyone on the corridor, including US17 and other roadways, structures, intersections, cultural resources, hazardous materials sites, wetlands, pasture lands, and places of interest. These were taken at all times of the day so that any pattern changes could be detected. While these photographs were necessary to record the existing physical conditions in the communities, it was surprising how few pictures were taken of residents. In most cases, residents were at work, shopping, going to the doctors or inside their houses. In order to document the public involvement activities, team members made a conscious attempt to record the residents and their activities.

In addition to being photographed, the project area was videotaped. The areas along both sides of every main road and secondary road were filmed down one side and up the other to record what was located along the corridor. Then a third and fourth filming was done looking straight down the center of the road to record the road conditions, pavement marking, shoulder widths and types, signs, driveways and so on. The video also helped to locate where the photographs were taken.

What was learned?

The photographs were extremely valuable during the preparation of the CIA report. They brought back memories that had been forgotten and corrected memories that had faded. Each of them was truly worth a thousand words.

What should be done differently the next time?

No matter how many photographs were taken, one more was always needed. In order to get the residents' perspective of what they consider important in their communities, they could be given throwaway cameras and asked to take pictures. These should be given to school children, older people, business owners, police, ministers, officials and so on. Everyone has a different perspective. When shown as a collage at a public involvement meeting, they will reaffirm that the CIA team was listening. The pictures also could be used to solicit comments from residents and provide anecdotal information.

Conclusions

While more and more information becomes available on the Internet and through demographic sources such as the US Census and the NC State Data Center, this information contains little if any insight into a community's human fabric, its character, values and personal history; only by pushing away from the computer, getting into the community and listening to the residents could this information be obtained.

Only by 'looking beneath the numbers' will a true picture of the workings and makeup of the community be uncovered. The interwoven pieces that compose the community must be identified and their relationship to the community's viability must be understood. Is that structure where the day-care center is located? It provides the opportunity for several of the mothers to hold jobs outside the home and stay off welfare. Is that the home of a resident that has the car? They provide their neighbors with a way to get to the doctor, the store, church or school.

The removal of local personal support services, the separation of family members, the changing of traffic patterns will all have an impact on the community that cannot be gauged by simply looking at a map, measuring acreage, and counting structures to be taken. None of these things provide insight into the heart, the soul and the spirit of a community – its human foundation. These can only be understood by getting to know those who live and work in a community.

References

Executive Order 12898 (1994) *Federal actions to address environmental justice in minority populations and low-income populations*, Washington, DC: The White House.

FHWA (Federal Highway Administration) (1996) *Community impact assessment: A quick reference for transportation*, Washington, DC: FHWA, US Department of Transportation.

FHWA/FTA (Federal Highway Administration/Federal Transit Administration) (1994) *Interim policy on public involvement and questions and answers on public involvement in transportation decision-making*, Washington, DC: FHWA/FTA.

NCDOT (North Carolina Department of Transportation) (2002) *Lessons learned in preparing the US17 community impact assessment*, Columbia, SC: Wilbur Smith Associates.

TWELVE

Crossroad blues: the MTA Consent Decree and just transportation

Robert García and Thomas A. Rubin

Standin' at the crossroad
I tried to flag a ride
Ain't nobody seem to know me
everybody pass me by.
(Robert Johnson, *Cross Road Blues*, 1936, alternate take)

Introduction

This chapter describes how a team of civil rights attorneys working with grassroots activists filed and won the landmark environmental justice class action Labor/Community Strategy Center v Metropolitan Transportation Authority (MTA). The plaintiffs alleged that MTA operated separate and unequal bus and rail systems that discriminated against bus riders who were disproportionately low-income people of color. The parties settled the case in 1996 through a court-ordered Consent Decree in which MTA agreed to make investments in the bus system that would total over $2 billion, making it the largest civil rights settlement ever. Metropolitan Transportation Authority agreed to improve transportation for all the people of Los Angeles by reducing overcrowding on buses, lowering transit fares, and enhancing county-wide mobility.

Despite the fact that MTA agreed to the terms of the Consent Decree, however, it has resisted bus service improvements for the seven-plus years the Decree has been in force. Metropolitan Transportation Authority has taken its arguments to set aside the Consent Decree all the way to the US Supreme Court – and lost every time. Ultimately, the MTA case was resolved through mediation and a settlement, not trial. The MTA case illustrates what can be accomplished under federal civil rights law in the US, when a community organizes to protest against environmental injustices. This is an important difference between the US and the UK, where no such legislation and litigation is available to populations that are discriminated against by transportation policies.

Background

Los Angeles may be regarded by many as the car capital of the world, but for the working poor and other people with limited or no access to a car who depend on public transit, it can be almost impossible to get to work, to school, to the market, to the park, to the doctor, to the church, to friends and loved ones, or to many of the other basic needs of life that many of us take for granted. At the time of writing, a transit strike had just been settled that gridlocked Los Angeles for 35 days and stranded approximately 325,000 commuters who rely on transit. Traffic – already the worst in the nation (TTI, 2003) – became measurably worse as the result of a 4% increase in cars and trucks that is enough to clog the roadways for everyone. Businesses across the city felt the pain, particularly where customers as well as employees depend on public transportation.

While everyone suffers from the lack of a decent public transit system, low-income people of color suffer first and worst. At the time the MTA Consent Decree was filed, the typical bus rider in Los Angeles was a Latina woman in her 20s with two children. Among bus riders, 69% had an annual household income of $15,000 – well below the federal poverty line – and no access to a car; 40% had household incomes under $7,500 (MTA, 1998a)[1]. The people who rely most on transit service are disproportionately poor – people of color, women, children, students, older people and disabled people.

Consider the case of Kyle, a 26-year-old single Latina mother of two and a bus rider in Los Angeles. She found work in a drug abuse prevention program after leaving welfare, which she described as 'hell', to face the new hell of her daily commute. At 6am, Kyle is at the bus stop with her children. Fourteen-month-old Ishmael is asleep on her shoulder; five-year-old Mustafa holds her hand. Two buses later, she drops off Mustafa at school in Inglewood. Then she rides two more buses to get Ishmael to his babysitter in Watts. From there it is half an hour to work. Kyle arrives about 9am, three hours and **six** buses after starting:

> The boys and I read. We play games, we talk to other people, we spend the time however we can.... In LA County, it's very difficult to live without a car. (Quoted in Bailey, 1997, p A1)

For small businesswoman Leticia Bucio, who recently opened a beauty shop in downtown Los Angeles, a mention in a downtown newspaper validated a risky investment in weak economic times. Then the buses stopped rolling. "And look at what happened", Bucio said, standing in her empty Letty's Beauty Parlour, where not a single customer had come in since the opening hour. "Now this comes. My God, I don't even know how I am going to pay the rent" (quoted in Bernstein et al, 2003, p A1).

When student Trevante Banks, 14, could not ride MTA buses and trains between his home in the heart of African American Los Angeles and his honors high school in the San Fernando Valley, Trevante found a roundabout way to school:

taking non-striking buses, which zigzagged more than 30 miles to the stop closest to his school. From there, he walked the remaining two miles to Woodland Hills. The one-way trip took more than four hours, but Trevante said it was worth it because he does not want to attend the academically inferior and gang-plagued school near his home (Liu, 2003).

At the nine meal centers that are run by Jewish Family Services for older people, as many as one third of those who regularly come for hot meals have been unable to make it for lunch or dinner since the strike began. Other kitchens and food banks report even more dramatic drops in attendance (Bernstein, 2003a).

Before the strike began, worker Freddie Summerville's workday started at 4:30am with a mile-long walk from his North Hollywood apartment to the Red Line subway. He would take the subway downtown and transfer to the Gold Line light rail to Pasadena and walk another mile to the construction company where he works as a laborer. On the first day of the strike, he walked eight hours to get to work to avoid losing his job. Since then he has rented a car that he cannot afford to reach a job that he cannot afford to lose (Bernstein, 2003b).

A better, cheaper, safer, clean-fuel bus service is the backbone of the transportation system in Los Angeles. Over 90% of MTA's riders ride buses. Subway, light rail, and commuter rail systems depend on buses to get people to and from stations. Buses reduce the need for single-occupancy cars on streets and highways. Without an effective bus system, the rail system will not work. Roads will become more congested. Pollution, related human health, and global warming problems will worsen. Janitors, housekeepers, day-care providers, factory workers and other low-wage workers are not be able to tend to the children, homes, offices, factories and work places of Los Angeles without an effective bus system. All the people who depend on these workers to get on with their lives – all the people of Los Angeles – suffer as a result. Buses keep Los Angeles moving.

In cities across the US, like San Francisco, Atlanta, Baltimore, Pittsburgh, and New York, the statistics vary, but the stories of transportation injustice remain the same and advocates are extending the lessons of the MTA case (Bullard et al, 2004). The plight of the working poor and others with limited or no access to a car throughout the nation illustrates the need for a transportation policy agenda to provide choices to people who currently lack them (Krumholz, 1982). Transportation is a social and economic justice issue because those who most rely on transit services are disproportionately poor. Transportation is a civil rights issue because the poor are disproportionately people of color. Transportation is an economic issue because a better transit service can increase the mobility of such people, enabling them to reach jobs, schools, training, shopping, and other activities. Transportation is an environmental issue because a better, cheaper, safer, clean-fuel transit service offers an alternative to the single-user automobile and can reduce congestion, pollution, and consumption of energy and other natural resources.

Transit policies leading to the MTA case

During the period 1980-96, the public transit decision-making process in Los Angeles County resulted in poor decisions on the type of transportation projects, including expensive rail lines that would provide little in the way of improved mobility for those who needed it most, expansion of bus service in suburban areas while reducing service and raising fares in the inner city areas of the County selected for implementation, billions of wasted taxpayer dollars, incredible missed opportunities, and massive damage to the most important components of the transit network and its users. In particular, the decision to devote over 60% of total transit subsidy funds to rail construction and operations for over a decade produced very expensive, relatively little used transit system components with paltry evident transportation purposes, while the extremely productive and cost-effective bus system – and its riders – suffered major harm to both quality and quantity of service. During a period when the largely transit-dependent populations of people of color in Los Angeles County grew almost 40%, these ill-considered and poorly executed decisions resulted in the transit ridership of the county's major transit operator falling by 27%[2].

The demographics of Los Angeles

The popular myth is that Southern California is a spread out, low-density region that is served by the most extensive freeway system in the nation, where virtually no one uses transit. This myth is simply not true, the Los Angeles region is the most densely populated urbanized area on the US mainland – almost 30% more densely populated than number two, New York City[3]. Los Angeles is close to last in the nation in all measures of miles of roadway per capita (FHWA, 2000).

The average bus passenger load of the MTA and its predecessors was the highest of the 'Top 20' US bus operators every year since the US Department of Transportation began collecting statistics in the late 1970s (UMTA, 1979-97) until the Consent Decree – with its overcrowding limits – was well into effect.

This huge difference between perception and reality had a major impact on transportation decisions in Los Angeles, particularly a belief that there was an essential requirement for something new (a rail network) as the way to solve the area's transportation problems. Unfortunately, the difference between perception and reality led to a course of action that not only did not contribute to the solution of the problems, but also made them significantly worse. How did this state of affairs – this massive difference between what everyone 'knows' about Southern California and the actual truth – come to be?

Transit history in Los Angeles

The story, of course, is long and involved, but the highlights begin with the Red Car/Yellow Car system, arguably the most comprehensive urban/suburban rail transit systems ever built. This formed an important basis of the early development pattern of Southern California, a collection of small settlements and real estate development joined by a transit system that allowed fast, easy, and relatively inexpensive travel between them. As the age of the automobile arrived and the original real estate developments connected to the rail system developers were built out, the region moved swiftly from reliance on rails to reliance on concrete and asphalt as the main foundations for transport. There was no shortage of plans for improved rail systems – approximately 18 from 1911 to 1978 – but all went nowhere, including at least four that were turned down by the voters (1922, 1968, 1974 and 1976). Interestingly enough, the original 1939 plan for the Los Angeles freeway system concluded that rail rapid transit was the key factor in meeting transportation needs. The need for immediate action, however, led to freeways being built first, with the more expensive rail lines to follow later (Green, 1985). (They didn't.)

After the Second World War, Southern California grew at an amazing rate of speed and the demand for automotive capacity grew with it. The 'Golden Age' of freeway construction lasted through the early 1970s, when the combination of environmental protection measures enacted by Congress, the first oil crisis, and a temporary, but significant, reduction in auto travel finally combined to end it.

After the first oil crisis began in 1973, a number of elements combined to limit the immediate response to the increasingly higher ratio of people to road capacity. First, the increase in the price of gasoline, and its occasionally limited availability, limited vehicle travel. This reduced at least the growth of congestion for some years. Second, the economic downturns of the late 1970s through mid-1990s (the latter had a far larger impact on the greater Los Angeles area than nationally) limited job growth. Third, public opinion moved against massive roadway construction as many people began to wonder where their next gallon of gasoline was coming from. The political decision makers heard and understood. Finally, bus mass transit in Los Angeles experienced a period of very rapid growth. During the six years from 1974 to 1980, for example, MTA's predecessor saw ridership increase from 217.7 million to 396.6 million – 82% overall, a sustained compound growth rate of over 10% per year (UMTA, 1978-97).

The other major change in Los Angeles during this period was a major shift in demographics. The non-Hispanic white population has actually decreased steadily in absolute numbers since 1970, as the population percentage fell from 70% to 32% in 2000, on its way to a projected 16% in 2040 (see Figure 12.1).

The most significant change is the over seven-fold growth of the Hispanic population, from 15% in 1970 to 46% or more in 2000, to a projected 64% in 2040. The black population is projected to increase only 2% in total, with the population percentage dropping from 11% in 1970 to 9% in 2000 to a projected 6% in 2040. The Asian population shows very rapid growth from a small base, from 4% in 1970 to 13% in 2000 to 18% in 2040 (DMU, 2001).

As people of color became the overwhelming majority of the Los Angeles

Running on empty

Figure 12.1: Los Angeles population by ethnicity (1970-2040)

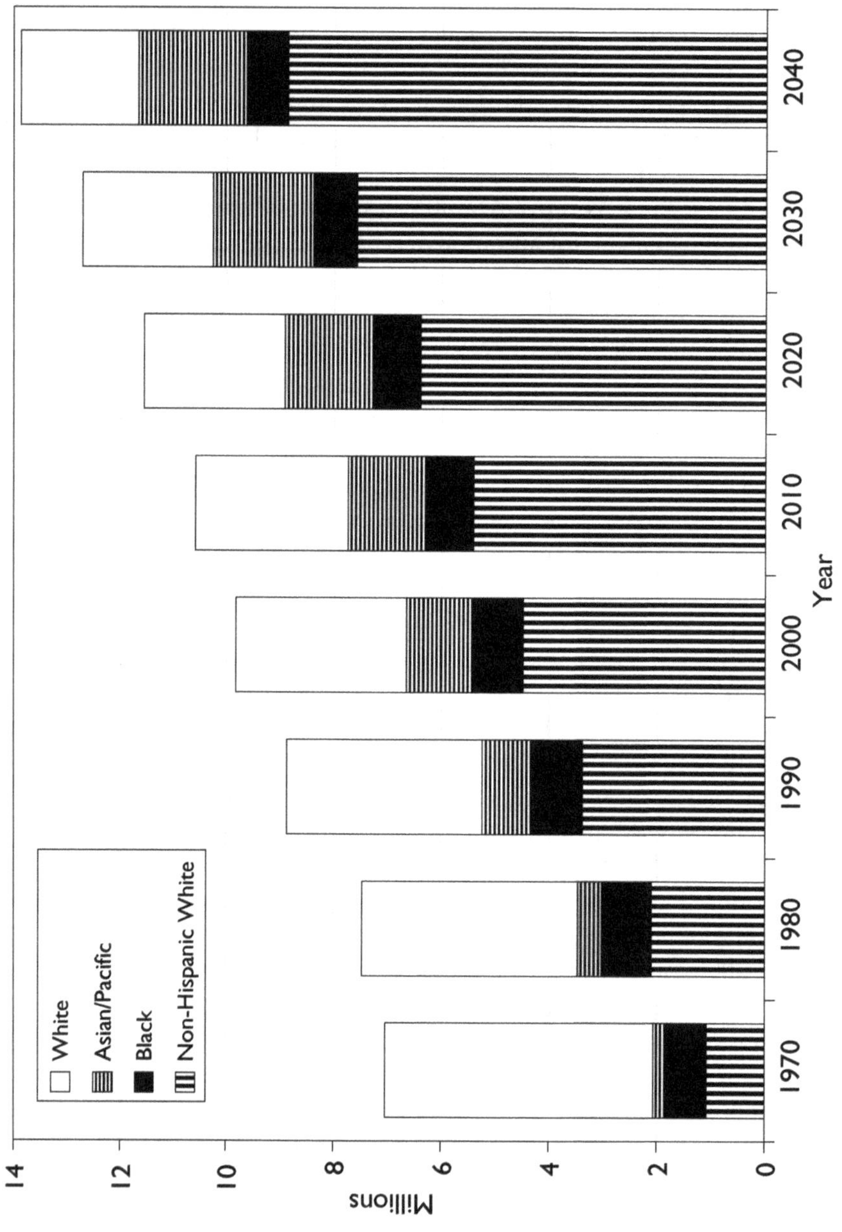

County population, transit usage has become, overwhelmingly, a minority phenomenon, far more those than in virtually any other major US mainland urbanized area. Although minority transit usage is virtually always significantly higher than the minority urban area population in the US (with the exception of largely suburban transit systems, such as commuter rail and water ferry operators, that serve overwhelming non-minority areas), the percentage of people of color who use transit is far higher for MTA than for the average of other US transit systems (APTA, 2001; DMU, 2001).

By 1980, however, transit in Los Angeles was running out of funding. The major public funding source was the quarter-cent state-mandated the 1971 Transportation Development Act sales tax. The limitations of these funds led to fare increases throughout the late 1970s. Quickly, however, the buses became so overcrowded that service was added to handle the loads. Fares went up from $0.25 to $0.35 for 1977, $0.40 for 1978, $0.45 for 1979, and $0.55 for 1980. Ridership continued to increase every year, even as the price of riding increased.

In 1980, the voters of Los Angeles County passed Proposition A. This measure imposed a half-cent sales tax in Los Angeles County for transit purposes. Learning from past failures at the ballot box, the Proposition A promoters put something in it for everyone. First, they reserved 25% of the collections for 'local return' to each incorporated city and Los Angeles County Supervisor (for the unincorporated portions of the County). This ensured a very high level of support from local elected politicians, or at least defused much of the former suburban opposition to countywide transit plans and taxes. Second, they dedicated 35% of the funds for rail construction and operations, promising a network of no less than 11 rail lines reaching virtually every corner of the primary populated areas of the County[4] (see Figure 12.2).

Third, for the first three years of tax collections, bus fares would be reduced to $0.50 and a $20 monthly pass. The '$0.50 fare' program was funded out of the 35% rail 'pot', thereby delaying rail spending full implementation for three years. Finally, 40% of the funds were put into the 'discretionary' pot, to be utilized for any purpose allowed by state statute and Proposition A. As a result, the proponents of every transit project in the county were able to convince themselves – often with a little help from Los Angeles County Transportation Commission (LACTC) staff – that 'their' project would be one of the first to be favored with discretionary funding (LACTC, 1980, for distribution of funding only). Proposition A gained 54% of the vote in the November 1980 election.

The $0.50 bus fare program was instituted in 1982 after a court challenge to the tax was successfully resolved. The result was the greatest increase in transit utilization over a comparable period in the US in a non-wartime situation since the early decades of the century – a 40% plus increase in transit ridership in three years, adding over 143 million riders a year (UMTA, 1987)[5]. The increases occurred despite bus service mile increases of only 1.5% over the period, resulting in the most overcrowded US buses since the Second World War. The fare subsidy

Figure 12.2: Proposition A rail plan

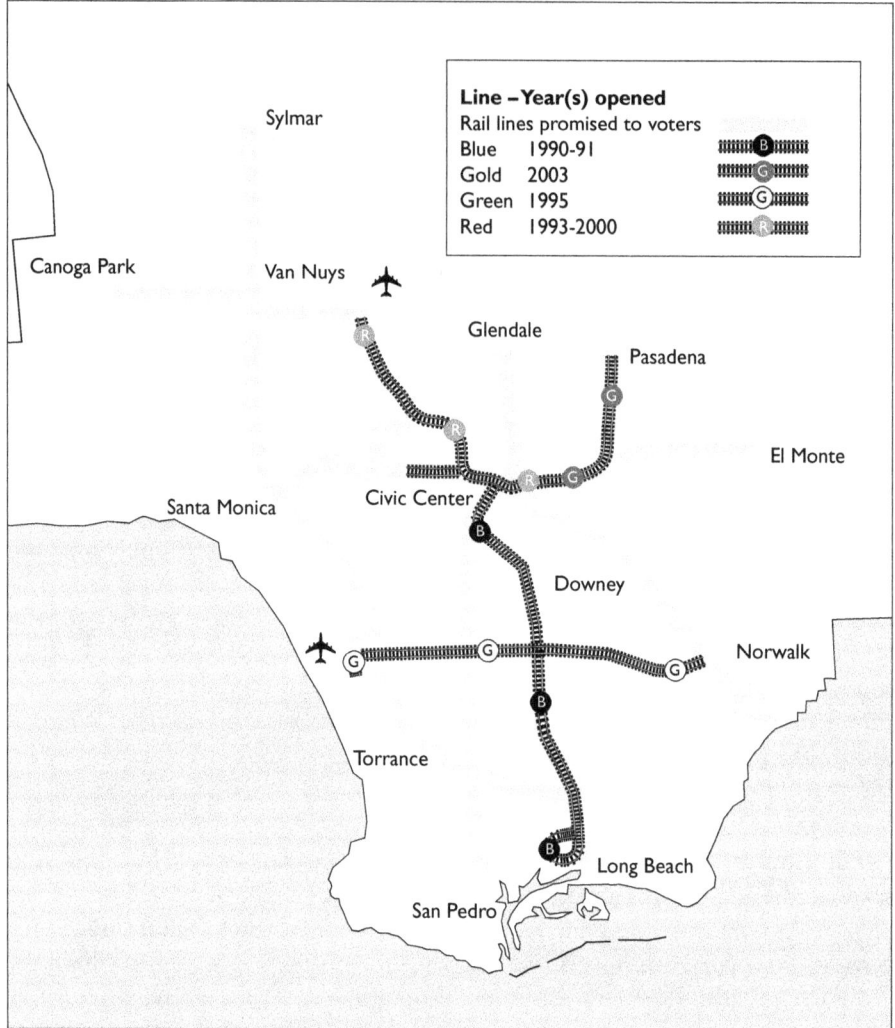

program required slightly under 20% of the Proposition A sales tax collections, or not quite a $0.001 sales tax – quite a bargain, to say the least.

At the end of 1985, the funding for the $0.50 fare terminated, under the terms of Proposition A, with the funds originally programmed for this purpose being used for rail construction. The first two projects to start construction were the Long Beach–Los Angeles Blue Line light rail and the Red Line subway from downtown Los Angeles to the San Fernando Valley.

Unfortunately, the combination of overly optimistic projections of rail construction costs, political expediency, and the lack of managers and staff with 'hands on' experience had already sown the eventual seeds of destruction of the

Proposition A rail plan. In order to gain the political support necessary to get Proposition A passed, it was necessary to include a very large number of rail lines. However, the costs of construction and operations of these lines far exceeded the funding that could be generated by Proposition A and other available funding sources. At the same time, the need to begin construction, to show the voters that they were receiving value for their money, and that their elected representatives were doing their job, served to ensure that expenditures were to be made, and committed, at a rate that far exceeded the ability of the funding sources to cover the costs.

The first problem that surfaced was the realization that the Proposition A 40% Discretionary Funds would not be available for rail construction. Financial reality required that the 40% funds be used to support the operations of the county's existing bus transit systems. The other major problem was the costs of rail construction were far higher than the original, technically deficient projections (and no one was willing to tell the emperor that he had no clothes!). For example, the earliest, informal estimates of the costs of the Long Beach–Los Angeles Blue Line light rail were approximately $125 million. The final approved budget was $877 million in 1990 – and the true cost is over $1 billion (Rubin, 2000).

Part of this increase of over 700% was due to changes in project design. A large part was due, however, to the original cost estimates just plain not being competent – and the reluctance of staff to admit to the governing board that costs were increasing. (These situations are known to anyone who has ever followed major capital projects for any length of time.)

The Blue Line light rail construction costs as a percentage of tax revenues rose from a 'best case' 6.75% of Proposition A sales tax rail funds over the construction period to over 115%. At the same time, the costs of the other rail programs were also growing. The Red Line subway Segment 1 had significant increases in costs of approximately $188 million over the $1.25 billion federal grant agreement cost (MTA, 1998b). The costs of the Green Line light rail line rose from a projected $178 million in 1986 to approach $1 billion (LACTC, 1986; Rubin, 2000).

These cost overruns began to require such high levels of borrowing that MTA's predecessor was approaching its debt limits. Proposition A's 11-line rail system would have soon come to a halt with only one line completed (Long Beach Blue Line light rail) and two others partially completed (Red Line subway and Green Line light rail) – and no funds to operate the lines that had been completed.

The result was what became Proposition C, a second half-cent sales tax that was placed before the voters in November 1990. The Proposition A success story was copied, including the local return (20%), dedicated fund 'pots' for specific interest groups (25% for 'transit-related' highway improvements which, as a practical matter, meant high-occupancy vehicle lanes, 10% for commuter rail/transit centers, and 5% for transit security) and discretionary fund (40%) tactics. Proposition C passed with a small margin, along with three state-wide measures that promised billions for transportation improvements, primarily rail construction, in Southern California.

One of MTA's predecessor agencies published a long-range transportation plan that was adopted as the 30-Year Integrated Transportation Plan in 1992. This became one of the all-time 'everything for everyone' planning exercises. The difficulty was in incorporating every project that all the many interested parties wanted while keeping within fiscal reality. The solution was, where there was a conflict, fiscal reality lost. Few knowledgeable observers believed that the projections in the 30-Year Plan could be realized, even before it was finalized – and it did not take long for its total lack of reality to be conclusively demonstrated[6].

When MTA started the next major plan process, it quickly discovered the extent of the problems they faced. The result was a document presented to the MTA board in October 1994 (MTA, 1994) that showed that, compared to the 1992 projection of $100 billion of revenues over the first 20 years of the 30-Year Plan, MTA was instead expecting $64 billion. MTA had overestimated the $64 billion it expected in 1994 by $36 billion, or over 56%. This is one of the largest, if not the largest, revenue forecast errors in the history of municipal finance.

Another major financial shortfall was the failure of the second and third parts of a $3 billion state transportation construction-funding program in 1992 and 1994.

The fare hike of 1994

During the first years of MTA's existence after its formation in 1993, the continual problem faced by the board and management was how to keep the rail construction program going at full speed. In his first major action before the Board, presenting the first MTA budget (for the 1994 fiscal year), the new chief executive officer stood tall and told the members the truth – that the agency was in deep financial trouble and the only way out was to live within the agency's means. Specifically, there was not sufficient funding to begin construction on the Pasadena light rail line and it would have to be delayed. The board refused to accept this and, led by the new Los Angeles Mayor, Richard Riordan, ordered staff to come up with a way to start the project. Staff returned with a plan that probably no one believed would work (or cared if it would), which the board immediately adopted, and work began on the Pasadena line – and the 'plan' to finance it was promptly forgotten by all[7].

In the budget process for the next fiscal year (1995), the big problem, once again, was to find ways to keep the rail construction projects going. One tactic was a fare increase. There had been no bus fare increase since the beginning of 1989, six years earlier.

One thing that all transit agency managers soon learn is that all transit board members absolutely detest being asked to approve fare increases. The MTA board proved no exception to this rule, taking the better part of a year to study alternatives before finally approving a major fare increase to become effective on

1 September 1994. It appeared that perhaps the one thing that bothered board members more than having to vote for a fare increase was stopping or slowing construction of rail projects.

This time, however, MTA had gone too far. Its ridership had been falling rapidly since 1985. The fare increases of 1985 and 1989 were prime causes of the decline in ridership and the 1994 fare increase would be far larger in impact. For the people of Los Angeles who depended on transit for their everyday mobility, this was the time to draw the line.

The fare increase that MTA attempted to implement, effective 1 September 1994, was huge. While the MTA documents focused on the cash fare increase from $1.10 to $1.35 – a 23% increase – the real crusher was the proposed total elimination of almost all pass programs. The MTA standard monthly pass cost $42 – and the average pass user took almost exactly 100 trips per month. The savings from passes was and is extremely important to MTA's very low-income ridership. For one type of 'typical' pass user, the cost of replacing the $42 monthly pass with $0.90 tokens and $0.25 transfers would be $57.50 – a 37% increase; for another, the replacement cost would be a $68.25, or 63% increase[8]. A small percentage of transit riders would encounter 100%, and even larger, fare increases.

The median MTA passenger household income was approximately $10,000 per year at the time of this action (MTA, 1998a, 1998c, 1998d, 1998e)[9]. An increase of $26.25 per month for transportation would run to a $315 increase per year – over 3% of household income. For a two-transit rider household (a very common situation), the impact of such a cost increase would be over 6% of household income. This was 6% of household income for households that were having great difficulty in putting food on the table for their children, let alone having a table to put the food on and a home to put the table in.

As a practical matter, of course, transit use would decline, even for these riders who are the most transit dependent of the transit dependent. Once a passenger has purchased a monthly pass, each use is 'free' – there is no additional cost to taking it. However, when each trip must be paid for on an individual basis with real cash money, care will be taken in taking unnecessary bus trips – for example, walking a mile or more may be preferable to spending $0.90 in scarce funds, or even $0.25 for a transfer.

This proposed increase was the direct precipitating event of the MTA lawsuit.

The MTA Consent Decree

The organizing effort

The MTA case is a prime example of how a highly organized grassroots campaign can team up with creative civil rights lawyers, academics, and other experts to achieve social change. Together, the participants collected and analyzed the data, organized the community, made political connections, presented the case to the media, and won the groundbreaking lawsuit that is helping to bring transportation equity to Los Angeles (for other perspectives on the MTA case see Lee, 1997; Hair, 2001 and Mann, 2004).

For years, MTA and its predecessor agencies had been favoring rail over bus service. These policies and practices came to a head in 1994. MTA approved a $0.25 increase in the cash bus fare, eliminated the $42 monthly bus pass that provided unlimited rides, and reduced the bus service to help overcome a claimed bus-operating deficit of $126 million. The following week, MTA allocated $123 million to build the new Pasadena Blue Line light rail line (now known as the Gold Line). Despite the chief executive officer of the MTA informing the board that the Pasadena line was beyond the agency's fiscal capacity, the MTA nevertheless proceeded with the light rail project and further burdened those riders who could least afford it.

A grassroots advocacy group called the Labor/Community Strategy Center (LCSC) and its transportation equity project, the Bus Riders' Union, had been organizing support for improved transit service and increased funding for buses since 1991. The Billions for Buses campaign advocated for a first-class, clean-fuel, bus-centered transit system for Los Angles.

The 1994 public hearing on the proposed fare increase was the catalyst for the organizing effort to join a legal challenge to MTA's transit policies. The passionate testimony of bus riders pleading against a fare increase, coupled with the indifferent response of the MTA board members to their plight, reflected the sharp dissonance between MTA policies and the needs of the community. The Los Angeles Times reported that "the Board's conduct while pushing through a fare increase … was so outrageous that it's hard to single out its most offensive act" (Boyarsky, 1994, p B1).

Unable to persuade MTA to stop the proposed fare increase, the LCSC turned to civil rights attorneys at the NAACP[10] Legal Defense and Educational Fund, Inc. (LDF) and others in search of a remedy through the courts.

Stopping the fare increase in court

On 31 August 1994, the day before the proposed fare hike was scheduled to go into effect, LDF filed a civil rights class action seeking to prevent the fare increase and to secure the equitable allocation of public funds for the bus system. The plaintiffs included the LCSC, Bus Riders Union, Southern Christian Leadership Conference, Korean Immigrant Workers Advocates, and various individual bus riders. The case was filed as a class action on behalf of all bus riders, as discussed below.

Federal District Court Judge Terry Hatter, an African American judge appointed by President Jimmy Carter, issued a temporary restraining order and a preliminary injunction against MTA to prevent the fare restructuring. The District Court enjoined MTA's proposed fare increase because the increase would:

> ... cause minority bus riders substantial losses of income and mobility that, for a significant number, will result in the loss of employment and housing, and the inability to reach medical care, food sources, educational opportunities, and other basic needs of life.

The Court held that plaintiffs presented "more than sufficient evidence" to support their disparate impact claims and "raised serious questions going to the merits" on the claims of discrimination:

> Plaintiffs have presented the Court with more than sufficient evidence to meet their burden of preliminarily showing that MTA's actions have adversely impacted minorities; that MTA's actions were not justified by business necessity; and that the MTA has rejected less discriminatory alternatives. (LCSC v MTA, 1994, pp 1-2, 4-5)

Metropolitan Transportation Authority agreed to settle the case after mediation, on the eve of trial, after all discovery was complete, after the District Court denied MTA's motion for summary judgment, when it faced near certain liability and extensive public disclosure and media coverage of its discriminatory, inefficient, and environmentally destructive transportation policies. After almost two years of extensive discovery and dozens of depositions, the parties settled the case through mediation in October 1996[11].

Through the Consent Decree, MTA agreed to roll back the price of the monthly unlimited-use bus pass from $49 to $42, to roll back the price of the biweekly bus pass from $26.50 to $21, and to institute a new weekly pass for $11. It agreed to purchase 102 buses for the most congested lines over the next two years and to reduce overcrowding by specified goals and specified times. Metropolitan Transportation Authority agreed to expand the bus service to new areas throughout the county. Finally, in a victory for democratic decision making, MTA agreed to work directly with bus riders in shaping transit policy through the Joint Working Group over the 10-year life of the decree.

The MTA case was settled with broad support that included Republican Mayor Richard Riordan, the libertarian Reason Foundation, free market efficiency advocates at the University of Southern California, self-described "bleeding heart liberals" at University of California, Los Angeles (UCLA), Cardinal Roger Mahony, and the grassroots groups who were plaintiffs in the case.

Several professors of transportation and urban planning, including Martin Wachs and Bryan Taylor of UCLA and James Moore II of University of Southern California (USC), and Professor Richard Berk of the UCLA Program in Statistics, prepared important expert reports and provided other vital assistance to the plaintiff class. The former chief financial officer for MTA's predecessor agency, Thomas A. Rubin, provided invaluable analyses of MTA's policies and insider knowledge of its practices.

While LDF led the legal charge, LCSC continued organizing and conducted a massive public relations campaign. This included appearances at virtually all MTA board and committee meetings, pushing the 'no fare increase' agenda and opposing MTA's actions to fund rail construction and other non-productive projects out of monies that could be utilized for bus operations. The LCSC prepared information flyers and reports, organized community meetings, met with other activist groups, continually pressed their story to newspaper, magazine, radio, and television reporters and editors, and ran a website. It took the message to the streets, and to the buses, with members and staff spending hundreds of hours at bus stops and on buses. Sit-in protests at MTA meetings resulted in Bus Riders Union members and staff being dragged off in handcuffs before the media.

On the eve of trial, the legal team recommended that plaintiffs and the class settle the case. Plaintiffs LCSC, the Bus Riders' Union, and Korean Immigrant Workers Advocates disagreed and retained separate counsel to recommend to the District Court that the case go to trial. This was a tense moment in the case. As counsel to the class, LDF's obligation was to represent the best interests of the class; it believed that the settlement terms were as good or better as anything the District Court could order after trial. A trial would take weeks or months and the inevitable appeals on the merits would drag on for years. On behalf of the Southern Christian Leadership Conference and the class, LDF recommended that the District Court accept the proposed settlement. The District Court agreed and signed the Consent Decree. LDF then resumed representing all the organizational plaintiffs in monitoring compliance with the Consent Decree.

Since the signing of the Consent Decree, despite determined MTA efforts to gut the Consent Decree through legal means and massive failures to meet its requirements, MTA transit ridership has increased by 22% – a net turnaround of over 25 million annual riders per year over the prior 11-year period – at very low cost per added bus rider, particularly compared to the rail system.

For the bus, the average subsidy per new passenger for fiscal year 2004 is a hair over $1.00; for the average of four MTA rail lines Blue, Gold, Green, and Red, the average subsidy is just over $19.00[12]. Since signing the Consent Decree, MTA has expanded its fleet by 140 buses.

Unfair disparities in transit service

The lawsuit allowed the plaintiff class to present a well-documented story about MTA's pattern and history of inequitable, inefficient, and environmentally destructive allocation of resources. The legal team documented the ridership disparities in a massive 226-page brief in opposition to MTA's motion for summary judgment and in support of the Consent Decree. The evidence was largely undisputed and is summarized below (LCSC v MTA, 1996).

Racial disparities

While over 80% of the people riding MTA's bus and rail lines were minorities, most people of color rode only buses. On the other hand, only 28% of riders on Metrolink – the six-county Southern California commuter rail line, which MTA has provided with over 60% of the local subsidy funding, for only about a third of the riders and an even lower percentage of the passenger-miles – were people of color. Thus, the percentage of minorities riding Metrolink varied by 173 standard deviations from the expected 80%. The likelihood that such a substantial departure from the expected value would occur by chance is infinitesimal (Castaneda v Partida, 1977).[13]

Subsidy disparities

While 94% of MTA's riders rode buses, MTA customarily spent 60-70% of its budget on rail. Data in 1992 revealed a $1.17 subsidy per boarding for an MTA bus rider. The subsidy for a Metrolink commuter rail rider was 18 times higher, however ($21.02). For a suburban light-rail streetcar passenger, the subsidy was more than nine times higher ($11.34); and for a subway passenger, it was projected to be two-and-a-half times higher ($2.92). (The actual figures, after operations began, were far higher.) For three years during the mid-1980s, MTA reduced the bus fare from $0.85 to $0.50. Ridership increased 40% during the period, making this the most successful mass transit experiment in the post-war era. Despite this increase in demand, MTA subsequently raised bus fares and reduced its peak-hour bus fleet from 2,200 to 1,750 buses.

Security disparities

While MTA spent only $0.03 for the security of each bus passenger in fiscal year 1993, it spent 43 times as much ($1.29), for the security of each passenger on the Metrolink commuter rail and the light rail, and 19 times as much ($0.57), for each passenger on the Red Line subway.

Crowding disparities

MTA customarily targeted peak period loads of 145% of seated capacity on its buses and that 'target' was very commonly exceeded. In contrast, there was no overcrowding for riders on Metrolink and MTA-operated rail lines. Metrolink was operated to have three passengers for every four seats so that passengers could ride comfortably and use the empty seat for their briefcases or laptop computers.

The history and pattern of discrimination

Such disparate treatment has devastating social consequences. The Governor's Commission on the 1964 Los Angeles riots and rebellion found that transportation agencies *"handicap[ped minority residents] in seeking and holding jobs, attending schools, shopping, and fulfilling other needs"* (Governor's Commission, 1965, p 75), and that the inadequate and prohibitively expensive bus service contributed to the isolation that led to the civil unrest in Watts (Governor's Commission on the Los Angeles Riots, 1965). Thirty years later, following the riots and rebellion in the wake of the acquittals of the police officers involved in the Rodney King beating, MTA commissioned a new study on inner-city transit needs that echoed the recommendations of the Governor's Commission. Metropolitan Transport Authority, however, did not comply with the recommendations of either report.

Efficiency and equity prevail

Buying more buses under the Consent Decree reflects sound transportation policy to offset decades of overspending by MTA on rail and unproductive road projects. Metropolitan Transport Authority's policies have focused on attracting automobile users onto buses and trains, to the detriment of the transit dependent who are MTA's steadiest customers. The dissonance between the quality of service provided to those who depend on buses and the level of public resources being spent to attract new transit riders is both economically inefficient and socially inequitable. Policies to attract affluent new riders decrease both equity and efficiency because low-income riders are, on average, less costly to serve. The poor require lower subsidies per rider than wealthier patrons. Moreover, the loss of existing ridership brought about by increased fares and the reduced quality of bus service, as in Los Angeles, far exceeds the small number of new riders brought onto the system (Garrett and Taylor, 1999).

Title VI of the Civil Rights Act of 1964 and just transportation

Title VI of the Civil Rights Act of 1964 and its implementing regulations prohibit both (1) intentional discrimination based on race, color or national origin, and (2) unjustified discriminatory impacts for which there are less discriminatory alternatives, by applicants for or recipients of federal funds such as MTA and most transportation agencies across the US. In the MTA case, the plaintiff class alleged both forms of discrimination.

The Title VI statute provides:

> No person in the United States shall on the ground of race, color, or national origin, be excluded from participation in, be denied the benefits of, or be subjected to discrimination under any program or activity receiving Federal financial assistance. (US DOT, 2000)

The Equal Protection Clause of the Fourteenth Amendment to the US Constitution also prohibits intentional discrimination. Section 1983 of the Civil Rights Act of 1871 prohibits intentional discrimination and unjustified discriminatory impacts.

Similarly, California state law now prohibits both intentional discrimination and unjustified discriminatory impacts for which there are less discriminatory alternatives by recipients of state funds under California Government Code § 11135. In addition, California law now defines environmental justice as "the fair treatment of people of all races, cultures, and incomes with respect to the development, adoption, implementation, and enforcement of environmental laws, regulations, and policies", under Californian Government Code § 65040.12. (These state law provisions were not in effect, and thus not at issue, at the time of the MTA litigation, but they now provide potential remedies for public resource inequities in light of the roll backs in federal civil rights protections since the MTA case was settled, as discussed later in this chapter.)

To receive federal funds, a recipient such as MTA must certify that its programs and activities comply with Title VI and its regulations (Guardians Ass'n v Civil Service Commission, 1983). In furtherance of this obligation, recipients must collect, maintain and provide upon request timely, complete, and accurate compliance information (see also Executive Order 12898 on Environmental Justice, 1994). Gathering, analyzing, and publishing such information can provide a powerful tool to illuminate inequities and to enable democratic participation in the decision-making process, as illustrated by the MTA case.

Unjustified discriminatory impacts

It is necessary to examine three components under the discriminatory impact standard under Title VI regulations, and by analogy, under parallel state laws:

1. whether an action by a recipient of federal funds, such as MTA, had a numerical discriminatory impact based on race, ethnicity or national origin;
2. if so, the recipient bears the burden of proving that any such action is justified by business necessity;
3. even if the action would otherwise be justified, the action is prohibited if there are less discriminatory alternatives to accomplish the same objective. (Larry, P. v Riles, 1984)

In support of the Consent Decree, the plaintiff class argued that the evidence established both discriminatory impact and intentional discrimination.

a) Discriminatory impacts. The racial, subsidy, security, and crowding disparities documented in the MTA case through statistical analyses have been outlined earlier in this chapter. The plaintiff class also produced anecdotal evidence, the

human stories of individual bus riders who faced incredible difficulties riding the bus and paying for transit service.
b) *No business necessity.* MTA was unable to provide any public transit or business necessity to justify the disparities outlined above.
c) *Less discriminatory alternatives.* MTA had less discriminatory alternatives: MTA could allocate resources to improve the bus service and reduce the transit fare.

Intentional discrimination

In order to evaluate an intentional discrimination claim, courts consider the following types of evidence:

(1) the impact of the action – whether it bears more heavily on one racial or ethnic group than another;
(2) the historical background of the action, particularly if a series of official actions was taken for invidious purposes;
(3) any departures from substantive norms, particularly if the factors usually considered important by the decision maker strongly favor a decision contrary to the one reached;
(4) any departures from procedural norms;
(5) the decision maker's knowledge of the harm caused by its decision;
(6) a pattern or practice of discrimination. (Village of Arlington Heights v Metropolitan Housing Dev. Corp., 1977; US Department of Justice, Civil Rights Division, 1998)

(1) *Impacts.* The evidence of discriminatory impacts has been discussed earlier in this chapter.

(2) and (6) *History and pattern.* The plaintiff class argued that the evidence discussed above – the discriminatory impacts and the Governor's Commission on the 1964 Los Angeles Riots – documented the continuing history and pattern of intentional discrimination against communities of color and low-income communities in the provision of transit services.

(3) and (4) *Substantive and procedural irregularities.* The plaintiff class argued that the decisions to increase the bus fare and to allocate resources to bus over rail were replete with procedural and substantive irregularities. Metropolitan Transportation Authority routinely proceeded with rail and commuter bus programs that had either marginal or no rider, fiscal, environmental, economic, or other benefit. For example, MTA approved the increase in the bus fare to meet a claimed budget shortfall, and almost simultaneously allocated millions of dollars to build a new Pasadena light rail line that the MTA chief executive officer described as "idiocy".

(5) *Knowledge.* The plaintiff class maintained that MTA's own documents analyzing the impact of fare increases established that MTA knew the harm caused to low-income people of color.

The class of all bus riders

While the MTA case was based on civil rights laws prohibiting discrimination based on race, color, or national origin, the case was also fought on behalf of poor white bus riders, who constituted almost 20% of the ridership. The District Court certified the case as a class action on behalf of all poor minority and other riders of MTA buses who were denied equal opportunity to receive transportation services because of MTA's operation of discriminatory mass transportation system, a class of approximately 350,000 people. The definition of the class included white bus riders because discrimination against any one diminishes everyone. Metropolitan Transport Authority did not challenge the class definition.

The MTA case highlighted the complexities of race, class, and the environment that are common in resource equity disputes around the nation. Racial and ethnic exclusion is often symptomatic of a larger, structural unfairness that affects all people who are powerless to protect themselves, including disadvantaged white people. This is why it was important to define the class to include all bus riders, not just riders of color.

Attention to racial and ethnic exclusion is often dismissed as being unduly confrontational, divisive, or at best opportunistic because race no longer matters. Some people believe race no longer matters in contemporary society, that racial discrimination is a thing of the past. Whatever vestiges of racism remain should be adequately addressed (if at all) through protections against invidious intentional discrimination against insular minorities.

While people of color stood to benefit from the suit, people of color with power and money held decision-making roles within MTA and were responsible for decisions that unfairly impacted low-income people of color; they, in particular, resented being accused of racial discrimination. Some also felt that, while MTA's transit policies might be inefficient, irrational, and indefensible, they were not intentionally discriminatory based on race or ethnicity despite the adverse impact the policies had on people of color and low-income communities.

Environmental justice is about race and ethnicity. The likelihood that the transit disparities documented in the MTA case would occur by chance is infinitesimal, as discussed earlier. Arguments dismissing adverse impacts on the grounds that they do not constitute racial discrimination fundamentally misunderstand discriminatory impact laws and the dynamics of interracial bias in contemporary society (Krieger, 1995).

Contemporary racial justice efforts focus on ferreting out institutional practices that systemically disadvantage individuals or groups based on race or class. Commonly referred to as 'institutional' or 'environmental' racism, these structural inequities are the result of a pattern of collective thought, action, or inaction, which are characteristic of many institutions like municipalities, state governments, or private corporations. Individuals in decision-making positions may not personally be racist, but by carrying out established institutional priorities they perpetuate and extend patterns of environmental inequity and injustice (Weiskel, 1999). Discriminatory impact law focuses on the cause and effect rather than just the racial animus of the actor. The fact that personal biases are not at stake does not make efforts to combat discrimination any more palatable to the actors.

The aftermath of the Consent Decree

Metropolitan Transportation Authority has resisted complying with the Consent Decree for over seven years. Three years after signing the Decree, MTA admitted that it violated the provisions of the settlement that required MTA to reduce overcrowding by specified levels and specified dates on 75 of 78 monitored bus lines. The Special Master monitoring compliance with the Decree ordered MTA to buy more buses to remedy the overcrowding violations. Metropolitan Transportation Authority asked the Special Master to reconsider, but then refused to comply with the Special Master's decision.

Metropolitan Transportation Authority appealed to the District Court, which ordered MTA to buy 248 more buses. The authority again appealed, this time to the Ninth Circuit Court of Appeals. Plaintiffs and the class filed their response, supported by a friend of the court brief filed by a broad multicultural alliance of environmental, environmental justice, civil rights, and grassroots advocates. When the Court of Appeals denied the appeal, MTA petitioned for a review by both the original three-judge panel and a special en banc hearing. Both refused to consider MTA's petition, voting 3-0 and 25-0 against, respectively. Ultimately, MTA sought review in the US Supreme Court, which refused to hear the case (LCSC v MTA, 2001, 2002). At every stage of the seven-year litigation, MTA has illustrated the only successful defense tactic from the time the suit was filed in 1994 to the present date – delay.

Most recently, Special Master Bliss has ordered that MTA purchase 145 40-seat buses as soon as possible (but no later than December 2005) and operate a total of 370,185 additional in-service bus hours for load factor reduction (Bliss, 2004). The MTA board has voted (with the bare majority seven affirmative votes) to appeal the portion of the order requiring it to buy additional buses (MTA, 2004).

The Consent Decree fare increase protections ended in late 2003, and effective from 1 January 2004, MTA implemented a significant fare increase, raising the price of monthly passes $10, to $52, and doing away with $0.25 transfers in favor of $3.00 day passes. The adult cash fare was reduced from the current $1.35 to $1.25 (which, due to the rather strange method of allocating transit operating subsidies to bus operators in Los Angeles County, MTA believes will actually increase total MTA revenue) (MTA, 2003a, 2003b).

Metropolitan Transportation Authority has also decided to delete bus services wherever it can. While the requirement that MTA reduce overcrowding under the Consent Decree provides protection against reductions in service on most bus lines during peak hours, MTA has concentrated on lower utilized lines and off-peak and weekend service. Metropolitan Transportation Authority has reduced bus service hours more than it is adding hours to comply with overcrowding requirements – in effect, MTA is forcing the Consent Decree to serve as both a floor to reduce, as well as a ceiling to limit, overcrowding.

Throughout the struggle, however, MTA has never lost its appetite for expensive guideway transit projects. Indeed, even as MTA continues to plead that it does not have the fiscal resources to buy and operate the buses required by the Consent Decree, it is actually borrowing hundreds of millions of dollars against promised state grants that were eliminated as part of the current $38 billion California budget shortfall work-out package. Instead of getting these funds on a reimbursement basis as MTA funds are spent, MTA is borrowing and paying interest in the hope – but not the certainty – that the funding for these grants will appear in some future state budget.

Even in fiscal year 2004, over 54% of the transit subsidies for MTA's own transit services capital, operating, and financing expenditures are going for guideway transit (MTA, 2003c). 'Guideway transit' includes expenditures for a $337.6 million San Fernando Valley 'Rapidway', or the 'Orange Line', a Bus Rapid Transit/Bikeway project that MTA keeps renaming.

Metropolitan Transportation Authority's past and proposed billions of dollars in rail capital and operating funds, well over half of all MTA expenditures for a period of decades, would, according to MTA, eventually carry 18% of MTA system-wide passenger trips. These projects are demonstrably inferior to many bus projects that MTA is refusing to even consider.

This combination of MTA decisions produces a very strange result. It is utilizing high-risk borrowing techniques to fund expensive, but non-productive, guideway transit systems. In the process, MTA is using up funds that could be used for transit operations both now and in future years, while pleading inability to finance the operating costs of the Consent Decree that MTA voluntarily entered into. Yet, if MTA allows these projects to be constructed, the projects will significantly increase MTA's operating expenses in the near future. The fear is that MTA will then reduce bus service to respond to the operating funding crisis it created, a fear compounded by a newly released MTA transit service policy (MTA, 2003d).

While the Consent Decree has protected the transit riders of Los Angeles from grievous harm to the bus transit system that they depend on and also produced very large improvements, the battle to obtain the full measure of improvements promised in the Consent Decree is obviously an ongoing war with many major battles yet to be fought.

Beyond MTA

Equal justice after Sandoval

Equal access to public resources including transportation dollars remains as important today as ever. A conservative 5-4 majority of the US Supreme Court in Alexander v Sandoval (532 US 275, 2001) took a step to close the courthouse door to individuals and community organizations challenging practices that adversely and unjustifiably impact people of color, such as transportation inequities, police abuse, racial profiling of drivers on the highway, and unequal access to parks and recreation. The majority, led by Justice Antonin Scalia, held there is no right for private individuals like José Citizen and groups like the Labor/Community Strategy Center under Title VI to enforce the discriminatory impact regulations issued by federal agencies under the Title VI statute.

Although the Sandoval holding is a serious blow to civil rights enforcement, it is more important to keep in mind that intentional discrimination and unjustified discriminatory impacts are just as unlawful after Sandoval as before. Recipients of federal funds, like MTA, remain obligated to prohibit both. Even now, after Sandoval, individuals still can sue a recipient of federal funds under Title VI to challenge intentionally discriminatory practices. Known discriminatory impact continues to be among the most important evidence leading to a finding of discriminatory intent.[14]

Aside from private lawsuits, there remain other ways to enforce discriminatory impact regulations. Recipients of federal funds are still bound by the regulations under Title VI. Every recipient signs a contract to enforce Title VI and its regulations as a condition of receiving federal funds. This provides an important opportunity to use the planning and administrative process to resolve discriminatory impact issues.

There are important strategic considerations in the quest for equal justice after Sandoval. Elected officials should be increasingly sensitive to and held accountable for the impact of their actions on communities of color, especially now that people of color are in the majority in 48 out of the 100 largest cities in the US. Los Angeles is about 50% Hispanic, 70% people of color, and only 33% non-Hispanic white, according to 2000 Census data. People of color are increasingly being elected to positions of power. Congress should pass legislation to reinstate the private cause of action to enforce the discriminatory impact standard. State civil rights protections can be enforced and strengthened. Civil rights and environmental claims can be combined in future cases in the wake of the MTA case and Sandoval. Similar kinds of evidence are relevant to prove both discriminatory intent and discriminatory impact. The same kinds of evidence can be as persuasive in the planning process, administrative arena, and court of public opinion, as in a court of law.

The complexities of equal justice after Sandoval require far-reaching strategies that include building multicultural alliances, legislative and political advocacy, strategic media campaigns, research and analyses of financial, demographic, and historical data, and strengthening democratic involvement in the public decision-making process in addition to litigation. Societal structures and patterns and practices of discrimination are significant causes of racial injustice and should be principal targets of reform.

The planning and administrative processes

Outside of the MTA case, others are working toward transportation equity. In 1998, for example, the Southern California Association of Governments (SCAG) adopted a regional transportation plan that is committed to complying with Title VI of the Civil Rights Act. The SCAG is the first transportation agency in the country that explicitly analyzes the impact of transportation proposals on low-income communities and communities of color in its regional transportation plan. It demonstrates how agencies can incorporate transportation equity and public participation into the planning process (US DOT, 2000).

While SCAG, the other metropolitan planning organizations that have begun to conduct environmental justice analyses, should be congratulated for beginning this important step in transportation and urban planning, there is still a great deal of work to be done to ensure that the processes that are being utilized will actually be meaningful tests of environmental justice. Unfortunately, in the early stages of environmental justice analyses of large-scale transportation plans, the evaluation is often limited to testing if the recommended program of projects appears to work *against* the interests of minority, low-income and other protected classes, rather than modelling alternative projects to determine which could provide the *most benefits* to these groups. This compounds a common problem in such long-range transportation planning, as well as corridor-specific planning exercises. Many schemes, that there is good reason to believe could be financially viable, are frequently suppressed, by staff, and/or consultants, who do not wish to see competition for their, or their Board's, pre-selected 'winners'.

Highways and land use

Just as transportation decisions affect social equity, economic vitality, and environmental quality, those decisions are affected by other factors, such as highway spending. Governments should consider all feasible options, including different mixes of roads and transit, to determine which is best for each region and its people, with a major emphasis on informed public input in the decision-making process.

Land-use planning and patterns also affect transportation policies and vice versa. Consequently, they should be addressed together. For example, sprawl in Los Angeles was initially generated not by the freeway system, which started in 1943, but by the Los Angeles and Pacific Electric Railway system, which served

Southern California from Long Beach to San Fernando, and from Riverside to San Pedro, from 1901 through the mid-century. The electric interurban (Red Car) and streetcar (Yellow Car) system made residential sprawl possible far from the urban core of Los Angeles (Wachs, 1997).

Los Angeles also pioneered the use of racially restrictive covenants in deeds, which restricted African Americans and other people of color from buying homes in white neighborhoods. Through the 1930s, the Federal Housing Authority subsidized racially homogenous neighborhoods[15]. Some economists have estimated that the federal government has spent more than $2 trillion subsidizing the flight of white people from central cities. As a result, Los Angeles and other cities today face a spatial mismatch between jobs, homes, and transportation (Waldinger and Bozorgmehr, 1996; García, 1997; Powell, 1999). By planning for multicultural, multiuse communities that are better suited to transit, walking, and biking, we can create healthier communities with more mobility, greater access to jobs, reduced congestion, cleaner air, and greater justice.

It is also necessary to recognize that orders of magnitude of more low-income people and people of color depend on the automobile than on public transportation. Many minority people live in rural areas, small towns, and other out-of-the-way places, nowhere near transit services. Transportation equity cannot be defined solely in terms of the experience of large, metropolitan areas. It is also necessary to look at the delivery of transportation services in small towns and rural areas and elsewhere.

For many highway projects, transit is not a viable alternative. Deciphering which communities are harmed by the negative aspects of highways and which communities get service is critical even in communities where no transit service exists. Highway projects generally do not displace houses and businesses in upper-middle-class neighborhoods to connect lower-income minority residents to jobs. Instead, highway projects displace lower-income and minority residents. There are no freeways in Beverly Hills, but the Latino Barrio of East LA is dissected every which way by freeways.

Finally, airports raise transportation equity issues that fall squarely within the transportation equity framework. For example, the proposed expansion of Los Angeles International Airport will affect not only communities of color and low-income communities but in fact all the people of Southern California. Major issues of concern include human health, air pollution and climate change, water quality, biodiversity, open space, noise pollution, job creation, ground transportation to flights and jobs, and displacement of communities and homes. Los Angeles World Airways, the city agency responsible for operating the airport, included a chapter on environmental justice in the draft environmental impact report/environmental impact statement published in 2001, but the expansion plan covered in that draft was abandoned in the wake of the 11 September terrorist attacks and the emphasis on security over airport expansion (US DOT FAA and the City of Los Angeles, 2001).

Beyond transportation

The lessons of the MTA case for ensuring equal access to public resources extend beyond the transportation context. One of the broadest and most diverse alliances ever behind any issue in Los Angeles has joined together to create parks in underserved communities of color. Los Angeles is park-poor, with fewer acres of parks per thousand residents compared to any major city in the country, and there are unfair disparities in access to parks and recreation based on race, ethnicity, income, class, and access to transportation. People in neighborhoods without parks or school playgrounds lack access to cars and to a decent transit system to reach the neighborhoods with parks and playgrounds. Activists are fighting to bring open space to the people and to provide transit to take people to the open space.

The urban park alliances stopped warehouses to create the state park in the 32-acre Chinatown Cornfield (Sanchez, 2001; García et al, 2003). The *Los Angeles Times* called the Cornfield "a heroic monument, and maybe even a symbol of hope" (Ricci, 2001, p 6). Robert García from the Center for Law in the Public Interest led the coalition that challenged the project as being one more product of discriminatory land-use policies that long deprived minority neighborhoods of parks (Sanchez, 2001). An alliance stopped a commercial project to create a 40-acre park, as the first step towards a planned 103-acre park in Taylor Yard along the 51 mile Los Angeles River. The alliance helped stop a power plant and a city dump in favor of a two-square-mile park in the Baldwin Hills, the historic heart of African American Los Angeles, that will be the largest urban park in the US in over a century – bigger than Central Park in New York City or Golden Gate Park in San Francisco.

The urban park movement is relying on strategies refined from the MTA case. First, there is a vision for a comprehensive and coherent web of parks, playgrounds, schools, beaches, and transit for the region. Second, the campaign is engaged in active coalition building that includes civil rights, environmental, environmental justice, religious, business, and economic interests. Third, the campaign engages in public education and advocacy outside the courts through the planning and administrative processes. Fourth, strategic media campaigns sharpen public debate and help build alliances. Fifth, extensive financial, demographic, and historical research and analyses provide hard data to support reform. Sixth, the urban park movement creatively engages opponents to find common ground. Litigation combining civil rights, environmental, and other claims remains available as a last resort.

Urban issues like transportation, parks and recreation, and sustainable communities are genuine civil rights issues of race, poverty, and democracy that are interrelated in Los Angeles and the American economy. The urban park movement, like the MTA case, is part of a broader struggle for equality, democracy, and livability for all (García, 2002a, 2002b, 2004: forthcoming; García et al, 2003).

The struggle continues

Clearly, transportation equity is about more than concrete, asphalt, steel, buses, trains, and cars. It is about investing in people and providing the opportunities to pursue better lives.

In fact, transportation equity is part of the continuing struggle for equal justice that goes back more than 100 years to the 1896 Plessy v Ferguson decision upholding segregated railroad cars and legitimizing the "separate but equal" treatment of white people and people of color[16]. Indeed, the modern civil rights movement has roots in the Montgomery bus boycott led by Rosa Parks and Martin Luther King Jr, who recognized transportation as an issue that lies at the intersection of civil rights, economic vitality and the environment. Addressing the need for structural reforms to deal with race and poverty, Reverend King wrote:

> When you go beyond a relatively simple though serious problem such as police racism … you begin to get into all the complexities of the modern American economy. Urban transit systems in most American cities, for example, have become a genuine civil rights issue – and a valid one – because the layout of rapid-transit systems determines the accessibility of jobs to the black community. If transportation systems in American cities could be laid out so as to provide an opportunity for poor people to get meaningful employment, then they could begin to move into the mainstream of American life. (Washington, 1991, pp 325-6)

Decades later, the experience in Los Angeles demonstrates that some transportation policies continue to nurture an environment that is not only separate, but starkly unequal. Nonetheless, as efforts in the wake of the MTA case show, there is hope. Transportation equity can be achieved and with it improvements in social justice, economic vitality, and environmental quality for all.

Conclusion

Has the Consent Decree been a benefit or a detriment to transportation and transit in the MTA service area? Not surprisingly, the plaintiffs and the defendants have very significant differences on this question.

For an unbiased evaluation, let us examine what Special Master Donald T. Bliss, the man who was appointed specifically to resolve disputes between the parties to the Consent Decree, has concluded, following presentations by both parties to him on this matter. The following is from his most recent order (Bliss, 2004, p 32), specifically Footnote 22 (detailed citations and emphasis notations have been deleted):

MTA's new management apparently is not pleased with the way the Consent Decree entered into by its predecessors has been implemented. In his declaration, David Yale states that 'the Consent Decree has had no benefits that could not have been achieved without the Decree, and it has diverted significant financial resources in process to questionable bus service expansions', which are 'a poor investment of scarce public funding'. Moreover, according to Mr Yale, 'the Consent Decree has, and will continue to have, detrimental impacts on the Regional Transportation System in Los Angeles County for many years to come'. Without the Decree, Mr Yale states that the MTA 'would have had additional financial resources' for highway construction. Mr Yale candidly acknowledges that 'the MTA has carefully developed a *short range plan* that balances these needs as best it can under the constraints of the Consent Decree....'. However, Mr Yale continues, 'any further unanticipated financial changes that are needed for the Decree *will have to be undone as soon as the Decree expires in early FY 2007....* (emphasis in the original)

Given these views on the alleged shortcomings of the Consent Decree presented by an MTA planning official in the record of this proceeding, it is all the more imperative that the MTA commit to a specific bus capacity expansion program that will provide lasting improvements in the quality of bus service for the transit-dependent – in accordance with the letter and spirit of the Consent Decree – beyond the expiration of this Decree. It should be noted that Mr Yale's views present an interesting contrast to what the MTA staff apparently wrote, at least with respect to the procurement of new buses, in a briefing for the MTA Board on the Consent Decree. The staff outlined the benefits of compliance with the Decree, including the transformation of the MTA bus fleet from 'the oldest to the newest fleet of major bus companies', and stated that 'MTA's new buses are worth every penny'.

Furthermore, the Bus Rider Union and its expert, Thomas Rubin, who have been sharply critical of the MTA's implementation of the Decree, also have presented a more positive view of the benefits achieved by the Decree in improving bus service for transit-dependent riders, which is, after all, the singular purpose of the Decree. In his Declaration Re Reallocation of MTA Funds, Mr Rubin analyzes in detail the effects of the Consent Decree, finding that in the six year post-Consent Decree period, the MTA has gained a total of 81.6 million annual riders. According to Mr Rubin, MTA ridership increased from 364 million in 1996 to 445 million in 2002, resulting in an increase in total fare revenues of $100.5 million over the six year period. This in stark contrast to a loss of 133.6 million annual passengers over the eleven year period preceding the Consent Decree. Mr Rubin also shows that, even taking into account what he views as 'extremely overstated' Consent Decree expenditures per new rider, the cost per new rider – 83% of whom are bus riders – is still far below other transit modes. Mr Rubin describes other benefits of the Consent Decree: 'The [Consent Decree] has made great progress in reducing overcrowding, and pass-by's, on MTA bus routes ... MTA service has also become more reliable and the condition of MTA's bus fleet improved substantially as the average age has decreased. The fares to ride MTA bus and rail have been kept low for MTA's huge numbers of extremely low-income riders. The service added for Consent Decree compliance has meant shorter headways, and the reduced overcrowding has decreas[ed] running times, speeding travel for these bus riders. The Rapid Bus Program, which MTA has claimed as a [Consent Decree] cost ... is another significant benefit for bus riders. Many new bus lines have begun service. The speed-up of bus replacement has meant cleaner air for all Los Angeles County residents.... All in all, hundreds of thousands of MTA bus and rail riders each day, and many more non-transit users, are receiving benefits in lower cost transit; a faster, higher quality, and more reliable transit experience; access to new destinations; and improved environmental quality and traffic flow – all due to the workings of the [Consent Decree].

Hopefully, these benefits are not the temporary results of a 'short range plan' due to expire at the end of the Consent Decree but rather are permanent improvements in the quality of bus service that will be sustained well beyond the Decree's expiration.[17]

As the ridership data clearly shows, the Consent Decree has been, by any measure, a tremendous success for the plaintiffs and other transit users in Los Angeles County. Indeed, an analysis of MTA ridership patterns demonstrates that the ridership under the Decree is almost 50% higher than ridership would have been without the Decree (Rubin, 2003).

During the period of the Consent Decree, MTA has never been in compliance with its requirement to reduce overcrowding. The plaintiffs are currently in the process of petitioning Special Master Bliss to extend the Consent Decree for six years to provide the full benefit of the Consent Decree for the full period that MTA had agreed to provide. It is expected that MTA will oppose this action.

The graph on page 249 (see Figure 12.3) includes two projection lines. The first is a simple extension of the 'least squares' (simple regression) trend line for the 11 years immediately preceding the implementation of the Consent Decree. The second is a 'judgment project' based on my expert analysis and report on what would have likely occurred if the Consent Decree, and the legal action that led to it, had never existed.

Figure 12.3: Los Angeles County MTA passenger trips: fiscal year 1985-2002, with and without Consent Decree

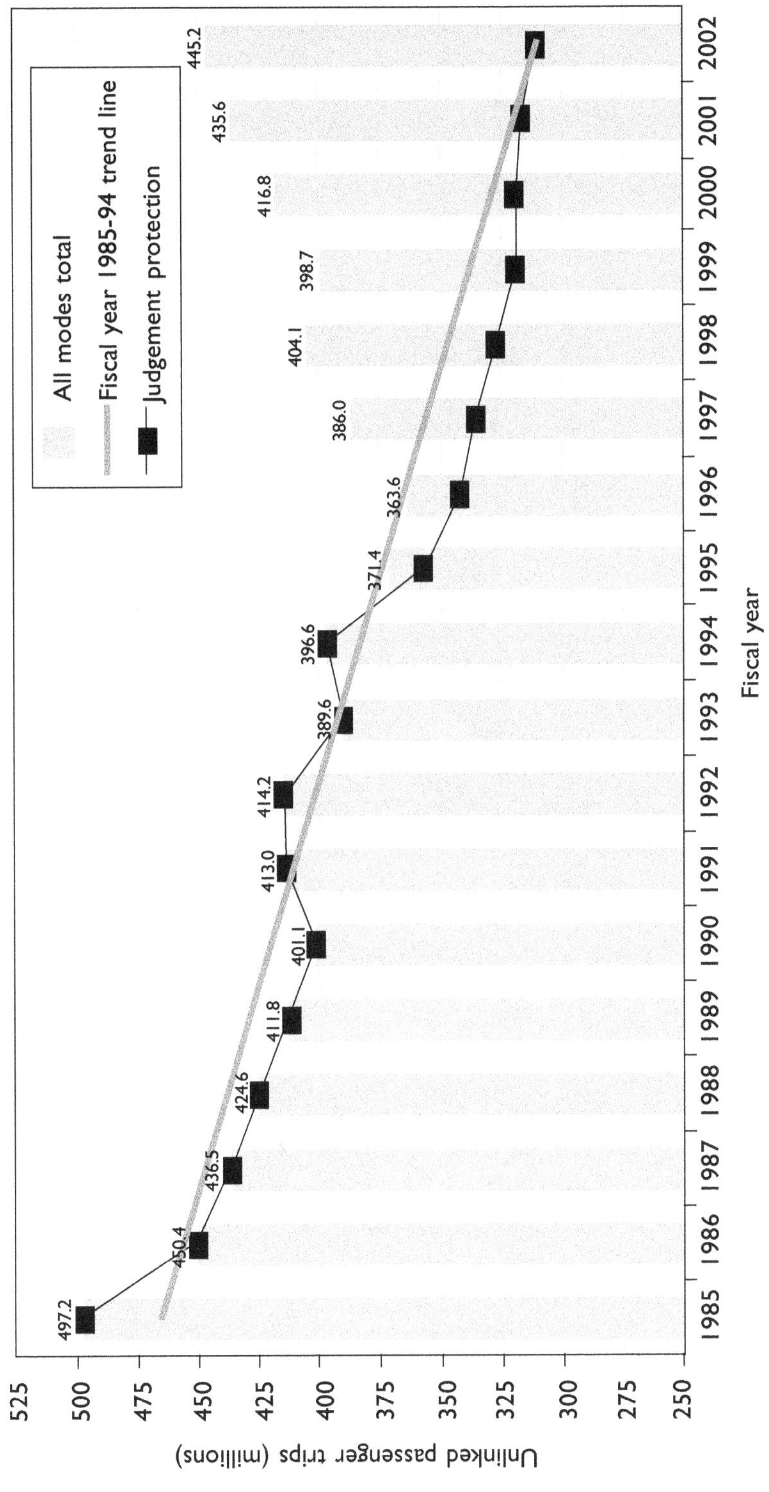

Fiscal year	Unlinked passenger trips (millions)	Trend line
1985	497.2	
1986	450.4	
1987	436.5	
1988	424.6	
1989	411.8	
1990	401.1	
1991	413.0	
1992	414.2	
1993	389.6	
1994	396.6	
1995	371.4	
1996	363.6	
1997	386.0	
1998	404.1	
1999	398.7	
2000	416.8	
2001	435.6	
2002	445.2	

Legend: All modes total; Fiscal year 1985-94 trend line; Judgement protection

Lessons from the MTA Consent Decree action that can be applied to other environmental justice struggles

Four of the central lessons of the environmental justice movement are that communities of color and low-income communities are:

- disproportionately denied the benefits of public resources like just transportation systems;
- disproportionately bear the burdens of environmental degradation;
- are denied access to information to understand the impact of decisions on all communities;
- are denied full and fair participation in the decision-making process.

The MTA case is one example of communities and attorneys working together to change the relations of power, to give people a sense of their own power, and to bring real improvements in people's lives. The case depended on a multifaceted approach that put affected communities at the center. The MTA case provides valuable lessons that go beyond transportation equity for strategic campaigns in and out of court to achieve social change. First, the mission of achieving equal access to transportation is just one aspect of a broader vision for the distribution of public resources' benefits and burdens in ways that are equitable, protect human health and the environment, promote economic vitality, and engage full and fair public participation in the decision-making process.

Second, the campaign must engage in active coalition building, both to learn what people want and to find collective ways of getting it. The coalition works to build bridges between civil rights, environmental, environmental justice, business, civic, religious, and economic leaders. Third, the campaign shows people how to participate in the planning and administrative processes so that they may engage in public policy and legal advocacy outside the courts. Fourth, strategic media campaigns focus attention and build support. Fifth, multidisciplinary research and analyses illuminate inequities.

Following the money clarifies who benefits by the investment of public resources and who gets left behind. Extensive financial, demographic, and historical analyses also connect the dots to demonstrate how cities and regions came to be the way they are and how they could be better. Finally, it is necessary to engage opponents creatively to find common ground. Ultimately, the MTA case was resolved through mediation and a settlement, not trial. Litigation nevertheless remains available, and reserved as a last resort, in the context of a broader campaign.

[Editor's note: subsequent to the submission of this chapter it has been announced that MTA has agreed, by unanimous decision of its board, to comply with the federal court order to add 145 buses to its network by 2005.]

Notes

1. In contrast, the typical Metrolink commuter rail rider was a white male who had an annual household income of $64,000 and owned at least one car.
2. In this chapter, 'ridership' means unlinked passenger trips. For example, a transit user that takes a bus to the Blue Line light rail and then transfers to the Red Line subway will create three *unlinked* passenger trips – and one *linked* passenger trip.
3. The data here covers the Los Angles-Riverside-Orange County Urbanized Area.
4. To ensure that this point was not lost on the voters, the rail lines on the Rail Rapid Transit System map as drawn would have been approximately one and a quarter miles wide in reality, generating a false visual impact that all points in the core densely populated areas of the county were relatively close to one or more rail lines.
5. To provide perspective, if the 143 million increase in bus ridership was a separate transit agency, it would have been the fifth-largest bus operation, and the tenth-largest transit system in the US in 1985 (UMTA, 1987).
6. The MTA's two predecessor agencies merged to form MTA in 1993.
7. At the end of 1997, MTA finally had to admit that it did not have the financial capacity to complete even the 'limited' number of rail projects that it had started and put the Red Line Segment 3 Eastside and Mid-City and Pasadena line projects on what later turned out to be indefinite hold. This decision was made after the Federal Transit Administration had refused to accept three separate MTA attempts to structure a financial plan to complete these three rail lines while meeting its other obligations. The newly appointed MTA chief executive officer, Julian Burke, was forced to submit this suspension of work to the board after spending his first several months at MTA attempting to get to the bottom of MTA's financial situation.
8. The original proposal was to increase the price of tokens from $0.90 to $1.00; the adopted fare structure kept the token price at $0.90.
9. In the 'Bus' survey, which represented over 90% of riders, 40% of respondents had household incomes under $7,500 and 29% had household incomes between $7,500 and $15,000. Respondents to the three rail surveys had somewhat higher income patterns, but it is such a small portion of total MTA ridership that the bus survey population controls the distribution.
10. The NAACP Legal Defense and Educational Fund, Inc. began as the legal arm of the National Association for the Advancement for Colored People, but is now a totally separate organization.
11. Donald Bliss, former Acting General Counsel to the US Department of Transportation, served as the mediator and later as the Special Master monitoring compliance with the Consent Decree.
12. Mr Rubin's calculation using Federal Transit Administration 'New Starts' costing methodology and data from MTA Approved Budget 2003-04.
13. Differences of two or three standard deviations are suspect.
14. Arguably, individuals can sue to enforce discriminatory impact regulations against recipients of federal funds through the 1871 Civil Rights Act, a matter not decided in Sandoval. Subsequent decisions suggest this theory might not prevail, however

(see for example Gongaza University v Doe S36 US 273 (2002); Save our Valley v Sound Transit, 335 F.3d 932, 936-937 (9th Circuit, 2003).

[15] The Federal Housing Administration Manual of 1938, for example, states: "If a neighborhood is to retain stability, it is necessary that properties shall continue to be occupied by the same racial classes. A change in social or racial occupancy generally contributes to instability and a decline in values". See also Davis (1990, 2000).

[16] Plessy v Ferguson, 163 US 537 (1896), was overturned 59 years later in Brown v Board of Education, 347 US 483 (1954).

[17] The last paragraph is *not* quoting Mr Rubin, but is the opinion of Special Master Bliss.

References

Alexander v Sandoval (2001) 532 US 275.
APTA (American Public Transportation Association) (2001) *Transit fact book*, Washington, DC: APTA.
Bailey, E. (1997) 'From welfare lines to commuting crush', *LA Times*, 6 October, p A1.
Bernstein, S. (2003a) 'Seniors struggle to cope with LA's transit strike', *LA Times*, 4 November, p B2.
Bernstein, S. (2003b) 'Coping with MTA strike takes ingenuity, gumption', *LA Times*, 28 October, p B2.
Bernstein, S., Pierson, D. and Hernandez, D. (2003) 'MTA strike derails business', *LA Times*, 6 November, p A1.
Bliss, D.T. (2004) *Memorandum decision II and final order on remedial service plan to meet 1.25 and 1.20 load factor target requirements*, Los Angeles, CA: US District Court/Central District of California.
Boyarsky, B. (1994) 'MTA's rude behavior shows it is out of touch with its riders,' *LA Times*, 17 July, p B1.
Bullard, R., Johnson, G. and Torres, A.O. (eds) (2004) *Highway robbery: Transportation racism and new routes to equity*, Cambridge, MA: South End Press.
Californian Government Code § 65040.12.
Castaneda v Partida (1977) 430 US 482, 496 n.17.
Chong, J.R. and Liu, C. (2004) *LA Times*, 23 July.
Davis, M. (1990) *City of quartz*, London: Verso.
Davis, M. (2000) 'How Eden lost its garden', in *Ecology of fear*, London: Picador.
DMU (Demographic Research Unit) (2001) State of California, Department of Finance, Demographic Research Unit, Race/Ethnic Population with Age and Sex Detail, 1970-2040.
Executive Order 12898 on Environmental Justice (11 February 1994).
FHWA (Federal Highway Administration) (2000) *Federal Highway Administration Highway statistics 2000: Urbanized area summaries-selected characteristics, Table HM-72*, Washington, DC: FHWA.

García, R. (1997) *Riots and rebellion: Civil rights, police reform, and the Rodney King beating*, Chicago, IL: Center for Computer-Assisted Legal Instruction.

García, R. (2000) 'Mean streets: transportation equity improves social justice, economic vitality, and environmental quality', *15 Forum for Applied Research and Public Policy*, vol 75, p 15.

García, R. (2002a) 'The Rodney King legacy and a testament of hope', American Bar Association, *Goal IX*, vol 8, no 2, p 6.

García, R. (2002b) 'Equal access to California's beaches', *Proceedings of the Second National People of Color Environmental Leadership Summit (Summit II)*, 10 October (www.ejrc.cau.edu/summit2/Beach.pdf).

García, R. (2004: forthcoming) 'Building community and diversifying democracy: strategies from the urban park movement', in R. Bullard (ed) *Wasting away: Environmental justice, human rights, and the politics of pollution*, San Francisco, CA: Sierra Club Books.

García, R., Flores, E.S., McIntosh, K. and Pine, E. (2003) *The heritage parkscape in the heart of Los Angeles*, Los Angeles, CA: Center for Law in the Public Interest (www.clii.org).

Garrett, M. and Taylor, B. (1999) 'Reconsidering social equity in public transit', *Berkeley Planning Journal*, vol 13, pp 6-24.

Gonzaga University v Doe (2002) 536 US 273.

Gordon, P., Poole Jnr, R.W., Moore II, J.E. and Rubin, T. (1999) 'Improving transportation in the San Fernando Valley', Study no 249, Los Angeles, CA: Reason Public Policy Institute (www.rppi.org/transportation/ps249.html).

Governor's Commission on the Los Angeles Riots (1965) *Violence in the city: An end or a beginning? A report by the Governor's Commission on the Los Angeles riots*, Los Angeles, CA: The Commission.

Green, M.L. (1985) 'A history of rail setbacks', *Mass Transit*, September.

Guardians Ass'n v Civil Service Commission (1983) 463 US 582, 629 (Justice Marshall, concurring in part and dissenting in part).

Hair, P. (2001) *Louder than words: Lawyers, communities and the struggle for social justice*, New York, NY: Rockefeller Foundation.

Krieger, L.H. (1995) 'The content of our categories: a cognitive bias approach to discrimination and equal employment opportunity', *Stanford Law Review*, vol 47, p 1161.

Krumholz, N. (1982) 'A retrospective view of equity planning', *Journal of the American Planning Association*, vol 48, no 2, p 163 (quoted in M. Garrett and B. Taylor [1999] 'Reconsidering social equity in public transit', *Berkeley Planning Journal*, vol 13).

LACTC (Los Angeles County Transportation Commission) (1986) *$700,000,000 Los Angeles County Transportation Commission sales tax revenue bonds, Preliminary Official Statement* (POS), Los Angeles, CA: LACTC.

LACTC (1980) *Los Angeles County Transportation Commission Ordinance 16*, Los Angeles, CA: LACTC.

Larry, P. v Riles (1984) 793 F.2d 969, 983 (9th Cir.)

LCSC (Labor/Community Strategy Center) v Los Angeles County Metropolitan Transportation Authority (1994) 'Findings of Fact and Conclusions of Law re: Preliminary Injunction' (September 21, 1994) at 1-2, 4-5.

LCSC v MTA (1996) 'Plaintiffs' Revised Statement of Contentions of Fact and Law', filed with Plaintiffs' Memorandum in Support of Proposed Consent Decree on October 24.

LCSC v MTA (2001, 2002) 263 F.3d 1041 (2001), cert. denied, 535 US 951 (2002).

Lee, B.L. (1997) 'Civil rights and legal remedies: a plan of action', in R. Bullard and G. Johnson (eds) *Just transportation: Dismantling race and class barriers to mobility*, Stony Creek, CT: New Society Publishers, pp 156-72.

Liu, C. (2003) 'MTA stoppage puts up roadblocks for students', *LA Times*, 7 November, p B14.

Mann, E. (2004) 'Los Angeles bus riders derail the MTA', in R. Bullard, G. Johnson and A.O. Torres (eds) *Highway robbery: Transportation racism and new routes to equity*, Cambridge, MA: South End Press, pp 31-45.

MTA (Metropolitan Transportation Authority) (1994) *Metropolitan Transportation Authority total revenues available: Adopted 30-year plan v Projected long range plan, 20-year period*, FY 1993-94 through FT 2012-13, p 14, Los Angeles, CA: MTA.

MTA (1997) *Metropolitan Transportation Authority FY 96-97 bus on-board passenger survey*, Los Angeles, CA: MTA.

MTA (1998a) *Metropolitan Transportation Authority FY 96-97 bus on-board passenger survey*, MTA Service Planning Market Research Program, p 16, Los Angeles, CA: MTA.

MTA (1998b) *Metropolitan Transportation Authority restructuring plan: Appendix E, executive summary – Rail program status as of January 1998*, Los Angeles, CA: MTA.

MTA (1998c) *Metropolitan Transportation Authority 1998 metro red line passenger survey – Preliminary summary report*, Los Angeles, CA: MTA.

MTA (1998d) *Metropolitan Transportation Authority 1998 metro blue line passenger survey – Preliminary summary report*, Los Angeles, CA: MTA.

MTA (1998e) *Metropolitan Transportation Authority 1998 metro green line passenger survey – Preliminary summary report*, Los Angeles, CA: MTA.

MTA (2003a) *MTA staff revises metro fare restructuring recommendation*, MTA Press Release, Los Angeles, CA: MTA.

MTA (2003b) *MTA adopts austere FY04 budget that still pushes forward with major transit projects*, MTA Press Release, Los Angeles, CA: MTA.

MTA (2003c) *Metropolitan Transportation Authority FY2003-04 Proposed Budget*, Los Angeles, CA: MTA.

MTA (2003d) *Metropolitan Transportation Authority draft transit service policy*, Los Angeles, CA: MTA.

MTA (2004) Metropolitan Transportation Authority Press Release – MTA Statement, Los Angeles, CA: MTA (www.mta.net/press/2004/02_february/mta_020204.htm), Los Angeles, CA: MTA.

Plessy v Ferguson (1896) 163 US 537, overruled by Brown v Board of Education (1954) 347 US 483.

Powell, J. (1999) 'What we need to do about the "burbs"', *ColourLines*, vol 2, no 3, Oakland, CA: Applied Research Center, Fall (www.arc.org/C_Lines/CLArchive/story2_3_01.html).

Ricci, J. (2001) 'A park with no name (yet) but plenty of history', *LA Times Magazine*, 15 July, pp 5-6.

Rubin, T.A. (2000) *Environmental justice and transportation decisions – The Los Angeles experience*, Presentation to the Transportation Research Board Annual Meeting, Washington, DC.

Rubin, T.A. (2003) Thomas A. Rubin declaration for Special Master Donald Bliss, October 14, 2003, Los Angeles County MTA Actual/Budgeted Ridership v Projected Ridership Without the Consent Decree.

Rubin, T.A. and Moore II, J.E. (1997a) *Rubber tire transit: A viable alternative to rail*, Los Angeles, CA: Reason Public Policy Institute, no 230 August (www.rppi.org/transportation/ps209.html).

Rubin, T.A. and Moore II, J.E. (1997b) *Better transportation alternatives for Los Angeles*, Los Angeles, CA: Reason Public Policy Institute, no 232 September (www.rppi.org/transportation/ps209.html).

Sanchez, J. (2001) 'LA's Cornfield Row: how activists prevailed', *LA Times*, 17 April, p A1, A12.

Save our Valley v Sound Transit (2003) (9th circuit) 335 F. 3d 932, pps 936-7.

TTI (Texas Transportation Institute) (2003) *Texas Transportation Institute 2003 urban mobility study*, College Station, TX: TTI (mobility.tamu.edu/ums).

UMTA (Urban Mass Transportation Administration) (1979-1997) Urban Mass Transportation Administration (now FTA), annual Section 15/National Transit Database reports, 1979-97.

UMTA (1987) Urban Mass Transportation Administration (now FTA) Office of Grants Management, National Urban Mass Transportation Statistics – 1985 Section 15 Annual Report, August 1987, Table 3.16, Transit Operating Statistics: Service Supplied and Service Consumed Details by Transit System, pp 3-277, 306.

42 U.S.C. § 2000d (1994).

US Department of Justice, Civil Rights Division (1998) Title VI Legal Manual, pp 49-53 and authorities cited.

US DOT (Department of Transportation) (2000) US Department of Transportation and Environmental Justice 4-1 to 4-23.

US Department of Transportation Federal Aviation Administration and the City of Los Angeles, California (2001) *Draft Environmental Impact Statement – Environmental Impact Report*, California State Clearinghouse No 1997061047.

Village of Arlington Heights v Metropolitan Housing Dev. Corp. (1977) 429 US 252, 265.

Wachs, M. (1997) 'The evolution of transportation policy in Los Angeles', in A.J. Scott and E.W. Soja (eds) *The city: Los Angeles and urban theory at the end of the twentieth century*, Los Angeles, CA: University of California Press.

Waldinger, R. and Bozorgmehr, M. (eds) (1996) *Ethnic Los Angeles*, New York, NY: Russell Sage Foundation.

Washington, J.M. (ed) (1991) *Martin Luther King, a testament of hope: The essential writings and speeches of Martin Luther King*, Jr, pp 325-6, New York, NY: HarperCollins Publishers.

Weiskel, T. (1999) 'Environmental racism: an interpretation', in K.A. Appiah and H.L. Gates, Jr (eds) *Africana: The encyclopedia of the African and African American experience*, New York, NY: Basic Civitas Books, p 679.

THIRTEEN

Women's issues in transportation

Stephanie Ortoleva and Marc Brenman

Introduction

This chapter looks at transportation in the US through the lens of a women's rights perspective, challenging transportation providers, funders and regulators to consider and assess impacts on women in the community in planning, research and regulation. The chapter discusses policy approaches that create parallels to civil rights laws in the US, as well as social exclusion theory, community and social impact assessment procedures, avoidance and mitigation of damage, and valuing women's transportation. It makes recommendations on where changes should be made to existing policy and practice. It presents a case study of successful implementation in the field and describes what a new feminist paradigm for transportation might look like.

An historical perspective

An historical perspective reveals that transportation has been used to subjugate women historically and to the present day. Transportation can serve as a method of securing freedom, equity and an increase in rights and liberties to women. Examples can be seen in the developments in the right to travel cases that gave women the right to move from state to state in the US and to secure welfare benefits in their new communities (see Shapiro v Thompson, 394 US 618, 1969, and subsequent US Supreme Court cases).

Cars were marketed to women early in the development of the automobile, but these early electric cars had limited range based on the notion that women did not need to travel beyond the sphere of the home. Institutional sexism strongly relates to women's history in transportation. To this day, we are plagued by the stereotyping of, and jokes about, women drivers. Women in the sphere of transportation are also often stereotyped in culture and societal attitudes and images.

Folk, blues, and rock'n'roll songs provide a telling example of a misogynist attitude toward women. Blues singer Robert Johnson generally displayed misogynist attitudes toward the women in his songs (Lemon, nd, para 2):

> In songs such as Terraplane Blues, Johnson shows a misogynist attitude when he uses the sexual metaphor of a car as a woman's body. In Terraplane Blues, Johnson speaks of all the things he plans to do to this woman, even though it appears that she is not interested in doing anything with him.

Douglas Brinkley, author of *Wheels for the world: A biography of Ford Motor Company*, stated in an interview on *Morning Edition* on 3 June 2003 (para 3):

> Henry Ford was shrewd enough to see women as the great consumers of America. If the man was going to be working these 40 or 50 hour workweeks, that gave the woman the time to do the shopping, to be the one who perhaps bought the Model T or the family car, and he won a lot of women over to his product by doing that.

Similarly:

> Historians agree that the dominant gender ideology in America by the mid-nineteenth century and, with increasing ambivalence, into the early twentieth century, was that of separate spheres. The division of the world into public and private, male and female worlds, has created a tension for women using any means of transportation, because transportation has traditionally taken place in a public, male space. But ideology bent to convenience: women frequently, if less frequently than men, used trains, streetcars, wagons, or cars, even if their use of these means of transportation ran counter to the separate spheres concept. (Schlanger, 1998, para 1)

Feminist theory

In planning, where the press of work and current issues in the profession leave little time for philosophical examinations, basic theory gets understandably short shrift. Nonetheless, it is wise on occasion to step back and examine the theories and ideas underlying our practice, for they are important.

The aim of our research is not to examine the impact on specific areas such as land-use planning, but on the conception of transportation planning and the ways it is carried out. The challenges and contributions of this work have many implications for planning theory, going well beyond issues of gender and dealing with power, process, professionalism, and ethics. These issues reach to the foundation of many issues of current importance in planning: defining the public interest, citizen participation, equity, justice, and the legitimation of planning itself.

Vigorous debates around feminist theories have been found in many disciplines since the 1960s. All are motivated by a shared purpose: to challenge male dominance, to contribute to knowledge about women, and to construct a science in which gender and gender relations are seen as fully social and explanatorily important. The data and documentation establishing the extent to which gender bias has permeated the humanities and sciences and the impact this has had is now extensive and widely accepted.

There is no single 'feminist theory'. There are many areas of divergence and disagreement between Marxist feminists, radical feminists, women of color, materialists, idealists, postmodernists, and others. Despite the many differences between and within disciplines, there is a consensus (Snyder, 1995, p 92) on certain central ideas which have direct implications for research and practice:

- *Social experience is gendered.* That is, the social order creates, assigns, and influences our roles, values, opportunities, status, environments, and perspectives in part based on gender. Gender itself is a social construct distinct from the biological category of sex.
- *All theory, like all practice, is inherently political; it necessarily either perpetuates or challenges the status quo.* The development of knowledge and its application through action are social enterprises, and therefore have political and ethical aspects which cannot be disassociated from them.
- *Theory and practice cannot and should not be separated.* Feminist theory is explicitly emancipatory and critical. Most theorists believe that knowledge contains an imperative to action; theory and praxis are seen in a mutually reinforcing, reflexive relationship.
- *Subjects and objects are not and cannot be separated.* A relationship exists between knower and the object, and each necessarily affects the other. Theory and practice are more accurate and clear when this reflexivity is consciously accepted, rather than attempting the scientistic ideal of objectivity through separation. A corollary of the above is that personal experience and grounded research are valid forms of knowledge. Feminist thought directs attention to and admits a broader range of experience as legitimate and valid knowledge. Other forms of knowing and other knowers exist beyond the limited authorities and expert status granted by traditional scientific method and the dominant patriarchal culture.

Gender differences in travel behavior

US transportation studies clearly demonstrate significant differences in women's travel behavior, patterns and needs from those of men (see Chapter Two of this volume). For example, women drive less (21 to 38 miles per day); men drive longer (67 to 44 minutes per day) (US Department of Transportation, National Household Travel Survey, 2001-02). Other differences include variations in trip-chaining[1] travel patterns for working women with children, increased isolation for older women who live in suburban and rural communities and who no longer drive, transportation safety and security concerns of women, and numerous other issues. There are also variations among groups of women, using criteria such as disability, age, race, national origin, limited English proficiency, income, and family status. Many of these differences require a focused policy and practice response.

The Federal Highway Administration (Hanlon, 1997, p 651) finds:

> Differences between men and women in terms of the ways in which they use public transport have been well-documented. Increasingly, the typical public transport user is not only a woman, but also a captive customer being without access to a car or without a license. In fact, two thirds of all public transport trips are made by such captive customers.

Civil rights law

Statutory prohibitions against sex discrimination require that the US Department of Transportation (USDOT) ensures that planning and policy decisions and incentives in federally assisted transportation infrastructure do not discriminate against women. These statutes generally require non-discrimination on the basis of sex. However, the concept of environmental justice in the US encompasses minority and low-income communities, but not women. It should, however, since women earn only $0.72 for every dollar men earn in the US; being a woman is often a proxy measure for having a low income (US Census Bureau, 2002).

We have explored the US federal transportation civil rights statutes and regulations that prohibit sex discrimination and enumerate some of the transportation policy issues that are covered by these provisions. Our analysis links transportation programs covered by sex anti-discrimination provisions and programs that provide benefits to and concern women.

The legal implications of transportation policy developments

Policy developments in transportation that have discriminatory implications include certain Transportation Demand Management (TDM) approaches, such as flexible work schedules, that may not work for women travelers because of the unavailability of childcare for these alternative schedules since childcare facilities frequently are not available in the evenings or on weekends. Transportation Demand Management generally refers to policies, programs, and actions that are directed towards decreasing the use of single-occupant vehicles. It also can include activities to encourage shifting or spreading peak travel periods. Non-discriminatory transportation planning and policy development with a focus on customer need and community input demands consideration of women's transportation issues.

Enforcement of non-discrimination laws: federal

The fact that federal transportation funding statutes prohibit sex discrimination on the basis of sex in federally funded transportation programs has been ignored by researchers, advocates, some recipients of federal financial assistance, and to some extent by those charged with enforcing the laws. In the context of litigation challenging allocation of funds to urban and suburban communities as discriminatory, Jeffrey Brown, an advocate for equitable transportation planning (1998, pp 12-13) wrote,

> One class of bus riders whose needs seemed to disappear during the struggle is women.

Women make up 54% of Metropolitan Transport Authority (MTA) bus passengers. Women's transportation needs can differ quite significantly from the transportation needs of men. Perhaps most obvious in this regard are the different travel patterns and hence transportation needs followed by women who work in the household and/or serve as the primary caregivers for their children. These women have different transportation needs than women who commute to work on a regular basis, who themselves often have needs arising from domestic responsibilities. Yet agencies such as the MTA, in their zeal to serve commuters, often make decisions that negatively impact different groups of women. These negative impacts stem from the fact that, like racial minorities and the poor, women have often been traditionally excluded from the MTA's decision-making process (Brown, 1998).

Perhaps one reason gender disappeared from the discussion is because it is not a protected category under either the Fourteenth Amendment or the Civil Rights Act of 1964, the two statutory bases of the lawsuit. However, class is not protected either and this did not stop the Bus Riders' Union (BRU) from linking race and class. The BRU stresses its feminist agenda in its brochures and handouts and boasts about the important roles played by women in its leadership. Perhaps the transportation needs of women will be an area of mobilization for the BRU in the future. At the present time, however, the questions remain: how can we guarantee that individuals can make their own transportation needs heard? How can we recognize the diversity of individuals and needs of the transit-dependent? How can all of us work to guarantee that women's voices are being heard and women's needs are being met?

Jeffrey Brown, a strong transportation equity advocate, seems unaware that federal non-discrimination provisions of federal transportation funding statutes prohibit discrimination on the basis of sex.

Enforcement of non-discrimination laws: state and local

Another area of this research concerns the extent to which local, state, and federal civil rights laws that prohibit discrimination against women are enforced in the transportation context. State and local laws cover employment, pregnancy, equal pay, public accommodations, and services. Are governmental transportation entities and state and local civil rights agencies enforcing these laws efficiently and equitably?

Driving while female

In April 2002, a Virginia state trooper was indicted for soliciting sex from women in exchange for dropping traffic charges against them. At about the same time, a San Bernadino (CA) officer was charged with raping 11 women while on duty. On the East Coast, an officer from a department outside of Philadelphia was convicted of raping an intoxicated woman while on duty and in uniform. Last year, a case occurring in Suffolk County (NY) involved an officer accused of forcing female drivers to strip or face arrest. This prompted a study entitled *Driving while female: A national problem in police misconduct* (Walker and Irlbeck, 2002).

The problem of 'driving while female' parallels the national problem of racial profiling or 'driving while black'. Substantial evidence indicates that police officers stop African American drivers because of their race and not because of any evidence of illegal activity. In other parts of the country, police officers stop Hispanic/Latino drivers solely because of their ethnicity, a practice that has been labeled 'driving while brown' (a major part of the problem, according to the *Driving while female* study, is the failure of law enforcement agencies to investigate allegations brought to their attention). Departments do not take allegations of this discrimination seriously and deny officer wrongdoing, the study said. Moreover, such victims feel "particularly traumatized or humiliated" (Walker and Irlbeck, 2002). The study also points to a "pervasive sexist culture" (Walker and Irlbeck, 2002) that manifests itself in employment discrimination against women, tolerance of sexual harassment within the department, and systematic failure to investigate domestic violence when the alleged abuser is an officer within the agency. The US National Center for Women and Policing has recommended that departments hire more women not only to change from an aggressive style of policing to one that emphasizes communication, but also to stem the use of excessive force and misconduct.

Walker and Irlbeck (2002) recommended that the following steps need to be taken:

Step one: Data collection
Law enforcement agencies need to begin collecting data to determine whether there is a pattern of driving while female abuses by their officers.

Step two: Official policies and training
Every law enforcement agency should immediately issue a formal policy prohibiting 'driving while female' abuse. The policy should define driving while female as the use of law enforcement powers for the purpose of stopping female drivers where there is no suspect criminal activity or traffic law violation, and also taking advantage of women drivers who have been stopped for legitimate violations. The policy should clearly state that any form of sexual harassment or assault of an individual, regardless of gender, is impermissible conduct that will result in termination proceedings.

Step three: Better supervision
Law enforcement chief executives need to take immediate steps to ensure proper supervision of officers on the street. They need to ensure that supervisory officers are alert to the potential problem of driving while female and take the necessary steps to curb it.

Step four: An open and accessible citizen complaint system
Law enforcement chief executives should take immediate steps to ensure that the department's citizen complaint system is open and accessible to all members of the community. Where an independent citizen oversight agency does not exist, local communities need to create one that is open and accessible.

Other legal and quasi-legal issues

Professor Ian Ayres (1991) finds overwhelming evidence that, in a variety of markets (retail car sales, bail bonding, kidney transplantation, and Federal Communications Commission licensing) black people and females are consistently at a disadvantage. For example, when Ayres sent out agents of different races and genders posing as potential buyers to more than 200 car dealerships in Chicago, he found that dealers regularly charged black people and women more than they charged white men. He states:

> There was evidence of gender discrimination in my original pilot study....
> In that study, dealerships offered systematically higher prices to African American women than to African American men. (Ayres, 1991, p 35)

As a counterweight, a recent study by researchers at the University of California, Berkeley, and Yale University found that the Internet serves as an equalizer for those whose demographic characteristics might end up costing them at a car dealership, primarily African Americans, Hispanics, and women (University of California and Yale University, 2001).

Religious issues

In the US, photographs of one's face are required for a driver's license. Some women, primarily Muslims, who wear veils for religious reasons, refuse to expose their faces for such purposes. Although it is always difficult to find rational reasons for a religious injunction, modesty and avoiding being attractive to male non-family members are often given as reasons for the rule for some Muslims on the veil for women. A driver's license is a necessity for getting to work and full participation in society, as discussed elsewhere in this chapter. In Florida in 2002, a Muslim woman sued the state for suspending her driver's license after she refused to remove her face-covering veil for the photo (Freeman v State of Florida, 2003). She wore a niqab, or face veil.

The American Civil Liberties Union said the law is vague and pointed to another Florida law stating the "government shall not substantially burden a person's exercise of religion" (Freeman v State of Florida, 2003, Count II, para 2). At least three other Muslim women have been refused Florida drivers' licenses because of their headdresses, according to Altaf Ali, executive director of the Florida chapter of the Council on American-Islamic Relations, an advocacy group.

The plaintiff did not prevail in the Florida state courts (American Civil Liberties Union of Florida, 2003). In June 2003, Florida Circuit Court judge Janet C. Thorpe ruled that Sultaana Freeman's right to free exercise of religion would not be infringed by having to show her face on her license. Thorpe said the state "has a compelling interest in protecting the public from criminal activities and security threats" (Sultaana Freeman v State of Florida, 2002), and that photo identification "is essential to promote that interest". The Florida Assistant Attorney General had argued that Islamic law has exceptions that allow women to expose their faces if it serves a public good, and that arrangements could be made to have Freeman photographed with only women present to allay her concerns about modesty. Interestingly, a driver's license can be obtained without a photo in 14 states. The story excited a great deal of commentary on the Internet, much of it negative about Muslims. The issue shows the interesting overlaps of women's issues, religion, privacy, and security. The more rabid criticism was also interesting because it confused the nationality of the woman (a native-born American), saying she should "go back to her own country". This shows the delegitimising risks women take when they try to stand up for their beliefs.

One could say that wearing the veil and obtaining a driver's license is not truly a women's issue, if one adopts the tortured reasoning in the Supreme Court decision stating that discrimination against pregnant women because of their pregnancy is not sex discrimination, because pregnant women are a category apart from 'women'. One could also ask if men will be required to shave their beards and moustaches in order to present a truer picture when they obtain a driver's license.

Differences across the lifespan

Women outlive men by several years, creating a significant impact on the conditions under which older women live, suggesting the need for new strategies for providing a decent quality of life for poorer, older women. In a society in which quality of life is determined to a significant degree by mobility, lack of convenient transportation is an important detriment. In the US, unlike anywhere else in the world, the percentage of women who hold drivers' licenses is very close to that of men. However, research demonstrates that women give up their drivers' licenses at an earlier age then do men. Analysis of applicable civil rights laws is necessary to determine if this situation presents potential issues of sex and/or age discrimination.

Older women give up drivers' licenses earlier than men. Women drive cars less often than men do, and have the option of driving less often than men have. This discrepancy is especially blatant among the older generations, partly due to the very gendered process of driving cessation. Anu Siren delivered a paper on this topic at the June 2002 Conference on Reconceptualising Gender and Ageing (Siren, 2002). She noted that, whereas men tend to drive as long as their health allows them to, women give up their licenses at younger ages and for less pressing reasons. Early, voluntary driving cessation can have a strong, negative effect on women's independent mobility and thus on their well-being.

There is some possibility that this is a 'habit-related' rather than gender-related phenomenon, in which older women give up driving unnecessarily soon. Perhaps they have a more realistic view of their driving abilities, decrease in vision and increase in reaction time, and so on, as opposed to older men, who may have an unrealistic view of their abilities.

Stutts (in University of North Carolina Highway Safety Research Center, 1998) also reported that men are particularly reluctant to stop driving, and often deny any deterioration in their driving skills. Some seniors continue to drive "in spite of everything", regardless of physician recommendations against driving and injury-producing, at-fault crashes. On the other hand, there is one subset of older drivers, typically women, whose giving up driving prematurely has been studied. Generally, these drivers never really enjoyed driving, are uncomfortable in today's driving environment, and have a spouse who drives. Although an event like a hospitalization may trigger their decision to stop driving, often they just drive less and less until they no longer feel comfortable behind the wheel. Due to lack of public transit in the US suburbs, where an increasing percentage of Americans live, driving cessation can create basic subsistence problems, due to lack of availability of shopping. This is discussed in more detail below in regard to the specific example of grocery shopping.

Older women have some greater accident risk than men because of some auto-design and auto-safety design issues, such as seat belt and air bag placement, and increasing accident rates among women (Staplin, et al, 1999). With percentage crash fatalities down due to air bags, but lower body injuries significant, there may be differential impacts on women due to osteoporosis (brittle bones, especially in hips) of older women drivers and passengers. There are data indicating that older women are more timid drivers than men and that older women might benefit from older driver education programs.

Part of the phenomenon of women giving up licenses prematurely or ahead of men may be due to the current generation of older women, who may not have started driving or become as habituated as their age-cohort men. If the statistics change over time, with fewer older women giving up their licenses, then there will be some reason to believe that the phenomenon is based on social practices. Today, as most US young women begin to drive when young men do, and drive continuously throughout their active lifespans, the discrepancy in driving cessation may gradually end.

Differences due to child-raising responsibilities

As noted earlier in this chapter, women frequently do not rely on public transportation because it is difficult and inconvenient for those who need to travel to work, childcare, shopping, and so on, known as trip-chaining. To determine what might be an effective solution to meet this need, the US Federal Transit Administration and the National Council of Negro Women Inc. (NCNW), conducted a study of the effectiveness of locating childcare services at transit hubs (Transportation Research Board of the National Academies, 2002). The project sought to determine if such an approach was desired by women in the several communities investigated and to determine if such childcare center placement was effective in increasing public transit usage and made travel more convenient and efficient for the women. The NCNW outreach into urban areas through its community-based national affiliates and its network of collaborative organizations provided an opportunity to obtain community input on the needs for safe, accessible and affordable childcare services that also facilitated use of public transit.

There have been proposals for – and limited experiments with – 'transit villages', which are clusters of apartments, townhouses, offices and stores near transit hubs. They can provide ready transit access to stores, services and community resources such as libraries, clinics and day-care centers, which can save time and travel expenses for commuters who pass through the transit village on the way to and from home or work. In Oakland (CA), most of the original Bay Area Rapid Transit (BART) parking area at the Fruitvale station will become part of an innovative project with a senior citizen center, a health clinic, a day-care center and a branch library in addition to almost 250 residential units (including lofts) and 70,000 square feet of commercial/retail space (Stewart, 2002).

A similar plan has been proposed for the Cincinnati (OH) area, called MetroMoves (Trapp, 2001). MetroMoves calls for a web of routes running east and west and from suburb to suburb, connecting most of Hamilton County and beyond. Serving the connections would be 26 transit hubs occupied by businesses tailored to each community's needs, such as day-care centers, newsstands and dry cleaners. Similar ideas are in various stages of consideration and development in Toronto, Ontario; Minneapolis (MN); and Detroit (MI).

Time spent chauffeuring children to activities also comprises a surprisingly large component of parental (mostly female) time (Budig and Folbre, 2002). Results from the *Child development supplement of the panel survey of income dynamics* (CD-PSID) show that:

> ... in 1997 children under the age of three in the US spent about as much time with their mothers on a weekday in transportation as they did in personal care. (Fuligni, 2000, cited in Budig and Folbre, 2002, p 11)

Most of this transportation time was time spent riding in a car with parents who were on their way to childcare, shopping, or errands.

Having children in the car is also a contributor to 'distracted driving'. Distracted driving is under some discussion now because of the growth in the use of cell phones. Distracted driving may contribute to accidents, due to perception blindness caused by the distraction.

Trip-chaining

Combined trips are referred to as 'trip-chaining'. Trip chaining creates complex trip patterns, making transit time consuming, inconvenient or impossible. For example, stopping at the dry cleaner or grocery store is combined with picking up children on the way home from work. Incentives to trip chain include lack of practical transit. Women trip chain much more than men. For women without cars, the problem is magnified. For example, a stop at the dry cleaner is combined with picking up little Johnny after school. Some impulse trips can be delayed or combined. Historically, the incentives to trip chain include an individual's personal time management and the physical unavailability or impracticality of transit options. The complex trip patterns of time-pressed two-worker households that involve multiple stops along the commute route often make the use of transit time consuming, inconvenient – and often impossible. Trip chaining especially affects women with small children.

Spatial mismatch

Spatial mismatch is an increasingly serious barrier to employment. It refers to the location of suitable jobs in areas that are inaccessible by public transportation. This is a result of the growth of new service jobs in areas outside the city, in new outer suburbs and airport industrial parks. Service jobs are heavily held by women and in particular lower-income women leaving welfare-to-work (WtoW) programs.

There is concentrated poverty in the historic center of cities, but de-concentrated opportunity in the form of job suburbanization toward the metropolitan periphery. This phenomenon is most prevalent in larger metropolitan areas that tend to be fragmented by multiple political jurisdictions, because that fragmentation helps to create disequilibrium, a market failure, in the labor market. Being female, especially being single and a mother, is often a proxy measure for being poor. While poor people and black people, on average, live closer to currently existing jobs than do white people, they are generally located farther from areas of net employment growth. Job vacancy rates and wages are also higher in less-skilled jobs that are located in predominantly white suburbs rather than cities or racially mixed suburbs, suggesting better labor market opportunities for those with access to the former. For instance, potential workers without cars have more difficulty gaining suburban employment than do potential workers with cars, and employers located near public transit stops attract more new employees than do those located further away.

The access of low-income inner-city residents to suburban employers depends not only on the proximity of employers to mass transit stops, but also on the distance of various employers from low-income neighborhoods and the extent to which direct public transit routes are available between these sites (that is, without the need to change buses or trains one or more times). Harry J. Holzer, chief economist at the US Department of Labor, stated (1999, section, para 1):

> Unskilled workers, especially inner-city minorities, face a variety of barriers on the demand side of the labor market relative to their own characteristics: high-skill demands of employers, racial discrimination, lack of transportation to and information about suburban jobs, and lack of effective networks and contacts. Taken together, these factors generate difficulties for unskilled workers in gaining or keeping employment, especially at wages/benefits above the most minimal level.

These issues have a disproportionate impact on indigent women, especially those now placed in so-called WtoW programs. Women returning to work after participation in welfare programs face numerous barriers, including domestic violence, lack of childcare, limited job skills and education, all of which are enhanced by lack of transportation.

Some of these transportation issues are being addressed to a limited extent by the WtoW programs (see Chapter Ten of this volume).

Personal safety issues

Some researchers on women's safety state that women's fear of using public transportation is unfounded because transit crime is decreasing (Anderson, 2003). Others indicate that women are afraid of isolated bus stops, transit parking garages and crowded mass transit. Surveys support this latter contention. Sexual harassment on transit is not always reflected in crime statistics. A common fear of women who use public transportation is car-jackings in rail and other transit parking lots. The crowded conditions on trains create opportunities for invasion of personal space. When surveyed, men rarely list safety and security as a reason not to take transit. Women do, however, express this fear, particularly in relation to using bicycles (Anderson, 2003, Fear of Attack section, para 1 and 2):

> Another occasionally expressed reason for bicycling attracting such a small percentage of females is fear of attack in remote places. Driving through a dark neighborhood in a car with locked doors gives a sense of security hard to match on a bicycle.... This is not entirely an unfounded fear. Women do report a certain amount of harassment while riding, usually in the form of remarks shouted from passing cars.

In addition to traffic safety, fears surrounding the level of safety and crime in an area may deter walking. A study conducted in five US states showed that residents who perceived their neighborhoods to be unsafe were significantly more likely to be physically inactive (Neighborhood Safety, 1999). This physical inactivity was highest among women, older people, people of color, people with a high school degree or lower, and people with annual incomes below $20,000.

Access to healthcare and abortion services

Lack of transportation deprives many women of necessary health services, resulting in greater need for emergency healthcare and poor health. The Kaiser Women's Health Survey (Salganicoff et al, 2002) clearly points out the dramatic effects of lack of transportation on women's health, finding that transportation difficulties resulted in delayed care for 21% of women in fair or poor health, four times the rate of women in better health:

> Women are major consumers of healthcare services, in many cases negotiating not only their own care, but also that of their family members. Their reproductive health needs, greater rate of health problems, and longer life spans compared to men make their relationships with the health system complex. Their access to care is often complicated by their disproportionately lower incomes and greater responsibilities juggling work and family concerns. Because of their own health needs, limited financial resources, and family responsibilities, women have a vested interest in the scope and type of services offered by health plans, as well as in the mechanisms that fund health care services. (Salganicoff et al, 2002, p vii)

Innovative programs help to link women with free and low-cost breast health-screening services in the community: for example, arranging transportation and case management for women who have access problems and bringing mobile mammography screening to a facility in the community. Bringing healthcare to transit-deprived women is one effective way of addressing healthcare needs (Kramer and Wiatr, 2002).

Another area of healthcare that is limited for some women, especially those in rural communities, is access to abortion services. The combination of laws that require so-called 'waiting periods' between the initial visit to the abortion provider and the performance of the abortion procedure, along with lack of access to transportation, frequently results in denial of abortion services, increased costs and/or substantial delay in obtaining the abortion. These 'waiting periods' frequently require two separate trips to the abortion provider: the first for 'counseling', and the second for the abortion. This often requires two trips to the provider or an overnight stay in a hotel. For women without a car or unable to drive or with a car in disrepair and long distances to transverse, this is impossible.

The declining number of clinics and the growing concentration of clinics in cities mean that many women must wait longer and travel farther to exercise their right to end a pregnancy. Ninety-four percent of the counties in Georgia, for example, have no abortion provider, a percentage that mirrors that found in many states, according to National Abortion Rights Action League (NARAL) Pro-Choice America Foundation (2004). Nationwide, 87% of US counties have no abortion provider, according to Physicians for Reproductive Choice and Health and The Alan Guttmacher Institute (2003).

Given the declining number of clinics, Karen Shugart (2003, para 5) states:

> Amid such declining access to clinics, the need for such transportation services is growing. Many organizations are responding to that need in the same way as the Volunteer Drivers Network [in Georgia] and some are providing even more extensive services.

Volunteer driver networks are an example of an effective and supportive approach to resolving a difficult situation for many rural women. Unfortunately, the programs that exist are not able to assist many women, resulting in unnecessary denial and delay.

Time poverty

Women suffer from time poverty, in part due to transportation problems. As Jeff Turner and Margaret Grieco (1998, Abstract section, para 1) have noted:

> Women have different transport and travel patterns to men in the developed world. Women are involved in poorly resourced, highly complex, multiple purpose trips, men make single purpose trips on higher cost and superior modes of transport. These differences in transport and travel patterns are generated out of the differential accesses of the genders

to economic resources, social resources and time resources. Women are time poor as a consequence of the disproportionate level of household tasks they are required to perform within present social structures.

The location of childcare centers at transit hubs, as discussed elsewhere in this chapter, is partly designed to alleviate this problem.

Examples of good practices in addressing gender biases in transportation delivery

Childcare services

Although there are many women's transportation issues that still need to be addressed, there are some successes in obtaining community input in transportation planning. As noted earlier in this chapter, women frequently do not rely on public transportation because it is difficult and inconvenient for those who need to travel to work, childcare, shopping, and so on, known as trip-chaining. To determine what might be an effective solution to meet this need, the Federal Transit Administration and the NCNW conducted a study of the effectiveness of locating childcare services at transit hubs (Transportation Research Board of the National Academies, 2002). The project sought to determine if women in the several communities desired such an approach, to investigate and determine if such childcare center placement was effective in increasing public transit usage and made travel more convenient and efficient for the women. The NCNW was able to outreach into urban areas through its community-based national affiliates and its network of collaborative organizations provided an opportunity to obtain community input on the needs for safe, accessible and affordable childcare services that also facilitated use of public transit. Although this project was not undertaken under a formal community impact assessment process, it provides a model for including the needs and concerns of women in transportation planning.

Assistance with shopping

There have been pilot programs to assist older women and women without cars with shopping, through grocery store shuttle systems (Winkler, 2002). Since women still have primary responsibility for household tasks, including grocery shopping, poor access to grocery stores because of lack of transportation has a significant impact on women's lives, health and time management.

Some supermarkets in inner-city areas including New York, Savannah, Houston and Los Angeles operate a shuttle for their customers. Mohan and Cassady (2002, pp 4-5) state that:

> ... despite the financial success of current shuttle programs around the country, the shuttle concept is not familiar to many storeowners operating

in inner city areas who may be searching for means to improve sales.... It appears that shuttle programs improve customer loyalty; reduce costs from shopping cart loss and retrieval; and win new customers.

Shuttle programs can improve the health of low-income consumers facing transportation barriers to purchasing fresh fruit and vegetables and other healthy foods.

Residents of lower income and minority neighborhoods in many urban areas face a double bind that limits their access to fresh, healthy food. Full service supermarkets are scarce in low-income areas, and residents in low-income, urban areas are less likely to own cars than their suburban counterparts, making it difficult to travel to supermarkets outside of their immediate neighborhoods. Residents of urban neighborhoods with few supermarkets have to travel farther to shop for food.

According to a US Department of Agriculture study, only 22% of food stamp recipients drove their own car to purchase groceries as compared to 96% of non-food stamp recipients. Transportation planners rarely plan bus routes around community food needs, leaving residents little choice but to carry their groceries long distances, use precious resources on taxi rides or make multiple transfers. Transportation via taxis and/or buses or paying for a ride can be costly, reducing a family's food budget by up to $400 per year.

Another study (Calgary Regional Health Authority Health Promotions Initiatives Fund, nd, p 2) made the following recommendations:

1. Create a systematic method of compiling, disseminating and updating information on current grocery shopping services and transportation services for use with seniors and their support workers.
2. Establish inter-sectoral partnerships with government agencies, seniors' organizations, retailers and volunteer organizations to communicate the grocery shopping needs of seniors and to develop a range of community-based programs to address the needs.
3. Work with existing services such as the grocery store shuttle buses and milk delivery service to increase awareness of these services to seniors and investigate possibilities of expanding services to improve access.

The role of intermediaries

Low-income workers in general, and especially low-income working women, tend to benefit from supports and services such as childcare and transportation. Many of the 'mismatch' problems associated with spatial issues, such as transportation and information, can be addressed with assistance from labor market 'intermediaries'; that is, third-party agencies that can help bridge the gap between workers and potential employers along a variety of dimensions (Pavetti et al, 2000). These agencies can assist workers with job search or job placement, particularly if they develop good relations with local (often suburban) employers. They can also provide workers with transportation assistance.

Prior to the implementation of TANF (US welfare reform law) (Pavetti et al, 2000, p vi):

> some welfare offices used intermediaries (often referred to as employment and training service providers) to operate all or part of their Job Opportunities and Basic Skills training (JOBS) programs. Intermediaries also provided services to welfare recipients and other low-income job seekers through the former Job Training Partnership Act (JTPA) programs. In addition, some community-based organizations act as intermediaries, helping unemployed community residents (some of whom are welfare recipients) find employment, often in conjunction with participation in other programs.

Intermediaries are both non-profit and for-profit entities. They are less commonly used in rural settings. As the 1998 Workforce Investment Act is implemented, its One Stop job centers are supposed to establish coordination with transportation entities. It remains to be seen how well they do this.

Methods to deal with the problems identified

Consideration of women's issues in regional transportation planning

Based on this review, we recommend the following considerations for dealing with these transportation issues.

Metropolitan planning organizations

A significant issue is whether women's needs are considered in the transportation planning process, especially through metropolitan planning organizations (MPOs). These are currently required to consider a wide range of needs, including those concerning minorities, people with disabilities, and people who have limited English proficiency, but do not specifically address the needs of women.

Community impact assessment

The FHWA encourages the use of community impact assessment (CIA) in transportation planning (FHWA, 1996). There is a question of whether CIA currently includes assessing the needs of women and whether anti-discrimination laws require the inclusion of this input.

Consider additional car ownership programs

There are a growing number of low-income car ownership programs across the country, but most of these are small programs with limited funding and capacity, and many are facing cuts due to state budget crises. Equal Rights Advocates (ERA), a San Francisco (CA) women's advocacy law firm, has recommended the expansion of existing loan programs that assist welfare recipients in purchasing cars and increase accessibility to public transportation. To achieve this, counties should expand their existing programs or create new programs that lend money to welfare recipients and other low-income families to purchase cars. Counties should also explore savings accounts that enable recipients to save for purchasing their own cars, without jeopardizing their financial eligibility for welfare cash aid. Also recommended by ERA is that counties partner with transportation agencies to translate transportation information and resources into other languages.

Older women

Demographic projection and forecasting techniques should be enhanced to define for the next few decades, not only the population size and survivorship of older women, but also family and social network size and availability, the levels of transportation-related disability and economic access to personal and public transportation. Additional targeted research is needed on the personal perceptions of older women with respect to access, acceptability and utility of all modes of transportation and other sources of mobility, as well as personal mobility needs and desires, in order to more effectively plan for mobility needs (Wallace and Franc, nd). More study is also needed on the evolution of urban and regional design changes that affect the mobility of older women. Changes that promote safe mobility should be championed. Also, the impact of assisted living facilities and other newer modes of residential design for older persons in general and older women in particular should be evaluated for their impact on transportation needs.

Communication

Enhanced communication on these issues is needed and greater interaction with established groups interested in women's transportation issues. These groups should include the Women's Transportation Seminar, the National Organization for Women Legislative Agenda, and the Transportation Research Board Women's Transportation Issues Committee.

Conclusions

In transportation, there is a general, but not universal, disadvantage to women. Women generally lack opportunity in transportation and we have argued that a new paradigm is needed to address this; a feminist approach to transportation. Data must explicitly be collected, breaking out a wide variety of transportation statistics by gender. We must avoid the problem Margo Schlanger points out of the 'erase of gender'.

The future does not bode particularly well for women's issues in transportation in the US, however, but there are interesting and useful experiments and pilots underway in the US. External influences may affect the situation, such as women's participation in the US workforce having reached a peak and declining slightly, perhaps temporarily. National security concerns appear to be draining resources away from local endeavors. Appropriators in Congress appear to be most interested in highway funding concerns. Transit funding does not appear to be very popular. There are opportunities to influence this legislative dialogue, and introducing more women's issues into the mix.

Demographic changes include a growing number of older women, who may flood and overwhelm local entities' ability to bring about necessary changes. Necessary childcare issues, closely tied to trip-chaining, are not being solved. Studying the problems and introducing a new public policy architecture and paradigm, such as this chapter has done, are useful steps in the right direction, but ultimately changes will have to occur on the ground, and these changes cost money, in a time of declining governmental resources and revenues. However, for those action changes that do not require government funding, some can be brought about by increased alliance and coalition building among women, disability groups, and other transportation-disadvantaged groups. While linking women's issues to environmental justice in the US is clearly a good idea, it may not be effective because environmental justice itself is in a state of disrepair, having suffered losses in the courts. Legal attacks through the sex discrimination civil rights statutes show a little more promise, but who will bring them? Federal agencies have the responsibility, power, and authority to do so, but have not. Private plaintiffs face obstacles created by the US Supreme Court in bringing civil rights cases alleging discrimination based on disparate impact. Under disparate impact theory, rules which are neutral at face value, but which have a disparate impact on legally protected classes, such as women, in practice, are illegal. In addition, individual women litigants and women's rights advocacy organisations often lack the financial resources to bring such law suits. The authors strongly encourage federal agencies to fulfill all their civil rights law enforcement responsibilites. As they had noted, numerous disparate impacts of transportation exist.

Note

¹ The term trip-chaining is used to describe a journey which combines a number of different journey purposes, for example, including a stop-off at a day-center with the journey from home to work.

References

American Civil Liberties Union of Florida (2003) 'ACLU says Orlando court decision in veil case permits government to needlessly restrict religious freedom without enhancing security', Press release, 6 June (www.aclufl.org/news_events/archive/2003/freemanruling060603.cfm).

Anderson, J. (nd) 'Where are the women?' (www.bicyclinglife.com/NewsAndViews/Gender.htm).

Association of Metropolitan Planning Organizations (nd) 'More information about AMPO and metropolitan planning organizations' (www.ampo.org/who).

Ayres, I. (2001) *Pervasive prejudice? Unconventional evidence of race and gender discrimination*, Chicago, IL: University of Chicago Press. Brinkley, D. (2003) 'Henry Ford's "Wheels for the world" interview on Morning Edition, National Public Radio', 3 June (discover.npr.org/features/feature.jhtml?wfId=1280498).

Brinkley, D. (2003) *Wheels for the world: Henry Ford, his company, and a century of progress, 1903-2003*, New York, NY: Viking Books.

Brown, J. (1998) 'Race, class, gender and public transportation planning: lessons from the Bus Riders Union lawsuit', *Critical Planning*, vol 5, Spring (www.bol.ucla.edu/~jrbgeog/busriders.pdf).

Budig, M.J. and Folbre, N. (2002, September) 'Has parental time devoted to children remained unchanged?' (pascal.iseg.utl.pt/~cisep/IATUR/Papers/budig12.PDF).

Calgary Regional Health Authority Health Promotions Initiative Fund (nd) 'Creating community supports for seniors: a needs assessment on the food shopping assistance needs of community dwelling seniors', Calgary, Alberta, Canada: Calgary Regional Health Authority (www.calgaryhealthregion.ca/hecomm/nal/esni/pdf/FinalReportFinalReport.pdf).

FHWA (Federal Highway Administration) (1996) *Community impact assessment, a quick reference for transportation*, Publication no FHWA-PD-96-036, Washington, DC: FHWA.

Freeman v State of Florida, Case No: Cio02-600/ Writ No: 02-4 (Petition filed by American Civil Liberties of Florida, 2003) (www.aclufl.org/legislature_courts/legal_department/briefs_complaints/freemancomplaint.cfm).

Fuligni, A. (2000) *What's time got to do with it? Children's time use and parental involvement*, New York, NY: Center for Children and Families, Teachers College, Columbia University.

Grahn, W. (nd) 'The terms of traveling: gender and public transport' (www.tft.lth.se/kfbkonf/2weragrahn.PDF).

Hanlon, S. (1997) 'Where do women feature in public transport?', in US Department of Transportation, FHWA, Office of Highway Policy Administration (ed) *Women's travel issues: Proceedings from the second national conference*, Washington, DC (www.fhwa.dot.gov/ohim/womens/chap34.pdf).

Holzer, H.J. (1999) 'Mismatch in the low-wage labor market: job hiring perspective', in D.S. Nightingale (ed) *The low-wage labor market: Challenges and opportunities for economic self-sufficiency*, Washington, DC: The Urban Institute, December (aspe.hhs.gov/hsp/lwlm99/holzer.htm).

Kramer, E.J. and Wiatr, A.R. (2002) 'New York State Office for the Aging promotes older women's breast health awareness', *New York State Office for the Aging archive* (aging.state.ny.us/news/letter/an000208.htm).

Lemon, A. (nd) 'Misogyny and respect in Robert Johnson songs' (xroads.virginia.edu/~MUSIC/blues/lemon.html).

Mohan, V and Cassady, D. (2002) *Supermarket shuttle programs: A feasibility study for supermarkets located in low-income, transit dependent, urban neighborhoods in California*, Davis, CA: University Of California, Davis Center for Advanced Studies in Nutrition and Social Marketing, November. (socialmarketing-nutrition.ucdavis.edu/Downloads/ShuttleReport.pdf).

National Abortion Rights Action League (NARAL) Pro-Choice America Foundation [Georgia] (2004) *Who decides? A state-by-state report on the status of women's reproductive rights* (naral.org/yourstate/whodecides/states/georgia/index.cfm).

Neighborhood Safety and the Prevalence of Physical Inactivity – Selected States, 1996 (1999) *Morbidity and Mortality Weekly Report*, Centers for Disease Control and Prevention, vol 48, no 7, pp 143-6.

Pavetti, L., Derr, M., Anderson, J. and Trippe, S.D. (2000) *The role of intermediaries in linking TANF recipients with jobs: Final report*, Report submitted to US Department of Health and Human Services, Office of the Assistant Secretary for Planning, Washington, DC: Mathematica Policy Research, Inc (www.mathematica-mpr.com/PDFs/intermediaries.pdf).

Physicians for Reproductive Choice and Health and The Alan Guttmacher Institute (2003) *An overview of abortion in the United States*, Washington, DC: The Alan Guttmacher Institute (www.agi-usa.org/pubs/abslides/abort_slides.pdf).

Saenz v Roe (1999) 526 US 489, 119 S. Ct. 1518, 143 L. Ed. 2d 689.

Salganicoff, A., Beckerman, J.Z., Wyn, R., and Ojeda, V.D. (2002) *Women's health in the United States: Health coverage and access to care Kaiser Women's Health Survey*, Menlo Park, CA: The Henry J. Kaiser Family Foundation (www.kff.org/womenshealth/loader.cfm?url=/commonspot/security/getfile.cfmandPageID=13969).

Schlanger, M. (1998) 'Injured women before common law courts, 1860-1930', *Harvard Women's Law Journal*, vol 21, no 79 (www.law.harvard.edu/faculty/schlanger/publications/injuredwomen.htm).

Shapiro v Thompson (1969) 394 US 618, 89 S. Ct. 1322, 22 L. Ed. 2d 600.

Shugart, K. (2003, June 26) 'Volunteer drivers hold keys to abortion access', *Women's e-news* (www.womensenews.org/article.cfm/dyn/aid/1395/context/archive).

Siren, A. (2002) 'Older women: independent community related mobility and its vulnerability', Paper presented at the Reconceptualising Gender and Ageing conference, Centre for Research on Ageing and Gender, University of Surrey, 25-27 June, University of Surrey, UK.

Snyder, M.G. (1995) 'Feminist theory and planning theory: lessons from feminist epistemologies', *Berkeley Planning Journal*, vol 10, pp 91-106 (dcrp.ced.berkeley.edu/bpj/pdf/10-Snyder.pdf).

Staplin, L., Lococo, K.H., Stewart, J. and Decina, L.E. (1999) *Safe mobility for older people notebook*, DOT HS 808 853, Washington, DC: Office of Research and Traffic Records, National Highway Traffic Safety Administration (www.nhtsa.dot.gov/people/injury/olddrive/safe).

Stewart, L. (2000, October/November) 'Where the action is: development near transit', *Bay Area Monitor*, San Francisco, CA: League of Women Voters of the Bay Area (www.bayareamonitor.org/oct00/devel.html).

Transportation Research Board of the National Academies (2002) *Daycare services at transit hubs*, Contract/Grant Number: FTA-DC-26-1001 (rip.trb.org/browse/dproject.asp?n=5374).

Trapp, D. (2001) 'MetroMoves to you: putting public transportation where the public is', *City Beat*, vol 7, no 19 (www.citybeat.com/2001-03-29/news.shtml).

Turner, J. and Grieco, M. (1998) 'Gender and time poverty: the neglected social policy implications of gendered time, transport and travel', Paper presented at the International Conference on Time Use, University of Luneberg, Germany, 22-25 April (www.geocities.com/margaret_grieco/womenont/time.html).

University of California and Yale University (2001) 'Minorities benefit when buying cars on Internet, say researchers' (11 December 2001) *Silicon Valley/San Jose Business Journal* (sanjose.bizjournals.com/sanjose/stories/2001/12/10/daily20.html).

University of North Carolina Highway Safety Research Center (1998) 'HSRC study shows seniors seldom plan for life without a car', *Directions*, Summer (www.hsrc.unc.edu/directions/summer98/olddriver.htm).

US Airport (2003) 'US airport staff may get x-ray vision' (2003, June 26) ICNorthernIreland.cu.uk, http://icnorthernireland.icnetwork.co.uk/news/national/page.cfm?objectid=13105260andmethod=fullandsiteid=91603

US Census Bureau (2002) 'Table PINC-10 wage and salary workers – people 15 years old and over, by total wage and salary income in 2001, work experience in 2001, race, hispanic origin and sex', *Current population survey* (ferret.bls.census.gov/macro/032002/perinc/new10_000.htm).

Wallace, R.B. and Franc, D. (nd) 'Literature review of the status of research on the transportation and mobility needs of older women', Paper prepared for the National Safety Council and the National Highway Traffic Safety Administration, Washington, DC: National Highway Traffic Safety Administration.

Walker, S. and Irlbeck, D. (2002) *Driving while female: A national problem in police misconduct: A special report*, Omaha, NE: Department of Criminal Justice; University of Nebraska at Omaha; Police Professionalism Initiative (www.policeaccountability.org/drivingfemale.htm).

Winkler, A.E. (2002) 'Measuring time use in households with more than one person', *Monthly Labor Review*, vol 125, no 2, pp 45-52 (www.bls.gov/opub/mlr/2002/02/art3full.pdf).

Wong, S., Ma, T. and Hayden, C. (2003) *Shifting into gear: A comprehensive guide to creating a car ownership program*, Oakland, CA: The National Economic Development and Law Center (nedlc.org/Shifting.pdf).

FOURTEEN

Conclusions from the US experience

Karen Lucas

The environmental justice movement in the US has been recognising inequalities in access to transportation since the mid-1960s. The problem was even raised by Martin Luther King when he called for structural reforms to deal with race and poverty. The US case studies have shown that, since this time, there has been a gradual (but far from problem free) shift towards both formal government recognition of the problem and policy commitment to resolving it. The question is whether this has made a visible difference on the ground.

Clearly, there are numerous contributory factors in transportation disadvantage, including people not being able to afford their own vehicle; lack of public transportation to and from work or other means of transportation; public transportation not being offered on the weekends or evenings when jobs are available; lack of childcare; no public transportation in rural areas and the job market locating further distances from the centers of cities and urban sprawl. Equally evident, given the multiple and complex nature of the problem is that there is no single solution.

Improving access to employment

A particular focus of the US environmental justice in transportation agenda over the past 40 years or so has been on addressing the increasing problem of access to employment in the face of the increasing physical isolation of unemployed people from job opportunities. This is commonly referred to in the US literature as the *reverse-commute* phenomenon, although the spatial mismatch between people and jobs is not always as 'inner-city to urban periphery' focused as the title would suggest.

As Cervero has identified in Chapter Ten, Job Access and Reverse Commute (JARC) and other specialised transportation programs first arose as a policy concern in the wake of urban riots in the late 1960s. Despite limited proof of the success of these earlier programs, and following a period of transit subsidy cuts and campaigns to privatise services in the early 1980s, interest in reverse commuting regained momentum in the 1990s. This was, in part, prompted by 1990s federal public policy directives setting limits on welfare dependence, notably the setting of a five-year lifetime limit on cash assistance.

Most Welfare to Work (WtoW) programs in the US now fully embrace the notion that improved transportation services are a crucial factor in reducing joblessness. Federal programs have provided tens of millions of dollars for expanding transit connections between inner-city areas and suburban jobs over the last ten years or so. Presently there are three federal funding sources that can be utilised in assisting individuals from welfare benefits and into work:

1. The Temporary Assistance for Needy Families (TANF) Program administered by the Department of Health and Human Services;
2. The WtoW grants administered by the US Department of Labor;
3. The Job Access and Reverse Commute (JARC) Grant Program administered by the US Federal Transit Administration (FTA).

These have tended to concentrate on enhancing public transportation, developing bespoke paratransit and community transportation services and/or subsidising the individual to use such services. However, as both Cervero, and García and Rubin point out (Chapters Ten and Twelve), particularly in America's car-dominant society, the working poor often need access to cars. On the whole, strategies to assist job seekers with the purchase of a private vehicle have been seen as controversial, however, and thus, have been less eagerly pursued. The three main cited concerns are:

- that the ongoing cost of running, insuring and maintaining a car is often beyond the means of many low-income households over the longer term;
- many donated cars are gross polluters and are only a year or so away from expensive repair bills;
- moving people from public transportation into private vehicles will ultimately undermine the level and quality of the overall public transportation system.

In Chapter Ten, Cervero finds that the success of reverse-commute projects largely depends on effective collaborations between the numerous local agencies involved in WtoW programs. He finds that, by coordinating their efforts, local partnerships can increase productivity by tapping into scale economies and deliver more suitable and cost-effective transportation services to clients. However, experience also suggests that forming such collaborations is often easier said than done due to disagreements and power struggles between the different organisations that are involved. Institutional responsibilities can also create policy contradictions that are difficult to rationalise.

Funding issues

It is recognised that running wholly subsidised services is expensive, and yet fares need to be kept low – therefore, they are rarely self-financing. One solution is to competitively contract out services, so as to lower operating costs. However, experiences show that contracted services can compromise reliability, on-time performance and service quality. Sometimes contracted buses do not show up or are well behind schedule. Reliability is of utmost importance to many low-income workers, because the high availability of unemployed people means that they can be easily replaced if they arrive to work late more than once. Another problem is that private vendors tend to hire non-unionised, low-wage drivers to keep costs down and this can not only end up lowering service quality in the short term, but can eventually depress salary levels and take away jobs from unionised workers.

There is virtual unanimity among local interest groups, therefore, that more money is needed to subsidize such services, as well as changes to the present funding arrangements for these projects. The state's transit providers and county welfare departments claim they are financially stretched to the limit and need more funding assistance to be proactive in this respect. However, on the basis of the Metropolitan Transportation Authority (MTA) case study (Chapter Twelve), having the available funding may not always translate into better transportation for the disadvantaged. As García and Rubin point out, MTA has continued to fund expensive rail projects, while pleading an inability to finance the operating costs of the Consent Decree to enhance bus services that it voluntarily entered into. In fiscal year 2004, over 54% of the transit subsidies for MTA's own transit services capital, operating, and financing expenditures will go towards the development of 'Guideway Transit'. This and experience elsewhere suggests that high-profile infrastructure projects, predominantly serving middle-class and politically vocal sectors of society will always win out over less glamorous, but significantly cheaper, improvements to bus services to serve the transportation disadvantaged. Thus, if enhanced transportation services for the travel poor are to be provided, funds need to be ring-fenced and ear-marked solely for this purpose, rather than made available in the form of general transportation block grants or transfer payments.

Adopting a legal basis for environmental justice in transportation

Legal case history has played an important role in both challenging discrimination in the transportation industry and shaping federal and state policies in this respect. The MTA case study offers a working example of how civil rights attorneys, working with grassroots activists filed and won a class action against environmental injustice in transportation delivery. The authors of this chapter (Twelve) have engagingly described the considerable efforts that were required both leading up to and after settlement of the case in 1996 through a court-ordered Consent Decree.

Ultimately, however, the case was resolved through mediation and a settlement, not trial, and MTA has resisted bus service improvements for the eight years since the Consent Decree has been in force, taking its arguments to set aside the Consent Decree all the way to the US Supreme Court. Setting aside the considerable cost and effort of pursuing such a class action, it is difficult to say if grassroots movements of this kind will continue with the rulings made on the Sandoval and Camden cases.

Although the Sandoval holding is a serious blow to civil rights enforcement, it is more important to keep in mind that individuals still can sue a recipient of federal funds under Title VI to challenge intentionally discriminatory practices. Additionally, individuals can sue to enforce discriminatory impact regulations against state and local government recipients of federal funds through the Civil Rights Act of 1871, a matter not decided in Sandoval. Litigation, therefore, still remains an important available option, even if it is seen as something of a last resort due to its prohibitive costs and the level of effort involved. Recipients of federal funds are also still bound by the regulations under Title VI and this continues to provide an important opportunity to use the planning and administrative process to resolve discriminatory impact issues.

The emerging policy agenda

The US experience demonstrates that, despite legal successes and vast spending on special programs targeted at transportation-disadvantaged citizens over the last 10 years, transportation policies in the US continue to nurture an inequitable environment. This has been recognised by the 2004 Executive Order, which has set up an Interagency Transportation Coordinating Council (ITCC) within the Department for Transportation specifically to address this issue, and is due to report to the President in February 2005. A key focus of the work of the ITCC over the next year will be to ensure greater overall efficiency in the delivery of transportation services and on delivering a seamless, comprehensive and coordinated community transportation system. Interestingly, in the light of past legal case law rulings, the order explicitly states that it does not create any right or benefit, enforceable by law or in equity, by a party against the US government.

Widening the policy remit

Evidently, there is no one solution to the transportation problems underserved populations face. Ultimately success will rely on the government's ability to finance and manage numerous small systems of targeted delivery alongside large transportation systems that are already in place. However, the case studies suggest that, in order to make a real step-change in transportation-disadvantaged sectors, the US policy remit needs to go far deeper and wider than the latest Executive Order proposes in three key respects:

1. It needs to ensure a continued focus on racial discrimination, while simultaneously giving greater recognition to other disadvantaged groups and their activity needs, in particular women.

2. The influence of land-use planning, service delivery decisions and the effect of policy decisions in other key areas of welfare delivery on transportation disadvantage needs to be more fully recognised within the policy agenda.
3. The importance of other supporting initiatives, such as childcare provision, basic skills training and community involvement in the decision-making process need to be seen as an integral part in addressing transportation disadvantage.

More groups, activity types and transportation options

The struggle for environmental justice in transportation found its origins in the civil rights movement and some feel there has been a tendency in the past to over-emphasise the needs of black and minority ethnic populations over and above other disadvantaged groups. As García and Rubin (Chapter Twelve) point out, however, racial and ethnic exclusion in the US is often symptomatic of a larger, structural unfairness that affects all people who are powerless to protect themselves, including disadvantaged white people. It has been argued that over-attention to racial and ethnic exclusion is unduly confrontational and divisive, when the problem of transportation disadvantage is clearly experienced by other sectors of the population. It is noted that the latest Executive Order no longer includes race as a separate category.

In Chapter Thirteen, Ortoleva and Brenman argue that women should also be included as a special category within the policy remit, on the basis that women returning to work after participation in welfare programs face numerous barriers, which require special consideration. In particular, women need to 'trip chain' much more than men and, thus, frequently cannot rely on public transportation because it is difficult and inconvenient to combine the journey to work with childcare, shopping and other essential activities.

Furthermore, the journey to work may not always be the most important travel activity for many low-income groups, for example older people and children, neither of which are even officially recognised under the latest definition of transportation-disadvantaged groups. As Chapter Two demonstrated, healthcare trips and access to healthy affordable food can be equally important in ensuring active citizenship. There is evidence to suggest that public transit is not providing access to medical facilities for many poor people in the US and may even discourage some from seeking care.

It is also necessary to recognise that more low-income people and people of colour depend on the automobile than on public transportation. Many minority people live in rural areas, small towns, and other out-of-the-way places, nowhere near transit services. Transportation equity cannot be defined solely in terms of the experience of large, metropolitan areas where transit options are more viable. It is also necessary to look at the delivery of transportation services in small towns and rural areas and elsewhere, where automobiles might be the only viable travel option. To be completely comprehensive, programs to address transportation disadvantage need to include consideration of all transportation options, including the subsidies for the purchase, running costs and upkeep of private vehicles.

More areas of policy delivery

On the whole, efforts to improve access for the travel poor in the US have tended to focus on improving access to transportation, rather than on making changes to patterns of land use and the location of activities. However, as García and Rubin (Chapter Twelve) identify, achieving equal access to transportation is just one aspect of a broader vision for the distribution of public resources benefits and burdens in ways that are equitable, protect human health and the environment, promote economic vitality, and engage full and fair public participation.

In Chapter Thirteen, Ortoleva and Brenman identify some limited experiments with transit villages, designed to provide commuters with ready transit access to stores, services and other community resources. They rightly identify that such initiatives can be highly beneficial to time-poor, transportation-disadvantaged citizens, particularly women, who often need to combine a number of trips in order to facilitate their daily responsibilities. Providing a range of key services at one location, especially if this is within walking distance of the home location, probably represents the optimum solution for addressing many of the problems experienced by transportation-disadvantaged citizens. Clearly, however, this is often not viable in the delivery of all key services for reasons of economy of scale and is also far harder to enact in many instances. Transportation will always be an important part of the solution and perhaps more so in the case of the US, where lands uses are so dispersed, but should not be the only focus of policy attention.

More supporting initiatives

Moreover, addressing transportation disadvantage does not end by simply supplying improved transportation services. To offer a better chance of success, a range of supporting, and preferably integrated, measures are needed both in the planning and delivery of transportation services.

Across all transportation-disadvantaged groups, there is a need to ensure that the 'voices' of local people are heard during the transportation planning and implementation phases of projects. In Chapter Eleven, Morris describes how well-designed community impact assessments (CIAs) can help with this. Morris's experience suggests, however, that the traditional public involvement techniques used in CIAs need to be adapted if they are to secure the participation of disadvantaged groups and low-income and minority communities. In particular, she notes that most practitioners do not make the connection between low-income and low educational attainment and literacy levels. As such, too little consideration has been given to the fact that segments of the population may not be able to read, or if they can read, may not be able to read English.

Community impact assessment also does not address the ongoing need for intervention once transport systems are already in place. Special transportation masters, such as those appointed to monitor delivery of the MTA Consent Decree, can help to put pressure on operating companies to service the needs of transportation-disadvantaged people, in some instances, but will be of little help where there is weak political will and limited legal redress to follow this through, as the MTA case has demonstrated. This means that, while the Consent Decree has protected the transit riders of Los Angeles from grievous harm to the bus transit system that they depend on and also produced very large improvements, the battle to obtain the full measure of improvements promised in the Consent Decree is obviously an ongoing war with many major battles yet to be fought.

Future research

The US experience suggests that more evidence is also needed on both the nature of the problems and cost-effective and efficient ways to resolve it. From a welfare policy perspective, evaluations of the success of initiatives to address transportation disadvantage should be gauged on whether the project has been successful in moving unemployed people off welfare rolls and into gainful employment rather than on improving bus patronage levels. On this basis, recent research has found improved access to public transportation was positively associated with successful W to W transitions. However, owning and having access to a car was found to be even more important.

In Chapter Twelve, García and Rubin suggest that 'following the money' also helps to clarify who benefits by the investment of public resources and who gets left behind. They recommend that financial, demographic, and historical analyses can be effectively used to facilitate discussions between the providers of services and communities in need and to creatively to find common ground.

The 2004 Executive Order calls for greater evidence of what works and how the present program of support can be made more efficient and responsive to the needs of the transportation disadvantaged. This is likely to provide the key focal point for research activity in the short to mid-term.

Part Four:
Transferring the lessons

FIFTEEN

Towards a 'social welfare' approach to transport

Karen Lucas

There are more questions than answers

In my introduction to this volume, I suggested that a significant proportion of people living on low incomes in the UK and the US are effectively 'locked out' of the activities that enable a decent quality of life because of a lack of adequate transport. In the minds of myself and my fellow contributors to this volume, many of whom work on the frontline to assist such individuals, there is no doubt that this is the case.

The statistical evidence shows that people living on the lowest incomes, in both the UK and the US, spend a far greater (and often punitively high) proportion of their income to travel less often and over shorter distances than the average population. They also disproportionately suffer the disutility of our car-dominant transport systems. This is not only in terms of their over-exposure to noise, air pollution and accidents, but because of diminishing and increasingly unaffordable public transport services combined with a decline in local shops and amenities in the areas where they live. The effect of this 'travel poverty' is to significantly reduce their life chances because of a reduced opportunity to access a decent education, gainful employment, healthcare services and other amenities. In this way, the inequalities that are already evident within this sector of the population are reinforced.

In the past, transport policies have been blind to such issues because the theories and models that have informed them were more concerned with the efficient operation and maintenance of the system than meeting the accessibility needs of the people using it. Similarly, professionals concerning themselves with the anti-poverty and social welfare agenda have failed to recognise and address the important and dynamic role of transportation in creating and reinforcing social and economic disadvantage. This situation is now changing on both sides of the Atlantic; new policy and legislative frameworks are being developed in both countries in an attempt to address this previous oversight.

Clearly, US policy and practice is more advanced in this respect and the UK policy makers and practitioners have much to learn from the experiences of their US counterparts. Nevertheless, my colleagues in the US would be the first to admit that they are a long way from resolving the problems they have so clearly identified. The issue is complex and often throws up more questions than satisfactory answers.

Is the lack of transport being recognised as a social policy issue?

There is general acceptance that one of the most effective ways of moving people out of poverty is to increase their economic activity by allowing them better access to employment. Reducing unemployment lies at the heart of both the US and UK welfare policy agendas, in recognition that this is not only of benefit to the individual but also the state.

Part Three of this volume demonstrates that the US is already targeting considerable policy attention and public money at providing transport to work for 'travel-poor' individuals and communities. Part Two identifies that improving physical access to employment is also moving up the UK political agenda. This would suggest a growing acceptance among 'welfare to work' (WtoW) professionals that transport is indeed a social policy issue. It is my contention, however, that this policy focus is far too limited in scope. The impact of 'transport poverty' spans across the whole life cycle, contributing to the social exclusion of people living on low incomes from a very early age and continuing to reinforce this through their lifetime.

Chapter Two identifies an inverse correlation between access to educational and training facilities and student achievement, in both the UK and the US. While the research evidence to corroborate this claim is extremely poor, it suggests that a lack of transport during a child's formative years may be playing a vital part in creating the type of 'enclave mentality' so often witnessed among people living in low-income communities.

Not only do poor people travel less than the average population, they are also often unwilling to undertake activities outside their immediate neighbourhood. This can be due to both their lack of experience in using the transport system and the 'agoraphobia' referred to by Westwood. Few policy makers or practitioners give due attention to this issue and travel training is generally not a feature of educational, training or capacity-building programmes.

Equally, the role of poor physical access to healthcare facilities in the differential health outcomes of low-income sectors of the population is poorly understood. This means that far too little policy attention is paid to the contribution of 'transport poverty' in missed health appointments and delays in seeking medical attention. Health policies, however, are beginning to recognise the link between exposure to road traffic and unequal health outcomes. Programmes are also being introduced to promote walking and cycling as part of a healthy-lifestyles regime.

More fundamentally, if such inequalities are to be reduced, addressing 'transport poverty' needs to be seen as one aspect of a broader vision for the reorganisation of public service delivery. The professionals responsible for making decisions about the location and timing of education, health, and other public services need to include full consideration of the ability of poor communities to physically access these. This must be supported by planning, housing, neighbourhood renewal and regeneration policies that ensure that achieving equitable access lies at the heart of all future development and redevelopment activity.

Is better public transport the best way forward?

Even if this vision is achieved, it will be in the longer term and there will anyway be numerous instances where people on low incomes will need some form of transport in order to access goods and services. Currently, the policy agenda places heavy emphasis on the public transport network to provide this. This is not surprising, as there are already comprehensive (if flawed) institutional and administrative structures in place at the local level to deliver such policies. Both the UK and US case studies, however, make it clear that improvements to fixed route services alone will not solve the problems of many 'travel-poor' individuals and communities. As Grant points out (Chapter Four), even in urban areas conventional public transport is often poorly suited to the wide dispersal of activities necessary to support a reasonable quality of life. In rural areas, fixed route services are rarely an option, due to low-density settlement patterns.

Nevertheless, as the success and popularity of the BraunstoneBus initiative in Leicester (Chapter Six) and the Los Angeles MTA case study (Chapter Twelve) both demonstrate, affordable public transport is an important part of the overall equation. However, ensuring that public transport services match the travel needs of people on low incomes is not an easy task. This is largely due to the poor public accountability of such transport providers to this sector of the population, even though they are usually the main clients. This problem is not specific to the transport sector; it is a common phenomenon across a whole range of delivery agencies in both the public and private sector and a recognised area for policy reform within the social exclusion agenda. Nevertheless, it is a hard nut to crack because, as with the issues of racism (Chapter Twelve) and gender bias (Chapter Thirteen), it is often institutionalised within both the policy processes and the practices of such agencies.

What are the alternatives to conventional public services?

Chapter Seven has identified that community transport has long played an important role in providing an alternative transport option for people without access to transport in rural areas and also for those individuals who are unable to use conventional public transport. Increasingly, transport professionals are also recognising the potential of such services for meeting the travel needs of 'transport-poor' communities in urban areas.

However, as Chapter Ten identifies, the development and operation of such services can be fraught with difficulties. They are rarely self-financing, as fares must, by necessity, be kept low if they are to be affordable to low-income populations. This means that the level of subsidy needed to support them is often prohibitive in the revenue constrained funding scenario that operates on both sides of the Atlantic.

However, their cost is not the only issue. As identified by Ortoleva and Brenman in Chapter Thirteen, travel poverty is highly gendered. A large majority of 'travel-poor' individuals are women, many are lone parents with sole responsibility for childcare and other household duties. Flexibly routed services tend to have even slower journey times than conventional public transport; time that many of these women simply do not have to spare. Low-paid jobs can often involve night-shift working, when even door-to-door public transport services can be perceived as unsafe. Often 'trip chains' are needed to pick up and drop off children and for shopping, a luxury that even flexibly routed services cannot offer. In such instances, as well as for people living in more isolated rural areas, cars can often be the only viable means of transportation.

Is the answer just to give everyone a car?

This is clearly a highly controversial issue and one that generally does not sit easy with the transport professionals. Over the last ten years or so, they have been actively trying to encourage people out of their cars and onto public transport in the interests of both the environment and the economy. The last thing they want is to encourage more cars onto the road. Low-income households also tend to drive older vehicles, which are more polluting and less energy efficient. This is of environmental concern in terms of both local air quality and greenhouse gas emissions.

On the other hand, people on low incomes need and prefer to use cars for the same reasons everyone else does: they are cheaper, faster, more flexible, convenient and reliable than public transport, particularly for carrying passengers, shopping and other heavy goods. It could even be argued that, in car-dominant societies, lack of access to a car is in itself one of the key defining factors in social exclusion. The statistical evidence demonstrates that car ownership is strongly associated with successful welfare to work transitions. Experiences in the US have also demonstrated that car ownership reduces the amount of work time missed and increases job-training participation.

Having a car does not necessarily mean that it is affordable to use. Insuring, maintaining and operating a vehicle can be beyond the means of many low-income households. The statistical evidence presented in Chapter Two suggests that low-income households with cars spend a disproportionate amount of their income on motoring costs and that this may be to the detriment of other essential activities. Furthermore, a huge proportion of people experiencing transport poverty are too young, too old or simply unable to drive. For this reason alone, car-based strategies cannot be seen the only solution, but neither should they be ignored.

It is interesting to note, however, that even in California where car ownership is relatively high among low-income sectors of the population, subsidies, loans and car hire schemes to give low-income households access to cars are limited. Such initiatives are even more rare in the UK (the two examples cited in Chapter Seven are the exception rather than the norm). I would suggest this represents more of a bias in the minds of the professionals working with travel-poor individuals than the appropriateness and viability of such an approach.

Ultimately, transport policies need to adopt a balanced approach to allow for a certain amount of increased car ownership and use among low-income sectors of the population where this is appropriate for securing their social inclusion, while curtailing the environmentally damaging and excessive levels of car use among middle- and high-income households.

What financial resources are needed?

Both the UK and US policy agendas for addressing 'transport poverty' claim that large amounts of state funding are already being spent on addressing this issue. They identify that the problem is insufficient targeting of these resources and cost inefficiencies and that better coordination of the existing resource base is needed. On the other hand, transport authorities and the other delivery agencies responsible for delivering specialist transport services on both sides of the Atlantic are unanimous. In their opinion, considerably more money is needed if real reductions in 'transport poverty' are to be realised.

It is clear that the cost of providing such schemes is not cheap; the new routes provided by the BraunstoneBus initiative required £1.13 million of Urban Bus Challenge (UBC) money matched with £334,000 of neighbourhood renewal funds to deliver. This does not include paying for the staff time spent on securing funding for, setting up and running the project. In 1999, $150 million of federal funds were awarded to the US Job Access and Reverse Commute (JARC) programme, funding approximately 200 transit projects of various sizes. Even so, Cervero identifies that more, not less money, is needed for such schemes in the US (Chapter Ten).

Another problem is that, even where public funds are being made available for such transport projects, there is a bias towards funding new schemes rather than providing ongoing subsidies, on the basis that once projects have been set up they should become self-financing over time. However, many transport projects targeted at low-income communities are never likely to achieve this; it is, after all, the main reason why they needed to be set up in the first place.

Lack of recognition of the considerable ongoing staff resource implications of working 'travel-poor' groups and communities is also an issue within the present funding structures. Often personalised travel advice, booking, travel training and other support services are needed in addition to the provision of transport services.

This is labour intensive and requires skilled, dedicated and experienced staff. Drivers and project staff salaries are escalating year on year, as are vehicle, insurance and service tender costs.

In both the UK and US, however, governments are looking to cut back rather than increase their welfare spending. It seems unlikely, therefore, that large sums of additional state finance will be made available to address the problems we have identified. For this reason, considerable emphasis is being placed on bending resources from non-transport sectors and resource sharing.

This is not an easy prospect. Budget holders are usually fiercely protective of their funding allocations and take some convincing to hand over monies for other organisations to administer. There are some examples of where this has been successfully achieved. These demonstrate that hard evidence of the benefits of transport improvements to the delivery objectives of these other sectors (for example, statistical evidence that a new bus services to the hospital will reduce missed health appointments). Such cause-and-effect relationships are notoriously difficult to prove and the data and information for undertaking such analyses are often not available. Even where there is a willingness to resource share, the different funding timeframes, structures, rules, regulations, policy targets and performance monitoring regimes applied to each sector make the process unnecessarily time consuming, over-burdensome and difficult to administrate.

So, do we need more research and analysis?

As a researcher, I am bound to answer in the affirmative. There is still insufficient understanding of the dynamic role of transport creating and reinforcing social exclusion. The accessibility planning approach being recommended to local transport authorities in England by the UK government will clearly demonstrate the geographical distribution of transport disadvantage in the UK; however, this is only a first step. As we have seen from a number of the case studies, far more complex, detailed micro-analysis is needed at the level of the individual if we are to gain any real understanding of the issues.

Too little is also known about what works best in terms of securing transport justice and social inclusion and the cost effectiveness of different schemes in achieving these outcomes. The best way to achieve this is through meaningful and continuous public involvement of the people who are affected. How policy makers and practitioners engage these people, how we define their communities and how they are treated in a fair and equitable manner (perceived or actual) is at the heart of environmental justice and social inclusion.

Do strong legislative and regulatory frameworks help?

We have seen that, unlike the UK, the US has a longstanding legislative framework for civil rights, which aims to ensure that all US citizens receive fair treatment in the allocation of federal and state spending. The law provides that communities can bring lawsuits against the providers of transport services if they feel they are being unjustly treated in this respect, albeit that the burden is on the plaintiff to prove discrimination.

The Metropolitan Transportation Authority (MTA) case is a prime example of how a highly organised grassroots campaign can work with transport-disadvantaged communities to achieve social change. García and Rubin (Chapter Twelve) suggest that litigation should only be seen as a last resort, in the context of a broader campaign for environmental justice in transportation. It can clearly be a very drawn-out process and success is never guaranteed. It nevertheless remains an option for US citizens experiencing discrimination in this respect, where no such luxury is afforded to 'transport-poor' communities in the UK. Legislation is also only as effective as the regulatory frameworks that support it. Unless there is true political will and commitment and adequate scrutiny of the agencies responsible for delivering this agenda, legislation is an empty gesture.

In the US, community impact assessments (CIAs) are used to help ensure that the interests and voices of low-income and minority communities are represented within transport planning. Although it can be argued these do not go far enough in protecting deprived neighbourhoods from the development of inappropriate transport infrastructure in their areas, they do at least ensure the mitigation of the worst environmental and health impacts of these. Once again, no attempt is being made to guarantee this in the UK, despite clear evidence that past planning decisions have often been against the best interests of low-income individuals and to the detriment of deprived neighbourhoods.

So, what is the best way forward?

In their chapter, García and Rubin (Chapter Twelve) put forward four universal lessons from the environmental justice movement. These can equally be applied to the transport disadvantaged in the UK and the US. Low-income communities:

- are disproportionately denied the benefits of public resources;
- disproportionately bear the burdens of environmental degradation;
- are denied access to information to understand the impact of decisions;
- are denied full and fair participation in the decision-making process.

Success in achieving visible reductions in 'transport poverty' will only be achieved if all four issues are fully and simultaneously addressed.

The message from frontline workers engaging with such communities is that it needs to be people-centred and solutions-led. People will say what they need, but they need to be listened to and not presented with a set of preconceived ideas about what will work. Otherwise, don't bother to ask!

Sometimes there may be enough people wanting the same trip to make taxi sharing or a minibus a viable solution. In other instances, a flexibly routed bus service or conventional public transport service may indeed be the answer. At other times, a car or motorbike really is the only viable option.

Over the longer term, however, it is equally important to ensure that key services and activities are located in places where they are easy for people without cars to get to. Without this, people on low incomes will be forced into owning and driving cars that they can ill afford, while the people who are unable to do this will be exposed to increasing environmental injustice and social exclusion.

Index

Page references for figures and tables are in *italics*; those for notes are followed by n

A
abortion services 270
accessibility auditing 44, 47-8
accessibility planning ix, 44, 47, 79, 81, 145-6, 151
 accessibility auditing 47-8
 benefits 51-2
 legislative and institutional barriers 147-9
 reconciling environmental and social concerns 149-51
 resource audits and action planning 48-51
 resources 147
 short termism and over-simplification 146
 under-resourcing and competing funding priorities 146-7
accidents 27, 28, 42
Acheson, D. 27
action planning 44, 50-1
African Americans 183
 driving while black 262
 US17 community impact assessment 198, 199-200, 206, 207, 208, 209, 212
age
 and car ownership 23-4, *23*
 see also older people
Age Concern 133
agoraphobia 91, 146, 292
Ahmed, A. 32
Aid for Families with Dependent Children (AFDC) 183, 185
air pollution 27, 33n, 97, 176
Alameda County, California 185, 188, 190, 191
Alan Guttmacher Institute 270
Alexander v Choate 172, 174
Alexander v Sandoval 175-6, 177, 242-3, 284
Ali, Altaf 264
American Civil Liberties Union 264
American Public Transit Association 184
American Public Transportation Association (APTA) 227
Anderson, J. 268, 269
Arriva North West 123
Ashman, L. 18
Atlanta 184
Audit Commission 29
Auto Response South Wales 124-8, *125*, *126*, *127*
Ayres, Ian 263

B
Bailey, E. 222
Balanced Budget Act 1997 (US) 162
Bania, N. 183
Banister, D. 9
Banks, Trevante 222-3
Beaumont Leys 102, 103
Berk, Richard 233
Bernstein, S. 222, 223
bicycling 269
Billions for Buses 232

Bingham, R. 18
bio-diesel 113-15
Black Caucus 212, 213
Blair, Tony 71-2
Bliss, Donald T. 240, 246-8, 251n
Blumenberg, E. 29, 30, 183, 185
Boston 184
Boyarsky, B. 232
Bozorgmehr, M. 244
Braddock, M. 28
Braunstone 95-6, 100
Braunstone Community Association (BCA) 52, 95-7, 98-100, 104, 107, 109, 110, 112, 115-16
Braunstone Working Project 99, 101
BraunstoneBus 146, 293, 295
 the dream 96-7
 impact on social inclusion 116-17
 making it happen 100-4
 new technology 113-16, *115*
 the reality 98-100
 on the road 107-10, *108*, *109*
 six-month review 110-13, *110*, *111*, *114*
 tendering process 105, 107
 unexpected opportunity 104-5, *106*
Breakthrough (Merseytravel) 64
Bridges to Work 182
Bringing Britain together (SEU) 41
Brinkley, Douglas 258
Brown, Jeffrey 261
Brown v Board of Education 252n
Bruton, M. 9-10, 11, 28
Bucio, Leticia 222
Budig, M.J. 267
Bullard, R. 223
Bus Riders' Union (BRU) 232, 234, 247, 261
buses
 access to employment 86-9, *87*, *88*
 college shuttles 86
 Ealing PlusBus 130-2
 fares 26, *26*
 Job Link 65-6, *65*
 legislative and institutional barriers 147-8
 Los Angeles 223, 224, 225, 227-8, 230-1, 283
 Merseyside *59*, 60, 64-5
 MTA Consent Decree 233, 234, 235-6
 NWACTA 136-8
 reverse commute 188-91
 subsidy review 147
 see also BraunstoneBus
Bush, George W. 156
Butte County, California 192
Button, K.J. 11
Byrne, Shaun 131, 132

C
Cache Creek Casino *189*
Cahill, M. 42
Cairns, S. 157-8

Calgary Regional Health Authority Health Promotions Initiatives Fund 272
California
  car ownership schemes 295
  discrimination law 237
  job access and reverse commute programs 181, 183, 185-93, *186*, *188*, *189*, 193-5
  Workfare 182
  see also Los Angeles
Callender, C. 31
CalWORKS (California Work Opportunity and Responsibilities to Kids) 182, 186, 187, 190-1, 193
  bus pass assistance 188
  mobility options 192-3
  paratransit 192
Camden case 176, 177, 284
car ownership 32-3, 149-50, 294-5
  households and social groups 22-5, *22*, *23*, *24*, *25*
  and land-use patterns 15-16
  Merseyside 58
  strategies 191-2, 274, 282
car schemes 133-5
car sharing 69, 72, 82-4, 127
Carrara, Mark 97
case law history 177
Cassady, D. 271-2
Castaneda v Partida 235
Cervero, R. 182, 185
childcare services 266-7, 271, 275, 285
children 285
  pedestrian accidents 27, 28, 42
  transport concerns 45-6
  and women's transportation difficulties 266-7
Chinatown Cornfield, Los Angeles 245
Chung, C. 18
Church, A. 42
churches 208, 209, 210-11, *210*
Cincinnati 266-7
cinemas 140-1
Cinemobile 140
Civil Rights Act 1871 (US) 236-7, 251-2n, 284
Civil Rights Act 1964 (US) 155, 177, 261
  see also Title VI
Civil Rights Act 1968 (US) 175
civil rights legislation 260-3, 296-7
classical market theory 7
Cleveland, Ohio 183-4
Coalfield Community Transport (CCT) 138-41
coalition building 245, 250
Coalition of Concerned Citizens Against I-670 v Damian 175
Commission of the European Communities 39-40
communication 274-5
Community Fund 141
community impact assessments (CIAs) ix, 163-4, 165, 197-8, 220, 286, 297
  evidence of previous research 200-1
  gathering new information 206-8
  holding workshops 208-10
  identifying income-sensitive programs 215
  involving elementary school students 215-17
  lessons learnt in preparation 202-5
  newsletters 214
  project maps 218-19
  recording the project area 219-20
  regularly scheduled events 213
  scope 199-200
  special events 211-13
  undertaking 201-2
  US17 198, 199
  using churches 210-11, *210*
  using grocery stores 217-18
  utilizing information of record 205-6
  women 274
Community Links Team 57, 61
community severance 27, 28
community transport ix, 119-21, 141-2, 145, 148, 293-4
  Auto Response South Wales 124-8, *125*, *126*, *127*
  Coalfield Community Transport 138-41
  Cornwall car scheme cooperation 133-5
  LIFT 121-4
  NWACTA 135-8
  Sure Start 128-32, *129*
Competition Act 1998 (UK) 147
Consent Decree *see* MTA Consent Decree
Contra Costa County, California 192-3
Cornwall 120, 133-5
cost benefit analysis 11
costs *see* transport costs
Cotterill, R. 18
Coughlin, J. 183-4
Council on Environmental Quality (CEQ) (US) 159, 165, 166, 168
Countryside Agency 141
Crain, J. 184
crime 18
Crime Concern 57
Crime and Disorder Reduction Partnerships 44
Cumnock 138
cumulative impacts 165-6

D

Davis, J. 42
Davis, M. 252n
Davis case 172, 173, 174
Demographic Research Unit (DMU) 225, 227
dentists 16
Department of Agriculture (US) 217
Department for Education and Employment (DfEE) (UK) 30
Department for Education and Skills (DfES) (UK) 74, 86
Department for the Environment, Transport and the Regions (DETR) (UK) 27, 41, 63
Department of Health and Human Services (US) 162, 170, 199, 215, 282
Department of Housing and Urban Development (US) 170
Department of Justice (US) 238
Department of Labor (US) 162, 282
Department for Transport (DfT) (UK)
  accessibility planning 47, 49
  community transport 133, 148
  Merseyside 61
  Mobility and Social Inclusion Unit 96
  UK National Travel Survey 16, *17*, *19*

Index

Department of Transportation (DOT) (US) 11, 169, 183, 243, 244, 259
   DOT Final Order on Environmental Justice 164, 166, 171-2
   Environmental Justice Strategy 166, 170-1
   Interagency Transportation Coordinating Council 156-7, 284
   NEPA regulations 166, 168
   Planning Regulations 166, 169
   Title VI regulations 166, 167
   women 260
Department for Work and Pensions (DWP) (UK) 126
Deptford 42
Detroit 267
Dial-a-Ride 135, 136, 137
direct effects 165
disabled people
   community transport 119, 120
   transport concerns 45-6
   US 160, *160*
distracted driving 267
doctors 16, 17, *17*, 31
driver's licenses 264, 265
driving while female 262-3
Duvall, John 121, 122, 124

E

Ealing 128-32, *129*
Ealing Community Transport 130-1
East Ayrshire 138-41
East Bibb Twiggs Neighbourhood Association v Macon-Bibb County Planning and Zoning Commission 174
Eccles by the Sea 137
ECMT 33n
education 40
   Halton 70
   improving access 85-6, 102
   and transport inequalities 30-1, 42, 292
Edwards, Jeff 124-5, 126-8, *127*
electric vehicles 97
Elkins, T. 10, 17
employment
   BraunstoneBus 101, 116
   and community transport 142
   Halton NTT 70, 86-9, *87*, *88*
   improving access 281-2, 292
   Job Link and NTCs 52, 65-6, *65*
   suburbanization 181-2, 267-8
   and transport inequalities 17, 29-30, 42
   UK 16, 40
   US 157
   Welfare to Work initiatives 161-3
   Wheels to Work 121-4, 126-7
   see also reverse commute
England 39
Environ 113
environmental injustice 177, 181
environmental justice ix, 2, 151, 155, 157-9, 177, 275, 281, 285
   case law history 172-6, 237, 250, 283-4
   community impact assessment 163-4
   Executive order human service transportation coordination 156-7
   federal policies and legislation 166-72
   highways and land use 243-4
   planning and administrative processes 243
   public involvement exercises 164-5
   race and ethnicity 239-40
   Welfare to Work initiatives 161-3
   women 260
Environmental Protection Agency (EPA) (US) 169, 170, 176
equal justice 242-3, 246
Equal Rights Advocates (ERA) 274
ethnicity *see* minority ethnic and faith groups
European Conference of Ministers of Transport 33n
Eversole, B. 181
Executive Order 12898 (US) 166, 169-70, 171, 177, 198, 199, 237
Executive Order Human Service Transportation Coordination 156-7, 177, 284, 285, 287

F

Fair Housing Act (US) 175
Federal actions to address environmental justice in minority populations and low-income populations (Executive Order 12898) 166, 169-70, 171, 177, 198, 199, 237
Federal Aid Highway Act 1956 (US) 203
Federal-Aid Highway Act 1962 (US) 11
Federal-Aid Highway Act 1970 (US) 166, 167
Federal Aviation Administration (FAA) 244
Federal Highway Administration (FHWA) 165, 224
   community impact assessments 197-8, 200, 274
   FHWA actions to address environmental justice 164, 166, 172
   Interim policy on public involvement 164, 197
   women's travel behavior 260
Federal Transit Administration (FTA) 161, 251n
   childcare services 266, 271
   Interim policy on public involvement 164, 197
   Job Access and Reverse Commute program 162, 163, 187, 282
feminist theory 258-9
Folbre, N. 267
food stores 17, *17*, 18, 42, 101-2, 271-2
Franc, D. 274
Franklin, A. 18
Freeman v State of Florida 264
Frost, M. 42
funding 11, 146-7, 194, 282-3, 295-6

G

García, R. 244
Garrett, M. 236
gender
   and car ownership 23-4, *23*
   feminist theory 258-9
   and travel behavior 259-60
   see also women
Georgia 270
Gonzaga University v Doe 252n
Goodwin, P. 10, 42
Gorz, A. 10
Gottlieb, R. 18
Governor's Commission on the Los Angeles Riots 236, 238

Gray, Paul 135, 136-8
Green, H. 29
Green, M.L. 225
Grieco, Margaret 42, 270-1
Guardians Association v Civil Service Commission 172, 174, 237

H

Hackney Community Transport (HCT) 120-1
Hair, P. 232
Hall, P. 9
Halton 69, 70, *71*
  Neighbourhood Travel Team 73-92, *87*, *88*, *89*
Halton Pathfinders Post 16 Transport Partnership 86
Hamer, L. 42
Hamilton, K. 42
Hanlon, S. 260
Hatter, Terry 232
Hay, A. 16
health 27-8, 70, 165, 292
Health Action Zones 44
healthcare facilities
  and community transport 135-8, 142
  and transport inequalities 31-2, 42, 285, 292
  women 269-70
Highland and Islands Arts 141
Highway Act 1962 (US) 11
highways 244
Hill, Michael 7, 8-9
Hillman, M. 27, 42
HM Treasury 11, 147
Hodge, D. 28
Holman, C. 27
Holzer, Harry J. 268
hospitals 16, 31
  improving access 102, 104-5, 112-13, 133-5, 136
Hutton, W. 17

I

income
  car ownership *22*
  journey distances and travel times 19-20, *19*, *20*, 21-2, *21*
  and transport costs 26
  and transport inequalities *159*
  and trip rates 59, *59*
  women 260
  see also low-income groups
indirect effects 165
inequalities
  education 30-1
  health 31-2
  see also transport inequalities
Institute of Employment Research 42
Interagency Transportation Coordinating Council (ITCC) (US) 156-7, 284
Interim policy on public involvement and questions and answers (FHA/FTA) 164, 197
Intermodal Surface Transportation Efficiency Act (ISTEA) 1991 (US) 164, 197
Internet 205, 206, 263
Irlbeck, D. 262

J

Jackson, Glenda 119
Jacksonville, North Carolina 198
jitney services x, 192
job-access programs 182-95, *186*, *188*, *189*, 192-3
Job Access and Reverse Commute (JARC) program 162, 163, 187, 194, 281, 282, 295
Job, Enterprise and Training Centres (JETs) 65
Job Link 65-6, *65*, 67, 67n, 88-9, 146
JobCentre Plus 44, 67n
  Job Link 65, 66, 88, 89
  and NTT 77, 78
Johnson, Robert 221, 257-8
Jones County, North Carolina 198
Joseph Rowntree Foundation 25-6
journey-sharing database 69, 72, 82-4

K

Kaiser Women's Health Survey 269
Kamerman, S.B. 8
Kaufman, P. 30
Kim, W.D. 28
King, Martin Luther, Jr 246, 281
Knowsley 56
Korean Immigrant Workers Advocates 232, 234
Kramer, E.J. 270
Krieger, L.H. 239
Krumholz, N. 223

L

Labor/Community Strategy Center (LCSC) 232, 233-4
Labor/Community Strategy Center v Metropolitan Transportation Authority 221, 232-3, 234, 240
Labour Force Survey (UK) 24, *24*
Lacombe, A. 184
land-use cases 174
land-use patterns 15-19, *17*
land-use planning 148, 149, 243-4, 285
Lang, R. 181
Learning and Skills Councils 44
Lee, B.L. 232
Leicester 52, 95
  see also BraunstoneBus
Leicester City Council 95, 96, 98, 104, 107, 110
Lemon, A. 257-8
Lewis, Ann 133, 134, 135
LIFT Valley Wheels scheme 121-4
Liu, C. 223
Liverpool 52, 55-7, 121-4, 146
Liverpool Housing Trust 62
Local Transport Plans (LTPs) 44, 63, 147
  Merseyside 60, *61*, 64
Los Angeles
  airport 244
  car ownership 191
  commute times 183
  demographics 224, 242
  fare hike 230-1
  land-use planning 243-4
  MTA Consent Decree 221
  parks 245

reverse commute 184, 185, *186*, 188, 190
transit history 224-5, *226*, 227-30, *228*
transit policies 224
transportation injustice 222-3
Los Angeles County Transportation Commission (LACTC) 227
low-income groups
  car ownership 22-3, 32-3, 294
  definition 198-9
  reverse commute 183, 186-7
  transport concerns *45-6*
  transport costs 25-6, 59
  transport inequalities 21-2, 159, 291, 297, 298
Lucas, K. 21, 26, 42, 44, 47

M

McCone Commission 182
McCray, T. 31
Mahony, Cardinal Richard 233
Making the connections (SEU) 57, 63, 64, 67, 71-2, 91
Mandanipour, A. 39
Mann, E. 232
Margaret BEAN v Southwestern Waste Management Corporation 174
markets 7-8
mass transit *see* public transport
Maysville, North Carolina 200
Medi-Ride 136, 137
Meier, K.J. 31
men
  car ownership 23-4, *23*
  travel behavior 259
Mersey Partnership 60
Merseyside 55-6, 66-7
  practical applications 65-6, *65*
  transport and wider social programmes 60-5, *61*, *62*
  travel 58-60, *58*
  see also Halton; Liverpool
Merseyside Community Transport 62, 67, 121
Merseyside Health Action Zone (HAZ) 63
Merseytravel 55, 57, *59*, 60, 67, 145
  Job Link 65-6, *65*, 88
  Merseyside Community Transport 62
  Pathways Transport Group 62-4
Merthyr Tydfil 124-8
Metrolink 235, 251n
MetroMoves 266-7
metropolitan planning organizations (MPOs) 273
Metropolitan Suburban Bus Authority 184
Metropolitan Transportation Authority (MTA) 177, 221, 224, 230-1, 251n, 283, 297
  see also MTA Consent Decree
Milwaukee 183
Minneapolis 267
minority ethnic and faith groups 285
  car ownership 24-5, *24*, *25*
  discrimination 262, 263, 264
  Los Angeles 225, *226*, 227
  MTA Consent Decree 235, 239
  pedestrian accidents 27, 28
  reverse commute 186
  spatial mismatch 183, 244
  transport inequalities *45-6*, 159-60, 223
  transportation equity 243
  see also African Americans
Mohan, V. 271-2
Mooney, John 74-5, 86
Moore, James, II 233
Mott Macdonald 73
MTA Consent Decree 221, 224, 246-8, *249*, 283, 287, 293
  aftermath 240-1
  class of all bus riders 239-40
  intentional discrimination 238
  lessons 250
  organizing effort 231-2
  stopping the fare increase in court 232-4
  Title VI 236-7
  unfair disparities in transit service 234-6
  unjustified discriminatory impacts 237-8
Murray, S. 16
Muslims 264
Myers, S.L. Jr 18

N

NAACP Legal Defense and Educational Fund, Inc. (LDF) 232, 233, 234, 251n
Nashville 28
National Abortion Rights Action League (NARAL) Pro-Choice America Foundation 270
National Council of Negro Women Inc. (NCNW) 266, 271
National Environmental Policy Act (NEPA) 1969 (US) 159, 165, 166, 167, 168, 177, 203, 271
National Household Travel Survey (US) 20, *21*, *22*, *23*, *24*, *25*, 259
National Organization for Women Legislative Agenda 274-5
National survey of American families (Urban Institute) 161
National Travel Survey (DfT) 16, *17*, *19*, *22*, *23*
National Trust 120
Neighborhood Safety 269
Neighbourhood Renewal Fund 74
Neighbourhood Renewal Unit 17
neighbourhood travel coordinators (NTCs) 66
Neighbourhood Travel Team (NTT) 69, 70, 72-3
  access to education 85-6
  access to employment 86-9, *87*, *88*
  achievements 89-90, *89*
  journey-sharing database 82-4
  lessons learned 90-2
  people, innovation, transport 74-5
  Personalised Journey Planning 75-82
  purpose and aims 73-4
  strategic positioning and funding 74
Netherly 121-4
New Bern, North Carolina 198
New Deal 40, 44
New Deal for Communities (NDC) 95-6, 97, 98, 100, 101, 102, 113, 116
new deal for transport, A (DETR) 41
New York City 184
NHS Trusts 44
Noble, B. 42
noise pollution 27-8
Norfolk 135-8
North Carolina Department of Transportation (NCDOT) 198, 199-200, 202, 205, 212

North Walsham Area Community Transport Association (NWACTA) 135-8

O
Oakland, California 266
Objective One programme 56, 60-1, 62, 64, 65, 121
Office of Fair Trading 147-8
Office for National Statistics (ONS) 16, 30, 31
older people 285
  pedestrian accidents 27
  transport concerns 45-6
  women 23, 24, 265-6, 274, 275
Olson, L.M. 28
Ong, P. 30, 183, 185
Onslow County, North Carolina 198

P
paratransit x, 192
Parks, Rosa 246
parks 245
Pathways areas 61-2, 62, 63-4, 65, 65, 66, 67, 121
Pathways Transport Group 62, 63
Pavetti, L. 273
pedestrian accidents 27, 28, 42
people of color x
  see also minority ethnic and faith groups
people with disabilities see disabled people
Personal Responsibility and Work Opportunity Reconciliation Act (PRWORA) 1996 (US) 162, 182, 187
personal safety 268-9
Personalised Journey Plans (PJPs) 69, 72, 75-6, 83-4, 86-7, 90, 91
  hidden benefits 79
  marketing 76-8
  setting parameters 79-81
  spotting the gaps 81-2
  user satisfaction 78-9
Philadelphia 184
Physicians for Reproductive Choice and Health 270
Pisarksi, A. 181, 183
Plessy v Ferguson 246, 252n
PlusBus 130-2
Pollocksville, North Carolina 200, 216
pollution 27-8
  see also air pollution
Pontypridd 120
poverty see low-income groups
Powell, J. 244
Price, Pam 133, 134
Primary Care Trusts 44
Proposition A 227-9, 228
Proposition C 229-30
public involvement 203-5, 285, 286, 296
  see also community impact assessments (CIAs)
public transport ix, 160-1, 293
  cost 26, 26
  decline 19-22, 19, 20, 21
  Los Angeles 224-5, 226, 227-30, 228
  Merseyside 55, 56-7
  reverse commute 185, 186
  women 260
  see also buses; rail

Public Voice for Food and Health Policy 18
Pucher, J. 19-20

R
R.I.S.E., Inc. v Robert A. Kay, Jr. 174
race see minority ethnic and faith groups
rail
  Los Angeles 223, 224-5, 227, 228-30, 228, 232, 235, 241, 243-4, 251n, 283
  Merseyside 59
Ralph W. Keith v Volpe 175
Reason Foundation 233
regeneration 138-41
religion 264
Renne, J.L. 19-20
resource audits 44, 48-50
reverse commute x, 162, 163, 181-6, 186, 267-8, 281, 282
  action agenda 194-5
  car access and automobility 191-2
  implementation and coordination 193
  initiatives 187-8, 188
  new targeted bus routes 190
  paratransit 192
  profiles 186-7
  schedule extensions 190-1
  transit-based strategies 188-90, 189
Ricci, J. 245
Rich, M. 184
Richard Armitage Transport Consultancy 73
Ridge, T. 42
Riordan, Richard 230, 233
Rodger, J.J. 8
Root, A. 9, 10
Rosenbloom, S. 183, 184
Rossetti, M. 181
Route 422 190
Rubin, Thomas A. 233, 247-8, 251n
Runcorn 70, 81, 92n
Rural Bus Challenge 96

S
Sacramento 185, 186
safety 268-9
St Helens 56
Salganicoff, A. 269
San Bernardino County, California 191
San Diego 184-5
San Diego County 185, 186, 188, 190-1
San Fernando Valley 190
San Francisco Bay Area 185, 186
San Joaquin County, California 191
San Mateo County, California 191
Sanchez, J. 245
Sanchez, T. 185
Sandoval case 175-6, 177, 242-3, 284
Santa Cruz County, California 192, 193
Saunders, Kate 129, 130-1, 132
Save our Valley v Sound Transit 252n
Schlanger, Margo 258, 275
Scotland 39
Scottish Executive 139, 142n
Screen Machine 141
Sefton 56
Shapiro v Thompson 257

Sheffield Hallam University 30
shopping 17, 271-2
  see also food stores
short termism 146
Shugart, Karen 270
Single Regeneration Budget (SRB) 63, 65, 74, 78, 121
Siren, Anu 265
Snyder, M.G. 259
social enterprise model 141-2
social exclusion x, 1-2, 39-40, 155
  accessibility planning 44, 47-52
  Halton 69, 70
  and health 135-8
  and transport 41-4, *43*, *45-6*, 57, *58*, 71-3
Social Exclusion Unit (SEU) *26*, 27, 28, 44, 145
  accessibility planning 47, 48-9, 79, 81, 147, 148
  Bringing Britain together 41
  establishment 40
  Making the connections 57, 63, 64, 67, 71-2, 91
  Omnibus Survey 16, 29, 31
  Policy Action Team on Jobs 17, 18
  transport 42
social inclusion x, 116-17
  see also accessibility planning
Social Inclusion Partnership (SIP) 139
social policy 7-9
South Camden Citizens in Action v New Jersey Department of Environmental Protection 176, 177, 284
South Eastern Pennsylvania Transportation Authority 184
South Northolt 128-32, *129*
Southern California Association of Governments (SCAG) 243
Southern Christian Leadership Conference 232, 234
spatial mismatch 183, 267-8, 273, 281
Stafford, B. 29
Stafford Act 1988(US) 199
Staplin, L. 265
StarTrak 115-16, *115*
Steer Davies Gleave (SDG) 133
Stewart, J. 42
Stewart, L. 266
Strategic Investment Areas (SIAs) 61, *62*, 63, 65, *65*
student travel packs 85-6
suburbanization 181-2, 183
Suffolk 120
Summerville, Freddie 223
Supreme Court (US) 172-6
Sure Start 128-32, *129*
Surface Transportation Policy Project 25
Sustainable Food Centre 18

T

Talen, E. 31
Taylor, Bryan 183, 233, 236
Temporary Assistance for Needy Families (TANF) 162, 163, 282
Texas Transportation Institute (TTI) 222
Thoreau Institute 160, 161
Thorpe, Janet C. 264
time poverty 270-1
Title 42, US Code 176

Title VI 158, 166, 167, 199, 205, 243, 284
  case law history 174, 175, 176
  DOT Planning Regulations 169
  MTA Consent Decree 236-7
  Sandoval 242
Toronto 267
TRaC 22, 25, 42, 44
transit villages 286
transport
  environmental and social concerns 149-51
  indirect effects and cumulative impacts 165-6
  policy-making tradition 10-12
  and social exclusion 41-4, *43*, *45-6*, 57, *58*, 71-3
  and society 9-10
Transport Access Patients (TAP) 120, 133-5
Transport Act 1985 (UK) 135, 136
Transport Act 2000 (UK) 147-8
transport costs 25-6, *26*
  Merseyside 58, 59, *59*
  US 160
transport inequalities 28-9, 32-3, 145-6, 291-2
  accidents, pollution and community severance 27-8
  car availability 22-5, *22*, *23*, *24*, *25*
  combination effect 15, *16*
  and educational attainment 30-1
  and employment 29-30
  and health inequalities 31-2
  journey distances and travel times 19-22, *19*, *20*, *21*
  land-use patterns and services 15-19, *16*, *17*
  Los Angeles 222-3
  MTA Consent Decree 234-6
  as social policy issue 292-3
  US 155, 156-7, 159-61, *159*, *160*, 281
  women 265-71, 275
Transport Research Board, Women's Transportation Issues Committee 275
Transport Studies Unit 57
Transportation Demand Management (TDM) 260
Transportation Equity Act for the 21st Century 1998 (TEA-21) (US) 163, 164, 166, 168-9, 182
Transportation Research Board of the National Academies 266, 271
Trapp, D. 266
TravelWise 44, 75
TraVol 120
Treasury 11, 147
Trinder, E. 16
trip-chaining 259, 266, 267, 271, 275, 276n, 285, 294
Troutt, D. 18
Troy, P. 10
Truelove, P. 11
Turner, Jeff 270-1
Turvey, Irene 131, 132

U

UK National Travel Survey (DfT) 16, *17*, *19*, *22*, *23*
United Kingdom 145-51
  accessibility planning 44, 47-52
  accessibility planning in Merseyside 55-67, *58*, *59*, *61*, *62*, *65*

accidents, pollution and community severance 27-8
BraunstoneBus 95-105, *106*, 107-17, *108*, *109*, *110*, *111*, *114*, *115*
car ownership 22-5, *22*, *23*, *24*, 32
community transport 119-42, *125*, *126*, *127*, *129*
educational attainment 30, 31
employment barriers 29
Halton NTT 69-92, *71*, *87*, *88*, *89*
health inequalities 31
improving access to employment 292
journey distances and travel times 19, *19*, 20-1, *20*
land-use patterns and service delivery 16-19, *17*
public transport 293
social exclusion 39-40
transport costs 25-6, *26*
transport policy 11-12
transport as social problem 41-4, *43*, *45-6*
United States 2, 281, 287
  accidents, pollution and community severance 28
  car ownership 22-5, *22*, *23*, *24*, *25*, 32, 294
  case law history 172-6, 283-4
  civil rights legislation 296-7
  community impact assessment 163-4, 197-220, *199*
  educational attainment 30, 31
  employment barriers 29-30
  environmental justice 151, 155, 157-9, 177
  federal policies and legislation 166-72
  funding 282-3
  health inequalities 31-2
  improving access to employment 281-2, 292
  indirect effects and cumulative impacts 165-6
  job access and reverse commute 181-95, *186*, *188*, *189*
  journey distances and travel times 19-20, *20*, *21*
  land-use patterns and service delivery 18-19
  MTA Consent Decree 221-5, *226*, 227-48, *228*, *249*, 250
  policy agenda 284
  public involvement exercises 164-5
  public transport 293
  transport costs 25, *26*
  transport inequalities 156-7, 159-61, *159*, *160*
  transport policy 11-12
  Welfare to Work initiatives 161-3
  wider policy remit 284-7
  women's issues in transportation 257-75
University of California, Berkeley 263
University of California, Los Angeles (UCLA) 233
University of North Carolina Highway Safety Research Center 265
University of Southern California 233
Urban Bus Challenge (UBC)
  BraunstoneBus 52, 96, 97, 98, 100, 105, 107, 295
  Halton NTT 74
  Job Link 65, 67n
  NTT 86, 88, 92n
  Urban Institute 161

Urban Mass Transportation Administration (UMTA) 184, 224, 225, 227
US17 198, 199-220, *199*
US Census Bureau 160
US DOT *see* Department of Transportation
US National Center for Women and Policing 262

V

Village of Arlington Heights v Metropolitan Housing Development Corporation 172, 173-4, 238

W

Wachs, Martin 233, 244
Waldinger, R. 244
Wales 39
Walker, S. 262
Wallace, R.B. 274
Waller, M. 29
Washington v Davis 172, 173, 174
Weiskel, T. 240
Welfare to Work 161-3, 182, 187, 190, 191, 192, 195, 268, 281-2, 287, 292
Wheels to Work (W to W)
  East Ayrshire 140
  Liverpool 121-4
  Merthyr Tydfil 126-8
White, D. 27
White, Sheila 138, 139, 140, 141
Whitelegg, J. 10
Whitty, Anna 128, 130-1, 132
Wiatr, A.R. 270
Widnes 70, 86-7, 88, 92n
Williams, Rob *127*
Winkler, A.E. 271
Wirral 56
women 284, 285, 286
  car ownership 23-4, *23*
  civil rights law 260-3
  legal and quasi-legal issues 263-4
  lifespan transportation differences 265-71
  regional transportation planning 273-5
  transport inequalities 45-6, 159, 257-8, 275, 294
  transportation delivery good practice 271-3
  travel behavior 259-60
Women's Transportation Seminar 274
Workforce Investment Act 1998 (US) 273
Working Links 126, 127

Y

Yale, David 247
Yale University 263
Yim, Y. 18
Yolo County, California 189, *189*, 190-1
younger people *45-6*
Yuba-Sutter Transit 185

Z

Zhang, Z. 18

www.ingramcontent.com/pod-product-compliance
Lightning Source LLC
Chambersburg PA
CBHW080355030426
42334CB00024B/2886